*International African Li*
General Editors: J. D. Y. Peel, David P:

# CHRISTIANS AND CHIEFS IN ZIMBABWE

Ul A. D

The *International African Library* is a major monograph series from the
International African Institute and complements its quarterly periodical *Africa,*
the premier journal in the field of African studies. Theoretically informed
ethnographies, studies of social relations 'on the ground' which are sensitive to
local cultural forms, have long been central to the Institute's publications
programme. The *IAL* maintains this strength but extends it into new areas of
contemporary concern, both practical and intellectual. It includes works
focused on problems of development, especially on the linkages between the
local and national levels of society; studies along the interface between the
social and environmental sciences; and historical studies, especially those of a
social, cultural or interdisciplinary character.

# International African Library

*General Editors*

J. D. Y. Peel, David Parkin *and* Colin Murray

# CHRISTIANS AND CHIEFS IN ZIMBABWE
## A SOCIAL HISTORY OF THE
## HWESA PEOPLE c. 1870s–1990s

DAVID MAXWELL

EDINBURGH UNIVERSITY PRESS
for the International African Institute, London

For my parents

© David Maxwell, 1999

Edinburgh University Press Ltd
22 George Square, Edinburgh

Typeset in Plantin
by Koinonia, Bury, and
printed and bound in Great Britain by
the University Press, Cambridge

A CIP record for this book is available
from the British Library

ISBN 0 7486 1130 4 (paperback)
ISBN 0 7486 1129 0 (hardback)

The publication of this book has been
assisted by a grant from The Scouloudi
Foundation in association with the
Institute of Historical Research

# CONTENTS

# LIST OF MAPS, PHOTOGRAPHS AND TABLES

**Tables**

# ACKNOWLEDGEMENTS

Numerous people helped to make this study possible. My greatest debt of gratitude is to Terence Ranger. He has been a great source of encouragement and inspiration to me ever since I first attended his lectures and seminars as a history undergraduate in Manchester University in 1983. It was the dynamic way in which he taught African history which inspired me to go to live and teach in rural Zimbabwe for three years on graduating in 1986. As my supervisor in Oxford, his friendship and support extended far beyond that which a student could expect. His continued encouragement helped me to find the stamina necessary to return to the study once more and turn it into this book.

The final stages of the thesis, and book, were completed on research fellowships at the International Centre for Contemporary Cultural Research in Manchester University. I am indebted to Richard Werbner, who as director of the centre secured the fellowships for me and helped to give my intellectual journey so far a pleasing 'African-like' circularity. Throughout my return visits to Manchester he has also shown great interest in my research and commented on numerous drafts and re-drafts.

I have been extremely fortunate to work alongside a group of dynamic Zimbabweanists. Three friends in particular: Jocelyn Alexander, Ken Wilson and JoAnn McGregor have been tireless critics of my work, continually pushing me towards new conclusions and greater clarity. Others in the wider community of Oxford Africanists have influenced my work in seminars and informal discussions. These were: Jeremy Brickhill, George Deutsch, Alice Dinerman, Marieke Clarke, Wolfgang Döpcke, Phyllis Ferguson, Geoffrey Manase, Ruth Marshall, Nyasha Masiwa, Bella Mukonyora, Victor Ralushai, Elsbeth Robson, Heike Schmidt and Christine Sylvester. Of these, Alice Dinerman and Ruth Marshall have been supportive friends and challenging critics.

Outside of Oxford (and Manchester) many others have commented on conference papers and draft chapters. Thanks are due to David Beach, Carl Hallencreutz, Adrian Hastings, Donald MacKay, David Martin, David Mazambani, Janice McLaughlin, David Moore and Lynn Schumaker. Carl Hallencreutz read the whole doctoral thesis and made very helpful suggestions concerning the book's possible structure. John Peel and Tony

Kirk-Greene made useful comments as my doctoral examiners, and thereafter John Peel has gently encouraged me on the painful journey towards its publication. Thanks are also due to the anonymous readers of the first draft of this manuscript.

I have also been fortunate in the support provided by the History Department of the University of Zimbabwe through my affiliation as a research associate. Ngwabi Bhebe and Gilbert Pwiti have done much to make my times in Zimbabwe both profitable and comfortable. David Beach, Paul Gundani, Ken Manungo, John Mukumbe, Christopher Newell and Martin Rupiah have all been good friends and colleagues.

In 1994 I took up a lectureship in the History Department at Keele University. John Briggs, Malcolm Crook, Mark Roseman and Jackie Sheehan have provided a warm welcome and a supportive environment.

Sabina Alkire and Christiania Whitehead have been invaluable proof readers throughout the various stages of writing. I am grateful for their long-suffering kindness and their advice on presentation. I am also indebted to Andrew Lawrence for help with cartography.

The process of research was aided by many. In the field Shupikai Chikutirwe, Joseph Chitima, Augustine Mabvira and Samson Mudzudza all acted as research assistants and taught me much about Shona culture in the process. Shupikai was also a dedicated teacher of ChiShona. Tom Riyo made a useful survey of local churches in 1993. The staff at the National Archives of Zimbabwe, the Jesuit Archives, Harare, and the Commission for Justice and Peace, Harare, were of the greatest assistance. Both mission organisations I researched proved extremely hospitable. Elim Headquarters in Cheltenham created an archive for me, and provided an office, photocopier and innumerable cups of tea. Philip Walker, Paul Stevens and Ruth Wittal were particularly supportive. In Dublin, the Priests at the Carmelite Priory at Dundrum gave me a warm welcome. Peter O'Dwyer, Paul Lennon and Luke MacCabe showed great interest in my work and made many helpful suggestions.

Joy Bath, Peter Egan, and Brenda and Steven Griffiths generously provided me with access to their personal correspondence or diaries. A number of scholars also allowed me to use documents in their possession. David Beach kindly translated, and discussed with me, the major Portuguese sources referring to Katerere, and A. E. Hallet wrote a lengthy and scrupulous translation of the key Portuguese text by Andrada, *Relatório*. Janice McLaughlin provided copies of Catholic documents used in her doctoral research. Marshall Murphree sent a vital delineation report from his archive, and Des Cartwright supplied missing copies of the *Elim Evangel*.

Numerous debts of gratitude are owed for hospitality. Pious Munembe and Ephraim Satuku did all they could to make my three years' stay in Katerere a pleasant one, while Geoff Saunders and Tom Riyo were excellent friends and colleagues. The Griffiths' home in Harare provided an excellent escape, and a second family. Ken Jenkins and Geoff and Erica Saunders were also extremely generous in opening their homes. On my return to Katerere in 1991 and 1996 Roger and JoAnn Drew, and John and Amy MacRobert were very gracious hosts. Geoff Saunders, Debbie Brown, Beth Lancaster, and Peter and Brenda Griffiths lent me transport when my truck inevitably fell foul of bush roads.

Funding came from a number of sources: the Beit Fund and Beit Senior Research Scholarship, the Spalding Trust, the Minos Trust, the Sir Richard Stapely Educational Trust, St Antony's College, Oxford, and the Society of the Sacred Heart. The Scouloudi Foundation kindly met the costs of cartographic work. My visits to Zimbabwe in 1995–6 and 1997 were made possible by grants from the Harry Frank Guggenheim Foundation and the British Social and Economic Research Council. But without the financial help of my father and sister, Catherine, and the support of my mother I would never have survived the early, hard stages of this research project when I was an impoverished graduate student.

The Norham Gardens Ecumenical Community provided a pleasant environment in which to work during my stay in Oxford. And during the final stages of thesis writing, Niall Cooper and Rachel Hockey graciously opened their home to me and provided a calming influence.

My 10 years of contact with Katerere has sometimes been painful. Three of my close friends: Peter Griffiths, Joy Bath and Augustine Mabvira, died tragically. Each in their own ways led courageous lives, and contributed much to building and protecting the local community. And each had a big part in making this study a successful one. I hope that in some small way it will act as a record of their struggles and what they achieved. For all its shortcomings and imperfections I accept responsibility.

Manchester and Keele,
August 1997

# LIST OF ABBREVIATIONS

| | |
|---|---|
| AFM | Apostolic Faith Mission of South Africa |
| Agritex | Department of Agriculture and Technical Services |
| ANC | African National Congress |
| AHM | Archivo Histórico de Moçambique |
| AHU | Archivo Histórico Ultramarino |
| BSAC | British South Africa Company |
| CCJP | Catholic Commission for Justice and Peace |
| CNC | Chief Native Commissioner |
| DA | District Administrator |
| DAI | District Administration, Inyanga |
| DC | District Commissioner |
| EAC | Elim Archives Cheltenham |
| JAH | Jesuit Archives Harare |
| LMS | London Missionary Society |
| NAZ | National Archives of Zimbabwe |
| NADA | Native Affairs Department Annual |
| NC | Native Commissioner |
| NDP | National Democratic Party |
| NGO | Non-Governmental Organisation |
| PA | Provincial Administrator |
| PNC | Provincial Native Commissioner |
| RENAMO | Resistencia Nacional Moçambicana |
| RF | Rhodesia Front |
| SRANC | Southern Rhodesia African National Congress |
| TTL | Tribal Trust Land |
| UANC | United African National Council |
| VIDCO | Village Development Committee |
| WADCO | Ward Development Committee |
| ZANLA | Zimbabwe African National Liberation Army |
| ZANU | Zimbabwe African National Union |
| ZANU/PF | Zimbabwe African National Union Patriotic Front |
| ZAOGA | Zimbabwe Assemblies of God Africa |
| ZAPU | Zimbabwe African People's Union |
| ZIPA | Zimbabwe People's Army |
| ZIPRA | Zimbabwe People's Revolutionary Army |
| ZRP | Zimbabwe Republic Police |

# PLACE NAMES

Numerous place names in southern Africa have been corrected or replaced in the last 20 years. Many have been returned their pre-colonial name (real or imagined) or are now spelt using a Shona orthography. Generally, I have tried to follow the convention of using the name appropriate to the period in question, thus before 1890 Mutoko, after 1890, Mtoko, after c.1980, Mutoko. Below are the colonial and pre- and post-colonial names:

| Colonial | Pre-Colonial/Post-Colonial |
|---|---|
| Gatooma | Kadoma |
| Gwelo | Gweru |
| Inyanga | *Nyanga |
| Manica | Manyika |
| Marandellas | Marondera |
| Mtoko | Mutoko |
| Northern Rhodesia | Zambia |
| Nyasaland | Malawi |
| (Southern) Rhodesia | Zimbabwe |
| Portuguese East Africa | Mozambique |
| Salisbury | Harare |
| Umtali | Mutare |

* After independence Inyanga district became Nyanga district but Inyanga town retained its former name.

Whenever possible, the maps in this book use Hwesa orthography. Hence, some of the spellings differ from those used on maps published by the Zimbabwe Surveyor General's Office, which have not been changed since the colonial period.

# INTRODUCTION

In 1951 the native commissioner for Inyanga district in north-east Rhodesia described the Hwesa as his 'Cinderella People'. The description, like so many other labels invented by colonial native administrators, was ironic. Neglect but future promise, the marginal condition of a people untouched by literacy, Western bio-medicine and Christian mission, a virgin awaiting Pentecostal penetration; all that and much more was intended by the native commissioner. The label was something of an enticement to missionaries, Elim Pentecostals, drawn by the Christian challenge of, in their own words, 'dirty uneducated spirit worshippers, bound by witchcraft and superstition' – 'a people crying out for living water'. The Hwesa themselves had their own agendas, their own idioms of empowerment, and their own moral economies, expressed in a rich array of proverb, myth, legend and folk-tale: stories of chiefly assassination and violation of the body; tales of angry leopards and talking baboons; images of bloodshed – *chishava* – and of restoration – *kutonhodza pasi* – the cooling of the earth. And, of course, the Hwesa were never comfortable with the imposed labels or the related fantasies of pristine encounter. Instead, a tension unfolds in their social history, encompassing a great deal of gradual, locally constructed interaction, subtle social and cultural negotiation of everyday life between chief and native commissioner, missionaries and local women, autochthons and migrant élites. Their history is much more than an account of externally introduced crises of great transformation. In studying the unfolding interactions, this book introduces a fresh critical approach to the much debated issues of state incorporation; the construction of identity; the foundation of popular Christianity; the relation between religious movements and politics.

The territory which, like the dynasty and its chief, is also known as Katerere is the stage for an extraordinary social history. Located in the remote and inaccessible north-east it was only brought under the political control of the British South Africa Company in 1904, 14 years after the Occupation. Even then it stayed marginal to the state's wider socio-economic project until the 1950s, which was very late in comparison with many other parts of colonial Rhodesia. Hwesa agriculture remained unhindered by state intervention and the area untouched by mission Christianity until 1951, by which time other parts of the country had decades of contact.

Even when mission Christianity finally did arrive it was not mainstream, but rather an Ulster-derived Pentecostalism. When predominantly southern Irish Catholic missionaries established a mission in Katerere the following year the relation between the two movements was to prove explosive. The Hwesa themselves were a small ethnic community, often classified as 'non-Shona' by the native administration. Their distinctive ethnic identity was to become particularly apparent in the 1950s, when missionised ethnic élites of Manyika people were removed to Katerere and their land given as a reward to British ex-servicemen. The subsequent internal Hwesa-Manyika clash is one of the key interactions studied.

The book focuses on religious and political developments. Broadly, it considers various modes of interaction: first, the encounter of mission Christianities with each other, and with traditional[1] culture and religion; secondly, the conjunctions of the institutions of the colonial state with Hwesa political and religious institutions. In this way, religious and political change is reconstructed from the pre-colonial period into the post-colonial era, c.1870s–1990s.

Two themes dominate: Christianity and chieftaincy. At present there is a growing preoccupation with religion amongst secular historians and social scientists after a long period of relative disinterest (Etherington, 1996). What can broadly be defined as intellectual history is reviving after several decades of materialist dominance. Scholars have begun to explore missionary contribution to ideas of ethnicity, environment, and gender (Ranger, 1994: 2–3). Nevertheless, despite the renewed interest in mission sources, there have been few in-depth studies on the social history of mission (Etherington, 1996: 203). Thus, while Zimbabwean scholarship boasts a lively tradition of denominational histories (Hallencreutz and Moyo, 1988; Zvobgo, 1991), little work has been done on reconstructing these churches' encounter with local African communities. What study has been done on the social history of mission in Zimbabwe comes predominantly from a splendid series of articles on Christianity in the eastern province, Manicaland, by Terence Ranger.[2] But this body of work awaits synthesis into a broader study before wider patterns and continuities can emerge.

Much of the explanation for the scholarly neglect of local level studies of mission Christianity lies in a still widespread notion amongst African clergy and religious studies departments (but not amongst secular scholars) that missions had a wholly negative impact on African societies and cultures (Etherington, 1996: 209–10). Another cause is a consequent undue emphasis on so-called independent churches, which Bengt Sundkler, in a review of over three decades of scholarship on African Christianity since the publication of his epoch-making *Bantu Prophets* in 1948, regretted as 'a modish scholarly hunt for something "authentically African"'! (Sundkler, 1987: 74)

A notable exception to the continued dearth of literature on the social history of mission is Jean and John Comaroffs' study (1991) of the encounter between the London Missionary Society (LMS) and the southern Tswana of South Africa. Their book has provoked lively and stimulating debate. One of the study's numerous strengths is that it gives as much consideration to the social sources and ideologies of the missionaries as to the ethnography of the Tswana; another is the innovative range of evidence used to reconstruct the drawn-out negotiation between missionaries and Africans. Nevertheless, the Comaroffs have been rightly criticised for their over-emphasis on the symbolic. Their study of how Tswana signs and practices came to be appropriated by missionaries seeking to establish a hegemonic order over them leaves little room for consideration of African agency and initiative in the making of Tswana Christianity (Peel, 1995; Elbourne, 1994).

Interestingly, the other significant[3] recent contribution to the social history of mission is Paul Landau's (1995) study of the LMS amongst the northern Tswana of contemporary Botswana. In comparison with the Comaroffs, Landau pays greater attention to the ways in which Christian ideas were seized upon and re-patterned by local agents in different contexts within the Ngwato Kingdom. To reconstruct the agency of Tswana pastors and evangelists he supplements the rich sources of the LMS with a considerable oral archive.

This study of the encounter between very different actors – Catholic and Pentecostal missionaries, and Hwesa and Manyika – in a very different context of north-east Rhodesia in the 1950s, builds upon the Comaroffs' and Landau's path-breaking work. But while it takes seriously the social context and ideas of missionary movements it makes a priority of reconstructing the African roots of Christianity. As Hastings observes in his recent magnificent history of the African church:

> We can chart the movement of Christianity into the interior of Africa rather easily with reference to European missionaries. We know their names, their backgrounds, the Churches and societies to which they belonged ... We have their journals, their letters home. But the reality of young churches was largely a different one and far less easy to chart or to describe. The Christian advance was a black advance or it was nothing. It was one in which ever so many more people were involved but very few of whom we can ever name ... in general the black advance was far more low-key and often entirely unplanned or haphazard. (Hastings, 1994a: 437–8)

This study is based on the fundamental premise that there were never enough missionaries or mission stations to account for the remarkable expansion of Christianity in twentieth-century Africa: 'The most important mental transformations occurred far from missionary eyes' (Etherington,

1996: 217). To capture the 'unplanned or haphazard' pattern of Christian advance, the focus moves beyond the actions of individual labour migrants and evangelists to the activity of youth, women and migrant elites. It moves from the mission station to village Christianity and the movements of Christians which often founded them.[4]

Despite a growing body of work considering the role of African agents in the foundation of a popular or vernacular Christianity,[5] some scholars, particularly theologians, remain convinced that Christianity in Africa is still an alien import (Sindima, 1994: chapter 4; Baur, 1994: chapter 14) awaiting absorption into some essentialised 'traditional' culture (Ranger, 1987a: 42). Consequently, they argue for a top-down process of inculturation: a theologically staged dialogue between gospel and culture. Such ventures often turn out to be as misdirected or as externally imposed as the early missionary enterprises themselves.[6] Instead, this study will investigate the often unexpected process of inculturation from below: a process by which Africans appropriated the symbols, rituals and ideas of Christianity and made them their own. It will consider how the extended dialogue between missionaries, African agents and traditional culture led to the founding of an indigenous Christianity. The resulting religious forms were not merely the result of incorporation of some traditional religious components such as witchcraft eradication or spiritual healing; they were also the product of the exclusion of others by demonisation, exorcism or the destruction of sacred objects. But whether local Christianity was constructed by means of inclusivity or separation it was nevertheless popular because the Hwesa and their neighbours practised it, both as a means of understanding the new world around them and making the best of it.

At this juncture it is also worth stating that this is not a phenomenological study of religion. Unlike Janice Boddy's fascinating account (1989) of the *zar* cult in Sudan I do not examine the meaning of possession; be that by the Holy Spirit or by ancestor and alien spirits. As the methodology section at the end of this book indicates I entered the field with the training of a social historian and did not gather the ethnographic data necessary to make such an interpretative analysis. Phenomenological insights into ecstatic and ritual phenomena are, of course, important but they will have to await a future study.[7] Instead, this book limits itself to a concern with the social significance of religion. It examines the effects of religious beliefs and practices on the workings of the social system, on the lives of societies and on their politics in particular.

There is no shortage of reflection on African chiefs. Unlike catechists and evangelists they were not written out of missionary narratives; rather, they were the key African characters representing the 'otherness' that missionaries encountered at the climax of their epic journeys from civilisation to the back of beyond. Chiefs figure, too, in the written accounts of adventurers, travellers and traders, even if the characters these Europeans encountered were given a grandeur they never really possessed. Finally, in the sources of colonial administrations, traditional leaders have a high profile as the focus of 'native affairs'. But chieftaincy has been misunderstood.

Both nationalist historiography and certain theories of imperialism have depicted traditional political leaders as reactionary: blocking the inevitable advance of Christianity, proletarianisation, and secular democratic political systems. Chiefs have been characterised as no more than stooges: tax collectors, labour recruiters and law enforcers, the unwitting local agents of colonialism run on a shoestring. This misrepresentation stems from a scholarly tendency to view religious and political processes in terms of oppositions between traditional and modern, rural and urban, tribal and territorial, collaboration and resistance.[8] Such interpretations are difficult to reconcile with the contemporary importance of chieftaincy. In Zimbabwe, and other post-colonial African states, chiefs are courted by government officials, politicians and the media. They are viewed as guardians of 'traditional culture', and hailed as spokesmen of important rural constituencies, ignored only at the state's peril.[9]

This book analyses the historical roots of chieftaincy's current importance. It explores chiefs' role in the invention of tradition, the imagination of ethnicity and the defence of local interests against an interventionist state.[10] The study also investigates the relation between the chiefly office holder and his wider network of kin and affines, examining the diverse ways in which the ruling royal faction can be imbricated in the politics of the state, church and ruling party. Traditional religion is also historicised. It is not viewed as a baseline with which to chart the inevitable triumph of Christianity but a dynamic phenomenon in its own right, responsive not only to the growth of Christian adherence but also to the needs of a changing political economy. As such, the religious sources of chiefly power become a key issue for investigation.

This study also innovates methodologically. By narrowing the field of study to one chieftaincy and its immediate setting, it has been possible to interview all of its major religious and political leaders and many of their practitioners and followers. This provides a particularly effective means of tracing interactions at the levels of faction, family and individual, making it possible to follow global and national forces to the point where they encounter people where they live: in villages, mission stations and rural townships. This scale of analysis not only identifies new religious and political processes but also deepens understanding of those identified in other studies made at the regional and district level.[11]

In focusing on a local setting, this research seeks to increase understanding of social differentiation and its change in African societies. 'The closer we get to a careful empirical concern with peasant discourse, the less uniform the peasantry appears', observes Steven Feierman (1990: 41. See also J. and J. Comaroff, 1991: 126). In a similar vein, this book explores the heterogeneity of Hwesa society and its neighbours. By so doing it offers new insights into how religious adherence has often been specific to gender and generation, and how protest against ruling elites has often taken the form of a religious struggle waged by women and youth.

However, this study is not content just to disaggregate society on the basis of eurocentric, unexamined divisions by age, gender and class. These categories themselves are deconstructed in order to recover multiple identities; to illustrate, for instance, how women form allegiances across social categories in pursuit of their interests. Thus, the study inquires how, at different times, conflict is differently structured, and how standard social divisions become more or less salient. Furthermore it explores how individual actors have influenced the meaning and deployment of social categories. In brief, the approach advances a growing mainstream in the literature, which rejects conventional assumptions about social uniformity and cultural consensus in localised processes of change.

Moreover, as with the 'local', so too with forces operating at a district, national or global level, it would be equally misleading to assume that these were monolithic (J. and J. Comaroff, 1991: 54); that, for instance, there was only one form of mission Christianity, or one unchanging colonial project. Mission Christianities were at least as diverse as their social sources and denominations, while there are a number of conflicting ideologies, both within the colonial state (Alexander, 1993), and between it and civil society (Jeater, 1993). Furthermore, missionaries' interaction with local societies shaped specific histories. Hence this study will not offer a standard history of the imposition of colonialism, mission Christianity and capitalism, but a situated history of mission movements in specific pre-colonial, colonial and post-colonial contexts.

The book is divided into seven chapters. Chapter 1 begins with a description of the Shona world of c.1870, moving on to the specifics of the Hwesa economy and society. It reconstructs factional politics within Katerere and explores the role played by royal ancestor religion – *mhondoro* cults – in this internal contestation. The chapter ends by examining how Katerere, and surrounding polities, interacted with the settler state during the first 14 years of its rule, again with reference to religious mobilisation. With the appearance of the colonial state the mediating factor of Katerere's marginality first appears, and consideration is given to its effect on the first decade and a half of relations with the new settler regime.

The second chapter traces the interaction of the colonial political economy with Hwesa political and religious institutions 1904–50. It inquires how Katerere's royal factions and *mhondoro* mediums, in alliance with the state, reconstituted their power bases which had been diminished by the advent of the new order. It summarises changes in the pre-colonial religious system brought about by colonialism, and considers the state's effects on gender relations. Finally it analyses how the local order was challenged by alternative religions and religious movements, both Christian and traditional, which contributed to the formulation of new identities for women, youth and returning labour migrants.

Chapter 3 compares and contrasts two markedly different, even anti-thetical, mission movements – Irish Carmelite Catholicism and Ulster-derived Pentecostalism – as they interacted with Hwesa society. The chapter begins with an exploration of the differing perceptions and agendas of both missionaries and local agents of Christianity on their first meeting. It then analyses how the two mission movements took local form, and asks how, in particular, the social sources of the two movements influenced the nature of the interaction between them, and the final patterns of missionisation.

The fourth chapter focuses on African responses to missionisation and the way in which they shaped its nature. It asks in what way women, youth and outsiders appropriated or localised Christianity in order to pursue their own agendas. Through considering the imagination and spread of Manyika ethnicity, it also explores how Christianity in eastern Rhodesia as a whole could enlarge identities as well as create local Christian communities.

Chapter 5 considers the interaction of local politics with guerrilla strategies of mobilisation during Zimbabwe's war of liberation, which began in Katerere in 1976. Tracing the interplay of peasant agendas with guerrilla ideology, it examines which was the more salient. 'Politics' are considered in a broad sense as meaning the struggles for political ascendancy between women, youth, young men, outsiders and autochthones, undertaken in order to pursue their own specific and conflicting interests. The chapter also returns to the issue of the interaction of religion and politics. Having examined the role of local ancestor cults in legitimating and contesting political authority in the first two chapters, it investigates how traditional religious *and* Christian institutions responded to guerrillas entering the area.

The sixth chapter returns to the study's opening theme, examining the competition amongst royal factions for control of the Katerere chieftainship in independent Zimbabwe. The struggle now takes the form of a succession dispute, played out according to normative rules in the late 1980s and 1990s. It explores how factional politics have been transformed by the mediating role of the independent state, but also how the struggle continues to be expressed in traditional idioms.

The final chapter shifts the focus back to religious change within the Christian religious field. Since independence, a new source of religious plurality has emerged in north-east Zimbabwe: African-led Pentecostal churches. The chapter investigates the rise of these churches from three perspectives: first, as the outcome of persistent social tensions within rural society; secondly, as products of the legacies of the liberation war; thirdly, as responses to the rapid transformations in Zimbabwean society since independence. Thus the proliferation of new Pentecostal churches is examined in terms of both continuity and change.

The conclusion relates the findings of this study to the wider literature on religious and political change in rural African societies.

# 1

# THE WARS OF THE FIELD MICE: HWESA POLITICS AND SOCIETY IN THE LATE NINETEENTH AND EARLY TWENTIETH CENTURIES

## INTRODUCTION

This opening chapter explores the dynamics of pre-colonial Hwesa politics and society, and analyses how they interacted with the colonial state during the first 14 years of settler rule. Throughout, developments in Katerere are set in the context of a broader history. This is because, in pre-colonial times, Hwesa was a local variant of a regional 'Shona' political and religious repertoire. The significant themes of Katerere's pre-colonial history: the territorial rather than genealogical nature of politics, the importance of mountain defences, the compromises made between autochthons and outsiders, the role of royal ancestor cults; all have parallels in other eastern Shona polities. Nevertheless, it will be argued that although Katerere's history was part of a wider set of processes and idioms, the polity arrived at distinct interactions with pre-existing landscapes, ecologies, shrines and peoples in order to establish itself. It is the particularity of Katerere's pre-colonial developments that so coloured its initial interactions with the colonial state.

## NINETEENTH-CENTURY SHONA POLITICS AND SOCIETY

In the 1880s the Zimbabwean plateau and the lowlands surrounding it were dominated by two African 'super-powers' – the Ndebele state in the south-west, and the Gaza state in the east. Between these two polities (see Map 1.1) lay a wedge of land stretching northwards towards the Zambezi, in which were as many as 200 smaller polities. These were mostly Shona, although a few were Sena and Valley Tonga. Some of these dynasties were subject to Gaza or Ndebele power, or at least to their periodic raids, while others – like Mutoko – exhibited great independence.[1] Territories like that of Nhowe or Muangwe were 70 kilometres across, while the smallest were as little as 10 kilometres wide, with as few as two or three settlements (Beach, 1991: 2–4). When viewed on a map this mosaic of dynasties appears both chaotic and fragile, yet some were as many as two or three centuries old and exhibited a great deal of resilience.

The term 'Shona' is something of an anachronism. It refers to the ChiShona language shared by the collection of territories bounded by the

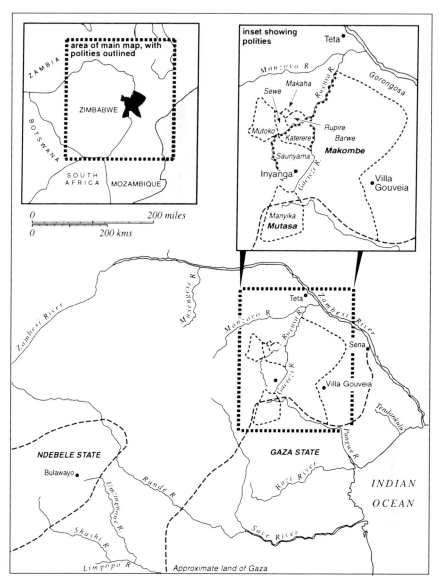

Map 1.1 States and Polities between the Zambezi and the Limpopo c.1890

Gaza and Ndebele states, rather than a single cultural or political identity (Beach, 1980: x). The Shona speakers were orientated in different directions by military and trading links, and would have defined themselves, 'as members of polities, whose boundaries could and did shift' (Ranger, 1993a: 72). Nevertheless, they shared a common political and religious repertoire.[2]

Succession was a key time in a Shona polity's political life, often prompting extreme instability. In 'theory' succession worked by means of collateral inheritance, in which the title passed from brother to brother of the ancestor who founded the dynasty. But in practice, each brother's house would try to retain succession for its own members (Beach, 1994a: 59–60). Sometimes there existed a state of equilibrium in which the title rotated between houses, but often inter-house warfare would take place. Such struggles would end in a tenuous peace, in which the winning head would take the title for his sons and the whole process would start again. Defeated houses would sometimes receive special hereditary titles and ritual functions, or special grants of land in compensation for their loss of rights to political succession. Alternatively, a defeated leader would migrate to found a new dynasty elsewhere, accompanied by some of his brothers and other close relatives, although the bulk of his following would not be tied to him either by blood or marriage. A more unfortunate outcome for the losing house would be its sinking into obscurity within the polity, eventually assuming commoner status (Beach, 1986: 48). As this study will reveal, antagonisms between houses could run so deep that they would resurface in different forms throughout the colonial and post-colonial periods.

A successful chief could sometimes pre-empt direct challenges for his office by means of a system of appointments whereby he awarded his younger brothers or sons control over subordinate polities (Kuper, 1982a: 52). The appointee became a headman over land given to him for the use of his house. Ideally this land would be seized from weaker foreign headmen, and/or carved out along the frontiers of the territory. This form of expansion by 'placing' seems to characterise the political history of the large Mutasa dynasty south of Katerere (see Map 1.1).[3]

The question arises: what was the effective unit of political action? For the best part of the last 100 years, scholarly analysis of the constitution of the pre-colonial polity has been dominated by discussion of 'clan' and then 'segmentary lineage' (Kuper, 1982b: 79). This is hardly surprising, because traditional leaders' claims to power in the colonial and post-colonial periods have been based on patrilineal descent. As Chapter 6 will illustrate, their highly idiosyncratic renditions of chiefly genealogies and legends function as an idiom – a language for talking about political power and property interests (Kuper, 1982b: 88).

Nevertheless, historians and anthropologists have been able to penetrate the clouded oral accounts of partisan informants to see the historical reality below. John Lonsdale offers a revised model of the pre-colonial past:

> The idea of culturally closed, self sufficient worlds of tribal descent has had to give way before the growing evidence of the demands of the close-fisted 'big men' of colonizing settlements, who were always striving for a legitimate hegemony of societal justice that they never quite achieved. 'Kin' or 'lineage' were the ideologies of authority that 'custom' later elaborated, not accurate descriptions of actual friendly societies. (Lonsdale, 1992: 212)

Drawing on research on southern Africa, Adam Kuper concluded that it was difficult to find any specific 'lineage' activity, 'which might not more readily be attributed to the homestead or neighbourhood or administrative ward' (1982a: 49). The lineage model of the pre-colonial past 'does not represent folk models which actors anywhere have of their own societies' (1982b: 92).

The effective political unit was *territorially* based rather than *descent* based. The notion that each territory was ruled by one chief, by means of kinship loyalty, is misplaced. Kinship was complicated by numerous other social ties. The reality was often that the polity was divided spatially between a number of patriarchs or 'big men' known in Katerere as *muzvinanzvimbo*, which literally meant 'the owner of this place': someone who controlled a portion of land. These leaders competed for political and economic power by raiding each other for women, children, cattle and control of trade, and amassing labour power through polygamy, infant pledging – *zvarira* – and bride service – *ugariri* (Beach, 1989: 33, 38; K. Wilson, 1990: 635). The territorial basis of these political units was vividly represented by the fact that these 'big men' and their followers made their homes on hill-top forts known as *aringa*[4] in Portuguese, and *zimbabwe* in ChiShona. Such a lifestyle was inevitable, given the degree of violence that underpinned so much of the society's politics (Beach, 1991: 4). The reality of factional warfare and political assassination in nineteenth-century Hwesa history is neatly summarised by a proverb about their totem: *imhoni dzarumana* – the field mice have fought (literally, the field mice have bitten each other).

The most appropriate term to describe the above political units would be *factions*. These were collections of 'big men' and their clients who sought after and enjoyed power, but lacked clear-cut political programmes. The groupings were thus short-term and unstable. They were made up of kin, real and fictitious, in combination with slaves, commoners and outsiders. Factional identity was thus made concrete though a combination of kinship, clientship and personal loyalties (Anderson, 1991: 76–7).

Marriage alliances were central to the construction of factions. Political marriages were arranged with outsiders and commoners at home, and the faction was reinforced through marriages made with rulers in other territories.

Commoners and outsiders gained influence through 'affinal and matri-lateral connections with the ruling line at various levels of the political hierarchy' (Kuper, 1982a: 58). Wives and sisters, then, were potentially the linchpins around which factional politics could operate. Moreover, their families provided a source of external support and refuge in time of flight.[5]

Diana Jeater's reconstruction of late nineteenth-century Shona gender relations deepens our understanding of the centrality of women to pre-colonial politics. She notes that those who held deep power – chiefs, 'big men' and male 'elders', or shallow lineage heads – derived it not by means of descent, but through the mechanism of bridewealth. Faction leaders 'could tie a labour force, particularly junior men from immigrant lineages, to their service through kinship links founded in a manipulation of marriage arrangements' (Jeater, 1993: 21). Here control over cattle was not as impor-tant as polygamy and the pledging of daughters. Male elders could accumulate women through poorer men pledging their daughters – *kuzvarira*. Jeater's model was derived from a study of the southern Shona in Mazvihwa (Ken Wilson, personal communication). Amongst the eastern Shona the pledged daughter was known as *mai nini* and her exchange often functioned as a means for a poor family to survive famine. Jason Machiwanyika, African evangelist and historian of the Manyika people of Mutasa, described the practice:

> A man used to go to someone he liked and said to him 'let us make a friendship.' And if the man agreed then various gifts were exchanged. The man who begins asking the others for a friendship usually espouses his daughter to the sons of his friend. He usually begins the friendship because of poverty and he begins to ask for cattle from his friend in exchange for his daughters.[6]

Although Machiwanyika describes the exchange of cattle in pledging, grain was also frequently used (Iliffe, 1990: 16). Moreover, men who paid the bride-price usually offered hoes and axes rather than cattle. Poor men, particularly outsiders, could do bride-service – *ugariri* – to obtain wives, thus increasing the labour supply of 'big men'. By commanding the loyalty of sons and sons-in-law through their provision of wives, or the means to obtain them, male elders established and perpetuated political authority. The surplus grain generated by clients meant that elder patrons could obtain more wives (Jeater, 1993: 22). Shona patriarchy, then, concerned elder male control of young men as well as women. And consequently some young Shona males preferred to settle amongst the Ndebele people and benefit from a life of raiding, increased access to women and beef eating (Beach, 1980: 132–3). This was an early indication of the structured generational conflict in Shona society which manifested itself in different ways through-out the twentieth century.

Jeater's pre-colonial model needs to be nuanced for the eastern Shona. The bridewealth system which circulated women between elders and 'big men' was not always the key to the construction of political authority. The number of women in circulation could be increased by raiding and theft. Prior to reaching Katerere in 1872, the German adventurer Carl Mauch traversed the adjacent territory of Chief Somali, who had just been a victim of one such raid by Mutoko. Somali told Mauch, 'We are in constant fear of him and are hungry, for he destroys our well built huts, kills the men and takes the women and young girls' (Burke, 1969: 235).[7] Alternatively, young men could circumvent the drawn-out processes of labour service to acquire either cattle or a wife. Rights over women's labour and reproduction could be bought from a local patriarch, but the personal ties of affinity between lineages could be overridden completely through the purchase of slave wives.[8] In 1903, a year of drought, the native commissioner (NC) Inyanga observed the arrival of 'matrimonial agents' from Portuguese territory with 'batches of wives for disposal' at three to six shillings each.[9]

To summarise, the most successful 'big man' would be the 'chief', although he was often no more than first amongst equals. Between 'big men' alliance and allegiance were interchangeable. As Beach notes: 'The habit of the *varungu* [Europeans] in the 1900s of calling every head of a few villages a 'chief' was not far from the mark, for the rulers could not always get obedience from their subordinates who often acted independently'.[10] Nevertheless, when a chief was strong, his office was an asset as a source of both human and material resources, not just to his kin but ultimately for the rest of his faction. Such resources could be demanded through tribute.

Often rival 'big men' to the chief were his own relatives. Kin could be both best friends and worst enemies (Beach, 1994a: 45). This seemingly contradictory state of affairs offers a clue to how polities could survive for such a long time, despite the fissile nature of their internal politics. It was in the interests of all the agnates of the ruling dynasty that it should continue. At times they would cooperate, and at times they would clash; they would do practically anything to secure the position of their own factions or houses, even allocate land or ritual positions to those who were a threat. However, it was no benefit to the members of the whole ruling dynasty if the entire dynastic structure broke up. Without a *mambo* – chief – of their clan, or worse still with a new *mambo* of another clan, members of the dynasty would lose the slight edge they had over local *vatorwa* – outsiders. Generally, though not always, as Katerere's political history will illustrate, they would probably unite to keep dynastic rulers in place, though very powerful rulers were not necessarily seen as an asset by rival factions.[11]

## THE POLITICAL ECONOMY OF KATERERE AND
## THE NORTH-EASTERN SHONA

Moving to the particular, Katerere was part of a north-eastern Shona political economy. The chiefdom lay between the Rwenya river in the west and the Gaerezi river in the east (see Map 1.1). Its population generally inhabited hills and mountains within a number of complexes. These were the Kwanda, Gujeza and Nyangaza ranges in the north, the Ruangwe range in the west and the Cherenje range in the east (see Map 1.2). Two spectacular mountains dominated the skyline: Mt Nhani, a dome-like granite outcrop in the west, and Mt Mhokore, a pyramid peak in the east. Beyond the large mountain complexes lay numerous hills, kopjes and smaller outcrops. Vegetation was particularly thick, growing eight feet high in places.[12] At the turn of the century, patrolling native commissioners found it so dense they had to leave their horses and proceed on foot.[13]

Although Katerere was one of the larger Shona territories, its dense vegetation, mountainous terrain and dry climate meant that it was very thinly populated. Its population c.1900 was probably no more than 5,000. It may well have been lower.[14]

The local economy was diverse. The major staples were rapoko – *rukweza* – and millet – *munga*. The latter was particularly cultivated along the Gaerezi valley. Beans, peas and groundnuts were also grown.[15] Shifting cultivation was widely practised. Small trees were cut and burnt, and seeds planted in beds of ash and soft soil. The ground was prepared with digging sticks and occasionally with locally produced iron hoes. Stock was extremely sparse.[16]

Hunting and gathering were important supplements to Hwesa cultivation. Herds of as many as 300 buffalo moved through the region in the 1870s. Elephant hunts were also organised (Burke, 1969: 232, 238). In times of famine, gathering was crucial. The baobab fruit – *chigogode* – and the Ndiya root became alternative staples.[17]

The Hwesa were also involved in a regional economy of trade and migrant labour, centred on the north-eastern Shona, but extending beyond them. Their pre-colonial trade relations had some orientation towards the immediate south. Hwesa traders moved amongst the Manyika of Mutasa selling their plates, sieves, straw mats, beads and bark fibres (Mukaranda, 1988: 9–107). However, far more trading activity was carried out to the east. With the peoples of Barwe and Sena, the Hwesa traded ivory, baskets and skins in return for beads and rights over women.[18] The accounts of the visit of the German adventurer, Karl Mauch, to Makombe, ruler of Barwe, underscore the centrality of the ivory trade to the region (Bernard, 1971: 229). The initial founding and subsequent success of the Katerere dynasty may well have hinged upon its control of a successful ivory trade.[19]

The Portuguese were more interested in the area's gold, which was still washed in the Rwenya and its tributaries as late as the 1880s. This was

1.1 Mt Nhani

1.2 Mt Mhokore

packed into feather quills and exchanged for guns, cotton cloth, or cash to acquire rights over women (Andrada, 1886: 10; Schmidt, 1992: 33–5; Burke, 1969: 234). Portuguese desire for gold caused them to penetrate into the north-east of Zimbabwe to secure its trade. A store was built in Katerere and the area took on a Portuguese name – Caetano. Another was constructed 30 miles north at the confluence of the Rwenya with the Gaerezi.[20] Further to the west lay Makaha, an ancient Portuguese *feira* – market town. Around it were gold fields which Mauch named after Kaiser William, in anticipation of German colonisation.

As Beach notes, while the southern African regional capitalist system began to establish itself on the plateau at the end of the nineteenth century, so too capitalist relations began to creep into the north-east, replacing an economy run on mercantile lines (Beach, 1984: 36). Hwesa men worked as carriers in a triangle of trade between Inyanga in the south, the Kaiser William Gold Fields in the west, and Tete in the east (see Map 1.1).[21] Moreover, the Portuguese adventurer and soldier, Captain J. C. Paiva de Andrada, noted when he visited Katerere in 1885 that the Hwesa used various Portuguese words and knew of Tete and Sena (Andrada, 1886: 6). Indeed when the NC from the adjacent Mtoko district made his first attempts to collect hut tax from the Katerere people in 1898 he was offered a selection of both Portuguese coinage and rupees.[22]

## RELIGION AMONGST THE HWESA AND OTHER NORTH-EASTERN SHONA

The complex political and economic relationships which defined Shona political economies were matched by equally intricate religious patterns (Ranger, 1993a: 73). Some scholars have been prone to romanticise pre-colonial religion, asserting a model of organic collectivity (Moyo, 1987: 67). However, the reality was more complex and dynamic. African religions symbolised relationships, and cults often articulated them (Ranger, 1993a: 73). The Hwesa, like other Shona peoples were involved in a range of religious interactions which began at the level of the family and faction but could extend to the polity and the region beyond.

In the homestead, family members believed their well-being was overseen by patrilineal ancestors. The veneration of these spirits legitimated male heirship.[23] However, even within the family, the authority of male ancestors was countered by alternative religious ideas. Outsider women marrying into Shona patrilineal society could ameliorate their inferior status by joining possession cults, and so gain recourse to a spiritual authority outside the home.

Beyond the village, men were involved in cults which reflected economic relations between polities. One such activity was hunting. Hunters of big game, such as elephants, joined guilds to coordinate their effort. The Hwesa guilds were associations of men who exchanged knowledge of charms and magic, and who jointly participated in the propitiation of *mashave ehombarume* – hunting spirits, or spirits of the land and waters – before embarking on the hunt. On return, successful hunters would also take part in the ritual distribution of the meat to the wider community, to celebrate the hunting spirit's benevolence.[24]

Like other Shona peoples, Hwesa ancestor cults also functioned at the scale of the polity, or intermediate levels within it. These were known as *mhondoro* cults. They centred on the spirits of dead chiefs or 'big men', who made their wishes known through a medium called a *svikiro*. When the spirit was not possessing its host, it was believed to possess a wandering lion, hence *mhondoro* also meant lion spirit.[25] In 1886 Andrada wrote the following on *mhondoro*:

> The *pandoros* [*mhondoro*] that I have already seen in the lands of district of Tete, that were in the Mazowe, that were in the Kingdom of Barwe, and that are to be found in all the lands of the small kings of this region, are certain men who hide themselves every now and again saying that they are going to the bush, and they transform themselves into lions, that when found in human form are almost always roaring, and they live at the expense of kings and peoples imposing themselves on them as supernatural beings. (Andrada, 1886: 8)

The reconstruction of Hwesa *mhondoro* cults over the last 100 years shows great variation over both space and time. There also seems to have been considerable differences *between* polities in terms of the cults' efficacy and function. Nevertheless, despite local variation in Shona royal ancestor cults, it is possible to identify common features amongst them. If we analyse Hwesa *mhondoro* religion using Matthew Schoffeleers's (1979: 9–10) classic typology of territorial cults which is based on their organising principle, it is clear that they had both 'local' and 'tribal' features. This seeming contradiction is to be explained by the fact that they performed different functions for separate constituencies. Moreover, different mediums within a cult's hierarchy of leadership could carry out distinct tasks.

In terms of the local dimension, village leaders sought out mediums as cult leaders, expecting them to use their connections with senior *mhondoro* spirits and the High God, Karuva, to produce rainfall. They also expected mediums to provide protection against famine, through use of anti-locust medicine and the provision of game in the dry season (Beach, 1986: 100–1, 134).

Senior mediums could also represent the interests of a wider 'ethnic' community, particularly to outsiders, thus fulfilling a tribal function. In this way *mhondoro* cults were often at the centre of the political stage. Mediums acted as intermediaries between the polity and outsiders, as advisors to the chief, and as military leaders.[26] Such political roles may well have taken on a greater significance in the event of a weak chief (Mudenge, 1988: 126).

However, given the fissile and heterogeneous nature of the pre-colonial Shona polity, mediums also mediated the interests of its constituent factions or royal houses, although not always siding with the chief or 'big man' leading the faction. Mediums and faction leaders could function in a balance of power.

There was an important territorial dimension to religious belief and practice in Katerere, with the Hwesa participating in what Schoffeleers (1979: 10) describes as a 'federative' cult which united different polities. It is now only possible to reconstruct this cult from fragments of evidence. Its membership was poly-ethnic and centred on the peoples in Barwe in Mozambique, and neighbours in the north-east of Zimbabwe. Today it is built from a bricolage of figures: Karuva, Dzivaguru, Murungu and Chikara.[27] In 1991, Katerere's most aged and senior medium, Diki Rukadza, recounted the story of the *Ambuya* – grandmother – Karuva who reconciled the warring dynasties of Mutasa, Saunyama, Katerere and Mutoko; nominated leaders; and gave them totems and land to live on. She sat at the apex of a spiritual pyramid and the *mhondoro* could approach her on matters of great importance. She would judge each *mhondoro* by making them jump over fire.[28]

This highly stylised account of Karuva may well have been embellished by Rukadza borrowing from Judaeo-Christian concepts of God gleaned by his contact with an adjacent mission, but the cult's prior existence can be corroborated by other sources.[29] Other elderly informants used the name Karuva, albeit more loosely. The Pentecostal missionaries who entered Katerere in the 1950s reported that the Hwesa referred to God as Chikara – a deified version of Karuva.[30]

Although Hwesa history can be contextualised within a wider set of economic, political and religious processes which comprised a broader Shona history, the actual establishment and consolidation of the Katerere dynasty hinged upon a specific set of interactions with pre-existing landscapes, ecologies and surrounding peoples. These will be reconstructed below.

## THE ORIGINS AND CONSOLIDATION OF THE KATERERE DYNASTY

It is likely that the Katerere polity post-dates the Inyanga Culture, which probably ended in the north of the district somewhere around 1750 (Storry, 1976: 16). Informants stated that the terraced mountain-sides located in the southern part of the territory were there when they arrived, and they could offer little explanation for their construction.[31] Most Hwesa seemed content, instead, to cultivate on the foot-slopes – *mujinga* – lying beneath the terraces, rather than the sides of the mountains themselves. The length of the genealogies, embellishments accepted, suggest that the polity was probably established sometime between 1750 and 1800.[32]

Accounts of the Hwesa's initial interactions with their environment are found in their oral traditions. Their myths of origin deal with a variety of Hwesa forefathers. They describe their migration into north-east Zimbabwe, their settlement on local mountains, the establishment of the Katerere family as the ruling line, and the pacification of the local autochthon and other large, but unvanquished, Hwesa families.

There are a number of Hwesa myths of origin. Their translations are reproduced, verbatim, in the simple narrative style in which the oral traditions were recounted. The three most common myths are included in Appendix 2. A collection of rituals concerning the coronation and burial of the chief and the first-fruits ceremony, which complement the myths, are found in Appendix 3.

In the late 1980s and early 1990s both the myths and rituals were the province of elderly members of 'big families', royal houses, their representative mediums and a few interested, but aged, outsiders. They were not common currency and a degree of secrecy is attached to them. This was because their concern was with élite politics: 'The need for rulers to be confident in their own legitimacy and to define their relations with other members of the ruling group.' (Ranger, 1993b: 8)

Following Roy Willis and Joseph Miller, the oral traditions are broken down into three strata: myth, repetitive legend and narrative chronicle.[33] The stories included in Appendix 2 concerning the origins and formation of the Hwesa dynasty, fall into the first strata of myth. Readings of the myths begin with the explanations of the informants themselves. From there we seek to decipher their implicit meaning, through the interpretation of their clichés. These Vansina describes (1985: 139) as 'stock phrases ... statements or episodes, indeed even narrative plots, that recur in other traditions of the same or different genres in the same or different cultures'. In time, a cliché can become a 'highly compressed and deceptively simple statement of meaning that refers to a much more complex reality'. In the case of the Hwesa myths, there appears to be a fairly strong correspondence between their implicit and explicit meanings (Ibid: 144–6).

All three Hwesa myths of origin exhibit structural similarities, sharing the two interrelated themes of authority and territory. In the stories, references to authority and land take the form of claims made by the 'big families', or factions, such as Sanhani, Sachiwo and Sadowera. These factions lose out as the Katerere dynasty consolidate their position as the dominant local power by means of a show of force, trickery or sheer weight of numbers. The losing factions' claims to authority and territory are legitimised by a number of clichés. These are first, traditions of origins from Mbire: 'They came from Mbire Dande while they were three men and after more people came';

Table 1.1 The Territorial Basis of Factional Politics during the Making of the Katerere Polity

| Faction | Progenitor | Location |
|---------|-----------|----------|
| Nyakasapa (*autochthon*) | Nyakasapa | Sanhani |
| Sanhani | Dembwetembwe | Mt Nhani |
| Katerere | Samavanga | Mt Mhokore |
| Sachiwo | Sakudzamba | Mt Cherenje |
| Sadowera | Chinoro | Mt Nyazingwe |

secondly, the bringing of fire: 'Dembwetembwe made him fire ... and was made chief because he was clever enough'; and thirdly, the march around the territory after settlement or conquest: 'After exploring the area Sakudzamba made fire ... Sakudzamba said that he should be made chief because he had explored the area.'

The clichés work in different ways. Assertions of origin from Mbire, the mythical Shona place of creation, give the factions' claims of descent a primordial quality; marching around the territory is a statement about its possession; whilst the civilising outsider bringing fire to the primitive autochthon represents the superior quality of the mastery of culture over nature.

The clichés in these stories are repeated in the founding myths of dynasties elsewhere in Zimbabwe (Beach, 1990a: 3–4). Their substance bears a particularly marked resemblance to those of the adjacent Maungwe Dynasty to the south (Abraham, 1951: 56–83), though each set of traditions offers a local variation of common Shona themes. For instance, the first and most sophisticated Hwesa myth of Dembwetembwe and Samavanga details specific interactions the polity had with the local environment. The two most spectacular mountains are settled, trade is established with the Portuguese, and the autochthon, Nyakasapa, is pacified.

Other attempts by the powerful factions of Sanhani, Sachiwo, Sadowera and Katerere to assert their legitimacy come about through *naming*. This works by means of etymologies (definitely false in some cases) which function by means of verbal equivalences. In the first myth, for instance, 'Katerere', the name of the dominant faction, is derived from *derere* – okra: 'When a spear was thrown at him it would slip off his body as if he was smeared with *derere*.'

The families of Sanhani, Sachiwo and Sadowera, who lose out as the Katerere faction comes to dominate the territory, overcome the difficulty of confronting the ignominy of their demise through the mystification of reality. In this mystification or *covering*, the vanquished administer to themselves a sop or a palliative. The Sachiwos and Sanhanis assert that they are in fact senior by virtue of arriving in the territory first, whilst the ousted Sadoweras convince themselves that they are indispensable to the polity's political and ritual functioning.

The rituals detailed alongside the myths (see Appendix 3) are inseparable from them, expressing the perceived yet unspoken, painful truth that the Katerere faction eclipsed the Sanhani, Sachiwo and Sadowera factions in accumulating political power. In the rituals, the patriarchs, representing each losing faction and the cloud of their ancestors, are forced by every new succession to acknowledge the authority of the Katerere chief. The final uncovering or, more appropriately, *undressing*, comes at the climax of the coronation ritual, through the agency of Nyakasapa – the original owner of the land. Nyakasapa is both the greatest beneficiary of Hwesa civilisation, and the greatest victim of the Katerere faction's dominance. His nakedness symbolises the 'primitive' state in which he was found, but it also exposes the *offering of fig leaves* made to the losers. In an anarchic act of 'ritual rebellion' (Gluckman, 1963): 'He encircles the chief's house with rattles. He is naked and shouts out both insulting and humorous things.'

The Katereres' victory is far from total. The rituals and myths exhibit a depth and plurality of reflection on the nature of pre-colonial politics. As Lonsdale observes:

> Even in the most powerful of Africa's old Kingdoms people argued passionately about the sources and purposes of power … Subjects espoused different theories of government … There was always conflict between centre and periphery, couched in a political language of rights and obligations. (Lonsdale, 1992: 210–11)

From an inferior position of power, the 'big families' *are* able to make social statements about the moral economy of the political system, particularly about the nature of chieftainship. The faction leaders, Sanhani and Sachiwo, are obliged to participate in the rituals underpinning chiefly rule, but also have autonomy in the rule of their own territory. There is a separation of power within the polity. These power relations are symbolised in chiefly rituals where the functions and qualities of a chief are impressed upon the office's incumbent. The eggs, baby baboon and phallic imagery of the chief astride a crocodile point to him (in his capacity as the living descendant of the *mhondoro*) as provider of fertility. The eggs in the hand symbolise just rule. Gripped too hard, they will break. From something as fragile as eggs emerges a powerful crocodile. A chief has to be careful not to alienate his followers and allies. The relationship between ruler and ruled is a delicate balance of power.

As illustrated below, it is likely, due to the nature of factional politics in pre-colonial Katerere, that these chiefly rituals rarely occurred. Nevertheless they would have had an important rhetorical value in times of alien threat and unjust chiefs. Such traditions could be said to underpin an unwritten

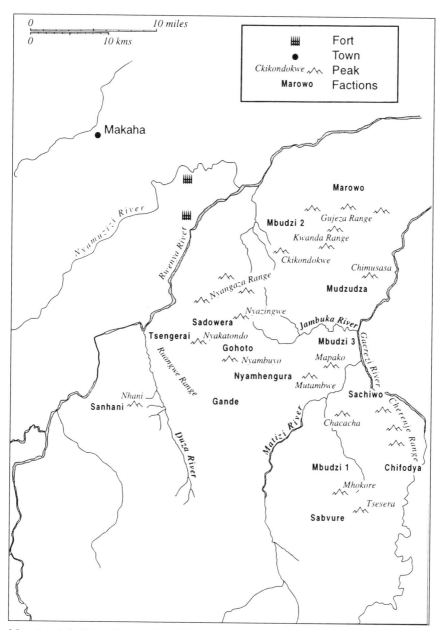

Map 1.2 A Political Geography of Katerere c.1880

Hwesa constitution. Moreover, commoners and outsiders, excluded from the concerns of Hwesa oral traditions, were able to make statements about their rights and rulers' obligations through other oral media. The dangers of greed and witchcraft; the rights of the powerless; and the importance of justice and mutual accommodation are central themes in Hwesa folk-tale, song and proverb.[34]

To summarise this section, the myths outline the historical process of migration into the area between the Rwenya and Gaerezi Rivers by a collection of peoples who subsequently formed the polity of Katerere. When informants were asked for their own explanation of the stories, they talked of fission from the Makombe people in Mozambique in time of war.[35] The migrants may have been a disaffected princely house and collection of followers. It is likely that Sanhani was the original focus of the polity. It was here that the first Hwesa people settled, building a faction with the autochthon Nyakasapa (see Myth 1, Appendix 2). Unlike other parts of Zimbabwe,[36] the autochthons were never numerous enough, or powerful enough, to exert any great influence over their conquerors, and were gradually assimilated. What power the Nyakasapas did have to make rain was eventually eclipsed by Hwesa *mhondoro* mediums. The territory's centre of gravity later shifted eastward towards the Gaerezi River, as the Katerere faction came to dominate.[37] Informants spoke of the Katereres having more wives and owning most of the few cattle there were. It also seems likely that they were the most effective traders and hunters. Informants also stressed the Katereres' trickery: the dominant faction were *slippery* like okra – *derere*. Along with the domination of the Katerere ruling line came a process of pacification, accompanied by devolution of territory to both Sanhani and Sachiwo. The losing factions remained powerful enough to argue their own theories of government and hold a balance of power. Their continued importance in contemporary Hwesa politics will be illustrated in Chapter 6.

Other later 'placings' occurred as the polity expanded. Moreover, new powerful factions of outsiders arrived in the territory. These events are remembered in the second 'legendary' strata of Hwesa oral tradition.

## FACTIONAL POLITICS IN KATERERE

This section deals with local faction politics in Katerere in the late pre-colonial period. Accounts of constant warring between rival Hwesa factions are found in the second strata of Hwesa oral tradition. This layer of legend has been defined by Miller as comprising 'certain classes of recurrent events … described … in a more or less standardised form …' (1978: 85). Similar legendary accounts of warfare between factions based in mountain strongholds in other polities can be found to match the Hwesa ones.[38] However, as is the case for Katerere's myths, the polity's legends again refer to specific sets of interactions with the landscape and surrounding peoples.

In the stories, the factions either perpetrate, or are the victims of, ghastly assassinations of rival faction leaders. The objective of such violence was political control of the polity represented by controlling the office of chief. A more benign alternative to the violence ends with the flight of the losing side.

A number of legends illustrative of these factional conflicts are present in Hwesa oral traditions. As legends they are composed of a combination of fact and symbolic material, with the comparative content of these two mediums varying in relation to where the story is located within this second strata of oral tradition. It is possible to create some time depth in the strata of legend through the construction of a genealogy for the Katerere ruling line. But it must first be noted that genealogical research is a hazardous enterprise. Family trees supplied by members of royal houses and their allied mediums also function as political arguments legitimating claims to succession. The Katerere case is compounded by the fact that data has been collected during a long-running succession dispute, when the material is particularly politically charged. It is consequently difficult to establish the lines of descent between the first and second generations as all the informants are intent on forging links with the senior ancestors. Nevertheless, there does appear to be something of an accepted order of seniority and obviously a real genealogy must exist, however difficult it is to recover. The four most common legends are found in Appendix 4. Accompanying genealogies are found in Appendix 5, including an attempt at a real one.

Informants mentioned other vague examples of assassinations of past chiefs,[39] but the legends considered here have been remembered because they also function as political arguments for houses retaining claims to the chieftainship. Since such claims are made to an audience beyond the élites of royal houses, the legends have a wider currency than the foundational myths. As political arguments, the legends display structural similarities, such as the gruesome nature of the chiefly assassinations, which will be analysed in Chapter 6. The intention here is to use the legends as a means of historical reconstruction. The stories lend themselves to this purpose because they share common historical themes, providing the basis from which to construct a narrative history.

The first shared theme is the flight of the losing chief and/or his family to his wife's or his mother's home, in three cases to Mozambique and in the fourth (Nyamhute) to Saunyama, south of Katerere. Intermarriage or the exchange of women with surrounding dynasties such as Makombe, Samanyanga and Saunyama was a common phenomenon, but more to the point, it was a means of both creating and reinforcing a faction with outside support.[40] Thus in Legend 2, Chimucheka's mother's family seek to protect him from his assassins: 'Chimucheka fled to Sangano and from there he went to Barwe... His mother had come from Barwe.'

The second common historical theme is the preponderance of mountains and caves in the stories. The Katerere polity's political history, from the outset, is a history of its hills. The relation of factions to mountains was a form of local politics in the vernacular which found expression in Hwesa praise songs sung in honour of mountains and their associated chiefs.[41] Political power was inseparable from the ownership of hill-top defences. The mythic assertion of delimited 'tribal' boundaries, which had been marked out by the conquerors marching around (see Appendix 2), was not historical fact. The nineteenth-century reality was that territory was an extension from hills at the centre, with only vague borders. Furthermore, through their association with past leaders, as places of their settlement, burial, and dwelling for their spirits, mountains were sources of political legitimacy. It is hardly surprising that the dominant families seized the highest and most visually impressive of peaks. Other less powerful factions lived on smaller mountains (see Map 1.2).[42]

Once established, the dominant Katerere faction rapidly expanded, Samavanga's descendants becoming very numerous. Some of the competition for power between royals seems to have been relieved by 'placing' from the Katerere faction. Samyamuwera and Sabvhure were given portions of land to govern, and the latter, a key role in the first fruits ceremony.

The chiefdom also expanded through the immigration of powerful outsiders. The Gande people – a group of Jindwe iron workers – were granted land in return for tribute of hoes and spears. Their own tradition reveals that they came from Mutare and met Chief Chikumbirike on Mhokore mountain.[43] Other important groups of outsiders were the Tsengerai faction who came to Katerere via Makombe in Barwe and made their home on Mt Nyakatondo, and the Mudzudza family who occupied the land around Chimusasa.[44] Much later, at the end of the nineteenth century, came Maroo from Mount Darwin, whose people were of the *Nhari* – buffalo – totem. Maroo was given land in the far north of the territory around Fombe, by Chief Tsarumunda Katerere. The new faction intermarried with the Katereres and the leader was made a *kotsi* – advisor – to the chief.[45]

As in the case of the adjacent Mutasa polity, the 'placings' and grants of land served to protect the heartland of the chiefdom, located between the Ruangwe, Cherenje and Kwanda ranges, by means of a barrier of loyal retainers (Storry, 1976: 26). However, the 'placing' of ambitious relatives did not satisfy every royal. Factional fighting occurred immediately amongst Samavanga's sons. Nyamhute was forced to flee to Saunyama, the home of his mother, and his people were eventually dispersed into Mutasa's territory. Ironically many were to return in the 1950s as migrant Christian élites evicted to the north after the implementation of the Land Apportionment Act (see Chapter 4). The second legend about Chimucheka also ended in flight, with his house vanishing into virtual obscurity until it publicly revived its claims in the 1980s.

Table 1.2 A Summary of Hwesa Legends with reference to Factional Politics

| Faction | Faction Leader | Location | Fate |
|---|---|---|---|
| Nyamhute | Nyamhute | Cherenje | Fled south; Kota succeeded. |
| Chirimunyati | Chimucheka | – | Assassinated, probably by Mbudzi. Family fled to Mozambique. |
| Mbudzi/Mberere (Matitima) | Gambiza | Chikondokwe River | Assassinated by Chifodya. |
| Chifodya/ Chikumbirike (Msirisiri) | Nyamande | Cherenje | Assassinated by Mbudzi or his faction. |

A narrative history can be reconstructed for this strata of oral tradition by interpreting the legends in combination with the differing genealogies. It appears that after Nyamhute had fled, Kota's faction united against the Nyaurimbo house. Once Nyaurimbo's family had been excluded from succession, the Kota faction split into two, with the progeny of Mberere (Mbudzi house) gradually excluding the Chikumbirike (Chifodya house) from succession (see Genealogy, Appendix 5).

The last two legends, concerning the factional warfare between the Mbudzi and Chifodya houses, merge with narrative history proper. This final strata of oral traditions recounts how the Katerere polity became embroiled in wars and conflict with the Portuguese and their agents. Thus, their content corroborates the written accounts of the adventurers and putative empire builders whom they were to encounter.

During the reign of Mbudzi, the polity was dominated by two factions: the descendants of Chikumbirike – Msirisiri (Chifodya) – and descendants of Mberere – Matitima (Mbudzi) (see genealogies in Appendix 5). The former felt particularly aggrieved that their house had not succeeded since the rule of their progenitor Chikumbirike. The Msirisiri or Chifodya house shared Cherenje ridge with another powerful family – the Sachiwos. From the perspective of the incumbent and enemy Mbudzi (Mberere) house, this was much too close to their stronghold on Mt Mhokore for their liking. Thus Chief Mbudzi appears to have made a prudent move across the Matizi river, first to a base in the Kwanda Range, and then to Mt Mapako (see Map 1.2). In consequence he moved the nerve centre of the polity.[46] This must have happened before 1872, because in that year the German explorer Carl Mauch was to encounter Chief Katerere on a mountain by the Chikondokwe river. Security was the order of the day. Mauch wrote: 'Thank God we were not forced to take up quarters in the rocky nest of Terere or Gaterere, who is enthroned high on a mountain height, but in another one of his half brother ...' (Burke, 1969: 237). The move also brought the Mbudzi house closer to their retainers – the Sadoweras on Mt Nyazingwe. The alliance was strengthened by a rare endogamous marriage. This may also have been the time when the Sadoweras took up their ritual functions.[47]

On the death of Mbudzi the Chifodyas made their bid for power. They recruited help from the powerful Mutoko polity west of Katerere (see Map 1.1), as well as from local families,[48] and assassinated Gambiza – the recently installed chief: 'They [the Chifodya faction] recruited soldiers from Mutoko and marched to Katerere. Gambiza was still alive and living at Chikondokwe ... A battle took place where the Chifodyas killed Chief Gambiza [of the Mbudzi house].' There was a great loss of life.[49] Nyamande of the Chifodya house appears to have then ruled for a while until the Mbudzi faction, with the help of the Nyawada *mhondoro* medium, regained political ascendancy through the assassination of Nyamande and the gruesome murder of his wife, Njesera. The Mbudzi faction made Tsarumunda chief. Nevertheless, the territory of Katerere remained effectively divided between the two factions throughout the twentieth century, even though the colonial regime formally recognised only the Mbudzi house as chiefs. The murder of Gambiza and the revenge assassination of Nyamande occurred in the 'time of Gouveia' who entered Katerere in the 1880s.[50]

## INTER-DYNASTIC POLITICS AND THE ARRIVAL OF COMPANY RULE

Hwesa politics cannot be considered in isolation. They were played out in relation to broader eastern Shona interests. Their pattern becomes apparent by tracing Katerere's interactions with surrounding polities in the wake of the arrival of the British and Portuguese colonial powers. The study of eastern Shona politics also highlights the role of traditional religious authorities in Katerere's affairs. We will see that *mhondoro* mediums in late nineteenth and early twentieth centuries *did* exercise some political and military leadership both independent of, and in cooperation with, the chief, though this varied over time and between polities.

This chapter has already shown how Shona polities were by no means unified, but riven with factions willing to appeal to outside sources of help. Even the political fortunes of dynasties far larger than Katerere could rise and fall quite rapidly. Describing the politics of the north-eastern Shona on the eve of colonisation, Beach captures both their fluidity and their interconnection. They were:

> [a] kaleidoscopic pattern of alliances and enmities, shifting from time to time and involving not only the ruling dynasty but subject lineages, neighbouring territories and any superpower that might be manipulated into aiding one faction or the other. (Beach, 1991: 4)

In the latter half of the century, Katerere's politics were entwined with those of four neighbouring powers, all of which could muster several thousand warriors in comparison to a mere few hundred Hwesa. The first of these polities was Makombe in Barwe, Mozambique, where the Hwesa originated. The adventurer, Carl Peters, described Katerere as a 'fief' of Makombe (1977: 150–1). Of the four surrounding powers Makombe was Chief Katerere's most consistent ally, and his territory a place of refuge in time of war.[51]

The second political power was Mutasa of Manica, whose kingdom was expanding northwards towards Katerere (Storry, 1976: 20). It had annexed Saunyama, and Katerere may have at one stage been under its control as a source of tribute.[52] The Hwesa were certainly a victim of Manyika raids (Beach, 1995: 18). Mutasa was also perhaps involved in the struggle between the Mbudzi and the Chifodya factions. The ethnographer, Michael Gelfand, was told that the king was called in to arbitrate and eventually favoured the Mbudzi faction, who consequently gave him a daughter to wed.[53] The third polity was Mutoko, lying to the north-west of Katerere. This large and independent polity much impressed the famous hunter and adventurer, F. C. Selous, in 1890. Capable of amassing as many as 5,000 men, it raided as far east as Gorongosa in Mozambique. Within its immediate vicinity Mutoko had a devastating effect on surrounding polities, raiding for women, girls and washed gold.[54] The kaleidoscopic nature of relations with external forces meant that, like Mutasa, Chief Mutoko could be an ally of one Hwesa faction and an enemy of another. Hence, there is also a tradition of a chief from the Mbudzi line fleeing there.[55] By the turn of the century, the Mbudzi house and Mutoko were on good terms. A family was sent from Mutoko to Katerere to aid the Hwesa chief in organising tribute labour to cultivate his fields.[56]

The last of the surrounding powers was led by Manuel António da Sousa, a Goanese *prazo* – estate – holder popularly known as Gouveia or Kuveya. By the 1880s he held a string of *prazos* stretching from his fort in Gorongosa to Sena and the Zambezi. Between 1880 and 1883 he conquered Makombe, thus bringing the north-eastern Shona territories into his sphere of influence (Beach, 1991: 8).

Insight into both the Katerere polity's relations with these surrounding powers, and the political function of *mhondoro* cults, can be gleaned from the records of J. C. Paiva de Andrada, the Portuguese soldier and adventurer, who recruited Gouveia to provide the necessary military backup for his company's exploration and conquest of the Zimbabwean plateau on behalf of Portugal (Beach, 1984: 37, 62). Andrada arrived in Katerere on 13 September 1885, professing friendship on behalf of Portugal. He was subsequently resisted by a collection of 'important people of Caterere' along with '100 armed men ... followed by a lion (or '*pandoro*')'. This delegation of 'important' people and a *mhondoro* medium, possibly asserting their independence from a weak chief, rightly claimed that he was friendly with Gouveia and had come to deceive them. (Andrada, 1886: 6–10)

It is possible that Andrada exaggerated the significance of the incident with the Katerere *'pandoro'* as an elaborate excuse for the failure of his first mission. Certainly when he returned in 1886 there was no recurrence of this confrontation, and Chief Katerere seems to have had his people and mediums under control.[57] Yet the confrontation did seem to make an impression on Andrada because he refers to it again in 1889.[58] Elsewhere on his first journey into the north-east he encountered *pandoros* as powerful intermediaries in the adjacent land of Rupire (Andrada, 1886: 9–10). Moreover, in his perambulations of 1887, he discovered that his elderly ally, Chief Chitsungo, lacked control over both his sons and *pandoro* who had killed two of his sepoys.[59] He subsequently described *pandoros* as figures who were 'believed to contain within themselves the souls of departed kings, and who, as such, determine all important questions connected with wars, the land ...' (Andrada, 1891b: 9). Likewise, when the adventurer, Selous, entered the region a year later, he had an equally frustrating experience of first being vetted by a powerful *mhondoro* medium before his negotiations with Chief Mutoko could begin. He wrote: 'No step of any importance is ever taken until this "Lion-god" has been consulted.'[60]

Despite their initial resistance, the Hwesa finally came into the Portuguese orbit. In May 1886, under Andrada's orders, Gouveia conquered the adjacent territory of Rupire. Katerere and three other chiefs immediately submitted to him. The statement recording Portugal's overall claims to the area read:

> Katerere will pay tribute when there is a fort in Rupire or Masahwa which is strong enough to guarantee his future security, seeing that he is more than any other constantly discommoded by raids from the people of Mutasa. (Portuguese Government, 1980: 264, no. 113)

This was the first phase of Gouveia and Andrada's plan to thwart the British South Africa Company's (BSAC) designs on the region (Henriksen, 1978: 83). The second phase did not go so well. In February 1887, Gouveia conscripted and armed Hwesa men to fight the powerful Mutoko polity. The campaign was a disaster which ended with most of Gouveia's allies fleeing in a state of panic, but Katerere remained loyal to the end.[61] In August 1889, Andrada gave Chief Katerere 100 Winchester rifles in return for his loyalty and was aided by Hwesa sepoys in his journey south.[62]

Chief Katerere's alliance with Gouveia and Andrada did not spring from any great love for them. He seems to have sided with what he perceived to be the most significant power, against his other two enemies. Mutoko, and perhaps Mutasa, had been involved in the near catastrophic factional struggle with the Chifodyas, and Mutasa's raiding was a constant threat to the

Katerere. In the absence of his ally Makombe, Gouveia thus offered Chief Katerere the best chance of consolidating his position. However, the Hwesa would be rid of the Portuguese threat as soon as the first opportunity arose.

The chance came when the BSAC began to interact with the north-eastern Shona in 1890, after its head, Cecil John Rhodes, had marched his pioneer column into Zimbabwe. However, in order to grasp the rapidly shifting alliances in eastern Shona politics at this time it is first necessary to understand the status of Rhodes's company on its arrival. During the first decade of its occupation of Zimbabwe, the BSAC was weak and under-capitalised. Its major concern was to consolidate its position against the Portuguese and the Boers in the Transvaal. This meant that 'the extension of its rule over the Shona was extremely gradual and uneven ... like the Portuguese ... [the company was] ... simply absorbed into existing political patterns' (Phimister, 1988: 12). Thus the British were not perceived in the north-east as a great conquering colonial force, but as one more local power to do business with – another, albeit strong, colour in the historical kaleidoscope. As late as 1899 it was believed that the British would leave, just as other white traders and explorers had done before them.[63]

After the Occupation in 1890, Katerere was supposedly administered by the Inyanga District Native Commissioner (NC). Yet the first Acting Resident Native Commissioner only arrived there in 1899 and the first substantive NC in 1902 – 12 years after the British arrival (Petheram, 1974: 41). Katerere remained remote from state control, a place that bandits fled to.[64] Indeed the Katerere polity's continuing links with Barwe in Mozambique caused the Portuguese to attempt to tax it in 1903.[65] Nevertheless the coming of the British immediately brought about significant shifts in the balance of power between the four large polities described above.

In 1890 Mutasa connived with the BSAC to have Andrada and Gouveia arrested at his mountain encampment. During the period of Gouveia's arrest and absence from Gorongosa, both Makombe and Mutoko raided his territory, leaving him severely weakened.[66] In 1892, Gouveia was killed by a coalition of WaBarwe princely houses. He had exacted tribute from Barwe throughout the 1880s, and at one stage assassinated King Makombe for his non-cooperation.[67] Chief Katerere, along with Taungwena, crossed the border and joined with his old allies in the uprising against the *prazo* holder.[68] There are a number of stories surrounding the killing of Gouveia, and the Hwesa proudly possess one of them. They joined the revolt in protest against the mutilation and rape of a prepubescent girl by Gouveia's men; a local warrior, Kambudzi, was responsible for Gouveia's death.[69] The rape of young girls at that time by Portuguese-led soldiers has been documented elsewhere.[70]

The addition of the BSAC to the kaleidoscopic pattern of relations between the north-eastern Shona enabled Katerere to gain six years of peace after the elimination of Gouveia. The Hwesa were not involved in the First Chimurenga – the 1896 war of resistance against the British. They had not yet been brought into the taxation system, and had experienced no forced labour or company stock raiding. 'The extremely uneven political and economic impact of the chartered intruders combined with Shona diplomatic and political considerations to bring about an extraordinarily complex and equally uneven response from Mashonaland's various African polities.' (Phimister, 1988: 19) Still marginal to BSAC administrative influence, the Hwesa doubtless perceived the Portuguese in the east to be a far more significant influence. The watershed in relations with the British came in the years 1898–1902.

In 1898 the British were still seen as a useful ally. Chief Tsarumunda Katerere offered them assistance in the border survey and the apprehension of the bandit, William Kober.[71] In August 1899, Tsarumunda Katerere died.[72] He was rapidly succeeded as Hwesa chief by another member of the Mbudzi faction, Chimombe. Two months later, 'a chief and his followers' appeared on the Portuguese side of the Gaerezi River and claimed the chieftainship. This was undoubtedly the Chifodya faction, as some lived on the east bank of the river. The challenger and his retainers were chased off by native department messengers.[73] The incident would have educated the new chief about the utility of an alliance with the settler regime.

Yet, at the same time, the British began to turn the administrative screw, prompting Hwesa disaffection. Hut tax began to be collected, albeit initially ineffectively, by the Native Commissioner for Mtoko.[74] By 1902 the collection was more effective, with Katerere brought firmly under the administrative district of Inyanga.[75] British insistence that the tax be paid in currency, rather than Portuguese coinage or rupees, seriously curtailed the dominant eastern dimension of the Katerere trade network, compelling the Hwesa to enter the Rhodesian money economy.[76]

Chief Katerere's response was immediate. Much to the distress of the Native Administration, he crossed over the border with his followers to aid the Makombe people in the 1901–2 war against Portuguese rule in Barwe. Police intelligence on the matter conjectured that the Hwesa hoped first to remove the Portuguese threat, and then pick a fight with the British over the tax issue. Such a plan was quite feasible from Katerere's perspective. Although only a small polity, Hwesa experience of the British presence had, to date, been restricted to a few mounted soldiers and porters, whilst they remained heavily armed thanks to Andrada.[77] Moreover, the Hwesa had spiritual assistance. Hwesa oral traditions recount how *mhondoro* mediums dispensed *mapfuwe* – magical charms to protect warriors going into battle.[78] In the event the Portuguese overran Barwe with great ease, crushing the rebellion. (Ranger, 1963: 59–60)

The Hwesa were finally brought to heel in 1904. Intelligence reports warned of an impending uprising which would be 'simultaneous throughout Mashonaland' and 'that Katarara, Souyama, Samembere, Sanyatwe, Sadamba, Zinde and others were to wipe out whites in this [Inyanga] district'. On the organisation of the revolt, intelligence warned that 'witch doctors were numerous and at the bottom of it all. Magando ... of Tshikomba's district ... and four others have been round stirring up people also a big one in Katarara's district, who is famous for feats with a basket which no others can lift'.[79] In swift response, Katerere was visited by a force of 32 BSAC police, 44 carriers and a maxim gun. The NC Inyanga described what happened:

> Major Straker instructed [Tpr] Bailiff of the BSAC police to fire the Maxim gun for the edification of Katerere, Marowa and their followers. About sixty-three rounds were fired in the space of one minute, which greatly impressed the natives present ... [Katerere] had nothing to say except that he was quite willing to pay the government tax ...[80]

It is possible that colonial officials over-reacted to intelligence reports, particularly to information that Chief Katerere had recently visited a 'witch doctor' in order to get spiritual sanction for his uprising.[81] The memory of the 1896 uprisings was fresh in their minds, and Native Department officials were somewhat 'obsessed with conspiracies and "superstition"' (Beach, 1986: 120). Nevertheless, BSAC intelligence was very effective (Isaacman, 1976: 143), and the NC Inyanga did engage in critical reflection concerning the rumours before stating that he was sure 'trouble of some kind of was brewing'.[82]

The 1904 unrest in Katerere, like the 1901–2 Makombe war before it, illustrates the complex interplay of local and regional agendas. Allen Isaacman's study on the politics of the Zambezi valley from 1851 to 1921 locates Hwesa political action against the Portuguese and British within an eastern Shona, and at times an even larger, Zambezi-wide movement. Katerere was one of 'many historical royal families' committed to remaining 'outside the sphere of effective European colonialism' (Isaacman, 1976: 59). Isaacman also contends that in the rising and the unrest, military forces were coordinated by a network of *mhondoro* mediums working through the Dzivaguru cult (1976: 60; see also Mudenge, 1988: 361).

Isaacman's arguments concerning the territory-wide scope of Shona politics and their religious organisation are plausible. Katerere did engage in coordinated political activity well beyond its borders, and the Hwesa did adhere to the multi-ethnic federative cult of Karuva/Dzivaguru. However, local agendas also affected the 1901–2 rising and 1904 unrest, in part explaining their failure. First, each polity was motivated by locally specific experiences of the colonial state, which of course differed in relation to which side of the Anglo-Portuguese border it was on (Isaacman, 1976: 144). Secondly, past rivalries between adjacent polities militated against a permanent broad-based coalition to oppose common colonial enemies (Ibid: 145). After 1904, any chance of Hwesa relations with Shona east of the Gaerezi River rapidly diminished with the BSAC's graphic assertion of its presence and borders.

## CONCLUSION

This chapter has outlined the internal dynamics of pre-colonial Hwesa society and introduced two important themes in this study. First, it has highlighted the durability of the institution of chieftainship. This resilience owed much to chiefs' and factions' skills in political survival. Hwesa chiefs were particularly adept in mediating the dangers of factional and inter-dynastic politics, and deft in playing off against each other the Portuguese and the British. These skills were to stand them in good stead when they were faced by colonial and post-colonial states.

The second theme to emerge is the dynamic interaction between traditional religious and political institutions. Traditional religion, more specifically *mhondoro* cults, did not merely provide legitimacy for pre-colonial chiefs. Rather, these 'tribal' cults oscillated between establishment religion and protest movement. Their tradition of resistance and innovation offers insight into how they were able to reassert themselves in response to the changing contingencies of life in twentieth-century Katerere.

This chapter also adds to a growing mainstream of literature[83] which reinterprets the immediate impact of colonial rule as less significant than previously thought. The arrival of the settler state in 1890 has diverted previous historians from the political realities of the late nineteenth century. Viewed from the reference point of the new Rhodesian capital in Salisbury, Katerere appeared a marginal polity in the remote north-east. Yet from its own perspective, Katerere was involved in a complex of inter-dynastic relations which centred on Barwe in Mozambique. Located within this frame of reference, the BSAC did not constitute a great transforming entity but another element in the regional balance of power.

State formation was slow and problematic. The BSAC was not able to establish direct political control over Katerere until 1904, and even then it was to remain marginal on a daily basis. Although the new regime, through its network of messengers, remained well-informed about population movements and crime, it was not until the 1950s that it intervened in agricultural production or built an infrastructure which opened the area up to missions. However, the pacification of Katerere in 1904 meant that the colonial state was able to disengage it from its previous sets of relations with surrounding polities, and slowly, though not completely, recast the Hwesa political economy to its own design.

# 2

# THE CINDERELLA PEOPLE: HWESA POLITICAL AND RELIGIOUS INTERACTIONS WITH THE COLONIAL STATE, 1904–50

## INTRODUCTION

When Chief Tsarumunda Katerere died in August 1899 the NC Mtoko reported the event with some regret. Tsarumunda had been a 'well known' chief, 'known favourably to all travellers by the east from the Zambesi to Mashonaland'.[1] Within a few years, the new state had asserted its borders and the route from the east was closed down. Fifty years later the Hwesa were little known and the NC Inyanga could call them his 'Cinderella People'.

This chapter begins by exploring in what sense the Hwesa's interrelation with the new colonial state rendered them a 'Cinderella People', and then outlines their own agendas and constructions of identity. Of course, colonial rule and its acceleration of capitalist penetration did bring about great changes in the Hwesa political economy, further privileging elders over women and youth, and sending men into the migrant labour system. But there was much room for negotiation, resistance and the playing out of local struggles. Hwesa elders revived their authority by allying with the Native Administration in the invention of a new customary order. The ruling Mbudzi faction strove to maintain its political dominance through the manipulation of both local and state perceptions of religious legitimacy, and through the elaboration of an ethno-history. Women worked out a number of economic and religious strategies to ameliorate the intolerable burdens of economic and biological reproduction placed upon them. And returning labour migrants attempted to separate themselves from the demands of traditional leaders by fostering witchcraft eradication movements and later a popular pentecostal Christianity. But while possession cults, witchcraft eradication and Christianity had an instrumental appeal to members of certain social categories we begin to see the multi-layered and contextual nature of identity in Katerere. Religious identities were complicated by allegiances of ethnicity and kinship.

THE NEW ORDER:
CHANGES IN THE POLITICAL ECONOMY

The settler state's assertion of authority over north-east Rhodesia in 1904 marked the end of a gradual process of pacification which had begun 14 years earlier with the Occupation. The imposition of colonial rule over the region brought about great changes in its political economy.

The collection of a Hut tax compelled adult males into the migrant labour system to earn the necessary money for its payment. Others migrated of their own volition, using their wages for bride-price, clothes, and security against drought. The majority gravitated to the colony's gold mines, principally those at Gatooma, but also to a lesser extent at Penhalonga, and Makaha in Mtoko. Other men worked on the *rarwe* – railway – between Marandellas and Umtali. The remaining few found jobs as *kitchiniboys* – kitchen boys – in the cities and towns.[2]

Where polities were near to Rhodesian markets, households had the option of becoming peasant producers (Ranger, 1985: chapter 1) In Katerere's case, its distance from settlement and mines made peasant agriculture an impossibility. A report of 1919 noted that the majority of males had entered the labour market, although a few continued in their 'age old' crafts as blacksmiths, bead workers and basket makers, which along with the possession of political office and/or ritual function were the main non-migrant options.[3]

Colonial rule was further consolidated by the disarming of the African population, rigorously enforced by native messengers and the BSAC police.[4] This erosion of the military basis of traditional leaders' power was part of a wider strategy aimed at limiting their authority. Chiefs were stripped of their rights to receive tribute, to distribute land and to hear criminal cases.[5]

However, in the third decade of colonial rule the state's policy towards traditional leaders went into reverse. There was no grand design for the settler regime's realignment with chiefs, nor did traditional leaders ever regain the full extent of their pre-colonial powers, although there was a gradual recognition of their potential utility. The Native Administration's increasing reliance on them can be attributed to a variety of reasons. First, by the mid 1920s it was apparent that the settler economy would not expand enough to sustain all Africans in plantation agriculture or mining. A new emphasis on 'tribal control' emerged from the post-1923 settler society, which did not wish to share its wealth with Africans. Advocates of a 'reconstituted "tribalism" and "traditionalism"' (Phimister, 1988: 149) got the better of those who, inspired by European individualism, had worked for a 'detribalised and proletarianised African population'.[6]

The second explanation for the state's accommodation of traditional leaders was its desire for political control of the African population. The movement of adult males into the migrant labour economy created opportunities for women and young men to break free from the tutelage of faction leaders. From the 1910s onwards, government legislation supported the endeavours of traditional male élites to reassert patriarchal control. (Jeater, 1993; Schmidt, 1992: chapter 4) Related to this was the state's concern for governance. Native Department officials were often over-stretched. Their contact with distant reserves was often limited to shows of force and the quarterly or semi-annual 'stage managed tour' (Fields, 1985: 54). Hence the state needed local agents in the reserves to implement its policies (Holleman, 1969: 35–7). Chiefs and headmen became tax collectors, labour recruiters and overseers of state intervention in agriculture. Lastly, the state realigned itself with the gerontocratic leaders of rural communities in order to gain legitimacy. 'The privileged never rest content – merely to enjoy their good fortune; they always demand to believe that it is merited.' (Fields, 1985: 41, paraphrasing Weber, 1963: 107)

Despite the fact that the power relations were far from equal, chiefs joined with their colonial masters in imagining an ideology to underpin this new order. Drawing on an idealised version of the pre-colonial past in which the rule of elder male élites went unquestioned, traditional leaders and the Native Administration created customary law. John Lonsdale describes the rationale behind the state alliance with traditional leaders:

> Rule through chiefs was defensible so long as they could be seen as the natural leaders of communal societies untroubled by a plurality of political ideologies, for whom consensus was an inherited state of mind rather than an inherited weapon of social conflict ... the codification of customary law was a weapon of present social control rather than a summary of past history. (Lonsdale, 1992: 209)

Though the Native Administration's realignment with chiefs and their consequent enterprise in the elaboration of a customary order occurred across the colony of Southern Rhodesia, the state had an uneven administrative impact which varied according to access from the administrative centre.

## THE CINDERELLA PEOPLE:
## THE EXTENT OF KATERERE'S MARGINALITY FROM COLONIAL RULE

Katerere remained outside the orbit of the BSAC for the first 14 years of the Occupation. Its inaccessibility made it an excellent refuge for bandits, safeguarded it from effective tax collection until 1902, and allowed it to stay involved in the politics of Barwe in Portuguese East Africa until 1904. After 1904 the colonial state had only two basic aims for Katerere: the maintenance of both its labour supply, and law and order.

In the first two decades of the twentieth century the Native Administration continually harangued Chief Chimombe Katerere to turn out his male subjects for work. The border was patrolled to ensure the smooth flow of Mozambican labour into Rhodesia, and to safeguard against the spilling over of Portuguese instability into the British colony. As the intelligence network of native messengers and BSAC police became more effective, there was a gradual increase in the flow of convictions for witchcraft accusation and the contravention of gun and game laws.[7] Occasionally whites would enter Katerere for some specific task such as the construction of the road from Nhani to the border at Fombe, or to work the mines of the Makaha gold belt. But those that did come were so few and far between that they rapidly engrained themselves in popular memory. One NC, *Mpondo Mbiri* – Two Pounds – was particularly remembered for his propensity for fining the Hwesa and their neighbours: two pounds whatever the offence. For a brief period, during the Second World War, the gold mines in Lawley's concession in the far west of Katerere, on the Fombe road, were worked by two white men: *Kuweni* – Cohen – and *Gekeke*[8] – Hooke. A small compound developed employing about 100 men. A few Hwesa worked there but the majority were Malawian and Mozambican. The Hwesa sold cow peas and other produce to this small market but the mine was forced to close down due to the difficulty of obtaining enough water to wash the gold.[9]

However, Katerere was still marginal to the state's wider socio-economic project. Hwesa agriculture remained free from state intervention until the 1950s, and the region was relatively untouched by the colonial 'civilising mission', receiving no education or health services until 1951. The north-east's marginality was directly related to its continued inaccessibility. A combination of dense vegetation, mountains and numerous streams made access by motor transport into Katerere from both the south-west and south-east extremely problematic. During the 1918 drought the NC Inyanga wrote, 'No European would consent to transport grain up to Mt Nhani privately as the road is very bad.' Seven years later he wrote, 'At present it is impossible to get to Nyamaropa Reserve or within several miles of it by wheeled vehicle.'[10] The territory's major road was the route to Fombe on the western edge of the territory, leaving the bulk of the chiefdom in the east, accessible only by foot.

When making their yearly visit to Katerere to collect taxes, Native Commissioners would be confined to camps on the western road. The chief and headmen would be summoned to them. To proceed further into the interior involved an arduous journey. It was not until the 1950s that roads and bridges were properly constructed, thus rendering Katerere accessible to the local administration on a permanent basis. It was only in 1951 that missionaries first successfully penetrated the area with the help of local people, who cut a road for their one-ton truck. In 1952 the Native Commissioner noted, 'this area has now been entered for the first time.'[11]

As will be shown below, Katerere's marginality was experienced in different ways by its inhabitants, and most profoundly by its women. But it was also felt by those colonial officials responsible for its administration. From the official perspective Inyanga district was a bad posting in the early decades of the twentieth century. Even the town of Inyanga in the south was seen as remote.[12] It was in this context that in 1951 the NC for the district, Meredith, did much to entice Elim Pentecostal mission into Katerere, explaining to the pioneer missionaries concerned that the Hwesa were his 'Cinderella People'.[13]

## CHIEFS, SPIRIT MEDIUMS AND THE RE-IMAGINATION OF TRADITIONAL RELIGION

The 'unspoilt' appearance of the Hwesa, to Native Department officials at least, gave their traditional leaders greater room to manoeuvre in the imagination of a new customary order. In the process, the old interaction between chiefs and mediums was redefined. Citing a number of incidents in Katerere, and adjacent polities, where outsiders were mediated by powerful mediums acting independently of chiefs, it was argued that there had often been less interdependence between chiefs and mediums in the pre-colonial period. Chiefs had their material and military bases of support, and were not dependent on ritual resources. And, since mediums were involved in a wider territorial cult system, they had relative autonomy from chiefs, even if they played host to 'tribal' ancestors. In the twentieth century, chiefs became more dependent on ritual legitimacy because they were unable to underpin their political control with material and military power. In a similar manner, mediums found their pre-colonial independence curtailed through the loss of their military influence, and through their restriction to one locality. Hence, the two parties moved closer together to re-imagine ritually supported chieftainship.

The imposition of colonial rule diminished the degree of political control chiefs could exercise over their subjects. Katerere's marginality to the local administration meant that such changes were only gradually effected there. In 1921, Chief Chimombe Katerere was indicted for the contravention of the Witch Suppression Ordinance of 1899. The details of the case provide fascinating insight into how pre-colonial chiefs may have used/abused their judicial powers, in this case through the cynical manipulation of the *muteyo* poison ordeal. Katerere's wife, Machangwe, accused a Barwe 'native' Muzaza and his wife Chakupotedza of poisoning their child. Usually both accuser and accused were forced to partake of the poison to determine guilt. But on pain of death, Muzaza alone was forced by the chief to go through with the poison ordeal. When the accused purged (vomited) violently, Katerere pronounced him guilty and sent his own relatives to exact a fine. This not only included a daughter, 12 goats and 30/- but also the entire contents of Muzaza's homestead: 11 loads of grain, four hoes and 20 fowls.

The Mozambican outsider was thus stripped of his entire wealth by the chief's immediate family. On pronouncing the sentence, Chief Katerere was reported to have said 'if we were not under the rule of a white man I would have killed you with an axe.'[14]

Although the above case is an extreme one, in that it directly involved Katerere's family, a large degree of a pre-colonial chief's political and economic power derived from his ability to dispense justice. Moreover, the case showed the considerable coercion to which the chief was able to resort without jeopardising his legitimacy. The gradual consolidation of colonial rule forced chiefs to look for new sources of power and legitimacy.

One new source of power was to be gained by moving location. In Katerere, the ruling faction moved quickly to secure control over land. When the adventurer, Carl Peters, reached Katerere in 1900, the chief's camp was no longer a 'rocky nest' (see Chapter 1) perched high on a mountain, as his German predecessor, Mauch, had encountered it, but a 'small shadeless dirty village' (Peters, 1977: 150). Another move, around 1903, saw the chief and his immediate following move south across the Matize River back into the centre of the chiefdom where they were located before they fled the hostile Chifodya faction.[15] Ken Wilson's research on Mazhiwa in southern Zimbabwe has shown that after the Occupation there occurred a period known as *kupaariria evanhu* – the spreading out of people – whereby young men moved out of the defendable hills into the *deve* – extensive woodlands. The new household system of production boosted crop yields and provided young men with a greater independence from the big men who ruled the mountain strongholds. In this process of dispersal, leaders of factions were often the first to move in order to secure tenure over the newly settled land and reassert their authority. (K. Wilson, 1988: 2)

A further source of power was the control of sacred wood lots and holy pools. Hwesa chiefs claimed sacred wood lots whose wood was only for their disposal.[16] Royal houses were often less concerned with conservation and more with symbols of legitimacy to compensate for their loss of direct political control over their subjects now living under *pax Britannia*. Moreover, the pools and trees did not simply have a symbolic value. After the 1950s when these resources became more scarce they were managed by royals as a means of amassing clients.[17]

Spirit mediums lent full support to ritual enterprises to reconstitute chiefly power. In Katerere, the Mbudzi house's desire to dominate the chiefdom from the territory's centre was to prove problematic. Their move had brought them onto Crown Land. When the state contested this, the chief was able to gain a dispensation by arguing that 'his ancestral spirits' did not allow him to live north of the river – an obvious invention, in the light of where his recent ancestors in the Mbudzi house had resided.[18] Mediums likewise helped sacralise the landscape to bolster chiefly power. Although mountains lost their immediate utility for providing defendable settlements, they were sacralised as burial sites of former chiefs. In the twentieth century almost all of the mountains associated with pre-colonial factions were sacralised in this way, evoking memories of a previous age when traditional leaders held considerable political power, and providing their descendants with a religious legitimacy by association. The mountains' religious significance was enhanced through strong taboos against the cutting of trees upon them. The taboos were enforced by *mhondoro* mediums.

The importance of the spiritual legitimation of the Hwesa chiefs is illustrated by the nature of the only officially recorded challenge to their leadership 1900–89. The opponents' case was made completely in the idiom of traditional religion. In 1936, Chief Chikata Katerere was accused by his relatives of not properly appeasing the spirits, wearing his crown too early, and failing to perform the coronation ritual of sitting on the crocodile – *gara [pa] ngwena*.[19] However, the opponents' argument was a lost cause on the Inyanga NC, who had already noted that the 'spiritual forces [*mhondoro* mediums] concurred' on Chikata's election, excluding the pretenders on the grounds of leprosy in their house.[20] Such contestation was very different from the pre-colonial reality of factional warfare and political assassination. Reflecting on 'the politics of custom', Karen Fields writes: 'Paradoxically, the role of the supernatural increased as Africa's history joined that of a secularised society' (Fields, 1985: 66. See also 61–5). A ritually supported chief is much more a twentieth-century construction than a nineteenth-century phenomenon.

The Mbudzi house, incumbent at the time of the Occupation, also strengthened its position by forming new alliances with particular spirits, and consolidating existing alliances. This was possible because the spirits remained within one family, with the grandson or nephew replacing the grandfather or uncle as host. In effect, the mediums' families joined the ruling faction with the alliance being tied through marriage to Mbudzi women. The medium not only gained wives but gifts of cattle, and new authority drawn from association with the chief.

The most long-standing and influential of these alliances that the Mbudzi house constructed was with a succession of mediums from the Rukadza family – host of Nyawada. As the 'Mbudzi House' legend in Appendix 3 suggests, this arrangement existed in pre-colonial times. The first Rukadza came from the adjacent Saunyama dynasty and joined the Hwesa chief as a warrior. The spirit next passed to one of his wives, Kadyiwa Kazipe, and then on to the last medium, Diki, who lived well into his nineties.[21] Another local family – the Chiwengas – 'played host' to as many as three *mhondoro* spirits, all of whom seem to have been sympathetic to the ruling house.[22] The benefits to families of mediums in terms of wives, cattle and authority derived from association with the ruling house also explains various anomalies in current factional politics in Katerere, discussed in detail in Chapter 6. Mediums whose spirits were the progenitors of other royal houses have realigned behind the incumbent house in return for material gain and political influence.[23]

The bureaucratisation of chieftainship, then, did not necessarily mean a separation of chiefs from *mhondoro* cults. Chiefs were adept at assuming multiple identities, appearing in one guise to colonial officials and another to their own constituencies, drawing legitimacy from local spiritual authorities at one moment and from access to state power at the next. One particular way in which traditional leaders used their ambiguous relationship with the state to reconstitute their power and authority was the elaboration of ethnicity. In Katerere this process, mediated by the territory's marginality, gave rise to an ethnic identity markedly different from other eastern Shona polities.

## CHIEFS, THE STATE AND ETHNICITY

After the Occupation, traditional political leaders seeking to retain their popular legitimacy were often compromised through unavoidable association with the colonial state. They were obliged to oversee the collection of the hated Hut tax, and to impose unpopular agricultural practices at the behest of local NCs. Hence it is often claimed that, under colonialism, chiefs became little more than stooges of the Native Administration, discredited in the eyes of their own people and lacking the necessary ability to reconcile the conflicting demands of 'tradition' and 'modernity'.[24] Yet this is only half of the story. We have already seen how Hwesa chiefs generated a new-found ritual legitimacy. With a similar pragmatism they used the state in the creation of ethnicity.

At the turn of the twentieth century Chief Chimombe Katerere was in a precarious political position. Only two months after his installation the Chifodya faction made a show of force to regain the chiefdom.[25] Whilst Chimombe was fortunate enough to have native messengers in the area who chased the challengers away, his chiefdom was still effectively split in two. The Chifodyas controlled the hills and plains around the Cherenje Range south of the Matizi River (see Map 1.2). The Mbudzi faction needed new allies.

After the failure of the 1902 Makombe uprising and the show of British military power two years later, Chief Chimombe Katerere seems to have shifted his loyalties to the Rhodesian State. This would have provided him with a number of benefits. The first was his privileged 'access to state officials' (Alexander, 1993: 16). Chief Katerere's move out of the hills not only consolidated his control over land distribution, but also increased his access to the state power over and against his rival. His domination of the land between the Ruangwe and Cherenje ranges blocked the Chifodya house's access to officials (and later missionaries), leaving them socially and physically marginalised in the remote border area. A key part of the Mbudzi strategy to retain the chieftainship was control of the native messenger. In his monograph on local government in Southern Rhodesia, J. F. Holleman remarks that, 'The role played in the local administration by these minor African civil servants merits more extensive analysis' (Holleman, 1969: 35). Native messengers became more important as sources of information, NCs became increasingly desk-bound under the growing weight of bureaucracy. And the rotation of NCs between districts further enhanced the messengers' value. Holleman writes:

> Their usefulness was immense, for being African and local, they unerringly found their passage along customary channels and centres of communication of the indigenous hierarchies and rivalries of power, of which the commissioner was only too often insufficiently aware. (Ibid.: 36)

Messengers also controlled the flow of information from the people to the NC: 'One of the practical and probably inevitable consequences was that such communications became "screened" and sometimes censored, before they reached the commissioner' (Ibid.: 37). Significantly, messengers were often recruited from prominent factions.[26]

On 1 November 1930 Tadzira Katerere from the Mbudzi house was made a native messenger. He remained in this position until the 31 October 1960 when, following the death of Chief Chikata, he was elected as Chief Njanji Katerere.[27] Until the 1980s, there were only two key moments when the ruling Mbudzi house's monopoly on the chieftainship could be threatened: the elections of 1932 and 1960. On both occasions it appears, both from official records and interviews, that the rival Chifodya faction had no knowledge of the key meetings and procedures for appointment. Thus Tadzira Katerere effectively screened successive NCs from the rival Chifodya claims to the chiefdom until he himself was ready to take up the office in 1960.[28]

In 1903, Chief Chimombe Katerere embarked on one of his characteristically pragmatic political juggling acts, and applied for a subsidy. Katerere was no doubt opportunistically making a definition of his subjects based on the number of taxable units – 1,084 males – arrived at in the first successful tax collection made in his chiefdom in that year.[29] The unimpressed NC Inyanga wrote curtly:

> I have not recommended this. He is only chief over 750 souls and has done nothing to warrant any recognition by the government to reward his services. Should he be granted, it would only cause mischief as I have at least five other chiefs in the district with as many people.[30]

Nevertheless, Katerere's association with the 1904 unrest appears to have increased his bargaining power. The Hwesa were now something of a liability and the NC doubtless realised that Katerere's influence did extend beyond the members of his immediate faction.[31] By 1907, Katerere had been awarded a subsidy.[32]

In the Inyanga administration's adoption of Katerere as a subsidised chief there is a prefiguring of what the Native Department was later to perceive as a general function of chiefs: as instruments of 'tribal control'.[33] The annual report of 1903 noted under the heading of 'crime' that the district was bordered on the east by a population of 200,000 in Portuguese East Africa, over whom the Portuguese had only 'nominal control'. Furthermore, the district was part of the highway from the north, and the border a conduit for illegal trade in guns.[34] Other concerns for the Native Administration were the movement of factions back and forth across the border as a strategy for tax evasion, and the constant influx of refugees from Barwe fleeing Portuguese rule.[35] The instability of the border population convinced the Native Department of the need to keep Katerere as a loyal ally.

Ironically, Chief Katerere's inclusive definition of his subjects contributed to the construction of Hwesa ethnicity. What had been a collection of territorially based factions, in which the 'chief' and his house were at times no more than first among equals, was transformed into an administrative unit, through which labour recruitment, local customary justice and tax collection were organised. As the century progressed, this official representation of the Hwesa 'tribe' gradually became a reality in the minds of the Hwesa themselves. In the past, the object of inter-factional politics had been the acquisition of resources: women, youth, cattle, trade and territory, by force of arms. The new political reality was more complex. Although these resources remained the goal of competing factions, the surest way of securing them was through the office of chief. And whereas in pre-colonial times succession had been determined by contest, it was now determined by a set of normative rules (Döpcke, 1991: 19). Those Hwesa factions seeking either to acquire or consolidate their power had to rapidly learn the rules of this new game.

A key rule was that royal factions needed to produce histories and genealogies which acted as legitimating charters or political arguments for their claims to power. This is not to imply that these traditions were nothing more than twentieth-century constructions which served to legitimate or challenge pervading political realities. As the previous chapter illustrates, they were by nature both historical and political. They were historical in the sense that they remembered repetitive processes or classes of recurrent events such as battles, migrations and assassinations. And they were political in that they made claims to power and legitimacy, by means of cliché and other symbolic statements. This new game could be termed 'lineage politics', a game whereby territorially based factions developed arguments about descent to satisfy the new chief makers – the Native Department.

Throughout the twentieth century, one can chart a growth in interest in history amongst gerontocratic African élites. Responding to the South African Native Affairs Commission of 1903, the Acting NC for Mtoko wrote to the CNC, lamenting his inability to discover information concerning 'the histories and genealogies of the tribes' in his district:

> I have frequently sought information of the nature required but for some inexplicable reason, the natives from whom I have tried to elicit some facts of their earlier history have pleaded ignorance of the past …
>
> With regard to a complete genealogy, I do not see how this information is to be obtained, to call all the chiefs into this office, and expect them to give in detail a complete genealogical tree of their forefathers is out of the question …
>
> They would probably demur at having to make a journey which does not interest them in any way …[36]

An ethnographic and historical survey, carried out in Inyanga district in 1908, was a little more productive, but still very vague on 'origins'.[37] Chiefs and headmen were not unaware of the past. In the early decades of colonial rule they were simply unwilling to divulge such information to a powerful and alien state. But by the late 1910s, at least in Inyanga District, they were willing to do so, because it was in their political interest.

Because gerontocratic élites remembered the past in order to make a set of political arguments about the present, their accounts were greatly embellished. Genealogies were lengthened, and traditions restructured in a way that disqualified or excluded the claims of other factions. Thus, the new rules of succession initially played into the hands of incumbent royal houses who benefited from their privileged access to state officials.[38] However, as the other Hwesa royal factions became aware of the rules, they too made claims of succession. In doing so the enterprise of imagining ethnicity became more widespread as more people became interested in asserting their credentials in terms of descent from a pre-colonial 'chiefdom'.

The Hwesa did have a pre-colonial identity as members of a polity with shifting boundaries. The maps drawn by those European explorers who travelled throughout the north-east in the late nineteenth century clearly show the 'Kingdom of Katerere' lying between the great polities of Mutasa, Mutoko and Makombe.[39] The Hwesa identity would have been reinforced in the 1880s by Goveia's collection of tribute from Katerere, and his conscription *en masse* of Hwesa into his war against Mutoko.[40]

However, the force of a pre-colonial Hwesa ethnic identity was checked by at least two others. The first identity was a larger one deriving from a regional polity; the second was the more local one of the faction. When the adventurer, Carl Peters, entered Katerere from the east in 1900, he was welcomed. He explained in his writings that this was because Katerere was a 'fief' of Makombe (Peters, 1977: 151–4). As Chapter 1 illustrated, Katerere was Makombe's ally in war, and Barwe a place of refuge for fleeing Hwesa factions. Of course, different identities asserted themselves in different contexts, but the primary identity of Katerere's inhabitants came through their membership of factions which competed for the control of stock, women and children, and trade and territory. Both local and regional identities had eroded with the Occupation; the first diminished by the closure of the border, the second by the dispersal of families onto the land between the ranges. Only those factions considering themselves to have claims to succession maintained a strong sense of this identity.

But Chief Katerere's inclusive definition of Hwesa ethnicity, which was intended to gain him a subsidy, was not shared by all of his subjects. The enterprise of imagining Hwesa ethnicity was restricted to royal élites and had little appeal to commoners and outsiders. This development of a 'soft' or limited Hwesa ethnicity is explained by factors outside of Katerere.

Now on the edge of the colonial state and marginal to many of its administrative interests, Katerere was defined out of the wider cultural field which we have anachronistically been calling 'Shona'. Whilst its neighbouring polities became part of a new Manyika identity, a more particular Hwesa ethnicity developed there. The construction of Manyika ethnicity will be considered in greater detail in Chapter 4; at this stage it is sufficient to outline its comparative differences from the Hwesa ethnic identity. Manyika ethnicity was primarily defined by its written language. This was pioneered by missionary linguists and spread by native pastors, evangelists and teachers between 1900 and 1930. Due to their proximity to a unique concentration of missions and to a large market at Umtali, the Manyika gained considerable advantages over surrounding ethnic groups, as educated labour migrants and peasant producers. (Ranger, 1989)

The force of Manyika ethnicity became particularly apparent in the migrant labour market where jobs were often awarded in relation to the workers' position in an ethnic hierarchy. In 1920 the NC Inyanga outlined the market's dynamics:

> Several Europeans in the district complained that they were unable to get extra labour ... There is a tendency to get northern natives from the Bureau. Undoubtedly the local natives are but little inclined to work for local farmers. The Manyika prefer to work in the towns and others generally go to the mines.[41]

Whilst the missionised Manyika could obtain the best in terms of pay and conditions, the Hwesa were generally only able to find poorer paid jobs in the colony's mines. At the bottom of the ethnic labour hierarchy came a fascinating reversal of status. The Hwesa gained a reputation as 'mining boys' and their pre-colonial over-lords, the Makombe people, along with 'northern natives', got the worst jobs as 'farming boys'.[42]

Whereas those Shona dynasties to the south of Katerere could claim to be part of the new Manyika identity because of their own exposure to mission education, it was not possible for the Hwesa to make such a declaration. As Manyika ethnicity rapidly expanded from its original restricted Mutasa base, colonial officials saw the Hwesa as distinct from it.[43] In his influential *Report on the Unification of the Shona Dialects* of 1929, the missionary and linguist C. M. Doke defined the Hwesa out of the Shona cultural field, classifying them as Sena speakers, not realising that the line dividing the two language zones ran through Barwe in Portuguese East Africa rather than through north-east Rhodesia. (Doke, 1931: 27)

The élitism of Hwesa ethnicity, combined with its position in the ethnic hierarchy, meant that there was no great rush to become Hwesa. Important outsider factions in Katerere like Tsengerai and Gande were content to maintain their immigrant identities. Moreover, in the imagination of Hwesa ethnicity, as in the making of its customary law, the voices of women were not heard. Remaining in the reserve, they had their own experience of changes in the political economy.

## KATERERE AND SHIFTING GENDER RELATIONS AMONGST THE EASTERN SHONA

There is an argument common to much research on gender in Africa, that 'colonialism intensified the sexual divisions and gender subordination of pre-capitalist modes of production' (Bayliss, Burgess and Roberts, 1984: 2). However, as this study has already shown, the colonial state was by no means as awesome and totalising as the early Native Commissioners would have us believe. Furthermore, white settler society was far from monolithic; it possessed competing and contradictory ideologies. Its collision with an already divided African community created and exposed fissures in which women found new opportunities, albeit often fleeting ones, to ameliorate their position. Recent studies on Rhodesia and further afield have high-lighted the new strategies available to women (Jeater, 1993; Schmidt, 1992; Wright, 1993). Although contradictory tendencies within the colonial political economy did throw up opportunities for eastern Shona women, Katerere's marginality prevented Hwesa women from taking them up. Thus between 1904 and 1950 sexual divisions and gender subordination were in fact intensified amongst the Hwesa.

Chapter 1 illustrated that the circulation of women within the bride-wealth system underpinned the political power of 'big men', and was the basis for the construction of their factions. Of course, many young women were far from content with their subordination. On pledging, Jason Machiwanyika wrote: 'Girls usually remain with their espoused men because of being forced by their parents. No girl likes to be espoused. All girls and boys have a good choice of lovers'.[44]

Flight was an alternative to secret lovers. New mines, farms, towns and mission stations threw up opportunities for this. Leaving their husbands and fathers, women fled to these places in search of alternative patrons, or a more independent lifestyle of prostitution or beer brewing. In 1901 the NC Umtali noted:

> The usual number of petty disputes have been settled. The native women are generally the cause of such cases, having now taken to exercising the right of choice in matrimonial affairs and refusing to make marriages 'de convenience'.[45]

Although women in Umtali and Inyanga districts later fled to mines at Penhalonga and the city of Umtali, women who first drew Native Department attention were those seeking refuge at the numerous mission stations in that vicinity. Almost as soon as missions were established, women sought them out.[46]

As the settler community established itself at the turn of the twentieth century, there commenced a number of debates about the nature of the regime its members wished to create. As we have seen, the first was between advocates of a progressive individualism and those arguing for a restored communalism. There was also a more particular debate about the nature of African sexuality. Influenced by their own late Victorian concept of sexual morality, settlers deliberated over the extent to which African male sexuality was 'immoral' and thus liable to an inevitable eradication by 'evolution' and education, or the extent to which it was simply perverse, needing to be dealt with by immediate state intervention. The debate appeared to be about morality, but its real concern was the type of African social organisation which would best suit the interests of the settler economy. (Jeater, 1993: 261)

Drawing upon mission evidence and a general fear of perversity, the BSAC legislated in its own interest. The emancipation of women from lineage control would facilitate its proletarianisation policy. Hence it framed the Native Ordinance of 1901 around the idea that African male sexuality was indeed perverse and in need of state monitoring. African women 'were presented largely as victims of this "perversity", whose individual sexual choices were to be respected, regardless of conflicting lineage interests' (Ibid.). Thus, initially, female flight from male control was tolerated and even encouraged by some sections of the white community, particularly missionaries.

However, the new regime of choice for women rapidly created tensions both from within and outside the settler community. First, the appeals for sanctuary made by women to missionaries undermined Native Administration authority. In 1912, D. H. Moodie, the NC Inyanga, sent minutes to the Superintendent of Natives at Umtali entitled, 'The Need of Regulations for Missions'. In them he argued:

> The practice of girls running away to missions and so annulling their marriage is becoming a common one. The proper authority for these girls to appeal to is the Native Commissioner and not the Missionary … The numerous missions among the Manyika are seriously affecting the status of Government officials and the natives are quick to realise that the sympathy of the missionary is directed towards them and … against the official.[47]

Secondly, although the Inyanga NC could rejoice in a 1908 report that the flight of women had the effect of making marriage a matter of choice, he was also forced to concede that it caused 'grave apprehension to the elder more responsible natives'.[48]

While Ranger argues (1981: 8–9) that 'there was no general revolt by Makoni girls against marriages arranged for them', other studies have shown that a considerable number of women did refuse to marry, or chose to flee their husbands (Schmidt, 1992: 115). Certainly one can conclude, as Marcia Wright does (1993: 129), for east central Africa, that: 'During the initial colonial decades, there was no issue more sensitive than the control of women.'

While existence of alternative patrons in mines, farms, towns and missions offered new opportunities for women, new sources of income also made it possible for young men to break free from the tutelage of male elders. Not surprisingly, chiefs and headmen were greatly antagonised by their subjects' new-found emancipation. This is clear from the transcripts of meetings between the Inyanga NC and traditional leaders. The 1925 meeting is a good example:

> Shiovu: Our wives leave us and go to Penhalonga. All the advice of the Native Commissioner is to get a divorce. Our wives go to Missions. We are prevented from taking them back.
> Mzindiko: SENA and other foreign natives take our women. Our sons away at work send no money.[49]

Chiefs and headmen resisted the erosion of their authority by attempting to stem missionary advance into their territories. In the same year as the above meeting, Chief Saunyama and Headman Zimbiti of Inyanga District refused to sanction the building of a Catholic school in their territory. They informed the NC that 'married men would have no control over their wives if the school were established, in view of the encouragement given of late by Triashill mission to runaway wives'.[50]

But in Katerere's case these options of flight for women did not exist. The nearest mission station was 100km away and the nearest substantial mine in Penhalonga, 140km away. Admittedly there was ample opportunity for contact with alternative patrons when Sena and other migrants passed through Katerere in search of work. But considering that labour migrants from Portuguese East Africa were located in a lower position in the migrant labour hierarchy than the Hwesa, the option did not have much appeal. Nevertheless, much to the chagrin of male elders, the lengthy absence of women's spouses enabled them to have extramarital affairs.

Even before the 1920s, the Native Department's sympathy for the plight of African women had diminished. Schmidt writes:

> The viability of the migratory labour system was predicated upon family stability. If the authority of patriarchs were undermined, so too would be the infrastructure of the colonial capitalist system …
>
> The convergent interests of African and European men thus set the stage for their collaboration in the control of African women. (1992: 98)

As the BSAC's strategy of family proletarianisation collapsed, African sexual identity was recast and enshrined through the law. The ideological sources of this new legislation came from the settler community. The individualistic manner in which whites understood sexual morality was in stark contrast to the communal African understanding. Whereas the settlers judged sexual acts, in themselves, as right or wrong, with little reference to their context, Africans judged them in terms of their impact on the lineage (Jeater, 1993: 260). In their collusion with European male administrators, African men found it advantageous to borrow from the former's ideology. Together they created a new 'moral realm' which judged sexual acts upon an individualistic basis and made female, rather than male sexual conduct a matter of concern. (Ibid.: 233–66)

The linchpin of the new legislation was the Native Adultery Punishment Act of 1916. The NC Inyanga explained its purpose to a gathering of chiefs and headmen in 1927:

> The meeting complained of the inability of husbands to control their wives, the latter becoming sulky on the slightest provocation, deserting to their husbands, and taking to prostitution on the mines [at Penhalonga]. I assured the meeting that they had the sympathy of the government and hence the passing of the Natives Adultery Ordinance, that where a man's wife committed adultery she and her lover would be severely punished.[51]

By the end of the 1920s, African patriarchs had won their campaign for control of women. The 1927 Native Affairs Act bolstered the authority of traditional leaders by insisting that their lawful orders had to be followed. In both the Native Adultery Ordinance and the development of customary law women were given the status of perpetual minors.

It would be erroneous to depict women as total 'victims' of the new legislation. Colonial rule had offered them new strategies for resistance. A survey of criminal cases for Inyanga from 1928 to 1933 showed that women used the courts to gain divorces, or to prosecute their husbands for domestic violence or incest. By far the biggest proportion of cases concerned bigamy. Here the law gave women who married at missions the option – not always taken – to prosecute husbands who subsequently took a second wife.[52] The frequency of bigamy cases caused the NC Inyanga to lecture chiefs and headmen on the dangers of forcing girls into an arranged marriage.[53]

Thus women did make some gains when it came to exercising choice of a partner. In 1920 Selwyn Bazeley, the NC Inyanga, noted that in the south of the district polygamy was in decline. This was not only due to church teachings but also to taxation, high rents and the cost of trade goods. The NC described how Manyika women dictated new terms for a successful marriage: 'Among the Manyika a husband who does not supply his wife with at least a cotton dress and a blanket is in serious danger of losing her'.[54] However the lateness of mission penetration into Katerere meant that Hwesa women, unlike Manyika women, lacked the bargaining power gained through monogamous Christian marriage.[55]

In the elaboration of customary law, as in the elaboration of ethnicity, it was men, more accurately the patriarchs, who were the architects of the new order. These 'elders learned in Native law'[56] were consulted as 'legal experts' by colonial officials who sought out 'customs' which would promote their own agenda (Schmidt, 1992: 107). Women were being forced back into a narrow domestic sphere with less access to formal politics, and to wage labour.[57] Such changes matched their new function in the colonial economy.

For many Shona in the east, particularly the southern portion of Inyanga district, the gradual encroachment of the settler economy threw up the opportunity for families to take up what Ranger calls the 'peasant option'. This will be discussed in greater detail in Chapter 4. But briefly, it involved a number of economic and ideological changes, made by the household, in order to become peasants producing a surplus for a rapidly expanding market. Schmidt argues that prior to the 1920s, the peasant option did not require changes in the gender division of labour. Labour was simply intensified within the existing framework, with much of it falling on women, who were given the extra work of having to stamp maize into mealie-meal.[58] But she has over-argued her case. The peasant option was often accompanied by technological innovations such as the plough, iron hoes and grinding mills, all of which could reduce women's toil,[59] although they did not always do so. (See Moore and Vaughan, 1987: 538)

But again in Katerere's case, the territory's marginality to the colonial economy limited the extent to which Hwesa women were affected by changes in technological and productive processes. Too far from the markets at Umtali and Penhalonga to make the peasant option viable, women continued to grow staples, such as millet and cow peas, more suited to the local environment.[60] Their digging sticks remained the major tool used in cultivation. Although some female-headed households were able to persuade elder male kin to clear their ground for cultivation (Moore and Vaughan: 539) others were not. The brewing of beer took on new proportions as women sought to attract what little male labour there was.[61] Whereas Manyika women in the south cultivated subsidiary staples and relishes in gardens, Hwesa women had no equivalent garden supplements, and were forced to rely on dried vegetables.[62]

The fragility of the agricultural component in the local Hwesa economy was exposed by changes in the political economy which left women to survive without supplements previously supplied by men. The absence of males gave women more autonomy in decision-making (Mazambani, 1990: 266) but in interviews and discussions it was clear that this autonomy was 'experienced as material and emotional deprivation by most women' (Jacobs, 1984: 39). Moreover, as we shall see, the declining viability of reserves like those in Katerere, which led to a high infant mortality, undermined the status women derived as mothers and rearers of children. (Phimister, 1988: 205)

Many of the options of flight from, and contest with, male authorities available to eastern Shona women were closed to the Hwesa. One domain, however, did exist in which they could exercise some autonomy from men and challenge their patriarchy: religion.

## COLONIALISM AND THE LOCALISATION OF HWESA RELIGION

Many scholars seeking to explain the phenomenon of 'conversion' to the world religions of Islam and Christianity in twentieth-century Africa were initially drawn to explanations based on the changes of scale and horizon which colonialism brought to African societies.[63] Adrian Hastings vividly summarises the case for such an explanation:

> The organization of large states, symbolised by government houses whose grandeur must have been quite astonishing to many who saw them, the railways the newspapers, the cathedrals, the sense of now falling beneath the authority of some remote potentate of seemingly infinite resource, the King of England or the Emperor of Germany, the sheer enlargement of scale, power, and knowledge within the space of twenty years, and the very numerous possibilities of participation within this new system of things, inevitably precipitated a pursuit of

new systems of truth, philosophy, and religion. The religions of tradition were not unchanging. They were not incapable of incorporating new elements and experience. But they were often closely tied to relatively small scale communities and, very often, to authorities which had now been deeply discredited. They had been appealed to and had failed to halt the white invasion. The new school of learning ignored or mocked them. (Hastings, 1994a: 404)

A particularly sophisticated version of this explanation of conversion is argued by Wim van Binsbergen in *Religious Change in Zambia* (1981). He contends that prior to the penetration of capitalist relations into Zambia, an individual's daily existence was contained within a microcosm, tied up with local kinship and political structures, and with the natural environment. The growth of trade, state formation, and the imposition of colonial rule shattered this microcosm. Africans became involved in large networks of tribute, trade and taxation. Households could no longer rely on the domestic mode of production and were increasingly sustained by male wage won in the money economy. Thus as the importance of old relations with the land declined, so too did eco-religion and related territorial cults. In response, spirits of the 'macrocosm', such as the High God cult, grew in importance to complement Africans' vastly expanded horizons. (Van Binsbergen: 24, 237)

Drawing from a mass of fragmentary oral and archival evidence[64] it will be argued in the final two sections of this chapter that, in the case of north-east Rhodesia, many of Van Binsbergen's propositions can be stood on their head. Chapter 1 argued that the pre-colonial Hwesa did have a sense of the High God, Karuva, as a creator-figure and judge.[65] Rather than experiencing an increase in significance, this monotheistic cult diminished relative to more locally based cults in the period 1904–50. The latter land-based cults *initially* rose in significance to legitimate waning gerontocratic male authority, and in response to the need for an explanation of the prolonged agro-ecological stress which the region was thrown into during the early colonial period. Moreover, the most microcosmic element of Hwesa religion – household-based ancestor cults – innovated to embrace the macrocosm. Finally, when Christianity did establish itself in the area in 1946, it came not as the conquering world religion but in popular form, in the hands of labour migrants responding to locally based needs and struggles.

This set of counter propositions rests on the argument that certain functions of African religion, which had always existed, became more important, either as other functions declined or as alternative means of expression disappeared. It will also be argued that *mhondoro* cults found new functions to retain their relevance. The federative, territory-wide, High God cult structures of communication broke down and were impeded, and hunting cults decayed. This left it to the spirit possession cults which operated at the level of polity/locality and the family, to do what was done before by the whole range, and also to meet the needs of the growing political economy. To illustrate these arguments we will consider changes in 'traditional' religion at the scale of household, locality/polity and region, and then proceed to explore the founding of a popular locally based Christianity.

In the pre-colonial political economy, household-based patrilineal ancestors – *mudzimu* – were venerated to secure family well-being, and functioned to legitimate male heirship. Informants described how, from the 1910s onwards, these family ancestor cults adapted to deal with problems thrown up by labour migration. The cults developed practices to ensure safe travel to work, success in finding employment and safe passage to the spirit world in the event of death in the work place (see also Bond, 1987). Annual family gatherings in honour of the ancestors also ensured the return of labour migrants with their remittances, which would be claimed by male elders.[66] As such, the innovations to family-based ancestor cults form a notable exception to the argument about the localisation of religion under colonialism. Hwesa elders also elaborated how the colonial political economy caused a decline in hunting guilds. This occurred as a result of the entry of young men into the migrant labour economy and the state's curtailing of subsistence hunting.[67]

In the previous chapter it was argued that there had been an important territorial dimension to pre-colonial religious belief and practice in Katerere and the region beyond it in the federative cult of Karuva. In the twentieth century, this cult experienced a severe fragmentation. The decline of its networks of communication cannot simply be explained as a consequence of erosion by mission Christianity. Both tribal and family cults have remained operative alongside Christianity. It is rather that the actions of the state in the first decades of the twentieth century severely curtailed the ability of cults existing at a territorial level to function effectively. The closing of the border and the swift arrest of itinerant holy men seriously impeded the Karuva cult's transmission.[68]

Important adaption also occurred in ancestor cults which functioned at the scale of the polity. Hwesa *mhondoro* cults had been organised on 'local' and 'tribal' lines. They were local in the sense that village leaders believed that *mhondoro* spirits could guarantee their ecological well-being, and they were tribal because mediums could lead and/or represent the polity in its military and political struggles with outsiders. However, following the territory-wide 1896 revolt against BSAC rule, and more regionally based attempts at armed resistance, the state became fixated with conspiracies and superstition. Such fears led to the privileging of local religion over territorial religion.[69] The colonisers feared religious institutions which could organise at territorial level and had the potential for multi-ethnic mobilisation (see Fields, 1985: 259–71). Their privileging of local religion was also an indirect product of a desire to organise Africans into discrete polities under the customary rule of chiefs. As illustrated above, one of the ways the Native Administration sought to bolster these local agents was to approve of, even require, medium/chiefly alliances.[70]

In the case of Shrugwi, in contemporary central southern Zimbabwe, it has been argued that 'tribal' or *mhondoro* cults were eroded almost to the point of extinction. There, cults were destroyed through state intervention in peasant agriculture, particularly through centralisation, and the spread of 'modern thinking' amongst the young.[71] State ideologies of ecology and state-sponsored agricultural practice undermined the hegemony of *mhondoro* cults of the land.

In contrast, Katerere provides an example of how locally based cults of the land could survive in a situation of colonial marginality. Its land was arid reserve, hence alienation of land to Europeans never occurred. Furthermore, its distance from white settlement and administration thwarted the state's penetration with its 'rationalist interpretation of ecology in the form of modern forms of land conservation and animal husbandry, which affected the moral and communal basis of the cults' (Schoffeleers, 1979: 36). Similarly, its isolation prevented the large-scale penetration of a world religion – Christianity – until the 1950s. It was only at this point that there arrived in Katerere migrant Christian élites unwilling to accept the legitimacy of Katerere's local cults. These élites were able to break the pattern of assimilation made by previous groups of immigrants from Barwe in Portuguese East Africa.

Indeed, in Katerere in the first half of the twentieth century, *mhondoro* cults not only maintained their relevance but developed a new importance as the traditional religious system adapted to the new political economy. As both the federative High God cult and the hunting guilds declined in influence, *mhondoro* cults rose in significance. This was possible because of a shift in emphasis in the latter's functions. As Kingsley Garbett also found in his research in the Dande region of the north-east, the cults' political and military activities (outlined in Chapter 1) were curtailed and their local ecological function took on a greater importance.[72]

The first explanation for the rise of eco-religion has already been alluded to on a number of occasions in this chapter – namely that the colonial political economy undermined the social and economic control of elders who elaborated *mhondoro* cults as a means of maintaining and re-establishing their authority. In the early colonial period, patriarchal faction leaders devoted much energy to establishing the political ownership of land, defined in chieftains and wards, to gain more control over young men who moved out of their jurisdiction to take up household-based cultivation. In the case of Mazvihwa, Ken Wilson argues that this élitist male strategy hinged upon two linked processes: 'the need to create legitimate ancestral cults able to "control" rainfall etc; and to persuade the colonial regime that they had traditional rights'.[73]

This chapter has already argued that *mhondoro* mediums helped bolster male élite power. As the Hwesa left their mountain-top defences and developed a greater dependence on agriculture, mediums adapted the local basis of their cults, developing well-defined spirit wards and flows of clients who participated in rituals to ensure rainfall and a successful harvest, or who came in search of explanation of communal or individual misfortune. The cults were thus in a better position to sacralise the landscape and control its resources. Through closer identification with the ruling factions, the cults also retained a tribal dimension; mediums provided the state with the normative rules of chieftainship. This elaboration of 'traditional' rights took the form of extended genealogies and other arguments about succession based on myth and legend, and elaborate rituals of coronation and burial.

The second series of explanations for the rise of eco-religion needs more elaboration. It became increasingly important for cults to offer a means of explanation, management and control over the environment by linking social and ecological stress to moral breakdown and disrespect to the land. Prior to the 1950s, Katerere had many more *mhondoro* mediums than today, both for the chieftaincy, and the Sanhani and Sachiwo sub-chieftaincies. Those that engrained themselves into the collective memory, like the Nyamhute and Nyaurimbo mediums, were remembered as being able to demonstrate considerable control over the environment: an ability to tame its 'wildness' and make rain from seemingly blue skies. Hwesa *mhondoro* were addressed as *mvura* – rain. They were believed to provide spiritual protection for labour migrants travelling to work, and safety for their crops and stock during their absence. Such ecological functions were part of their wider responsibility to provide a safe environment free from social and political strife in which their descendants could flourish. This provision of security and well-being was expressed in the rich image *kutonhodza pasi* – the cooling of the earth. This ecological innovation by Hwesa *mhondoro* mediums meant that what rain-making powers the Nyakasapa autochthons ever did have were now completely sidelined.

But the heightened emphasis on mediums as guardians of the land and its natural processes occurred not only through the decline of other elements in the 'traditional' religious system, but also because in the first half of the twentieth century Katerere was subjected to prolonged agro-ecological stress.

The causes of this agro-ecological stress were directly related to a decline in hunting.[74] The introduction of game and gun laws would have acted as a deterrent to hunters,[75] whilst dog tax and the decline of net making would have made the hunt less effective.[76] But the major cause was the forced entrance of Hwesa males into the migrant labour market. The absence of hunters not only led to an increase in large game, but also to changes in the crop and stock raiding patterns of smaller game and predators. Without their guns the Hwesa were unable to protect their stock from leopards, and baboons played havoc with their crops.[77] It is something of a cliché for peasants to stress their area's 'wildness' prior to white settlement, and hence difficult to calibrate the increase in wildlife from their reminiscences. Nevertheless, two detailed surveys of fauna in Inyanga district carried out in 1927 led the Assistant Magistrate to conclude: 'The Inyanga District has been free from serious hunting now, for several years, game and birds have been undisturbed, and are increasing naturally.'[78] Elderly women informants spoke of the distress the migration of their husbands caused them by leaving no one to kill or chase off baboons and wild pigs.[79] Their stories of hunger and pestilence, coupled with administrative comments on the problem, bear remarkable resemblance to conditions experienced by the Banyubi people in the Matopo hills of Matebeleland for the same period (Ranger, 1986a: 38). Moreover, the problem of crop raiding was compounded by changes of habitat. Hwesa movement out from their mountaintop defences made their shifting cultivation of the foot-slopes – *mujinga* – more vulnerable to baboons living in the hills.

Another contributory factor to agro-ecological stress was the location of Katerere on the edge of a zone prone to cyclical drought. The area stretched east into Portuguese East Africa and southwards into South Africa (Newitt, 1988: 15–35). A sequence of droughts can be reconstructed from the reports of adventurers entering the area in the last three decades of the nineteenth century. Carl Mauch encountered Katerere in a state of famine in 1870, likewise Andrada in 1884, and Carl Peters in 1900. (Burke, 1969: 238; Andrada, 1886: 4; Peters, 1977: 151)

The diversity of Katerere's pre-colonial economy had ensured that there were few deaths from such famines. Its weak agricultural base was supplemented by trade and a strong hunting and gathering component.[80] However the loss of men to the migrant labour system caused the curtailment of these crucial supplements, both of which had a high male labour input.

A recent study on the contemporary impact of labour migration on Katerere concludes that remittances do not always come, and when they do they are not used to develop local agriculture (Mazambani, 1990: 264). Elderly informants stressed that this was also true of the more distant past. It is impossible to gauge pre-colonial infant mortality rates, but old women talked of the death of their children as a common experience in the first half of this century. In 1915 infant mortality was at 50–60 per cent as a result of malnutrition and syphilis.[81]

In the face of ecological stress the Hwesa turned for explanation to *mhondoro* cults which linked relations to the earth with matters of morality. In this way, the two explanations for the rise of eco-religion, the crisis of chiefly legitimacy, and ecological stress, were linked. Ecological stress was often explained in terms of disregard for elder male authority.

Other elements in the 'traditional' religious system innovated in response to the ecological and economic changes outlined above. When missionaries and Christian immigrants arrived in Katerere in the 1950s, they encountered a large number of Hwesa and Barwe women in *shave* possession cults.[82] Briefly, *mashave* (*shave* sing.) were alien spirits, such as the spirits of neighbouring peoples, whites, or certain animals. Sometimes, as in the case of *mashave ehombarume* – hunting spirits – the spirit bestowed some skill on its host, but many had no special function. However, like all spirits, *mashave* could make their presence felt in the community. Participants in such cults were free from the hegemony of *mhondoro* cults, and operated in a distinct sphere with their own sets of clients (Bourdillon, 1987a: 242–7). *Mashave* mediums never danced with *mhondoro* or *mudzimu* mediums. (Lan, 1985: 38)

Possession cults such as these have been interpreted as an indirect strategy of attack on male authority and male-dominated religion. In his sociology of possession (1989), Ioan Lewis argues that the host may use the authority of her spirit to 'manipulate superiors with impunity' (p.104), temporarily attract attention, or escape the ceaseless toil of everyday life. He contends that peripheral possession occurs in situations of social stress (p.106).

There are a number of criticisms of Lewis's model of possession and these will be discussed in greater detail in Chapter 7. A useful reinterpretation of possession comes in Janice Boddy's account (1989) of the *zar* cult in Sudan. Her thesis, which does not necessarily invalidate Lewis's more functional analysis, links possession to female sense of selfhood. She argues that problems with biological reproduction or marriage threaten a woman's highly socialised sense of self (pp.183–6). Possession by *zar* spirits enables them to ameliorate these problems through communication with close kin, spouses and affines 'in ways antithetic to the harmony-preserving tactics of every day discourse' (p.236). Fundamentally, possession provides women with an alternative language with which they can contest the expectations placed upon them as wives or mothers. As Boddy argues, possession by spirits, generally amoral in nature and often immoral in type – such as the shades of gypsies or prostitutes – hints to women 'that they and the constructs which order their lives can hardly be one and the same' (p.308). Boddy's study has relevance to Shona society in the first half of the twentieth century, for it also placed a great premium on women's capacity to bear children in the face of high infant mortality. It is striking how, in their volume, Hwesa proverbs and folk-tales placed a greater emphasis on good motherhood than on just rule or common humanity. Stories abound of animals nursing children abandoned by negligent mothers.[83]

Thus, although prior to the 1940s spirit mediums remained dominant, the hegemony of the local eco-religion did not go unchallenged. Within the same 'traditional' religious system, women found room to contest the elder male authority legitimated by *mhondoro* cults. Challenges to the hegemony of this local eco-religion-cum-royal ancestor cult were also to come from the outside, in the form of Christianity.

### MENDICANTS, MIGRANTS AND MCHAPE: NEW RELIGIOUS CHALLENGES TO THE CUSTOMARY ORDER

By 1912 Inyanga district had seen a remarkable amount of mission activity. The Catholics had founded two missions at St Barbara's and Triashill, along with six out-stations. The Anglican mission at St David's Bonda had seven out-stations and the American Methodists at Old Umtali in Makoni district had six in Inyanga.[84] But all of these sites were in the south of the district. Nevertheless, although Katerere remained marginal to white settlers and missionary movements, its traditional religious institutions did not go unchallenged.

The first challenge in the colonial period began in 1908. In this year a new holy man, different from those who preceded him, made his way north. He was a German Trappist monk, Brother Aegidius Pfister, who stood in the South African Marianhill tradition which privileged the missionary ideal over the monastic one (Baur, 1994: 194–5). From Triashill mission in Makoni district Aegidius travelled throughout the unevangelised north as a mendicant preacher. Taking a stick and a bag, he travelled on foot, living with the people and sharing their food with them as the first monks in Europe had done.[85]

Aegidius was a central figure in the founding of popular Christianity in Manicaland. Every Catholic outstation constructed before 1929 owed its existence to him. He would spend six months away at a time, catechising and looking for new sites, only returning to Triashill for significant festivals like Pentecost and Easter. Once the festivities were finished, he would leave the mission accompanied by a group of mission-trained catechists to the site of a planned outstation. The subsequent 'village Christianity' was left in the hands of local chiefs and he would proceed further.[86]

Aegidius was still well remembered when the Irish Carmelites arrived in Manicaland in 1946. One of the Irish Pioneers described his style of evangelism and legacy:

> If Father remained for the night the word went round swiftly and early morning saw everybody, Christians and pagans, clad in their 'Sunday best' and making their way to the mass rock for it was upon a rock that the Fathers had to offer the holy sacrifice. Indeed even today Holy Mass must be said in such places.[87]

Thus, the first encounter northern Manicaland inhabitants had with mission

2.1 Brother Aegidius Pfister

Christianity differed considerably from their counterparts in the south. In the north, villagers encountered a Trappist missionary who stood in a Zimbabwean tradition of itinerant holymen. Doubtless, Brother Aegidius taught new and important ideas about the High God but the village Christianities he helped to found were not mediated by a hegemonic mission complex of schools and farms which both transformed the local political economy and spread the message of capitalist imperialism. Here, at least, mission Christianity remained separate from the wider colonial project.

Neither must it be assumed that the victory of the Christian religion was automatic. Although Brother Aegidius had reached Nyamaropa by 1911 and charted Katerere by 1914, his activities were curtailed for the period of the First World War, when he and his fellow German Trappists were interned. Undeterred, his work resumed when the war was over. In August 1924 another white priest, Brother Zacharias Reidel, was sent to Nhani, the sub-chiefdom of Katerere, to found the Mission of the Ugandan Martyrs, near the Duza River.[88] With the help of local people, Zacharias built a pole and dagga school and church, and commenced to teach prayers and Christian religion.[89] But he soon came to grief. On 3 September 1925 he was badly mauled by an injured leopard he had attempted to snare. He was carried half of the way to Triashill by eight local men who took it in turns to waft cold air onto his wounds. The remainder of the journey was possible by ox-cart. The ferocity of the attack caused Zacharias to lose the use of both his hands.[90]

What is important here are the numerous interpretations of the 'Zacharias' story, each making an argument for the religious legitimacy of their proponents. The following chapter will show how the failure of the Mission of the Ugandan Martyrs was read as an example of Catholic neglect of the north by a pro-Protestant Native Commissioner, whereas Zacharias's heroic efforts were seen by the Catholics as a legitimating charter for future mission work there. However, the Hwesa shared a different, and an unusually unified interpretation of the story.

Although successive Catholic missionary journals describe the activities of Zacharias's forerunner, Aegidius, in heroic terms, his contribution to the founding of Manicaland popular Christianity was not made without opposition from various sections of Shona society. Angered by his popularity with the youth, elders named him *Nyamusenga* – a type of ogre who cuts up children's bodies for medicines.[91] Zacharias met with similar opposition. His strange arrival, initial impact and dramatic departure was much discussed across the chiefdom. Soon the event was spiritualised. Brother Zacharias was said to have broken the cardinal rule of any new stranger settling in an area. He had failed to consult through the appropriate channels the *mhondoro*, the guardians of the land. His failure to do so meant that they had sent the leopard to punish him.[92]

There appears to have been no contesting of this interpretation of the story amongst Hwesa elders. There is but one remembered discourse which stated that *mhondoro* spirits were dominant and that their mediums legitimised strangers entering the chiefdom. Some informants, however, usually Christian women, stressed that the *mhondoro* were not specifically against the church but simply in favour of protocol.

Subsequent attempts at evangelism by outsiders also came to grief due to minor natural disasters in Katerere. In the late 1920s two black priests came on donkeys to work at the mission at Duza. Their books were destroyed and they left. Two Malawians tried to found an American Methodist church. The first developed a leg complaint and left, whilst the other's wife died in childbirth.[93]

The Ugandan Martyrs Mission was not a complete failure. Zacharias trained a handful of Hwesa youth who were to become school teachers elsewhere. Moreover, in 1927, two Catholic kraal schools were opened in Inyanga north reserve. Hence a 1929 survey of Triashill recorded 40 scholars and eight Christians.[94] However, a combination of the sheer distance between Triashill and Katerere, and the shortage of priests, made the maintenance of the mission work highly problematic. After 1929, there were a number of visits to the area by itinerant Catholics, one of whom had a penchant for baptising local children. In the absence of any organised church presence such baptisms proved meaningless and many of those concerned never attended a Catholic service.[95] These visits seem to have been as much about staking a Catholic claim to the area out of fear of a Protestant advance,[96] as about the maintenance of the faithful. There was a five-year gap in visits between 1935 and 1940, and in 1943 the lease on the mission site at Nhani was allowed to lapse.[97] The dagga school and church which Zacharias had built, slowly fell down. The gum trees he had planted remained the only visible sign of a brief mission presence.

Thus, prior to the mid 1940s, Hwesa *mhondoro* cults met little conceptual or physical challenge from Christianity. Unable to confront outsiders directly, as in the time of Andrada, they used their monopoly of interpretation of natural events as a means to de-legitimate Christian initiatives. However, in 1933 a new religious movement swept across the plains of Katerere. In the hands of outsiders, it moved with such rapidity and force that no local cult could contain it.

The major object of this new movement was witchcraft eradication, carried out by means of a multipurpose medicine dispensed by agents who called it Mchape. The movement originated in the Zomba district in Nyasaland, where its founder, named Robe, was said to have died and then risen, returning with Mchape medicine and a quest to cleanse the society of witchcraft. In Katerere the movement entered from the east, via Portuguese territory.[98] The NC in the adjacent district of Mutoko wrote that the movement had as its object:

> purifying native life, and ridding society of evil-doers and criminals, particularly witches and wizards, murderers, thieves and adultery. Mchape is alleged to overcome all evil influences, and anyone attempting to kill or bewitch another who has partaken of it will himself be destroyed.[99]

The Mchape movement spread throughout central and southern Africa during the period 1932–4. Amongst the Hwesa it displayed many of the features recorded elsewhere.[100] The agents moved from village to village, and within them, from homestead to homestead, dispensing their medicine. The people they encountered were obliged to drink, for fear of otherwise being labelled a witch. Peasants came forward with horns and charms and confessed to using them in witchcraft as a means of gaining advantage over their neighbours. These charms were gathered together and burnt in huge bonfires. Witches who refused to confess before drinking the medicine were said to have subsequently died. In response to receiving communal cleansing, the people of Katerere were obliged to sustain the Mchape agents with gifts of grain, and to brew beer for them.

The Mchape movement also developed some more particular qualities in north-east Rhodesia. One informant who drank the medicine described how hair was removed from each recipient's forelock, along with part of a finger nail, and inserted into stiff porridge, which they had to eat. Also, the husks which were a waste product of beer brewing were used to paint trees.[101] In the north-east, the Mchape movement exhibited few of the Christian ideas and practices recorded in other contexts. There is little evidence of a strongly salvationist doctrine, an elevation of the power of God or a millenarian mythology (Ranger, 1982a: 28). Such ideas would have found few resonances in an area yet to be effectively missionised. Moreover, the symbols of modernity, such as whistles and mirrors, utilised by Mchape agents elsewhere in central Africa and east Africa (Iliffe, 1979: 367) were conspicuously absent.

Terence Ranger has argued (1982a: 46) that it is fruitless to seek a monocausal explanation of a movement which swept across such a broad area. Mchape encountered diverse societies in very different social, political and economic contexts, appealing to different social categories within each. In the lower Shire Valley in Nyasaland, it is possible to situate Mchape within a long sequence of prophetic eradication movements, hostile to the poison ordeal as a means of detecting witches. Here, Schoffeleers argues that Mchape stands within a Mang'anga tradition of eradication which has mythical roots in the sixteenth century.[102] However, there is no evidence to suggest a similar tradition for Katerere; rather, Mchape marked the beginning of a series of witchcraft eradication movements which were to borrow from its initiative over the next 60 years. In north-east Rhodesia it is more likely that the innovative aspect of the movement was the key to its spread.

In the south-east of the colony the movement spread amongst the Ndau. Keith Rennie argues that the dilemma of the labour migrant was vital to the movement's success. Many migrants were laid off in the region during the world depression of the 1930s, and returned home in a difficult position. As labourers, they had been marginally better off than the rest of their community, who sought to gain part of the migrants' wealth by whatever means, legitimate or illegitimate. Commenting on their predicament, Rennie writes:

> Should he refuse numerous requests for gifts and loans, misfortune caused by the envious or resentful might strike him. Should he then go to a *n'ganga* [traditional healer] for remedy and protection, the *n'ganga* would demand a sum which would finish him on the grounds that he was being assailed by very powerful *mitombo* [magical power].[103]

In Katerere, the movement took on particular features which made it appeal to migrants. The agents dispensed a special medicine to protect those who worked in towns, and wife beaters and adulterers were vulnerable to the magic's punitive potential.[104]

Although labour migrants in Katerere seem to have played a key role in facilitating the movement's spread, it was not only migrants and their wives who drank the medicine. Its appeal was more widespread, addressing other tensions inherent in Hwesa society. Audrey Richards, who actually observed the movement as it operated in the field amongst the Bemba, understood it in terms of a response to colonialism. She wrote:

> Economic and social changes have so shattered tribal institutions and moral codes that the result of white contact is in many ways an actual increase in the dread of witchcraft, and therefore in the incidence of magic throughout the group ...
>
>   The Bemba chief could no longer administer the poison ordeal; nor charge any witch in a court; divination 'is discredited and in this transition stage its loss has certainly robbed the native of some of his moral certainties'.[105]

As this study will show, movements of witchcraft eradication and cleansing were cyclical phenomena in Katerere – a generational response to fears of witchcraft. Nevertheless, colonialism did play a role in the circumstances out of which the movement developed in the north-east. Mchape was shaped by colonial policies which did not take popular perceptions of witchcraft seriously. Attitudes to traditional authority and belief in a supernatural system of punishment were so challenged, that Africans were left in a constant state of longing for some sort of 'supernatural defence'.[106]

Though chiefs were able to reconstitute 'traditional' authority in new ways, their ability to deal with witchcraft accusation was limited by the Witchcraft Suppression Ordinance of 1899. In the case of Chief Katerere's conviction for contravening the act in 1921, the NC Inyanga hoped that his indictment would act as a deterrent to others wishing to make witchcraft accusations. The minutes of subsequent meetings of chiefs and headmen with the NC in the 1920s, record the anxiety 'traditional' leaders felt about their inability to counter locally perceived manifestations of evil. In 1925 Headman Mzindiko complained:

> In the past when everyone was thought to be a poisoner or a wizard we could make him drink a potion to test him and if he was proved guilty we could punish him. Now we are all dying of poison.[107]

Mzindiko's words were not heeded. On the eve of the 1930s Headman Gadzima protested that since the occupation, 'witchery' had become a greater evil:

> Formerly we put them [witches] through the ordeal and so cured their pranks, we used to have 'blood money,' those who assaulted each other were made to pay compensation but now they all come to the office with the result that things have become worse.[108]

Despite the suspicion and disapproval of Native Commissioners, Mchape agents were able to purge African societies of a popularly perceived crisis of witchcraft which colonial regulations prevented chiefs from remedying.

The state's detailed intelligence reports on the Mchape campaign, particularly its concern with the response of chiefs, expose the underlying structure of the colonial regime.[109] The Mchape movement did not merely reveal the inability of local religious/political institutions to deal with witchcraft but indirectly challenged the legitimacy of the state which had its local foundations in the new customary order (Fields, 1985). This threat becomes more apparent when Mchape is placed alongside other religious movements in the 1930s.

Although the Mchape movement was more widespread in eastern Rhodesia than Ranger asserts, he correctly observes that it failed to penetrate deep into the territory's interior. The explanation for this is that it was undercut by the existence of Christian eradication movements. Mchape's arrival in Rhodesia coincided with the emergence of the Apostles – *Vapostori* – of Johanna Masowe. Its members identified witches through prophecy, trance or the laying on of hands, and destroyed substances used in witchcraft. Masowe, or Shoniwa as he was often known, had been a lay evangelist in the Apostolic Faith Mission of South Africa (AFM) and many members of the *Vapostori* had previously adhered to the AFM. Together these two movements formed a zone of witchcraft eradication and cleansing around the capital. Indeed the two movements' teachings and practices were so similar that their own adherents, the colonial authorities, and chiefs and headmen often conflated the two.[110]

Like Mchape, the AFM and the *Vapostori* were often introduced by labour migrants who founded their own village gatherings. And they met with the same suspicion from chiefs and headmen, and missionaries. The movements' vilification of ancestor religion undermined chiefly legitimacy, whilst their fervent worship in hills, and practice of divine healing, subverted mission churches' 'civilising project'. In their different ways, both traditional leaders and missionaries were local agents of the colonial state (Fields, 1985), reinforcing its control over women and youth. Moreover, all three movements operated at a regional[111] level in Rhodesia and hence posed the threat of multi-ethnic assimilation. It is not surprising then that they were subject to a good deal of state surveillance and their activities were periodically banned or curtailed.

It is labour migrants who provide the next link in Katerere's religious history. In his work on Mchape amongst the Ndau, Rennie argued that migrant workers, who supported the witchcraft eradication movements, were at the same time key agents in the founding of popular Christianity.[112] Both movements were what Ranger describes as 'an attempt to restructure the spiritual economy of African rural societies in the interests of the returning migrant labourers' (1982a: 27). As new rural élites, labour migrants criticised mainline mission Christianity, which they perceived as failing to take the spirit world seriously enough. From their perspective Christian teaching should have precipitated the decline of witchcraft, but instead Christian practice created more tensions, providing rural Christians with a veneer under which to pursue their former 'evil' customs.[113]

By 1934, Mchape had gone, but deaths attributable to witchcraft re-emerged.[114] Twelve years later, an alternative religious response appeared. In 1946, labour migrants from Tsengerai village, Katerere, returned there to found a church of the Apostolic Faith Mission. They had encountered the AFM on the mines at Kadoma, one of the two key centres of the church's activity. Four men: Harry and Misheck Tsengerai, Timothy Marovha and Mateau Marongedza, played a key role in founding an intensely localised Christianity.

Acting independently of white missionaries who had always had only nominal control over the movement, they moved from their village base preaching the gospel, healing the sick through prayer and the laying on of hands, and exorcising demons. Their practice of witchcraft cleansing prefigured its later widespread use by mission-based Pentecostals in the 1950s, and by more locally based Pentecostal churches in the 1980s and 1990s. The church grew rapidly as new members, especially women, joined to experience this new healing power. Subsequently, leaders came from Umtali to baptise the new believers.[115]

The migrants' relative wealth meant that they returned with the status and independence necessary to challenge the more aged 'traditional' leadership of society. As new local religious leaders, they demonised[116] autochthonous beliefs and practices, ranging from the veneration of *mhondoro* and *mudzimu* to the consultation of *n'ganga*. Thus all spirits, whether considered benign or antagonistic within Shona cosmology, were collapsed into the category of demon. They were ascribed negative characteristics and pitted at odds with one true spirit – the Holy Spirit.

The Apostolic Faith Mission's critique of traditional religious institutions had a clear rationale stemming from its leaders' status as outsiders and young male labour migrants. In pre-colonial Katerere, the Tsengerais had been a powerful migrant faction from Barwe (whilst Marongedza was a Malawian). In the new political order the Tsengerais had less of a place in local politics, which were fought out in the idiom of descent. Harry Tsengerai was highly critical of beer brewing and other acts of traditional commensality, arguing that they inhibited development. His rejection of such practices took the form of a sophisticated argument against the chief-*mhondoro* medium alliance:

> We preached that God is greater than *mhondoro*. *Mhondoro* were created by chiefs who ate herbs prior to their deaths … We told people that those who wanted to follow *mhondoro* were free to do so but chiefs should not hinder people to come to God because he is supreme sovereign Lord.[117]

This group of migrants' contribution to the Christianisation of Katerere was to go one stage further. Their experience of the mines and cities of southern Africa had made them keenly aware of the operation of an ethnic hierarchy. Their Manyika competitors, on top of the hierarchy, had reaped the benefit of years of mission presence in their communities. Thus, as we shall see in the next chapter, the migrants chose to facilitate the entrance of Pentecostal mission Christianity in 1951.

## CONCLUSION

The imposition of the colonial political economy disengaged the Hwesa from a complex set of political, economic and religious ties with neighbouring polities centred on Barwe, and rendered Katerere marginal in a number of senses. In ethnic terms, the Hwesa were redefined as non-Shona by state officials, excluded from a wider Shona identity and a more immediate Manyika one. Economically, the territory's distance from markets at Umtali, Penhalonga and Rusape made the peasant option untenable. The majority of adult males were forced into the migrant labour economy, leaving women to eke out a subsistence from a declining economic base. The inability of the colonial administration to make its presence felt on a daily basis meant that there was no state intervention into Hwesa agriculture. Predominantly, female producers were left much to their own devices. Consequently, the development of what Ranger (1985: 177) has called a 'peasant consciousness' – an evolving collective sense of resentment over lost lands and state interference peasant agriculture – was postponed until the 1950s. This was the period when the state arrived in force along with the Manyika peasants it had evicted from Makoni and southern Inyanga districts.

In some respects the tightening of colonial rule on Katerere in 1904 turned it into a women's world: a place dominated by women's struggles for material and human reproduction, but nevertheless circumscribed by male elders. Within this new order there was no single consciousness but rather a number of competing consciousnesses, all of which drew heavily from religious idioms: an ecologically based communalism adhered to by elders; *shave* possession cults expressing female solidarity and autonomy, and challenging the overbearing expectations upon them as wives and mothers; and later a localised pentecostalism beginning to articulate the economic individualism of returning labour migrants and their families. The 1950s would bring yet more radical transformations to Hwesa religion and politics.

# THE SPIRIT AND THE SCAPULAR: PROTESTANT AND CATHOLIC INTERACTIONS 1950–75

## INTRODUCTION

The history of mission Christianity in Katerere is full of ironic variations upon the theme of the local and the global. Although representatives of a world religion, the mission movements which arrived in 1951 took a profoundly local form. Missionaries were initially thin on the ground, and the foundation of a popular Christianity which accompanied their presence was as much the product of African agents as of missionaries' own idiosyncrasies. Women, youth and outsiders rapidly adhered to churches which legitimated themselves in local terms.

Moreover, although the missions which established themselves were representative of perhaps the two most dynamic forces in modern world Christianity – crusading Roman Catholicism and its systematic opposite, Protestant Pentecostalism – the form which these forces assumed in Katerere had a paradoxical and imported localism. Catholicism was represented by nationalist Irish Carmelites, predominantly from southern Ireland, and Protestantism by Ulster Pentecostals. The introverted battles of Ireland were refought in Katerere, giving an extra edge to the inevitable clash between two totally contrasting Christianities.

The end result of Pentecostal/Catholic rivalries and of local Hwesa receptions and seizures of Christianity was a mosaic of competing Christian factions somewhat analogous to the political factions which dominated pre-colonial Hwesa politics. For Christianity in Katerere, whether Catholic or Pentecostal, was intensely rooted in the local environment.

## THE CHANGING NATURE OF STATE INTERVENTION

Before considering the ideas and social sources of the two missionary movements that entered Katerere in the 1950s it is worth sketching the rapidly transforming economic and political context which they were to encounter. Prior to the 1950s the state was not present in Katerere on a daily basis. It had made no attempt to centralise peasant agriculture as it had done in Makoni district to the south, principally because there were no prosperous Hwesa 'reserve entrepreneurs' who challenged the Native Department ideal of communal tenure. Moreover, because Katerere appeared such a bleak location to successive Native Commissioners in the 1930s and 1940s, they did not consider it necessary to redistribute land to make space for those due to be moved off the European land into reserves with the implementation of the Land Apportionment Act. Such a prospect was unimaginable (Ranger, 1985: chapter 2). In his submission to the Natural Resources Native Enquiry of 1942, L. V. Jowett, the NC Inyanga wrote: 'The great portion of Inyanga North reserve is arid and waterless and unsuitable for settlement by the Manyika people.'[1] Thus the state only entered Katerere for the purpose of labour recruitment, law and order and taxation. As one elder put it 'we could plant where we liked'.[2]

Jowett resisted the implementation of the Land Apportionment Act throughout the early 1940s. But the arrival of ex-servicemen seeking land, and the post-war boom in commercial agriculture meant that his successors could hold out no longer. In 1946 the Manhattan Syndicate began to sell its estates to the Rhodesian Wattle Company. Manyika peasants who had previously lived on the land as tenants were removed to Nyamaropa reserve. In 1948 Crown Land was given to ex-servicemen, and more Manyika were moved to Zimbiti Reserve. The further expansion of the Rhodesian Wattle Company in 1952 finally brought evicted Manyika into Katerere.[3]

The 1950s also heralded a period of greater state interest in reserves. Renewed intervention in peasant agriculture was exemplified by the Native Land Husbandry Act which allowed for rights of ownership of small plots in reserves, and enforced agricultural rules such as halting shifting cultivation and imposing contour ridging. The state also developed the infrastructure of reserves. Weirs, bridges, drains and irrigation schemes were rapidly constructed in Katerere.[4] It was with a view to developing the medical resources of Inyanga North reserve that Meredith, the NC Inyanga in 1951, helped persuade the Elim missionaries, the Drs Brien, to pioneer a station in Katerere. But as we shall see, the Hwesa also had their own agendas for the missionaries.

THE TWO CHRISTIANITIES:
ULSTER PENTECOSTALISM AND SOUTHERN IRISH
CATHOLICISM

The near synchronised arrival of the Elim movement and the Carmelite Catholics in Katerere in the early 1950s had a certain explosive quality about it. This was as much due to the similarities between the two movements as to their differences. Although theological opposites, both missionary organisations were fundamentalist in their sense of their own mission.

While scholars are beginning to take cognisance of contemporary Pentecostal movements sweeping across Africa (Marshall, 1993; Gifford, 1991), little attention has been paid to their missionary forebears.[5] Part of the explanation for this scholarly neglect of Pentecostalism is that, relative to the established and non-conformist missions, it is a new phenomenon representing a third twentieth-century wave of mission activity.

Pentecostalism arose within an ambience of interrelated waves of 'revivalist' activity, which occurred between 1900 and 1910 in places as diverse as Azusa Street in California, Oslo in Norway, and the Welsh valleys, in what became known as the Pentecostal Movement (Hollenweger, 1972; McGee, 1988: 58–61). This new Christian religion was a fusion of four theological antecedents: first, salvation, comprising the belief that forgiveness follows an act of repentance in the light of God's grace; secondly, sanctification, a second work of grace received by baptism in the Holy Spirit; thirdly, divine healing; fourthly, adventism, the belief in the imminent return of Christ (Dayton, 1987: chapter 1). It was this fourth strand, the imminence of the Second Coming, that rapidly transformed a Western-derived church into a missionary movement. More generally, Pentecostalism, along with Conservative Evangelicalism, represented the only expanding sectors of a generally declining Protestant missionary movement (Hastings, 1994a: 567). Thus Elim was not the only Pentecostal movement to enter Southern Rhodesia in the quarter of a century following the Second World War. It was joined by the Pentecostal Assemblies of Canada, the South African and American Assemblies of God, and a variety of smaller bodies. Scripture Union also began its evangelical work in government and mission schools immediately after the war.

The specific origins of Elim Pentecostalism are described by Bryan Wilson:

> The Elim Foursquare Gospel Church originally developed in Ireland about the time of the First World War, a period of great uncertainty in Irish History. It arose in an atmosphere of insecurity concerning political changes, and amid marked religious tensions. It was nourished by the old revivalist tensions of Ulster, and it spread by use of revivalist techniques in England and Wales in a period of economic unrest and depression in the twenties and early thirties, at a time when religion generally, and non-conformity in particular, were experiencing decline. (B. Wilson, 1961: 51)

The second movement, Southern Irish Carmelite Catholicism, was part of a wider revival of Catholic missionary activity throughout Africa, which had received a fresh[6] impetus under the papacy of Pius XI in 1922. Within this movement the Irish played a leading role. But despite being a twentieth-century phenomenon, the Catholic resurgence was little influenced by liberal theology or secularising influences. Hastings outlines the movement's features:

Narrowly neo-scholastic, papalist, Marian. Hell was not questioned, Protestants hardly noticed except as rivals, social and political issues avoided unless they were greatly affecting Catholics or the conversion process. The element of control and unquestioned obedience internal to the system was decisive. It was highly self-sacrificing, unself-questioning, supremely confident in the mission committed to it and the divine approbation of every element of the Catholic Church exactly as it stood. (Hastings, 1994a: 559–60)

Both the Elim Pentecostals and the Irish Carmelites were riding high on waves of recent expansion from within their own movements. In the first five years following the end of the Second World War, Elim had doubled its missionary effort.[7] Missionaries had gone to India, South America and Africa. And the Irish Carmelites, within their impressively extensive tradition, were also enjoying relatively recent success with missionary endeavours. Provinces had been founded in Australia and New York, and the order had re-established itself in England and Wales.[8] Both missions believed in the imperative of evangelism. Elim did so because of its strongly adventist theology (B. Wilson, 1961: 27), the Catholic impulse came, in part, from their belief in the absolute orthodoxy of their religion and the inadequacy of all others as a means to salvation.[9]

The movements also shared a sense of their own self-importance, both seeing themselves as part of great Christian traditions, even if they were somewhat invented. Elim claimed descent from the evangelical tradition of Wesley and Spurgeon and the revivalist tradition of Finney, Moody and Torrey (B. Wilson, 1961: 15; G. Jeffreys, 1933: 192–212). The Carmelites associated their mission enterprise with the '"Golden Age of Irish Civilisation" and specifically with its missionary content' (Hogan, 1990: 151). Despite historical evidence to the contrary, it was asserted that the modern Irish Catholic resurgence was a revival of an ancient missionary tradition which had cradled Christianity during the Barbarian invasions of the Roman Empire, later re-introducing it to Europe in the eighth century. An editorial in a 1946 edition of the Carmelite journal, *White Friars*, contended:

What Ireland did for Europe in those ages she must do for the whole world today. The work of Jesus Christ must be done and we are the nation most favourably placed to do it. Surely it is the supreme honour to be placed in such a position, to be the chosen nation for so great a work. If we contend that the organisation of the great Roman Empire, with its wonderful system of communications and roads and the famous Pax Romana, was no fortuitous circumstance, but a divinely designed plan to facilitate the spread of early Christianity, we must freely admit that on the present occasion we are the nation chosen, the chosen nation.[10]

Indeed, the Irish nationalism that informed, and was informed by, Carmelite Catholicism offers another clue to the intense contestation between the two movements. As Wilson noted (1961: 15, 94), the Elim movement emerged from Ulster in the 1920s in a period marked by religious tensions, and in part defining itself through opposition to the Catholic threat. Hence the Elim movement's exegesis of Revelation cast the Roman Catholic Church as the real entity symbolised by the Mother of Harlots drunk with the blood of the Saints. Whilst the *Elim Evangel*, the journal of the movement, asserted the existence of a 'Roman Catholic Curtain' which kept the people of Spain subject to a systematic religious oppression coordinated by Rome,[11] Irish Carmelites triumphally proclaimed:

> Irishmen can stand before mankind with a clear conscience on many things. We have never figured in history as persecutors of our fellow men, either in the interests of politics or religion. We cannot be accused of having political ambitions overseas.[12]

Finally both movements derived from what David Martin calls the 'resistant "peripheries"' of the British Isles, acting as vital components in the defence of regional cultures against the encroaching centre. The 'vigorous, participatory and egalitarian faith' which they developed in opposition to the hierarchical religion of the centre (D. Martin, 1990: 276) was, at times, replicated in Manicaland; usually in the absence of missionaries.

   Nonetheless, despite the bold rhetoric of both movements, their initial interactions with the Katerere were shaped by local agendas and local legacies. This becomes apparent in missionary accounts of their early encounters with the chiefdom.

### EARLY ENCOUNTERS:
### THE DIALECTICS OF POPULAR CHRISTIANITY

Mission correspondence and publications have proved an excellent archive for social historians of Africa. Such was their desire to convince their sending churches and the wider public of the value of their civilising mission, that missionaries wrote copiously on their interactions with the objects of their endeavour. The Carmelites and the Pentecostals were no different from their predecessors in this respect. However, the lateness of mission penetration into Katerere, a feature of its marginality, makes oral sources available to supplement missionary accounts. This archive of testimony from local agents of Christianity, along with ordinary Christian adherents, provides a very different explanation of the origins of the African church. Placed side by side, the different sources reveal that the founding of a 'vigorous African Christianity' arose out of the 'interaction between missionary and African consciousness' (Ranger, 1987c: 182). In order to come to terms with the operation of this 'dialectical process' (Ibid.) in Katerere, we first consider the missionary texts, and then turn to the alternative explanations of those Africans who witnessed the initial missionary encounters.

The Elim Pentecostal movement's first contact with the chiefdom was recorded by its pioneer missionary to Southern Rhodesia, Jesse Williams:

> When we had travelled about 100 miles we arrived at a small farm, the owner of which was known to one of my companions. This was the last bit of civilisation ... From then on the roads were almost impassable, and for many miles it seemed that we were travelling over a dried up river bed strewn with boulders, & we had great fears that the truck would not make it, but prayer got us through to within 5 miles of the Chiefs Kraal.
>
> The first village we came to was the one where the Christians belonged. It was 4:30 AM when we arrived, but within a few minutes nearly all the village was awake and had gathered around us. They began singing and praising God for sending a white missionary. It seems they had been asking God to send them a missionary for a long time, but had almost lost hope except for a native who had taken them the Gospel. He had encouraged them time and time again to believe that God would answer their prayers, and we felt greatly moved as we stood before them as he explained that God had at last answered their prayers ... They sang and prayed for two hours, and then through the interpreter I gave them the message ...
>
> After the service we told the headman that we wanted to see the Chief. So we left the truck and walked five miles through the bush until we came to the Chief's kraal. There we had to go through various ceremonies. First of all we had to sit down on the bough of a tree which was shaped like a bow & placed in front of the Chiefs hut. The two natives who had brought us sat down on the floor & commenced clapping their hands.
>
> After a time there was a movement in the hut & the Chief came out & sat on a chair in front of us. By this time several of the Chiefs councillors had arrived ... The Chief neither looked nor spoke to us & the conversation was carried on between myself, the ex missionary, the headman & the Chiefs head advisor ...
>
> Finally the Chief consented to allow us to work in his district, but only after a great deal of palaver & consultation with his advisors.
>
> We then presented the Chief with the gift we had taken along for him. This had to be handed to the headman who passed it to the runner. He in turn passed it to the Chiefs son & he passed it to the Chief.
>
> He seemed to be very pleased with the blanket & ordered that a cockerel be caught and given to us as a present. Then the Chief shook hands with us & we made our departure with the live chicken.[13]

Williams's account of his first arrival at the Hwesa chiefdom was similar to earlier missionary-encounter texts. His narrative took an 'epic form' describing in a highly personalised manner his conquests, in the name of civilisation, in the wilderness beyond (J. and J. Comaroff, 1991: 172). Where Pentecostal encounter texts often differed from those of established non-conformists was in the fact that the Pentecostals legitimated their presence in terms of a divine calling. With great triumphalism Williams also announced that his arrival in Katerere was an answer to prayer.

Williams's account also differed from other earlier missionary narratives (Ibid.: 182) in that it is apparent that whites were more of known entity in Katerere, and subject to a degree of suspicion. Although he minimalised the role of the Africans who had taken him ('the two natives who had brought us sat down on the floor and commenced clapping their hands'), their own account suggests that they were crucial to the whole enterprise.

The two African agents of Christianity who aided Williams in his deliberations with Chief Chikata Katerere have already figured in this study. They were Harry Tsengerai and Mateu Marongedza who, along with two others, founded a church of the Apostolic Faith Mission in Tsengerai village in 1946. They had preached a message of sobriety, hard work and religious freedom characterised by a refusal to submit to autochthonous Hwesa cults. All this was within keeping with their status as outsiders and young labour migrants. Having no part in the religiously ordained new political order they realised that they were better off outside it altogether, thus escaping from demands of traditional commensality. Their alliance with missionaries took this agenda one stage further. As migrants they were all too aware of the existence of an ethnic hierarchy in the labour market and of the advantage mission education had given to neighbouring ethnic groups like the Manyika. Missionaries represented material advancement.[14]

The Apostolic Faith Mission of South Africa had from its inception made evangelism its priority, and positively encouraged African initiative in this area. It viewed the maintenance of educational and health institutions as an encumbrance to be avoided if at all possible.[15] However Tsengerai and Marongedza were able to make contact with Williams, a Pentecostal missionary who could supply these services, through Jimmy Watson, the AFM's white representative in Umtali. As the first Elim missionary in Southern Rhodesia, Williams had cultivated close relations with the AFM.[16] Together, Watson and Williams drove north with their African companions.

Williams's account of his meeting with the Hwesa chief cast the missionaries as the heroic actors with the Africans providing no more than the backdrop to the story. The reality was that the encounter was controlled by Chief Katerere and mediated by the AFM evangelists. Tsengerai and Marongedza had remembered the fate of the mendicant priest Zacharias and the pervasiveness of the discourse that attributed his attack by a leopard to his failure to respect the political powers in the chiefdom. Thus although Williams saw the negotiations as something of a 'palaver', his African colleagues were keen to ensure that the 'various ceremonies' were carried out.

Throughout the negotiations Chief Chikata Katerere was in two minds about the missionaries. He was aware that, like the Apostolic Faith Mission before them, their presence could further diminish his political authority by undermining its spiritual legitimacy. At one stage he enquired whether they would 'send away his *mhondoro*'.[17] However, he was eventually swayed by the promise of a mission doctor, desperately needed by his people, and the opportunity of mission education for his sons.[18]

Tsengerai and Marongedza's mediation with the chief ensured that the first Elim missionaries in Katerere, Drs Cecil and Mary Brien, established themselves in a manner acceptable to religious and political authorities. One elder who acted as an acolyte to a *mhondoro* medium explained the church's subsequent success in the familiar discourse of a protective nature:

> When he came, he asked the people to give him to the *mhondoro*, to inform the *mhondoro* there was someone around. They did that and that's why the leopards sent by the *mhondoro* were harmless to him. And he would either shoot the leopards or set a trap for them ... It was only through the *mhondoro* that the lions be put down.[19]

It is doubtful that Cecil Brien instructed local people to 'offer him to the *mhondoro*' for, as will be illustrated below, the latter were to be recipients of a good deal of Pentecostal ire. Nevertheless, in the initial process of mutual accommodation between the local political authorities and the missionaries, Dr Brien employed men from the dominant Mbudzi house on the mission, and named the missions out-schools after local faction leaders. What the acolyte's description of Dr Brien's arrival represented was a widely felt perception amongst elderly people in Katerere that the Elim missionaries came in a manner acceptable to local custom. One old woman who lived close to Sanhani, the site of Zacharias's abandoned Mission of the Ugandan Martyrs, contrasted the 'disrespectful Roman Catholics' with Dr Brien 'who came with good manners'.[20]

In 1929 the Marianhill missionaries left Manicaland to be replaced by Jesuits. In 1948, the Carmelites took control. The latter seemed to have learnt something. In a brief Catholic history of the region written in 1958, the following appeared on the area of Katerere: 'The whole area is ruled by this chief and his sub-chiefs. Anyone wishing to found a school or mission in this territory must first negotiate with Katerere and then with the sub-chieftain of the particular district'.[21]

However the legacies of Zacharias's mission initiative did affect the pattern of interactions that the Carmelites were able to make. This becomes apparent in another early encounter story reported by the Briens for the *Elim Evangel*:

> For sometime we have heard that Chief Sanhani, whose village is thirteen miles from our station, desired us to meet him. He even sent his son to see us. About three weeks ago we left the mission station at 7 a.m. in the truck, reaching his place about 10a.m … On arrival we were told that the Chief was trying cases that day, but a few minutes after letting him know we were there, we saw an old man with a grey beard hurrying towards us. He has given us a very hearty welcome to begin work in his area … They have absolutely refused the Roman Catholics an entrance … The Chief is very old.[22]

Rejoicing at their victory in the first of many contestations with the Carmelites, the Briens failed to grasp that their success hinged upon Catholic legacies. The doctors' report went on to relate another remarkable episode linked to their visit to Sanhani:

> A Christian woman who accompanied us in order to show us the way, asked us to visit her village of Nyagwara on our way home, also in the Sananhi district. She said no lorry had ever visited the kraal, but all the previous week she had hacked a way through, using an axe … Numbers of young girls and women awaited us and at her invitation we gathered in the hut sitting on the floor … it was wonderful to hear them in that village – never before visited by a European – singing the grand old hymns and choruses in their own language … This Christian women, helped by another – the Headman's wife – holds a meeting every night for girls.

Again the Elim missionaries seemed unmoved by the paradox that in a village never before visited by a European the people were singing 'grand old hymns'. Likewise the text is striking for the degree of agency it ascribes to women in founding popular Christianity in Katerere – an issue explored in the following chapter.

Not surprisingly the story of the Catholic encounter with sub-chief Sanhani, in 1948, had a different conclusion. It was narrated by Donal Lamont, who later became renowned for his struggles with the state to protect the integrity of his priests and people during the liberation war. Lamont's opening did bear resemblance to the Pentecostal story, telling of an arduous journey into a dark unchartered land:

> We started off, the carriers leading the way, in a single file along the narrow path. Away ahead of us lay uninviting country, great jagged mountains heaped on top of one another in mad confusion, with dark valleys in between, which the sun would suddenly light up as it flung

through the fleecy clouds. It seemed that we were on the highest point
of the whole land, on top of the world, and a vast and fierce looking
world lay beneath us.[23]

But rather than end with evangelical triumphalism, Lamont's story had a
denouement of dashed hopes and lapsed Catholicism. The Carmelites were,
of course, aware of their Trappist forebears. Lamont's story began by noting
the actions of 'a German lay brother' who 'penetrated its [the north's]
uttermost extremity and in the course of his peregrinations baptised some of
the inhabitants'. But whilst the party were able to find the remains of the tiny
brick hut which brother Zacharias had built near Sanhani, 'nobody seemed
very clear about what the word Catholic meant'.

Finally, an old lady volunteers to search for an old man called Clement –
a hopeful sign. But with a heavy dose of irony Lamont brings the story to its
sorry conclusion:

> He hadn't what you would call a very prepossessing appearance ... We
> questioned him. Of course! he replied, he was a Christian. Hadn't he
> been baptised at Triashill long ago, in Brother's time? And then we
> told him we wanted to see the chief and headmen about opening up a
> kraal school in the village, Clement assured us that Providence could
> not have chosen a more opportune moment for it, nor a more
> influential intermediary than his humble self ... He would see the chief
> and assemble the headmen the very next morning. In fact he would go
> off and see the chief and headmen that very night ... They were all at a
> beer-party in the neighbouring village. But the bold Clement would
> dare the terrors of the bush and go and see them without delay ... He
> wouldn't accept hospitality. Beer? Tut-tut! Clement touch beer ...
> Clement would go and be back to the Fathers to discuss the joys of the
> Christian faith ... before the water had boiled for tea ... Clement
> returned late for Mass, and looking much the picture of *castigato mea in
> mututinis*, next morning.[24]

A year earlier, Lamont and Father Luke Flynn stumbled, by chance, upon
the remains of another Catholic mission, which much to their chagrin had
been named after St Patrick. The village station was located in the Honde
valley, an area equally as marginal as Katerere.[25] Of the 150 families in the
village only four remained Catholic. The movement of popular Christianity
which swept Manicaland in the first two decades of the twentieth century
was not sustained in areas distant from its source in Makoni district and the
southern part of Inyanga district. As Chapter 2 illustrated, the Church's
victory over 'tradition' was by no means always inevitable.

3.1 A Hwesa elder in front of his house, c.1951

3.2 Mary Brien in front of her house, c.1951

3.3 and 3.4 (top and above) The Founding and Early Days of Elim, Katerere

## PENTECOSTAL INTERACTIONS:
### THE LOCALISATION OF ULSTER PROTESTANTISM

The sacred texts of the Elim movement, those written by or about its founder George Jeffreys and his brother Stephen, provide excellent insight into the character of Ulster Pentecostalism. It was strongly dualistic in nature. There were only two possible sources of spiritual power (G. Jeffreys, 1933: 148), two possible masters of the body (G. Jeffreys, 1932: 49), and two sources of disease. (Ibid.: 37–46)

Despite its appearance, like other fundamentalist movements Elim was 'quintessentially modern' (Caplan, 1987: 5) in that it offered a response to contemporary conditions and events by means of demonising the perceived threat and defining itself in opposition to this 'notional and significant "other"' (Ibid.: 20). One significant 'other' was Roman Catholicism. The second was more nebulous, referring to the threatening modern world which the Pentecostals fought desperately to keep at bay.

As late as the 1950s, even perhaps the 1960s,[26] secularising forces outside and within the church were identified, and became the object of Pentecostal vitriol. Such influences were cinema and public house owners, and clergy who allowed their churches to become places for dancers and players of cards, billiards and bagatelle (E. Jeffreys, 1946: 30, 51, 57). Not surprisingly the movement's leaders and preachers were extremely adversarial in their defence of all that was good and Pentecostal. Thus victims of secularisation along with its agents were identified and castigated: 'Sinners of the deepest dye ... Magdalens, drunkards, lovers of pleasures and religious journalists.' (Boulton, 1928: 19)

Cecil Brien was no newcomer to evangelical campaigning. In Belfast he had spent much of his spare time distributing religious tracts, along with his best friend, a bus conductor. In Rhonda, Wales, he had scandalised his medical practice colleagues by preaching in the open air.[27] In Katerere, different categories of enemy were constructed, representing new threats. The spirit world replaced secularising influences, and Shona 'traditionalists' supplanted the British working classes. In this vein Cecil Brien referred to the Hwesa as 'bound by Satan' or 'worshipping Satan'.[28] Others were more adept in their turn of phrase. Katerere was 'the heart of savagedom and witchcraft' and the Hwesa were 'dirty uneducated, spirit worshippers, bound by witchcraft and superstition' who participated in the 'beating of drums and the wild frenzy of devil orgies'.[29]

New rituals were also found to emphasise the transformation of loyalties that conversion to Pentecostal Christianity brought. Substances that polluted the life of the British working classes were replaced with those which defiled the Shona. The rituals of burning pipes and tobacco pouches and of pouring home-made wine down the sink which accompanied British Elim campaigns (Boulton, 1928: 21) were transformed, under the initiative of Evangelists,

Obed and Buxton, local women, and itinerant Methodists from strongholds of Manyika Christianity to the South, into the burning of charms, fetishes and bracelets outside the church and hospital.[30] The public confession of sin, the day- and night-long meetings, and the destruction of polluted objects gave Elim's initial interaction with the Hwesa and Barwe the appearance of a witchcraft cleansing movement, not unlike Mchape 20 years earlier.[31] Describing a weekend of special meetings in 1954 which was attended by over 400 people, Elim missionary Winnie Loosemore wrote: 'We saw men and women coming forward; some to repent, some with greater desire to follow the Lord Jesus, whilst others bound by evil spirits were delivered and their witchcraft burnt.'[32]

In their demonisation of the African spirit world, the Pentecostals drew from both global as well as local sources. The missionaries both contributed to and learnt from the *Elim Evangel*, which recorded the progress of the worldwide Pentecostal movement through reproducing the stories of Elim missionary interaction with local cultures in Africa, Asia and South America. Other African set texts were the widely circulated accounts of one of the earliest Pentecostal missionaries to Africa, Willie Burton. This Congo pioneer's copious writings were faithfully published by Victory Press. (Burton, 1933, for example)

In interview, Mary Brien provided insights into how her theology could arise out of dialogue with local people:

> I was once sitting with an African woman ... and I said to her 'where are the spirits?' And she sat up and looked and said 'they are never beside water, but you see, where there's no water, where its very dry, that's where the spirits reside.' And the bible says the same: 'When a spirit goes out of a man, it will go looking for a new place and it will always seek a dry place'.[33]

In a similar manner her perception that African beer was just a nourishing drink was changed by an itinerant black Methodist pastor, together with some local women, to a more 'Pentecostal' view that it was a polluting substance associated with ancestor veneration.[34]

There was another reason why the Elim movement lent itself so easily to localisation. The missionaries' acceptance of the supernatural, and their Pentecostal practice, had immediate resonances with Shona cosmology. The Briens' own narrative of their journey to Katerere took the form of a sequence of divinely inspired prophecies, visions and dreams;[35] phenomena equally familiar to the Hwesa, but alien to many mainline missionaries. Drs Cecil and Mary Brien were also no strangers to the exorcisms, baptism in the spirit and tongues which they encountered in Katerere. They had experienced this Pentecostal power in Elim's British campaigns in Wigan during the Second World War, before coming to Southern Rhodesia to work for the

Evangelical Africa Mission on the Zambezi Escarpment in 1948. Indeed, it was the Evangelical Africa Mission's very rejection of Pentecostal practice that caused them to switch their allegiance to Elim in 1951.[36]

Thus, as Cecil and Mary Brien, along with their nurse Winnie Loosemoore, began their medical mission amongst the Hwesa, they proved extremely amenable to dialogue about local perceptions of evil. Perhaps the most remarkable Christian form to emerge out of this symbiosis between Elim Pentecostalism and local demand and creativity was a unique and powerful package of divine healing.

## THE DOCTORS BRIEN:
### MEDICAL SCIENCE AND PENTECOSTALISM JOIN FORCES

In Hwesa oral history, the surgeon, Cecil Brien, is remembered as a wonder-working figure. He is described in the same terms as an African prophet. The key to his beatification lies in the symbolic innovation he made in the domain of healing. Together with his wife, an anaesthetist, he brought to Katerere a sophisticated package of bio-medicine. But this knowledge of medical science was supplemented by a profound belief in divine healing.

The Briens' practice of divine healing had a dual pedigree. Its first line of descent came from George Jeffreys, the founder of the Elim movement, whose evangelistic campaigns in the 1920s and 1930s in the British Isles caught the attention of the national press because they were accompanied by extraordinary healings. The histories of the movement abound with citations from the press describing the abandoned bathchairs and crutches following the evangelist's ministry (Boulton, 1928; E. Jeffreys, 1947). Jeffreys' own writings on the subject of divine healing locate it within a heritage which he traced back through Andrew Murray to George Fox and John Wesley. (G. Jeffreys, 1932: 122–37)

The second pedigree had already been tried and tested in Southern Rhodesia in 1910–20. Whilst in Swansea the Briens lived in a Bible college run by Rees Howells. A product of the great Welsh Revival, and a noted healer, Howells had worked at the South Africa General Mission in Rusitu which was renowned for its scenes of revival in the years 1915–20. More importantly, in the post-war influenza pandemic, the mission station became transformed into a divinely protected zone, free from the virus, to which local chiefs and people fled for refuge (Grubb, 1973: chapter 24). The Briens were profoundly influenced by Howells.[37]

In the Briens' hands, Pentecost and medical science joined forces. Clinics were preceded by religious services and the hospital was transformed each morning into a place of singing, dancing, prayer and the Word. But the process went far deeper than this. In 1952 Mary Brien wrote in the *Elim Evangel* of their response to cases considered 'medically hopeless'; a woman with peritonitis, her kidneys diseased beyond medical repair, a woman with

3.5 (top) Medical Work and 3.6 (above) Afternoon Tea in Elim, Katerere

puerperal infection not responding to drugs. Here the only option was the laying on of hands. Miraculous healings followed.[38] In many cases of divine healings, the patient and even their family would join the church.[39]

Local perceptions of the Briens' medical practice often conflated it with divine healing, thereby greatly increasing the latter's spiritual efficacy. When in 1952 Cecil Brien revived a newly born baby, which had appeared to have been dead for 40 minutes, the local headman and his wife, whose child it was, believed that the doctor had breathed life into it.[40] Informants viewed as miraculous Dr Cecil Brien's ability to cut open a woman and remove a child from her womb. Such surgical expertise would rarely have been encountered even in the southern portion of the district. Adherents of the Apostolic Faith Church in Tsengerai village transferred their allegiance to Elim due to its superiority in the domain of healing.

When contextualised within the real and imagined agro-ecological stress in Katerere, discussed in Chapter 2, medical practice combined with divine healing had a remarkable relevance. Those who had for many years been troubled with aching teeth flooded into clinics for their extraction during the mission's early days.[41] Others who had problems with sight and hearing were also helped.[42] Indeed, this Pentecostal power intending 'to deal with pain and disease, sorrow and trials' (E. Jeffreys, 1947: 26) appeared very compelling, especially to Elim's staunchest enemies. Perceiving that the old religious system was no longer meeting the popular need, some local traditional leaders who practised traditional medicine converted to Christianity. Thus for instance, when a *n'anga* – traditional healer – found his wife's life had been saved in childbirth by Cecil Brien, he arrived at the hospital demanding to see the white doctor who was 'like Jesus'. He subsequently abandoned traditional healing, walking 13 miles to church every Sunday.[43]

The Elim missionaries' package of bio-medicine and divine healing complicates scholarly understanding of Pentecostal/healing churches. In an essay entitled 'Medical Science and Pentecost: The Dilemma of Anglicanism in Africa', Terence Ranger argues that Pentecostal Christianity redefined the meaning of African perceptions of disease by abolishing the dichotomy between diseases of God and diseases of man. He writes:

> What African Pentecostalism did was to make available the healing power of the Holy Spirit to counter all other spiritual agencies. Thus God was brought into the diseases of Man, not as willing them nor as eradicating them, but as regularly combating them through the openness of human beings to His Spirit. At the same time African Pentecostalism redefined the other category of diseases of God, where hitherto recourse had been both to traditional and Western medicine. Here, too, the Holy Spirit alone had power. African Pentecostals

repudiated all medicines. Thus the dichotomy was abolished. (Ranger, 1982d: 339–41)

Pentecostalism *per se* does abolish the dichotomy between diseases of God and diseases of man, but the example of Drs Cecil and Mary Brien also abolished the dichotomy between medical science and Pentecostalism.

### POSSESSING THE LAND:
### THE DEMISE OF CHIKUMBIRIKE

As well as transforming the bodies of its adherents, Elim Pentecostalism could also transform perceptions of the landscape. Recent social histories and historical anthropologies of mission have stressed the importance of missionaries in 'taking hold of the land'. (Ranger, 1987b: 117) This process had a political dimension concerned with the symbolic impact of 'seizing the centre' (J. and J. Comaroff, 1991: 200) and a spiritual aspect, involving the sacralisation of the landscape (Ranger, 1987b). The localisation of Ulster Pentecostalism stemmed, in part, from the Elim missionaries' seizing hold of the land, although it is again debatable how cognisant they were of the implications of their actions.

The Pentecostals' impact on the physical landscape was immediate and striking. Twelve schools were constructed around the chiefdom within the space of a few years. The station itself developed into a significant settlement with a boarding school, hospital and church. The missionaries appear to have had no designs to seize the old political centre: the chief's village remained more than 15 miles away. Instead they created an alternative or competing centre in the chiefdom. Older converts spoke with great approval of how Elim had changed the landscape, bringing a development comparable with Inyanga's administrative centre and township to Katerere. They pointed out that many had relocated in order to be nearer the mission.[44] The impression which both Pentecostal and Carmelite missionaries created, of inaugurating a powerful and immediate physical transformation of the landscape, was enhanced by the fact that they arrived in the 1950s, a decade in which the state intensively intervened in African reserves, building an infrastructure, as well as seeking to direct agriculture.[45]

Equally important was the Elim movement's seizure of the spiritual landscape. Their method of resacralising of the land is best described as the 'redemption of space'. The chroniclers of the history of the Elim Church in the British Isles record with sheer delight the irritation its evangelistic campaigns caused cinema owners and publicans, whose numbers dwindled due to the presence of George Jeffreys and his evangelistic team in an area. E. C. W. Boulton wrote with joy concerning the movement's ability to restore a picture palace in Belfast, previously a Methodist Chapel, to its former glory by turning it into an Elim Tabernacle. He notes in a postscript that after the first prayer meeting there, the caretaker and his wife (presumably unsavoury characters) 'developed a sudden desire to leave the premises, and as result made their departure under the cover of midnight darkness' (Boulton, 1928: 43). The redemption of space occurred through contestation, as chapter headings of Boulton's book illustrate: their titles include 'Invading England', 'Glorious Triumphs' and 'South Coast Conquests'.

In a similar vein, Winnie Loosemore wrote an article in the *Elim Evangel* entitled 'Possessing The Land'. Drawing on imagery of the Jewish occupation from Deuteronomy, she wrote:

> We have come to possess the land of Katerere, Inyanga North Reserve ... Many who were groping in the darkness of heathenism have been liberated from the chains that bound them and have been brought into the glorious light of the Gospel. We are so sad to see so many coming to the hospital weighed down with heathen charms and so obviously under the power of Satan ... We have also seen hell defeated and heaven gloriously triumphant in the deliverance of several people possessed and tortured by evil spirits.[46]

Cecil Brien shared a similar vision. One of his African evangelists described how the Doctor declared 'war' on the people of Gande, the nearest village to the mission:

> That was his object lesson almost every Sunday. On certain occasions at certain times of the year, when they would beat their drums all night appeasing the ancestors and so forth, the next Sunday you would know that this would be Dr Brien's sermon. So he would preach and hammer very hard.[47]

Every member of Gande village who came to the hospital was chided by Dr Brien for taking his medicine yet refusing his message. As the following chapter will illustrate, the Briens had strong allies in this war: local women, youth, and Manyika people.

The local representatives of the old order came under considerable pressure from their Pentecostal adversaries. The mission site by the Manjanja river in Ruangwe had strong associations with a *mhondoro* spirit, initially causing many to avoid attending church and hospital. Occasionally pots of beer were left along the upper reaches of the river.[48] The *mhondoro* in question was Chikumbirike, and his host, Razau Kaerezi, lived just outside the perimeter of the mission.

The coming of the Pentecostals spelt disaster for Kaerezi. First, his wife converted and refused to brew him beer. He persecuted her only to find his two daughters converting through their attendance at the secondary school. Things grew steadily worse: the pools along the river where pots of beer had once been placed became places of baptism, testimony and open-air services.

Later still the river was dammed. This great source of fertility was now clearly controlled by the Pentecostals.[49] None of the later missionaries knew that Kaerezi was a medium, but one could speculate that Cecil Brien at least understood something of his significance. He offered him a job as a school cook in the 1960s in order to win him.[50]

Whilst around the mission, Kaerezi was a sociable man, but at home he was known to fall into a trance. Chikumbirike would then speak, seeming to address the missionaries: 'What are you here for? You are disturbing us, our people are not following our traditions because of this teaching.'[51] Kaerezi soon left his job. Having seized the centre of his spirit ward, the missionaries had severely curtailed his activities around the mission. As Chapter 5 will illustrate, his powers were only restored through the agency of ZANLA guerrillas during the liberation war who relocated him. Around Elim the drums used to summon the spirits fell silent. In the 1980s one of Kaerezi's sons also converted, becoming a fervent Pentecostal preacher in Mutare!

## CATHOLIC INTERACTIONS:
### DIFFERENT MODELS OF INCULTURATION

The story of Carmelite interactions in Katerere is as ironic as the Pentecostal one. It is an account of contrasts, the significance of which can only be grasped through the reconstruction of the social history of Catholic mission in the southern part of Inyanga district and Makoni district prior to the Carmelites' arrival in 1949.

The process of the foundation of a popular Catholicism in Makoni and southern Inyanga district has been effectively reconstructed by Terence Ranger. Like the Pentecostals, Catholic missionaries also seized hold of the mystical landscape. In 1912, the Jesuit, Richard Sykes, wrote in *The Zambezi Mission Record* of his desire that:

> Before very long ... every mountain peak of the alpine country in which I am writing, in this corner of Rhodesia will have its Cross, planted on the summit and every valley its school, house, convent and resting place for the abiding sacramental presence.[52]

But in distinct contrast to the Pentecostals there was also a strong emphasis on veneration. The three orders who worked consecutively in Manicaland – German Trappists, German Jesuits and Irish Carmelites – each had a different form of veneration. But as Ranger writes:

> One emphasis however remained constant: the emphasis upon the Virgin of the 19th and 20th century apparitions. At Triashill both the Trappists and the Jesuits erected a Lourdes grotto and held torch-light processions to it. The Carmelites, of course, made the feast of Our Lady of Mount Carmel the highlight of their liturgical year. (1982d: 348)

3.7 The Hwesa-style Church at Avila Mission

3.8 Elim Baptism in a Mountain Pool

Another continuity was the veneration of St Therese, the Patron Saint of mission, which the Carmelites found to their surprise to have been initiated prior to their arrival. An article in *White Friars*, describing the celebration of the Feast of St Therese, illustrates the extent to which the people had already made it theirs:

> The members of ... [the Society of St Therese] were the 'Vakuru', or elders, men and women Catholics from surrounding kraals. On certain days they used to come to church and recite special prayers to the Little Flower before her statue, winding up in an attractive hymn to her in the native language ... and when we had finished with the Benediction, the 'Vakuru' stood up before the Little Flower and sang her hymn.[53]

In 1950, the Manicaland Catholic identity was further enhanced with a new Carmelite flavour through the founding of Brown Scapular Confraternities at Umtali, Triashill, St Barbaras and St Killians.[54] That the scapular (a monastic vestment) could be confused by some for a 'Papal Blessing' did not bother some priests, for along with the rosary it was eagerly taken up by the young and even the older generation, supplanting the metal bracelets that had hitherto been used to warn off evil spirits. Its use spread rapidly in the first few years of the Carmelite presence in the region.[55] Another Carmelite initiative was to share in the visit of the pilgrim statue of Our Lady of Fatima to Africa in 1950. In Rusape such large crowds turned out to venerate the statue that an outside altar had to be erected.[56]

One of the three Carmelite pioneers to Southern Rhodesia explained that the early missionaries had no formal instruction in missiology; nevertheless, they were trained priests with the New Testament as their handbook. Hence they were to be exploratory.[57] This left much to each priest's initiative. Generally, the early Carmelites worked with what was familiar to them, developing in Manicaland the Catholic symbolism and ritual imported from southern Ireland.

Irish Carmelite practice in Southern Rhodesia was not without effect. Its symbolic potential was explicitly recognised by its missionary priests. In an essay on 'mission' appearing in 1960 in *Zelo*, the journal of Carmelite novices, Father Tony Clarke wrote:

> Sacramentals, besides being efficacious, have a tremendous appeal to African people and can help us greatly in our battle to break the power of the witch-doctor and superstition ... A priest, when he goes to a village, should always be armed with the Ritual, ready to bless the sick, to bless the homes of the people, their animals, their crops, their children ... In time of drought processions should be organised to plead for rain, again turning the people's hearts and minds to God, the

Giver of all good gifts ... If the rains are exceptionally heavy, there is a blessing to prevent floods. For every occasion there is a blessing. In the past the Africans have been accustomed to going to their witch-doctor in every crisis – let us spread the word, through our catechists, through our teachers, through our own practice, that instead of going to the witch-doctor they should come to the priest, who has medicine that comes from above the blessing of God.[58]

Clarke was not advocating the open contestation with the leaders and practitioners of traditional religion practised by the Pentecostals, but rather that Carmelite Catholicism should supplant their major functions, rendering them redundant. Thus when he founded Avila mission in September 1953, a statue of Our Lady of Mt Carmel was erected at the entrance to the mission and local people wearing the scapular were encouraged to pray at this shrine.[59]

However, the founding of Avila and Regina Coeli missions in 1955, in the north of Manicaland, came at the end of an era. Clarke left Avila in 1959 to pioneer St Peter's mission in the south of Manicaland, and the new Carmelites who replaced him had very different missiological goals. These new men were profoundly influenced by the debates, deliberations and final proclamations of the Second Vatican Council. They were horrified by the brand of Catholicism they encountered in the southern portion of the district. One priest commented:

Vatican II had happened, it rubbed off on all of us in some ways. The non-essentials were non-essentials. I suppose when we went to Rhodesia we were shocked to see the things that were part of Catholicism in particular areas like Triashill for instance; that they were no different from a white European colonial church. We took the church from Ireland and planted it in Triashill with all the trappings of a pre-Vatican church – the Latin hymns. Go to Triashill today and some of the old people will sing Latin hymns. We came at the end of that era and the beginning of a new one. It was a different type of evangelisation. It was getting down to peace and justice, fighting injustice ... there was a move towards Africanisation, inculturation.[60]

Although the nineteenth-century Ultramontanist peasant cults, tried and tested in rural Ireland, had great appeal to the Manicaland peasantry, it was these 'non-essentials' which were the first religious forms to be dropped by the new men. The later priests did not realise the extent to which they had already been indigenised, and the degree to which they played a vital role in the founding of a folk Catholicism.

As Chapter 4 will illustrate, the strength of folk Catholicism in the south became apparent in the 1950s when Manyika Catholics evicted from

Triashill, after the implementation of the Land Apportionment Act, came to Regina Coeli mission in the north, bringing with them their scapulars and rosaries.[61] African Catholics thus introduced their own inculturation, from below.[62]

The post-Vatican II Carmelites had very different views on inculturation. Father Luke MacCabe, doctor at Regina Coeli mission in the 1960s and 1970s, provided insights into his perception of the process. Unlike the Briens who were at war with the *n'anga* – traditional healers – MacCabe believed that these healers were able to heal people from 'acute mental psychosis' and that they had some 'quite good medicines'. He never preached against ancestor veneration because, like many post-Vatican II missionaries, he saw a direct parallel between this and the veneration of the saints. In his doctoral thesis on medicine (1972: 26) he wrote: 'Pagan beliefs have many ethical points in common with Christianity; even the pagan concept of God is notably lofty and not far removed from the Christian concept.' MacCabe also assisted Michael Gelfand in his ethnographic survey of the Nyamaropa area.[63] More generally, words like 'pagan' and 'heathen' disappeared from the rhetoric of the movement in the 1960s as it strove to reappraise local culture and religion. In a similar vein, Father Berthold Dowd produced a series of learned articles on Shona religion for *The Scapular*, the Order's journal.[64]

There was also a conscious desire to develop African symbols and forms of worship in church. Thus catechists from Regina Coeli returned there from weekend liturgical seminars with drums previously banned from services. Priests pre-empted pastoral decree in allowing their use. In the same vein came Father Peter Egan's architectural masterpiece – the round church with thatched roof, in Hwesa style, constructed at Avila mission.[65]

Inculturation had unexpected, even ironic results. The development of African forms of worship was a slow process and there seemed little to show for it before the mid 1970s. In comparison with the older folk Catholicism in the south, Catholicism in the north of the district, particularly around Avila mission, appeared bleak and dry, devoid of the symbols which many of its non-literate practitioners could draw upon. It seemed as if the older pre-Vatican II priests, admittedly able to build upon the traditions of their German Trappist and Jesuit predecessors, were more successful in founding a popular Catholicism.

In the southern part of Inyanga district and Makoni, Catholic priests had constructed a more 'totalising' religion by controlling the lives of adherents living on their vast mission farms. The missionaries made demands not too dissimilar from those made by Pentecostals. Comparing life on the mission station with life in the reserves, Father Mel Hill made the following observations:

It is not uncommon for the whole village to be drunk for a week. In a place like Triashill Mission where the Prior is the Landlord and the natives are his tenants, some sort of check can be kept on the beer, but in the Natives Reserves things are completely wild ... If the parents refuse to send their children to learn they are threatened with expulsion from the farm ... The whole atmosphere of their village life militates against any sort of learning or religion ... Very few families say night prayers or even mention the name of Christ in their villages.[66]

On the mission station, Catholics attended daily mass and prayers. Priests monitored weddings and funerals and intervened if they did not consider the rituals suitably Christian.[67] Avila mission's most loyal supporters were second generation Manyika Catholics who had relocated to build stores in Katerere in the 1950s.

However, almost in spite of the later Carmelites' missiology, zones of popular Christianity were created around Avila and Regina Coeli missions. As Chapter 4 will show, this had much to do with the agency of local women, nuns and Manyika migrants. Nevertheless, the Carmelite missionaries did identify with Africans in ways the Pentecostals could not. This was because of the social context of southern Irish Catholicism. First, the rural background of many priests greatly enhanced their ability to relate to peasants. Peter Egan, for instance, won great respect for his ability to irrigate previously infertile areas of Katerere and create vegetable gardens. Secondly, the Carmelite's strong sense of Irish nationalism freed them from close association with the colonial state and offered greater opportunity for identification with the colonised people – a characteristic which was to become much more apparent during the liberation struggle.[68]

## THE SECT FROM THE BLACK NORTH MEETS THE MOTHER OF DRUNKEN HARLOTS: THE GLOBAL EXPORT OF A LOCAL STRUGGLE

Pentecostalism emerged at the turn of the twentieth century, in opposition to what it saw as the corrupting influences of priestly supremacy and liberal theology in the established churches (Hollenweger, 1972). It made a particular object lesson of Catholicism. Jesse Williams, the first Elim missionary to Southern Rhodesia, was in no doubt about the veracity of his pre-Reformation stereotypes of Catholic practice. In a 1952 report he wrote: '[The Priest] takes a bucket of water and sprinkles them, thus making them members of their Church of Rome. Sometimes he gives them a medal to hang around their necks. These poor souls do not know what they believe ...'.[69] But the Carmelites were equally assured of their own cause. The Irish Provincial's letter to *White Friars* set the tone of their work:

> The Fathers say that they are surrounded by schools under the care of Anglicans, American Methodists and Dutch Reform. These Fathers realise that they must do everything possible to keep the True Faith burning vigorously at St. Killian's mission and they appeal most earnestly for benefactors. And they send across the vast distance of land and sea this cry: Help us to defend our people by your prayers, sacrifices and alms. Your reward will be great in heaven.[70]

The inevitable conflict between the two movements was intensified by their social sources: Ulster Pentecostalism and predominantly Southern Irish Catholicism. It has already been noted that Elim Pentecostalism specifically arose in Northern Ireland in the context of post-First World War religious and political tensions. Elim was to clash with Carmelites who were unabashed in their promotion of the Irish cause. *Zelo* describes how the three Irish Pioneers celebrated their first St Patrick's Day in Southern Rhodesia in 1947. These 'true Irishmen' taught mission choirs to sing 'Hail Glorious St Patrick' and 'The Dear Little Shamrock', and choreographed a procession which culminated in the unfurling of the Irish Tricolour.[71] A decade later one of the few Northern Irish Carmelites, Donal Lamont, was consecrated Bishop of Umtali. The new bishop used the opportunity to pontificate on recent political developments in Central Africa. His speech, reported in *White Friars*, provides a fascinating insight into how he viewed colonial developments through Irish Nationalist spectacles:

> The Federation did not now need the Motherly care of England to the extent that she did when a small child, as it were. While she would not like to see her Mother attacked, she would still say 'Leave us alone,' and amid general laugher, 'As we would say in Ireland, "Sinn Fein!"'[72]

The battle lines were drawn in Ireland but Katerere was the site of this holy war between Pentecostals and Catholics. As soon as the Carmelites arrived on the scene, Elim missionaries moved onto the offensive. One missionary wrote in the *Elim Evangel*: 'The Catholics are fighting us desperately and have appealed to the government for school sites all over the reserve.'[73] In the following edition, the Drs Brien issued an 'S.O.S for Prayer' against the Roman Catholics, not too dissimilar from the Irish Provincial's exhortation of his faithful to prayer.[74] Whilst Elim sought preferential treatment in Katerere,[75] the Catholics felt aggrieved that their northward expansion throughout Manicaland had been thwarted. One Carmelite missionary indignantly wrote of the 'Elim Sect' stepping into Katerere whilst the Catholics were still pursuing negotiations.[76]

The contest was intensified on the ground by the personalities involved. The Elim missionaries were led by Cecil Brien, a staunch Ulster Protestant who informed *Elim Evangel* readers in 1952 that 'Unless we get permission

to go in [to Katerere] before the Catholics the whole of this vast unevangelised area will be shut off from the Gospel and all these tribes will remain
in utter darkness.'[77] His opposition to Tony Clarke, the able and determined
southern Irish priest based at Avila mission, was implacable and even
reached the annals of Carmelite history. A recent biography of James
Carmel O'Shea, a leading Irish Carmelite at the time, notes: 'He was very
anxious about Anthony Clarke who had moved up to a new area, Katerere
where he was experiencing particular difficulties from a Protestant mission,
the directors of which were doing their utmost to prevent him from
establishing schools there.' (O'Dwyer, 1989: 39)

The struggle between the two movements reached almost comic
proportions. On one occasion a missionary couple prayed that God would
give the Pentecostals victory over the Catholics' 'crack football team'.[78] On
another, Cecil Brien summoned the local NC informing him that the
Catholic mission at Avila had built a school within Elim's three-mile radius
– a serious breach of missionary protocol. The Doctor insisted on pacing it
out accompanied by the NC and the Catholic priest in question – Tony
Clarke. At one stage of the journey the proceedings became particularly
heated when Brien argued that they should walk straight through bush and
scrub rather than around it for the sake of accuracy. The Catholics were
found to have transgressed. Their newly erected school was torn down. It
was hardly surprising that Carmelite Priests complained bitterly to the NC
Inyanga about the 'man from the Black North'.[79]

The struggle between the missions also took the form of an extended
argument over the number and location of schools each organisation could
build. The struggle was so fraught because in the 1950s and 1960s schools
were viewed as the major means of evangelism.[80] Evangelism was, of course,
the primary concern of both missions.

The struggle for schools inevitably drew the state into the conflict, not
least because the Catholics believed that the Inyanga NC, Meredith,
preferred the Pentecostals.[81] As evidence they cited the NC's failure to refute
Jesse Williams's allegation, made at a meeting of the two missions, that
Catholic priests murdered 'indigenous natives' in Portuguese East Africa.[82]
The conflict widened as the fiery Donal Lamont went over Meredith's head,
writing a thunderous letter of complaint to the Native Affairs Department.
The major thrust of Lamont's letter concerned the contested Christian
history of the district, beginning with Zacharias's mission of the Ugandan
Martyrs. Where the NC saw a history of neglect, Lamont wrote of an
'unbroken tradition' of Catholic witness.[83] Finding the 'prevailing spirit …
quite un-Christian',[84] the exasperated Meredith wryly noted in a report to
the PNC, Umtali: 'It may also not be irrelevant to mention that Dr Brien is an
Orangeman and the Roman missions are staffed by Southern Irishmen'.[85]

The Catholic and Pentecostal missionaries who later emerged onto the scene were not from Ireland and found this rivalry between the movements distasteful. But by then it had already affected the nature of the interactions between mission Christianity and Hwesa religious and political institutions.

African reaction to Carmelite-Pentecostal rivalry was varied. NC Meredith thought it might have confused Africans,[86] but as we have seen, many quickly developed their own local versions of Christianity. One response from chiefs and headmen was to manipulate the rivalries to ensure a school in the vicinity of their villages.[87]

Another effect of missionary rivalry was to create African enemies. Elim's desire for doctrinal purity caused missionaries to intervene in the prospective marriages of their teachers. In 1964, the mission received a letter signed by 'Zimbabwean Sons of the Soil',[88] attributed to local inhabitants who were members of the nationalist movement ZAPU (Zimbabwe African Peoples Union) in Salisbury.[89] The writers singled out for criticism the Schools Superintendent, whom they said had chased off a school teacher for marrying a Roman Catholic girl. What was significant about the letter was not that it was anti-Christian – it even quoted scripture in one place – but that it strongly disapproved of missionary sectarianism:

> Do you think that we Africans come from Rome or Elim? We are all Africans, don't split us by your political churches. We Africans marry Africans; Colonials marry Colonials ... Do you think that your political club Elim is the only church which is loyal to God ... all the European Churches shall be disbanded and form an African United Church.[90]

These early nationalists resented the fact that they were being used as cannon fodder in an imported local struggle which was not of their making.

The final African reaction was to vote with their feet. Throughout the 1950s an African-controlled Pentecostal church, the *Vapostori* – Apostles of Johanna Marange – had spread like 'grass-fire' northwards throughout Manicaland.[91] The movement was initially unable to gain a foothold in Katerere, which already had its own strong Pentecostal heritage. However, in 1962 the *Vapostori* managed to establish themselves in Ruangwe, Katerere, in the shadow of Elim mission. Indeed, there is strong evidence that those 'Sons of the Soil' who wrote to protest about Elim's dismissal of its school teacher over his choice of bride may well also have been *Vapostori*. Their letter finished by recommending a passage of scripture – Deuteronomy 14:1–12 – and with the question: 'Do you ever preach these?'. The biblical text cited concerns Hebrew food taboos – a text central in the definition of *Vapostori* identity. Thus this group of African-led Pentecostals were also intent on challenging the content of the missionary message.

## FROM MOVEMENTS TO CHURCHES:
### PENTECOSTAL AND CATHOLIC MISSIONS
### IN THE 1960S AND 1970S

The bulk of this chapter has focused on the indigenisation of Pentecostal and Catholic mission Christianity. This process took place in the first few years of the missions' presence in Katerere, when missionaries were few and reliant on African agents. But we must also ask what became of the Christian movements in the following two decades?

The answer is not at first obvious. Once the missionaries were no longer involved in a great foundational moment – the creation of a popular Christianity – their correspondence to their home countries was reduced from a flow to a trickle, and changed in nature from excited accounts of religious transformations and encounters to more bland reports and surveys. Nevertheless, it is possible to discern a number of related changes from their records. First, as we have seen, there was a shift away from the building of churches to the founding of primary and secondary schools. Secondly, there was a marked drop in church attendance. Many who were initially converted to Catholicism or Pentecostalism subsequently joined one of the vast array of other churches brought into Katerere by displaced Manyika from the south, and returning labour migrants. In Elim's case where statistics are available, attendance dropped considerably from a peak of about 500 in the central church in 1956 to a low of 160 in 1966, recovering to 200 in 1972. Attendance at their out-stations remained at an average of about 30 members per church between 1966 and 1972.[92] The final change was a loss of Pentecostal practice in Elim Churches: divine healing, exorcism, and the destruction of sacred objects all declined. By 1970 the Briens wrote of the need of the Spirit to revive the church in Katerere.[93] They left in 1973 not seeing their prayers answered. As we have seen, this loss of Pentecostal vigour made the church of Johanna Marange particularly attractive to disgruntled Elimites.

Pioneer missionaries were something of an exception in Rhodesia in the 1950s. Much of the territory had been Christianised in the first two decades, and missionaries were now concerned with the management of their vast institutions, and the education of a tiny élite (Hastings, 1994a: 555). In building schools Katerere's Pentecostal and Catholic missionaries rapidly caught up with missionary concerns of the day. But demands of running large organisations also created a number of tendencies which 'disengaged' (J. V. Taylor, 1958: 12–15) them from local people.

The missionaries felt compelled to build schools. As early as 1952 Father Mel Hill argued in a wide-ranging description of the Carmelite enterprise: 'You must be clear on this point. If you have not got the schools and hospitals, you will not get the Christians.'[94] Both organisations observed that the 'words school and church' were 'synonymous in native language and native mind'.[95] But, the specialisation which educational work involved increasingly separated missionaries from their community and gave them little time to supervise out-stations.[96] In the same article cited above, Hill wryly noted: 'In most missions there are two priests, one of whom does the "treks" while the other does the work of the central mission ... there is not much time left for walking from village to village like Francis Xavier.'[97] By 1960, Antony Clarke, one of Avila's pioneers, was calling for a renewed emphasis on the use of catechists:

> How are we to reach our older people? I believe the answer to be *through Catechists*. With only one priest available on each mission to work in the reserves it is ridiculous to think that he can reach all the people *and* give them *adequate instruction* – he has too much territory to cover, too many schools to superintend, he must administer the sacraments ... without the gift of multi-location his efforts, mighty though they be, bear little fruit.[98]

This frustration with the demands of administration and teaching was shared by Elim missionaries. In her field report of 1974, Catherine Picken stressed that she would have liked to have gone out into villages but felt that it was 'impossible at present with missionaries occupied so much with institutional work'.[99]

But there were other factors alongside the growth of educational work which accounted for the stunting of the church life of the missions. The increased specialisation of missionary work was accompanied by a decline in status of black evangelists. Although revered by many, the Briens were very paternalist towards African workers, 'treating them like children'.[100] Though they were crucial to the founding of a popular Christianity (see Chapter 4), evangelists never lasted long at Elim. Ironically, the process of schooling itself militated against the establishment of a strong African male leadership. In 1962 Cecil Brien reported that of the 62 men who had passed through the mission's primary and secondary schools, only two had gone to Bible school. Others had gone on to normal jobs in the cities, and joined other evangelical churches. Brien reflected that the chiefdom's marginal economy had few jobs to offer except teaching, which paid a small wage.

At Elim the lack of indigenous leadership was intensified by the arrival of numerous missionaries to run the secondary school and the hospital. There were critical missionary voices on this issue. In 1972, Don Evans wrote: 'The answer [to church growth] is not to be found in advertising for professionally trained pastors ... but to train our own men ... The fraternal as opposed to paternal attitude is welcome and necessary if the work is to progress.'[101] But voices like Evans's were in a minority. Elim mission only ordained its first black pastor, Ephraim Satuku, in November 1975. Satuku's work was to prove invaluable to the survival of the Elim's churches in the Liberation War.

The Catholics were more enlightened than the Pentecostals when it came to black leadership. An African Order of nuns, the Handmaids of Our Lady, was founded in 1959 (see Chapter 4), whilst Antony Clarke was helped to pioneer Avila by Father Simon Tsuro, one of Rhodesia's first black priests, ordained in 1947. (Baur, 1994: 421)

There was a lay African leadership of hospital orderlies and primary school teachers around the mission stations but in Elim's case the growth of an African eldership also contributed to its loss of Pentecostal zeal. 'The young rebels' who helped found a popular Christianity 'became entrenched as elders' (Iliffe, 1979: 259) Now ironically threatened by Pentecostalism's egalitarian potential they became authoritarian in their leadership. Others grew tired of Pentecostalism's unceasing emphasis on personal transformation and secretly returned to idolatry.[102] In 1970–1, an ex-secondary school student, Paul Makanyanga, returned from the Evangelical African Mission bible college to work as an evangelist. A convert to Elim from Marange's *Vapostori*, Makanyanga was full of Pentecostal zeal and briefly instituted a revival in Elim's churches. Church elders and deacons confessed to idolatry and their charms and fetishes were destroyed.[103] However, the revival was short-lived. Makanyanga grew discouraged by his low status and poor accommodation, and moved to Scripture Union where he became one of the organisation's key workers.[104]

There was, however, a continuity in missionary practice in the move into education. The boarding school presented missionaries with the same opportunity as the former Christian village or mission farm (Isichei, 1995: 196), or perhaps the European monastery (Hastings, 1994a: 425). It provided the chance, through separation from the outside world, to create a new Christian culture. In Elim's case the experiment initially failed. The secondary school's strict regime of school and general work, devotions and church services, with little time for recreation, very quickly prompted its closure after the pupils, many of whom were grown men, rioted.[105]

The secondary school, Emmanuel, was reopened in 1966. Within a decade its new headmaster, Peter Griffiths, had gathered around him the most qualified teaching staff in the territory and developed one of the most academic mission schools. Links were formed with the Scripture Union, and along with American Board Biriwiri mission school in Chipinge, Emmanuel became one of the earliest and most potent sources of the Union's rural expansion in Manicaland. Under Griffiths's increasing influence of learned expository preaching, Elim mission became more evangelical than Pentecostal.

What Pentecostal practice there was in the school was introduced by the students themselves. In 1974 there was a remarkable revival in the boarding school in which young people 'had been filled with the Holy Spirit, speaking in tongues, some interpreting, prophesying, and a few seeing visions … Some had to confess sins, return stolen goods, bring out hidden witchcraft and destroy it before being filled'.[106] But the 'fire' never spread to the deacons and long-standing church members.[107] The burning of witchcraft remained restricted to the school playing fields.

The Elim missionaries had a clear strategy in concentrating on pushing a small élite though local and Cambridge examinations. They were aware of the nationalist movement growing from strength to strength in the reserves surrounding the mission,[108] and their response was to help prepare a Christian leadership who would inherit the nation. In an article for the *Elim Evangel*, Griffiths outlined the plan:

> Students come from up to 300 miles away and from many different backgrounds. Very few are Christians on arrival and many are from heathen homes. They are hand picked, drawn from the best ten per cent academically of those who entered primary school. So we see our work as strategic – winning souls for Christ and training potential future leaders.[109]

In developing a vast mission infrastructure, the Elim missionaries put themselves at odds with the British Elim movement which, in a sectarian manner, consistently pushed for the founding of local 'Elim' churches. Much to the disgust of the *Evangel*'s editor, an article by Griffiths entitled 'In Defence of Institutions' was removed by the executive just before going to print.[110] But those like Griffiths, and his colleagues who were massacred in the Vumba (see Chapter 5), had a larger vision. The fostering of a free-thinking Christian élite, many of whom eventually became church leaders in their own right, made an important contribution to the development of Zimbabwean civil society.

### CONCLUSION

When Elim Pentecostalism arrived in Katerere, it had the appearance of a religious movement. Africans rapidly adhered to the church as it legitimated itself in local terms, re-sacralising the landscape in Christian fashion, pitting itself against local demons, and making resonances with local concepts of illness. Likewise, the Catholic Church literally followed a movement of popular Catholicism north, as Manyika migrants from the south arrived with their medals, scapulars and village schools, demanding the founding of Regina Coeli mission along with priest-led churches. In the two mission Christianities different concepts of Africanisation were at work. Carmelite Catholics first sought to replace traditional rituals and symbols with their own, and then after Vatican II, to incorporate them into Catholic practice. In contrast, the Pentecostals arrived at Africanisation through the exclusion of traditional religious components by exorcism, demonisation and the destruction of sacred objects. By so doing the Elimites were perpetuating an African tradition of cyclical societal cleansing.

What is remarkable about Katerere's Christian movement is not that it happened, but that it occurred so late. As noted above, pioneer missionaries were something of an oddity in 1950s Africa, where the focus was now on the management of institutions, and the Africanisation of church leadership. Nevertheless, other parts of Southern Rhodesia also experienced their first encounter with mission organisations in the post-war period (Alexander and Ranger, 1998). It seems necessary to adjust the periodisation of pioneer work to accommodate later movements of revived missionary Catholicism, and movements of Evangelical and Pentecostal revivalism.

However, both movements did rapidly institutionalise. They caught the spirit of the age, competing to build schools and hospitals, staffed by an influx of expatriates. International agendas asserted themselves. Catholics versus Protestants, Loyalists versus Republicans fought out the 'Irish Question' on the plains of Katerere. By 1960, Elim had dampened its Pentecostal fervour, and Catholic priests had restrained folk Catholicism through a misplaced pursuit of their own brand of inculturation.

Nevertheless, the early days of the missionary movements had left their mark on Katerere in the form of zones of popular Christianity. The founding of these local Christian communities, particularly around mission stations, were as much the product of the creativity of women, youth and outsiders as the endeavour of the pioneer missionaries. The following chapter will focus on these local responses to mission Christianity.

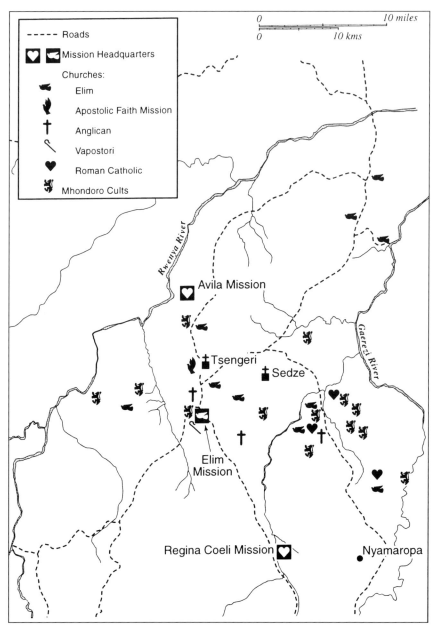

Map 4.1 The Distribution of Churches and *Mhondoro* Cults in Katerere in the 1950s and 1960s

**4**

# THE FIRST CHRISTIAN MOVEMENT IN KATERERE: LOCAL APPROPRIATIONS OF MISSION CHRISTIANITY IN THE 1950s

## INTRODUCTION

African reception of mission Christianity in Katerere further extends the range of ironic variations on the theme of the local and the global. Like the Carmelite and Pentecostal missionaries, the ways in which the Hwesa and Barwe responded to and shaped Christianity were also a product of 'tradition' and change. The impact of colonial capitalism was felt in Katerere as a series of shocks in pre-colonial structures and systems of thought. The new tensions it created in gender and generational relations first found expression in Hwesa religion and then in Christianity. Women, youth and returning labour migrants adhered to local churches further elaborating the mosaic of competing Christian factions.

But the effect of the impact of mission Christianity in eastern Rhodesia as a whole was to enlarge identities as well as to create local Christian communities. Through a well-studied process of language classification and codification, of the production of texts and of their diffusion through church and school networks, a new Manyika identity was created in the 1920s and 1930s. It was very much a Christian identity – literate, progressive, dynamic. Katerere, however, to which Christianity came so late, played no part in this Manyika identity. Excluded from it, the Hwesa became more peripheral. And when Manyika people from southern Inyanga district and Makoni district were evicted into Katerere, their form of African Christianity contrasted with and influenced Hwesa appropriations.

## WOMEN AND CHRISTIANITY IN KATERERE

In Chapter 2 it was noted that, prior to the arrival of missionaries, many women were involved in the *shave* possession cults. It was argued that female adherence to such cults was 'counter hegemonic' in that it contested the patriarchal social and political order which was underpinned by the male-dominated ancestor religion. This section extends the consideration of religion and gender relations. It will be argued that ancestor religion not only subordinated women but left them ritually and symbolically excluded from the central religious processes of Hwesa society. Hence, the arrival of the two mission Christianities in Katerere – Elim Pentecostalism and Carmelite

Catholicism – offered a new range of options to women to contest male authority, and to reinvent their identity.

David Lan's anthropological research on ancestor cults of the Korekore people in the Dande region of Zimbabwe can be generalised for the case of Katerere. Lan argues (1983: 179) that the mhondoro are the most important spirits and 'the rituals at which they attain possession are amongst the most significant moments in the social life of the people'. He contends that the relationship between the sexes which is displayed during these rituals contains crucial information about the way gender relations are conceptualised. Lan writes:

> At possession rituals, as at all public events, the important and individualised actions are performed by men and observed by a crowd of deindividualised women. The only participation of women in these is as brewers of beer, as singers and as dancers but never individually, always as member of a group. (Ibid.)

When the *mhondoro* speaks, men surround the medium at the edge of the mat, in conversation with him. Women sit quietly, as a group, removed from the action and assigned the role of mere spectators. Women can be excluded from rituals completely during times of pregnancy and menstruation.[1]

Lan's analysis of Korekore cosmology explains women's ritual exclusion from these pivotal religious moments. He identifies two types of life: the biological – blood-drenched – life associated with women as affines; and spiritual life associated with the *mhondoro*, which is controlled by men. Spiritual life is seen as superior, because through it the *mhondoro* makes the rain, thus controlling another kind of fertility. Biological life is inferior and rejected by the *mhondoro*, symbolically by dint of their abhorrence of blood, and empirically, by their exclusion of women from active participation in rituals (Lan, 1985: 91–8). Whether one accepts Lan's analysis or not, signs of women's fertility and reproduction are shunned by men, and seen as a source of ritual defilement.

Hwesa *mhondoro* rituals bear many similarities to those of the Korekore. Moreover, women's symbolic exclusion and subordination can be further traced to specific rituals in the political cycles of the chiefdom – the coronation and burial of the chief. The coronation ceremony is completely dominated by male officers. At a key moment, a figure resembling a jester encircles the chief's hut, shouting insults and shaking rattles. He is naked, and if anyone laughs they will pay a girl as a fine (see Appendix 3). When the chief dies, if those responsible for the drying of his body fail, they too must pay a girl.[2] Through the cults of the Hwesa royal ancestors (all of which are male) women are marginalised and de-individualised, and their fundamental contribution of biological reproduction is reduced to an inferior form of life-creation. Their spiritual dispensability means that they can be reduced to ritual objects, transferred from one lineage to another.

However the decades following the Second World War threw up new religious options for north-eastern Shona women to reinvent their identity by other means than joining *shave* possession cults. The first option concerned women drawing from the myths and stories of the Virgin, and creating from them a model on which to restructure their lives. Implicit in the analysis of popular Catholicism in Chapter 3 was the idea that it was predominantly a feminine religion by virtue of its continued emphasis on the Virgin. This emphasis was made explicit and further enhanced by the founding of the Handmaids of Our Lady, an order of African Sisters for the Umtali Diocese, based at St Benedict's Umfeseri.[3] Their establishment by Bishop Donal Lamont in 1959 had been preceded by half a century of controversy concerning the right of African girls to enter the Sisterhood. Their determination to make a break with the family network outraged both their parents and the local administration, and caused much debate over the legal status of unmarried women. (Ranger, 1981: 13–18)

Once established, the order was zealous in its veneration of the Virgin and other female saints. *White Friars*, the journal of the Irish Carmelites, records from the earliest days of the Order's foundation, the vigour with which novices took up Marianism. It describes the great joy with which the statues of St Bernadette and Our Lady of Lourdes were received at St Benedict's. The Sisters took the statues, which they carefully wrapped in blankets, and processed with them to a prepared grotto. A letter in the journal by one of the novices then takes up the story:

> The box in which St Bernadette was, was opened first, and everybody was excited to see the face of St Bernadette. We were so happy that we stretched out our hands to greet her. We were still longing to see Our Lady, and the box of Our Lady was opened ... There was dead silence. Mother started the Lourdes Hymn in Shona and we all joined at once ... Without exaggerating, we felt very proud, for the place where Our Lady and St Bernadette would be was well prepared beforehand. We started to prepare our grotto when we heard that Our Lady and St Bernadette were coming to stay with us. The whole kopje is flowering now. The grotto is noticed by many people because it is near the road. We have written Ave Maria in flowers and they are all flowering now ... Our Lady is looking towards our house. We go there very often to sing the Litany of Our Lady and a nice hymn. We say the Rosary on the way going there and coming back.[4]

Having taken their final vows, the nuns dispersed throughout Manicaland to work in the Province's numerous Carmelite mission schools and hospitals, founding local women's societies centred upon regular veneration of the Virgin.[5] By so doing, they reinforced and further propagated the Manicaland

Catholicism's strong Marian emphasis at a time when post-Vatican II Irish Carmelite priests were turning their backs on it.

This feminine religion is double-edged for women, as Marina Warner's classic historical reconstruction (1976) of the myth and cult of the Virgin Mary illustrates. The many personalities of the Virgin have lent themselves to both female subjugation and liberation. Nevertheless, alongside the Virgin's stoicism in the face of suffering, women informants also identified ideas associated with motherhood and the family which attracted them to Marian devotion.[6] Indeed in their pre-Vatican II mode, the Irish Carmelites do not appear to have been too directive in the interpretation of the myths and cult of the Virgin. Instead they seem to have noted its importance as a means of enhancing the position of women and tried to nurture it amongst male Catholics.[7]

By far the most remarkable accounts of women indigenising Christianity, however, are recorded for the first few years of the Elim movement's arrival in Katerere. Analysis of early encounters between Elim missionaries and the Hwesa in Chapter 3 noted the example of a woman axing a road through the bush so that missionaries could reach a meeting of women in her homestead. This was followed by numerous other instances of women inviting the Briens home to preach, of women bringing other women to church, and of women seizing the initiative by convening meetings.[8] Female agency was central to the founding of a popular pentecostalism.

It was also noticeable that the Drs Brien were subject to a good deal of adoration from the local women. Thus when they returned from sabbatical in 1956 they were greeted by a procession of dancing women which made its way to their door; later they were given 'love offerings' in church.[9] Much of this was due to the tireless dedication with which they worked. It can also be attributed to their brand of Christianity.

In Chapter 3 it was argued that one of the means by which Ulster Pentecostalism was localised in Katerere was by defining itself in opposition to local enemies, namely the Shona spirits and those involved in their veneration. Women played a key part in the enterprise of constructing a local demonology. Very quickly they banded together, exorcising other women, and instigating rituals in which charms, bracelets and other polluting substances were burnt. The terms of this contest between Shona spirits and the Holy Spirit were spelt out by one of the pioneer missionaries to Katerere, Winnie Loosemore:

> Those possessed by demons will speak in tongues and prophesy and it has been known for some to speak in English under this devilish power, but praise God we have the greater Power that can cleanse the hearts of these people and set them free.[10]

In casting the Shona spirit-world as the enemy, women living in Katerere were pursuing an agenda aimed at undermining the patriarchal social order that ancestor religion legitimated. The issue of authority is clearly apparent in the widely remembered testimonies of the first women converts. One husband was so angered by his wife's conversion, which gave her recourse to an authority outside his own, that he confronted her with a pair of thongs for plough oxen and the question: 'Who is greater, Jesus Christ or me?' For her persistence, this convert lost an eye in the domestic violence that ensued.[11] Discontented husbands came to the mission to complain about the behaviour of their wives, who were refusing to brew them beer due to its association with the veneration of ancestor spirits.[12] Older Christian women would even undermine their own son's authority, using their seniority to either connive with, or compel, their daughters-in-law to remove charms from young children, and discourage them from brewing beer.[13] The rapidity with which women adhered to the Pentecostal Church suggests that possession by the Holy Spirit represented a credible alternative to traditional possession cults. This idea will be pursued in Chapter 7, which draws upon the accounts of contemporary Pentecostals.

Women converts reconstructed their identity and challenged male expectations often at great cost. They could encounter more hostility from their husbands after their conversion than before. One female traditional healer felt compelled to burn her ritual paraphernalia after her contact with Pentecostalism. She had been a source of great income to her ageing husband and returned home to many beatings.[14] In a similar episode, another woman, exorcised of a lucrative healing spirit, so angered her husband that he refused to allow her to sleep in his hut.[15] This withdrawal of conjugal rights was the ultimate sanction a husband could place upon his wife, tantamount to divorce (Weinrich, 1979: 47). But despite domestic violence and potential loss in social status, Pentecostal women did gain a sense of empowerment through possession by the Holy Spirit. Such empowerment could be accompanied by an ability to heal, speak in tongues or exorcise evil spirits (Marshall, 1993: 231–2). And these displays of female power could now take place at the religious centre where women were able to exploit the spontaneity of church services.

Moreover, there was always the hope of the conversion of the spouse. A man's conversion to Pentecostal Christianity was usually accompanied by his domestication, replacing an old life of neglect or violence by one of nurture and education (D. Martin, 1990: 181). Such changes in turn renewed 'the innermost cell of the family' (Ibid.: 284). The prospect of social trans-formation was made immediately more tangible by the networks that the church created. Mary Brien's *ruwadzano* – women's fellowship group – was of immediate appeal to local women. In a society where women were divided by exogamy, polygamy and the fear of being labelled gossips or witches (Weinrich, 1979: 47), women relished the opportunity the *ruwadzano* offered for mutual support and solidarity. As such, the Pentecostal fellowship group was functionally similar to the Catholic women's societies for the veneration of the Virgin.

There is one final explanation for the strength of the Christian women's movement around Elim mission. It centres upon women's struggle for biological reproduction. In Chapter 2 it was noted that the infant mortality rate was extremely high for Inyanga district, estimated to be between 50–60 per cent in 1915. Young children often died from exposure, malnutrition and syphilis. A woman's capacity to produce children for her husband enhanced her status both within the polygamous household and the wider community. And failure to reproduce, in a culture which placed such a premium on motherhood, greatly diminished a woman's sense of self, and could often lead to her rejection by her husband's family. In Chapter 3 it was described how the Briens brought a sophisticated package of bio-medicine to Katerere. Their ability to specialise in gynaecology, obstetrics and paediatrics merged with their practice of divine healing, and won them widespread renown as great healers. A similar pattern emerges in that of women bringing others to church: women who had received the Brien's medical treatment rapidly spread the news to others.[16] As Mary Brien put it: 'As soon as the women saw their babies living, they started coming to church.'[17]

## RECASTING THE FUTURE:
## THE CHRISTIAN YOUTH MOVEMENT

The first adherents to the Catholic and Protestant missions in Katerere were marginal social categories: women, youth and young men sensitive to the egalitarian potential of the Christian message (J. and J. Comaroff, 1991: 240). But those young men who adhered to the new mission churches were marginal in a different sense than women. Excluded from authority by virtue of their age, young Hwesa and Barwe males had only the prospect of an eventual elevation in their status. Hence, the church represented 'an altogether new source of meaning, control, and influence' (Ibid.). For many, conversion to Christianity, when accompanied by schooling, provided a means of escape into 'the world'. For others, as we have already seen, it offered a means of obtaining local influence. In the latter case, it led to the formation of new mission élites.

On its arrival, young men rapidly adhered to Elim mission in a similar fashion to women. They approached missionaries asking for schools, and were prepared to walk great distances daily, as well as finance themselves, in order to attend.[18] One informant spoke of how he refused to speak to his father for weeks until he consented to allow him to attend school.[19] Another informed his father that he had chosen to attend school as a *fait accompli*.[20] Like the young male labour migrants from Tsengerai village who introduced

Elim missionaries to Katerere, these young men, zealous for education, perceived that mission Christianity provided the resources with which to construct a new social order in which they would be free from customary roles. (D. Martin, 1990: 283)

Karen Fields has argued (1985: 41) that Christian conversion in Central Africa was a cultural as well as a religious phenomenon. The conventional language of Christians 'coming forwards', 'setting themselves apart', and declaring for a 'completely changed life', took on a new meaning when fused with Christianity's individualist conscience (Ibid.: 41–6). It provided converts with 'principled grounds for denying customary obligations of all kinds' (Ibid.: 46) such as arranged marriages, funeral observances, ancestor veneration, and obedience to elders. It is clear from the testimonies of some of Elim mission's first young male adherents that they attached themselves to this new religion to break free from networks of traditional commensality.[21] One informant had an acute perception of the difference his conversion to Pentecostal Christianity had brought about:

> It separated me completely from believing in traditional religion, making me a very different person from my relatives who still drink and worship spirits ... I think it is true that ancestral spirits cannot change someone's life to become a better person ... Also when people believe in traditional spirits there is a lot of wastage ... they sacrifice to the spirits and get nothing.[22]

Pentecostal missionaries were fully aware of the potential for social transformation embodied in an assertive collection of Christian youth. As we have seen, missionary teachers groomed these 'gems'[23] to take power locally, and in the world.

Many of the young men who came in contact with Elim mission moved on into the cities. Others stayed as teachers, pastors, evangelists, hospital orderlies and drivers, eventually forming a local *petit bourgeoisie*. However, because so many moved out of the district into the world, class was not as significant a social category as it might have been in less marginal areas, at least until the 1980s. Those who stayed often enhanced their identity as members of new mission élites by relocating. They moved into the vicinity of Elim mission. Others were provided with houses on the station. Their homes resembled those inhabited by the missionaries, but were smaller and set apart from them. Their new-found status was often bolstered by missionary-arranged marriages to progressive Manyika women.[24]

Similar processes occurred at the Catholic mission at Avila, although here the mission élites were smaller because entrance to Holy Orders as nuns or priests was a far harder route.[25] Moreover, the Catholic school teachers and mission staff were less inclined to disentangle themselves from familial obligations.

## THE ARRIVAL OF THE MANYIKA AND THE RETURN OF
## NYAMHUTE: ETHNICITY AND MIGRATION
## AS STIMULI TO MISSIONISATION

In Chapter 2 the Manyika ethnicity was briefly mentioned in contrast to that of the Hwesa. Whilst Manyika identity was enlarged to cover large areas of Manicaland, the Hwesa were defined out of this wider 'Shona' identity, and categorised as 'Sena' along with their Mozambican neighbours. In this re-definition of pre-colonial identities the Hwesa became more peripheral; as a consequence they lost out on the material advantages that the Manyika could reap in the migrant labour market.

The final sections of this chapter describe the imagination of Manyika ethnicity by missionaries and their evangelists, colonial officials, labour migrants and peasants, and explores its meaning in three different contexts: eviction from the south; resettlement amongst the Hwesa; and the missionisation of the north.

### THE IMAGINATION OF MANYIKA ETHNICITY,
### AND THE PEASANT OPTION

In an article on the construction of the Manyika identity, Terence Ranger (1989) argues that the term *Manyika* did have a pre-colonial currency deriving from the territory and the people of Chief Mutasa. This area on the map was expanded by both the Portuguese and the British in order to control as large a land mass as possible for the purposes of trade and territorial rivalry. However, these newer definitions came to possess a 'degree of reality', 'due to the agency both of "unofficial" Europeans and "unofficial" Africans – of missionaries and their converts – and of African labour migrants'. Focusing on the use of language in inventing ethnicity, Ranger describes how, through the activities of missionary linguists, the gradual lexical and idiomatic change in the Shona language countrywide was turned into 'discrete dialect zones by developing written languages centred upon a number of widely scattered bases' (Ibid.: 121–7).

Thus the Jesuits at Chishawasa created Zezuru and the Dutch Reformed Church at Morgenster, Karanga. In the east, the vast concentration of mission resources – the American Methodists at Old Umtali, the Anglicans at St Augustine's and the Marianhill Fathers at Triashill – helped to create Manyika. In Manicaland native pastors, teachers and evangelists, respond-ing to the grassroots demand for education, took the new dialect out to the people in the form of tracts, catechisms, bibles and educational literature.[26] Ranger also considers ethnicity as a labour factor and shows how labour migrants from the eastern province, who were by no means all mission Christians, would 'attach themselves to the growing "myth of the Manyika" … with their irresistible "high sounding English"' in order to maximise their chances in the labour market. The Manyika came to be thought of as natural domestic servants (Ranger, 1989: 139–40). He concludes by noting that although by the 1950s there was a movement towards a Shona cultural nationalism, a loyalty to Manyika identity still existed beneath it (Ibid.: 144).

Many inhabitants of the southern part of Inyanga district who had been subjects of Chief Mutasa readily responded to the opportunities provided by the new Manyika identity. They joined the schools and churches provided at the out-stations of the central Anglican, American Methodist and Catholic missions of the region. Like their counterparts from Makoni district, many joined the labour market, making full use of the higher wages and better conditions that domestic service offered. In 1938 the NC Inyanga wrote of them:

> The younger people exhibit a very high level of intelligence, and generally speaking in employment command a much higher wage than other Rhodesian Natives. It has been said in hyperbole that the Manyika supply cook boys to half of Rhodesia and Johannesburg. They are also found as highly paid officials in mines and municipal compounds.[27]

Other Manyika preferred to take what Ranger describes as the 'peasant option'. This involved 'tribesmen' and women making a number of changes in their lifestyle in order to become peasants and produce for a market. These innovations ranged from a change of staple, to ideological changes such as converting to Christianity and appropriating a new work ethic, to transformations in the division of labour, and a conceptual departure from the authority of chiefs (Ranger, 1985: chapter 1). For some Inyanga inhabitants this meant moving to another district, such as Umtali, in order to be nearer the market or railhead.[28] For those who stayed as peasant producers in Inyanga district, a pattern emerged of a people living on alienated land, paying rent rather than working for a landlord. Some marketed maize at the railhead at Umtali and others realised the potential market for goats, milk, eggs, potatoes and green vegetables at the mines at Penhalonga.[29] Few European farmers took up the alienated land in the district leaving it ripe for peasant exploitation. In 1934, the NC Inyanga described them as having 'the free run of the district', able to farm extensively, graze cattle where they wished and evade rent.[30] It came as no surprise to the NC that these 'progressive farmers' were unwilling to take up land in Native Purchase Areas. Such areas, in the northern part of the district, possessed poor soils and were too remote from the market to attempt the peasant option.[31]

There was never a hard and fast division between Manyika who went for the labour market and those who went for the peasant option. It was possible for half the male workforce from a household to enter the labour market and earn wages which would also cover the taxes of those families choosing the peasant option. The male householders would rotate their period away from home so that the following year the other half could migrate to work.[32] Here the contribution of women in maintaining the cohesion of the household was crucial. Likewise, their labour in tending vegetable gardens was a vital component in the peasant productive system. Peasants worked out extra-ordinary strategies, such as the cultivation of mining claims, in order to make this possible.[33] However, what is most noticeable was the desire of many Manyika households to maintain the peasant option at all costs.

The independence and assertiveness that characterised these Manyika peasant producers was intensified in the immediate period following the Second World War. As we have seen in Chapter 3, alienated land in the south was taken up by companies responding to the boom in commercial agriculture, and by British ex-servicemen in what was known as the Second Colonial Occupation. Many peasants now found themselves described as 'squatters' on land they had assumed was theirs. Attempts made by their new landlords to entice them into labour agreements met with outright failure. The horrified NC Inyanga wrote:

> Not one native has so far come forward to say he is willing to go on a Labour Agreement with any of the new settlers. They are all determined to move next year after their crops have been reaped. It almost seems as if it is an organised form of passive resistance to keep the European farmers out of the district.[34]

The Native Commissioner was not wrong. Manyika peasants developed other strategies to challenge the Land Apportionment Act, making capital out of the fact that Section 49 stipulated that the Native Department could only evict 'squatters' if it had alternative land to relocate them on. The shortage of habitable areas in the district left peasants in the south in a strong position, and young men refused to fulfil labour obligations for foresters and commercial farmers, knowing that the threat of eviction had briefly diminished.[35]

Such acts of resistance were far from disparate or random challenges to the settler state, but part of an organised political response. As early as 1930 Manyika migrants had organised themselves into an ethnic association suited to their urban setting. In the Cape, Bulawayo and Salisbury, branches of the Young Ethiopian Manyika Society were founded whose objects the Inyanga NC described as 'political'. The constant interaction between town and country meant that Manyika peasants were also highly politicised by the late 1940s. A sophisticated ideological critique of the Land Apportionment Act was developed to accompany their acts of passive resistance.

In 1948 – the same year that young men began refusing to fulfil their labour agreements – a leaflet was circulating amongst Manyika resident in Salisbury. The tract was entitled 'Manyikaland: Memorandum to the Government' and contained a detailed attack on the implementation and effects of native land policy.[36] It began with criticism of the recent spate of removals, complaining about increases in Manyika mortality due to their movement from the cool high plateau to the hot dry lowlands infested with malaria, and devoid of medical facilities. It finished with a number of recommendations. These included: a thorough survey of the new area before relocation, security of tenure, and compensation for the cost of transportation and removal. The leaflet does much to explain both the appeal and *raison d'être* of Manyika ethnic ideology. It was couched in a language that stressed the historical integrity of the 'tribe' and its claims to land, and the sanctity of the family with its rights to possess land (see Vail, 1989: 14). The memorandum began by clearly stating its source as: 'The people and chiefs of Manyikaland ...'; it continued:

> The people of Manyikaland are definitely suffering from a sense of frustration. They have in another respect lost all allegiance to their hereditary chief, Mutasa. Owing to this removal, they have been forced to live under completely new conditions which have destroyed all tribal and family life as such.[37]

Yet the definition of Manyika identity was broader than this, containing a plurality of legitimating sources which, when considered out of context, could appear contradictory. In response to the eviction of Africans from land owned by missions, the document finished with the threat that: 'this [the evictions] has caused much frustration and hardship and is causing many *Christian Africans* to lose faith in the church.' This was indeed only a threat, for as shown below, the 'Christian' aspect of Manyika identity was to take on a greater significance when the mass removals began. Once estranged from their ancestral lands and the possibility of claiming allegiance to their 'traditional' chief, 'modernising Christianity' offered Manyika migrants a more viable source of identity.

It was in this state of heightened ethnic consciousness that hundreds of assertive, 'progressively minded' Manyika were evicted to the northern portion of the district. One group in particular – the Nyamudeza people – who had refused to plant wattle for their new colonial masters, were moved from near Bonda mission to a site adjacent to Elim mission.[38] The key to the impact of these migrant élites on the surrounding Hwesa and Barwe lies in the dynamics of the ethnic hierarchy.

## THE DYNAMICS OF THE ETHNIC HIERARCHY

The contrast between Manyika and Hwesa ethnicity has already been explored in Chapter 2. The differences were not only apparent to white employers but also, in a very graphic way, to the Native Administration in its daily control of the district. At an official level the ethnic hierarchy was perceived and described through oppositions. Whilst farmers in the south used fertiliser, ploughs and practised winter planting, those in the north retained the hoe, planted once a year and used no fertiliser. The northerners were 'less progressive', 'conservative', and 'backward', continuing to grow the pre-colonial staple of rukweza and not maize. By contrast, the Manyika were 'progressive', 'useful and intelligent'.[39] In an ethnographic survey of 1914, Moodie, the NC for Inyanga, divided the inhabitants of the district into two categories; 'raw natives' and 'semi-civilised mission natives'. He wrote:

> These two main divisions would also roughly represent the Northern natives (Katerere's, Sawunyama's and Tangwena's) the raw natives, and Umtasa's the Southern and partially civilized element. These two main divisions would be antagonistic to one another and not likely to act together.[40]

Whilst it is dangerous to use these administrative characterisations uncritically (there was nothing 'unprogressive' about not growing maize in an unfavourable environment such as Katerere), it is striking the extent to which Manyika informants were willing to reproduce them verbatim. The Manyika characterised their Hwesa neighbours as *karimbwi* – primitive.[41] Moreover, although the Hwesa did not necessarily share the sentiments of the Native Department characterisations, they were acutely aware of the operation of an ethnic hierarchy in which they were located somewhere near the bottom. The strong desire of the Tsengerai faction to accrue the benefits of mission education powerfully illustrates this.

The antagonism between the groups about which NC Moodie wrote, manifested itself in different ways over the course of the century. When the Trappist mendicant, Aegidius, had visited the Barwe of the Honde valley before the First World War, they refused to be baptised as Catholics in order to assert their difference from the Manyika who had converted.[42] When, in the 1950s, large numbers of Manyika were evicted to Nyamaropa reserve, some Hwesa and Barwe moved to Portuguese East Africa in protest.[43] However, by this date the imperative of modernisation was such that the Hwesa had only one real option, to imitate the Manyika. Such imitation would increase their chances of prospering in the settler state which, in the 1950s, finally managed to make its presence in Katerere felt on a daily basis through the construction of an infrastructure, and concerted intervention in local agriculture.

The extent to which the Hwesa imitated the Manyika lifestyle was staggering. They began to construct fowl pens, brick houses and toilets. In agriculture, those who continued to practise shifting agriculture on the foot slopes – *majinga* – relocated to the vleis or valleys – *madambo* or *mupata*. They began to use the plough, to cultivate maize and cotton, and to use manure and dip tanks. Hwesa women copied their Manyika counterparts and began keeping gardens on stream banks. Hwesa and Barwe men sought

Manyika wives.[44] But the process of imitation ran far deeper than this, influencing missionisation.

## ETHNICITY AND CHRISTIAN IDENTITY

The Hwesa and Barwe imitated the Manyika not only in their agricultural technique but also in their Christian practice. Just as the Manyika identity expressed itself in the houses they built with 'straight lines' (i.e. square), so too was it represented by their Christianity. Although the Manyika-Nyamudeza people's experience of Christianity was Bonda mission's High Anglicanism, they were not deterred by Elim Pentecostalism. They were pleased to find a mission at all. Mary Brien explained what happened on their arrival in Katerere:

> The Hwesa people said: 'We don't want our girls to learn.' The Nyamudeza people came from Bonda and said: 'Oh look there are schools' and sent their girls. The Hwesa followed. The Nymudeza people came to church and put on their best clothes. The Hwesa followed. The Nyamudeza people knew Dr Taylor at Bonda and wanted medicine so the Hwesa followed.[45]

In a number of instances, complete Manyika villages were evicted and often those displaced chose to be relocated as a whole village, simply retaining the name of the previous settlement. It is not surprising that a number of informants spoke of the 'Manyikaisation' of the north.[46]

The Native Department was well aware of the potential contribution inhabitants from the south could lend to projects in social engineering. It was with this in mind that Meredith, the NC in 1951, at the time of the founding of Elim mission, relocated the Nyamudeza people just a few miles outside the newly-pegged site.[47] Elim missionaries were also aware of the Manyika people's evangelistic potential. Mary Brien found the support of Manyika women crucial in organising meetings and spreading the message of bio-medicine.[48]

The degree to which a Christian identity was important to some groups of Manyika is illustrated by the case of Nyamudeza village. Here the people refused to submit to autochthonous Hwesa *mhondoro* cults – a practice usually expected of immigrant Shona groups (Schoffeleers, 1979: 5). One Nyamudeza informant justified their defiance as follows: 'There were some people [Hwesa] who trusted their spirit mediums. Their traditional life we found unsuitable for ourselves, so we came to an understanding with the Europeans and joined their church.'[49]

The Nyamudeza people were able to resist traditional religious assimilation, not simply because they came as migrant élites, but because the influence of *mhondoro* cults was also at an all-time low. The migrants' arrival coincided with two other important transforming forces: mission Christianity and state intervention in peasant agriculture. As described in the previous chapter, these two agencies massively transformed the landscape, and offered the Manyika powerful alternative (rationalist) interpretations of ecology with which to challenge the hegemony of *mhondoro* cults.

Other groups of Manyika more distant from Elim mission did not convert to Pentecostalism but maintained their former Church adherence. Sedze village remained staunchly Anglican. Its inhabitants consulted traditional healers and spirit mediums, but disapproved of the extent to which the Hwesa were willing to defer to them.[50]

Where Manyika were absent, the task of a missionary was far harder. Avila mission was even more remote than Elim, and surrounded only by Hwesa and Barwe peoples. There the founding missionary, Tony Clarke, struggled for many years to persuade headmen and fathers to send girls to school. Only when they encountered the example of a woman teacher did they finally yield.[51]

Far larger numbers of Manyika were removed to the irrigation project in Nyamaropa Reserve adjacent to Inyanga North Reserve. Here, the processes of imitation and 'Manyikaisation' also repeated themselves, although in this case the Manyika came in such large numbers that they were more able to bring and sustain their own locally led churches. Catholics evicted from the vicinity of Triashill mission not only brought with them their native schools with distinctive saints' names, but also their brown scapulars and rosaries. Other Manyika Catholics who had formed themselves into societies for the veneration of specific saints retained these sub-religious identities as well.[52] Hence elements from the folk Catholicism of the south were transplanted in the north.[53] But there was much more to this movement of Manyika popular Christianity than just the arrival of Catholicism. New churches ranged from Anglican and Methodist to the Apostolic.[54] The resilience of these local gatherings in the face of evictions meant that the migrants were later able to demand schools and hospitals, and other Christian infrastructures from ecclesiastical hierarchies initially removed from these processes.

The Manyika alliance with the state and with missionaries strengthened their position in the competition for material resources. The state awarded the Nyamudeza people access to grazing and irrigation schemes at the expense of surrounding Hwesa villages. And the Elim missionaries gave Manyika work on their stations, acting as marriage brokers between Manyika women workers and the new Hwesa mission élites. Missionary and state preference for the Manyika not unexpectedly generated ethnic tensions. The Hwesa too had their own derogatory name for the Manyika: *Watatsi* – incomers. But their resentment of the Manyika remained beneath the surface until the liberation struggle when the opportunity for revenge arose.

There is one final irony in the story of the Manyika migration to Katerere. Some of the Manyika families inhabiting the Nyamudeza village were in fact

Hwesa![55] Chapter 1 described how, in the early stages of factional warfare in Katerere, the Nyamhute house was forced to flee in the face of an attack by the Nkota faction (see Appendix 4). After taking refuge in Saunyama the faction dispersed, moving southwards to Inyanga and into Makoni district. The implementation of the Land Apportionment Act sent many of them home. However, the advent of colonial rule had brought about a loss in status for the Hwesa that remained in the north; they had been defined out of the wider Shona cultural field and their colonial marginality had placed them low down the ethnic hierarchy. Perceiving that no immediate benefits could be derived from claiming Hwesa ethnicity, the returned Nyamhute faction remained in Nyamudeza village, identifying themselves as Manyika.

The role played by the Manyika in the missionisation of the north has important consequences for the social history of African Christianity. Bengt Sundkler has long been at pains to point out the role of African agents in the continent's Christian history. To his 'refugee' and 'returnee' movements for Christianisation there must now be added 'eviction' movements (Sundkler, 1987: 75).

## CONCLUSION

Similar accounts of rapid Christian adherence to missions in southern and central Africa date from the final decades of the nineteenth century to the first decades of the twentieth century. It was with this in mind that Sundkler described nineteenth-century Christianisation as a 'youth movement' and twentieth-century Christianisation as a 'woman's movement' (Ibid.: 83). That the two processes should occur in tandem in Katerere, and so late, was a product of the chiefdom's marginality and, of course, the belated pioneering zeal of the two mission movements which arrived there in the early 1950s.

In Chapter 3 we saw that mission Christianity was by no means monolithic. Its impact was initially affected by its varying social sources, and later also, in the Catholic case, by theological innovation within the world-wide Church. This chapter further complicates the encounter between missionaries and Africans by showing how two contrasting Christianities interacted with a local society riven with tensions of ethnicity, gender and generation. The capacity of social categories, religious groupings, and individuals to ally with external agents, and to localise global ideologies in pursuit of local agendas, will be explored further in the following chapter, which focuses on the interaction of guerrillas with the people of Katerere during Zimbabwe's war of liberation.

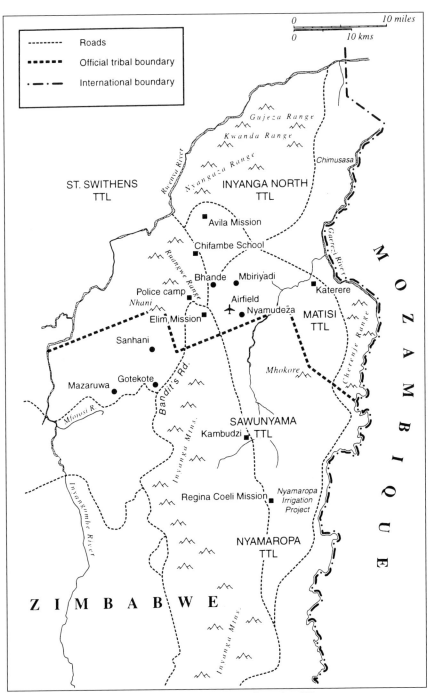

Map 5.1 Northern Inyanga District during the Liberation War

# 5

# LOCAL POLITICS AND THE WAR OF LIBERATION

## INTRODUCTION

The violent path taken by Zimbabwean nationalism followed the refusal of the Rhodesian state to acquiesce to the reformist demands of the early nationalist movements. The open mass nationalist period is usually dated from the founding of the Southern Rhodesian African National Congress (SRANC) in September 1957. This first nationalist party had relatively moderate aims. Though it pressed for universal suffrage and the repeal of racial legislation, it still declared its allegiance to the British Crown and advocated a mixed economy. In its programme of action, the SRANC coordinated opposition against the franchise laws, the Department of Native Affairs, and the Native Land Husbandry Act. Rhodesian reaction to this first breath of Zimbabwean nationalism was swift and ruthless. Acting on white fears for their land and jobs, and, of course, racism, the government of Edgar Whitehead banned the Congress in February 1959.

But African nationalism grew stronger and more revolutionary in the face of Rhodesian state repression. The National Democratic Party (NDP) was formed in 1960, only to be banned in December 1961. Almost without delay the Zimbabwe African People's Union (ZAPU) was founded under the leadership of Joshua Nkomo. It intensified its international diplomatic efforts and initiated a campaign of sabotage against church and government property – school buildings, dip tanks and the plots of agricultural demonstrators. ZAPU was banned in September 1962 and rather than form another party the nationalist leaders decided to carry on the struggle 'underground'. In August 1963 the nationalist movement split over questions of strategy and doubts about Nkomo's leadership. Zimbabwe African Nationalist Union (ZANU) was formed with Ndabaningi Sithole as President and Robert Mugabe as Secretary General. Both ZAPU and ZANU established themselves in exile in Zambia the following year.

Meanwhile, white racism grew more entrenched with the rise to power of the Rhodesia Front (RF). In October 1965 the RF, led by Ian Smith, issued the Unilateral Declaration of Independence from Britain. The nationalist movements were unprepared for Rhodesian intransigence and though there were a few small-scale acts of violence from 1964 onwards, sustained guerrilla war did not break out until 1972, and this was only confined to the far north of the country. It was not until 1976 that the war covered most parts of the country. Over the nationalist period, which was to end in 1980, ZAPU gradually, though not entirely, came to establish itself and fight the war in the west of the country. Likewise, ZANU was increasingly based in the east. By 1972 ZANU had come to espouse a Marxist Leninist rhetoric. Though notably, popular mobilisation was based on a Maoist strategy.[1]

In early 1976, guerrillas (also known as comrades) entered Katerere. They were from ZANU's military wing, commonly known as ZANLA (Zimbabwe African National Liberation Army), although for a period between November 1975 and January 1977, when ZANU's old guard seemed to lose their way, the armed struggle was coordinated by ZIPA (Zimbabwe People's Army) whose younger leaders held a distinctly different ideological position (see D. Moore, 1995). The guerrillas stayed amongst the Hwesa, and their neighbours in this part of the north-east, until early 1980 when a cease-fire was established.

Inquiry into the nature of interactions between rural societies and guerrillas is now a central concern of scholars working on southern Africa. And the study of Zimbabwe's liberation war in Katerere contextualises a number of debates. First, there has been a good deal of research into the fate of churches and mission communities in Zimbabwe's war-torn rural areas. Together these studies have demonstrated a range of factors which help explain the survival or demise of rural Christianity during the liberation struggle (Ranger, 1983; Bhebe, 1988; Bourdillon and Gundani, 1988; Maxwell, 1995a; McLaughlin, 1995).There has also been a good deal of scholarly debate concerning popular mobilisation in Zimbabwe's liberation war. Briefly, Terence Ranger claimed (1985) that there was a broad consensus between peasants and guerrillas. David Lan argued (1985) that 'traditional' religious authorities played a key role in mediating between them. Norma Kriger, on the other hand, contended that the guerrillas did not have political legitimacy, but were manipulated by sections of an internally divided peasantry in pursuit of their own agendas. This resulted in the coercion of specific categories of society within rural communities (Kriger, 1988, 1992; see also Alexander, 1992). More recently the study of such interactions has become a central theme in Mozambican historiography.[2]

This chapter investigates the fate of ZANLA's/ZIPA's strategies of rural mobilisation as they interacted with what we have seen to be the diverse range of agendas and ideologies of Katerere's inhabitants. Its argument will bear out a number of propositions. First, guerrilla strategy changed over time and place because their ideology was essentially weak. On the ground, ZANLA's/ZIPA's attempts at mass mobilisation were pragmatic rather than ideologically determined. This pragmatism emerged as guerrillas grappled with the complex socio-political dynamics of the society they sought to mobilise. At the commencement of the war, peasant ideologies and interests asserted themselves in response to the comrades' attempts to secure the widest possible legitimacy. These often conflicting peasant agendas, based upon ethnicity, religion, social stratification, gender and generation, acted as the motor of change for guerrilla strategy. Although the guerrillas were fighting to seize the state, local agendas proved more salient. From this perspective it will be argued that a critical factor determining the fate of mission communities and mission infrastructure was the depth or shallowness of popular Christianity.

Secondly, the weakness of guerrilla ideology and its consequent pragmatism is explained in two ways. The first was the limited appeal of ZANLA/ZIPA Shona cultural nationalism, which was an attempt to gain political legitimacy by appealing to a particular version of African culture. It offered only the deferred gratification of restored land and political autonomy but gave little hope of immediate gain (Kriger, 1992: 95–101, 168–9). The second explanation of the weakness of guerrilla ideology lies with the divisions within the guerrilla armies themselves, which needed to be disaggregated as much as the peasant societies with which they interacted.

Thirdly, the result of the weakness of ZANLA/ZIPA ideology as it interacted with local politics, meant that guerrillas missed opportunities to transform the structures of rural society.

Although this argument rests on the proposition that the dynamics of guerrilla mobilisation can only be understood in relation to the specifics of the rural societies in which they operated, the last part of this chapter will explore what other lessons the Katerere case has to offer to the general debate on wartime mobilisation, and what modifications it suggests to the existing historiography.

## GUERRILLAS TAKE CONTROL OF KATERERE

A central contention of this chapter is that in the relative security of Katerere, ZANLA/ZIPA guerrillas were able to work out very specific strategies of rural mobilisation. Thus, before introducing material on mobilisation, it is necessary to detail the extent to which guerrillas were in control of the area for the majority of the war between 1976–80.

As this study has shown, the remoteness of the Katerere chiefdom in the north-east of Rhodesia was a recurrent and significant factor affecting the area's development. During the late 1970s it was to profoundly affect the processes of the war. The area's mountainous terrain made it relatively easy for the guerrillas to seize control of communications. By the end of 1976 all the major roads leading to Katerere had been mined,[3] and numerous bridges destroyed.[4] The comrades controlled virtually all civilian movement by forcing travellers to move along the road beside the Mozambican border where they were easily monitored.[5] The colonial state's administrative grip over Katerere, which had only gradually increased throughout the century, was lost within a year.

The comrades replaced the local political structure. State-imposed headmen were killed.[6] In contrast, other 'traditional' leaders whose positions were the product of hereditary succession and thus endowed with 'traditionally' legitimate status, were just relieved of their badges of office, and local committees formed in their place.[7] These committees channelled resources to guerrillas from stores, missions and the peasants themselves. Uncooperative store owners were killed, or their stores burnt down.[8] Some committees were given the responsibility for agriculture, health and women's affairs. A ruthlessly effective intelligence network was constructed using *mujiba* – teenage boys who worked in alliance with guerrillas.[9]

Guerrilla control of Katerere was extensive. By early 1977 they had created a semi-liberated zone between the Rwenya River, and the Cherenje and Ruangwe ranges (see Map 5.1). The police camp perched on the top of the Ruangwe range was effectively in a state of siege from that point onwards. As the guerrillas became more established, their mobilisation rallies – *pungwe* – grew in size, so that as many as 10 villages could be brought together at one time.[10] An international delegation which visited Elim Pentecostal Mission in 1976 noted: 'The whole of the African population in the area is in sympathy with ZANU and there is evidence that the school children are in contact with them.'[11] Guerrilla control of the area was impressive, but the question remains how *did* the comrades mobilise such a socially and ideologically diverse population into providing them with active support?

## MOBILISING THE MANYIKA:
### POPULAR MOBILISATION AND ETHNICITY

Narrative accounts of guerrilla mobilisation in Katerere given by ex-combatants stress the initial importance of the progressive Manyika immigrants. The Manyika were crucial to guerrilla strategy for two reasons. First, ZANLA were able to build on their strong tradition of nationalist politics and secondly, they were able to use the Manyika to politicise the local Hwesa and Barwe. The guerrillas used the Manyika to widen the horizons of other ethnic groups in Katerere.

In the previous chapter we saw that the Manyika were a collection of literate progressive élites who were removed to the north-east in the 1950s following the implementation of the Land Apportionment Act. Located near the top of the ethnic hierarchy they secured the best jobs in the labour market, and when evicted northwards they were favoured by both the district administration and missionaries. Once established in the north-east, their Christian identity hardened through their choice not to submit to autochthonous Hwesa ancestor cults. Missionary and state preference for the Manyika created a deep-seated ethnic resentment amongst the host peoples. Nevertheless, the Hwesa and Barwe imitated these ethnic élites in their agricultural techniques, desire for clinical medicine, and mission education.

The comrades initially preferred the Manyika because this ethnic group's previous struggles with the state, to defend the peasant option and resist eviction, had made them more politicised in comparison with the local Hwesa and Barwe. In Chapter 4 we saw that they had been politically active from the 1930s onwards, through the activities of the Young Ethiopian Manyika Society which derived its organisational base from the ethnic associations functioning in southern African cities.[12] By 1957 the Manyika Society had formed to coordinate rural grievances at an ethnic level against the state.[13] This ethnic radicalism developed into nationalism. The Manyika reserves in the south of the district, and particularly those in the north to which they were evicted, became NDP strongholds.[14] They were also the sites of the greatest militancy against the Native Land Husbandry Act.[15] The clearest personification of a Manyika nationalist tradition was Herbert Chitepo – chairman of ZANU until his assassination in March 1975. Chitepo, a leading member of the NDP, had a considerable following in his home area in central Manicaland. When he returned there on one occasion in 1955, to act as an advocate in a legal hearing, the Inyanga courtroom was too small 'to accommodate his numerous admirers who had travelled far to hear him in action'.[16] During the war, Inyanga district was named 'Chitepo Sector'.

It was logical that the comrades should first turn to the immigrant Manyika rather than the autochthonous Hwesa in Katerere. When guerrillas entered northern Inyanga in early 1976 they already had the names of ZANU sympathisers. These were Manyika store-owners who had followed their people north from Makoni or the southern part of Inyanga district. Others were businessmen of Ndau and Shangaan origin who now claimed to be part of a wider Manyika identity which functioned at a provincial level.[17]

After these initial contacts with store-owners the comrades had two strategies. The first was to make contact with the black Christian élites who worked in the territory's two missions (see below).[18] The second was to visit Manyika villages. Significantly, they deferred mobilising the Hwesa until later. Hence they used the Manyika villages as stop-overs on their journeys to Nyatate and Nyamutowera – strongholds of Manyika nationalist support in the south. It was only after these areas were consolidated that they returned to the Hwesa in the north.[19]

One reason for the delay was that the comrades found the Hwesa far harder to mobilise. One ex-combatant explained:

> People among the Manyika are more prosperous, with more schools, property, for example, shops and had more radios. Katerere is less

developed than Nyamaropa where there is irrigation. Even in Nyatate there are lots of schools and well established business centres. So it was not proper to use a similar approach to those in Katerere, rather you have to start from the base and teach them everything.[20]

The Hwesa needed 'a lot of expertise' because '[they] had been [there] for a long time and had no grievances against the white people except the tax question. Secondly, they were people who had never had problems such as eviction from their home.'[21] Katerere had figured far less in the 1961 militancy in reserves and what party activity did take place can be generally attributed to the Manyika.

The comrades also had their own material reasons for preferring the Manyika. Because they were a more prosperous people, the guerrillas received better care from them in terms of food, blankets and washing facilities.[22] These material benefits which the Manyika had to offer seem to have protected them from the worst excesses of guerrilla violence in the latter stages of the war. By this later stage, the comrades had taken to mobilising the autochthonous Hwesa who attempted to use them to settle old scores.

Guerrilla strategy toward the Hwesa was two-fold. First, they approached the spirit mediums, especially one named Diki Rukadza.[23] Comrade Shaka explained: 'The Hwesa were more linked to their ancestral spirits. When we went to their area we looked for the eldest person possessed and followed his instructions. Once we followed his instructions we found no problems at all.' Secondly, and more fascinating, ZANLA used the Manyika 'to get hold of the Hwesa'.[24] Thus, for instance, they took the Manyika Nyamudeza people living in the vicinity of Elim mission, who one ex-combatant described as 'intellectuals', and mixed them with the Hwesa of Mbiriyadi village. This mixing occurred at *pungwe* where Manyika elders explained to the Hwesa the intricacies of ZANU's case. From such interactions the comrades gained a better perception of Hwesa grievances such as contour ridging.[25]

As the war progressed, political ascendancy shifted in favour of the Hwesa who far outnumbered Manyika immigrants. As a result intense ethnic conflict occurred. The Hwesa had been humiliated by years of missionary and Native Administration preference for the Manyika. On their arrival from the south, the Nyamudeza people had been given grazing land belonging to three nearby Hwesa villages. Seizing their opportunity for revenge, the Hwesa informed on this Manyika village to a group of comrades.[26] They were labelled as sell-outs due to their close association with missionaries. These comrades responded by kidnapping all the Nyamudeza youth and taking them across the border for a while.[27]

Jeremy Brickhill has argued that the continuities between earlier open mass nationalism and the guerrilla nationalist army were broken in

Manicaland. This is because ZANLA were entering a zone where the nationalist elders belonged to other nationalist parties such as ZAPU, or the UANC (United African National Council). Guerrillas thus had to break existing links with the nationalist tradition and forge new strategies of political mobilisation, often through the idiom of religion.

Brickhill argues that, in contrast, ZAPU continued to operate underground in Matabeleland. Here there was a nationalist tradition which had remained unbroken for two decades and was ripe for exploitation by ZAPU's military wing – ZIPRA (Zimbabwe People's Revolutionary Army).[28] In some instances, this analysis works for Manicaland. ZANLA/ZIPA guerrillas did run into opposition from ZAPU elders in Tanda, although they became sympathetic once they experienced security-force harassment.[29] However, the manner in which guerrillas interacted with Manyika from the north of the district diminishes the stark contrast between the east and the west of the country, and suggests a more complex picture for ZANLA/ZIPA mobilisation. In Katerere, Manyika had a nationalist tradition malleable enough to facilitate rapid cooperation with the guerrillas. Villages of highly politicised Manyika who were ready for, and responsive to, guerrilla cultural nationalist appeals, were able to serve the same function as ZAPU branches.

Nevertheless, the strategy of using the Manyika to politicise the Hwesa was not sufficient to secure wide enough mobilisation. The Hwesa were not completely ready for the Manyika's brand of nationalism. Hence the guerrillas also turned to local religious institutions.

## MISSIONS AND MOBILISATION: ELIM MISSION[30]

Along with mobilising the Manyika, the guerrillas were also quick to make contact with Christian missions. Missions were a great source of logistical support to ZANLA/ZIPA, providing them with food, medicines, money and access to the towns and cities. Where popular Christianity was strong, missions and churches were also a potential source of religious legitimacy for guerrillas, and sometimes they were influential enough to make their own demands on the comrades. Nevertheless, compared to adherents of Shona traditional religions, rural Christians were at an immediate disadvantage when it came to relations with guerrillas. Nationalist leaders had vilified missionaries as key agents in the colonial project, and those political commissars schooled in Marxist Leninism viewed Christianity as a regressive ideology. Traditionalists were far better positioned to makes claims of legitimacy based on a Shona cultural nationalism. Thus Christian leaders had to work hard to establish a *modus operandi* with the comrades. And if they were too successful there was always the danger of reaction by the security forces.

A platoon of guerrillas first visited the Elim on the night of 27 April 1976, making contact with a handful of the missionaries. The missionaries withdrew the following day and henceforth sought to maintain a policy of neutrality *vis à vis* the guerrillas and the security forces. The majority of these white Christians were not antagonistic to the goals of the nationalist movement. As Chapter 3 illustrated they envisaged the event of majority rule, and sought to educate a Christian élite in preparation for it. However, their intellectual response to the war was limited by their conservative evangelical theology which focused their energies on individual transformation to the exclusion of social justice and structural change. There was a tendency to depoliticise issues. Thus Elim missionary, Phil Evans, who had talked at length with an ex-Methodist guerrilla during the initial encounter, commented: 'Do we talk about Rhodesia in political terms? The fundamental problem is the heart of man – the revolution must occur there. Only God's message of repentance will remove the hatred and bitterness and distrust' (Thompson, 1979: 46). Evans's response illustrates what the sociologist Bryan Wilson describes (1961: 89) as the Elim Movement's general disdain for, and disinterest in, social and political issues excepting, of course, the Irish Question.

In fact, relations between Elim missionaries and guerrillas turned out to be good, predominantly because Elim's relations with the local community were sound. When platoons entered a new area they would interrogate its inhabitants about the conduct of the missionaries. Power relations between black and white were inverted and a bad report could spell disaster for missionaries. Ian Linden makes the point well:

> The daily life and safety of rural missions increasingly depended on the good-will of the population to the point where traditional dependence relationships had been turned on their heads. Missionaries survived by the Grace of God and the grace of their parishioners who recommended them to guerrillas, or condemned them. (Linden, 1980: 246)

After half a century of state neglect the inhabitants of Katerere desired a mission, and as Chapter 3 illustrated some even solicited missionaries. Moreover, the new arrivals in the chiefdom, the Manyika, immediately treated missionaries as allies in their struggle to maintain a progressive Christian peasant identity. The Briens' remarkable package of divine healing and bio-medicine won the mission much credibility, whilst the dedicated educational work of later missionaries meant that local goodwill continued. Those older, more conservative whites who would have been a liability had left before the war.

Although the missionaries maintained the appearance of wartime neutrality, they closely identified with the plight of the people. The contribution of the secondary school headmaster, Peter Griffiths, to the establishment of a good rapport with Elim's neighbours was crucial. Increasingly, Griffiths represented the grievances of local people, often church members, to the police. Such complaints concerned the harsh treatment they received from the security forces. On one occasion his action led to the arrest of soldiers responsible for the rape of two girls; on another, the early release of a man suspected of aiding guerrillas. He also protested about the behaviour of Rhodesian Grey Scouts who terrorised the mission while looking for terrorists.

In July 1977 J. C. Smyth, a representative of Elim's International Mission Board, visited Katerere and interviewed black and white staff there. Concerning Griffiths he wrote:

> Peter is in good standing with the terrorists. He has given himself so fully to the local people representing them before the Security Forces and by virtue of the fact that he was a witness in the defence for a Rev. [sic] Michael Pocock ... [who was prosecuted for aiding the guerrillas] ...[31]

Griffiths's actions did bring him into conflict with senior missionaries no longer on the station; nevertheless, as long as he headed the mission community in Katerere, relations with the comrades had most chance of working. When Griffiths and the primary school headmaster, Pious Munembe, met with guerrillas in their base at Kambudzi (see Map 5.1) in July 1977, and mentioned that Elim's authorities were considering moving the secondary school to keep it open, the comrades tried to persuade Griffiths to stay. The reality of these good relations was seen in the reduction of ZANLA activity on the days surrounding the beginning and ending of school terms, and the detailed information Griffiths received concerning mined roads and guerrilla movements.[32]

Despite the missionaries' determination to stay in Katerere, circumstances conspired against them. Two valued African staff resigned, unwilling to risk their lives any longer; new enrolment figures dropped dramatically; and finally the mission's five-ton truck which supplied the school was blown up on its way to Salisbury. The driver had failed to take the longer but safer route along the border. Logistically it was becoming impossible to keep the school open.[33] The missionaries decided to relocate their educational work in the premises of the Eagle preparatory school in the Vumba. And so began the long train of events which was to lead to their horrific massacre at the hands of a rogue group of ZANLA guerrillas. (see Maxwell, 1995a: 61–70)

The departure and then death of the Elim missionaries, marked the end of the missionary era and the beginnings of the black church. The Africanisation of Elim's leadership had speeded up as the missionaries came to rely on black Christians for advice and protection, and was completed, somewhat prematurely, with the Vumba tragedy. It was up to those African leaders remaining in Katerere to work out a new *modus operandi* with guerrillas, and strive to keep the mission open.

Even while the missionaries were still present in Katerere the African mission staff had formed a support committee for the comrades. Each working person gave $20 per month for the purchase of food and medicines, and many attended *pungwe*. In return the guerrillas promised to keep away from the mission. After the missionaries had departed, relations with guerrillas were intensified. In particular, Munembe and Satuku, the African pastor, sought out and cultivated guerrilla leaders they could work with. These commanders were often sympathetic towards the church because of their mission education. Some were seeking self-legitimation through their Christian faith. These guerrilla leaders also used the Christian idiom as a means of mobilisation. Drawing on a long tradition of creativity and innovation in Shona protest song (Kalhari, 1981: 82–9), hymns were rewritten to carry a political message for *pungwe*. Another facet of good working relations with guerrillas was trustworthy local people, who would act as the mission's representatives to the guerrillas and, when the need arose, as 'go-betweens'. Again Munembe and Satuku drew upon a network of local Christians, who belonged to the Apostolic Faith Mission.

However, the good working relations between guerrillas and black Christians around Elim mission were not replicated in all of its out-churches. Many of these were a good distance from the mission and led by overworked missionaries who only visited them once a week, on Sunday. And in a number of these out-churches, there never developed local Christian communities resilient enough to withstand the pressures of the war. By 1 January 1977, the church at Chifambe was closed and another at Mbiriyadi 'shaken to its foundations'.[34] Only a year later it appeared to one missionary, now stationed in the Vumba, that only two churches, the one on the station and another nearby at Bhande, remained open.[35] Of those which were closed, one was done so on the orders of a guerrilla commander; others outside Katerere, to the south at Gotekote and Mazaruwa, were closed in the early stages of the war for fear of attracting security force attention. Whilst some of their adherents bided their time until the end of the war, others participated in the revival of certain *mhondoro* cults, considered below.

In fact one other out-church did survive the war, although its continued existence may not have been apparent to a missionary returning on a brief visit. This was the church at Kambudzi, an area approached through steep mountain ranges and across many rivers. The area's bridges had been destroyed in the war and it was so difficult for security forces to get there that one ex-combatant described it as 'liberated zone'. Right in the middle lay an Elim church, which the people had proudly built with their own hands. It had its own clinic and primary school and had been the site of a very successful convention in 1973. In many respects Elim Kambudzi could be seen as a sub-station of the main mission. Its leader was not a missionary but Ephraim Satuku, who had lived there for a while. He had instructed his flock well, warning them to form 'cells' in time of war. When it came, they met in homes when afraid and openly in the church when safe. It was in this environment that Munembe and Griffiths visited guerrillas, and felt confident enough to negotiate arrangements with them which would ensure the safety of the mission. Thus, where Elim Pentecostalism was most localised, it had most chance of co-existing with guerrillas.

## MISSIONS AND MOBILISATION: AVILA AND REGINA COELI[36]

The war came to Avila mission before Elim in April 1976. The station was en route from ZANLA/ZIPA's border crossing at Chimsasa. When one evening they arrived asking for medicines, Father Peter Egan was totally unprepared:

> Three guerrillas with machine guns took me outside and put me up against a wall. It was very traumatic ... I hadn't done anything to the people. I had lots of black friends and those guys came with machine guns. It scared me. The whole world was going mad.[37]

Egan immediately reported the incident to the authorities, fled to Salisbury, and boarded the first plane which would take him to Ireland. The security forces promptly took revenge on the mission. Soldiers arrived there the following day and began to arbitrarily beat and interrogate people. Thus, Avila's initial interaction with the comrades, and Egan's response, precipitated a crisis within the order and prompted its members to devise a policy which would enable them to continue their work whilst at the same time limiting the degree to which their staff and local community were exposed to danger. The policy was 'sympathetic to not reporting the presence of guerrillas'.[38] In this context Carmelites were not only making a practical response to the justice and peace themes of Vatican II theology, but were also expressing a sense of Irish nationalism which had always manifested itself in the Order's distance from the colonial state.[39]

Priests, nuns and black lay Christians at Avila and elsewhere, aided the comrades with food, medicines and money, accepting with good humour their rhetorical attacks on the evils of Christianity. However the Rhodesian authorities became increasingly aware of this collaboration and sought to silence Manicaland's Catholic leader, Bishop Donal Lamont, and destroy the Justice and Peace Commission he headed. The opportunity came when the Superior of the Irish Presentation Sisters inadvertently admitted to police officers that her nuns did help the guerrillas with the Bishop's knowledge. Lamont was prosecuted and later deported, but not before his stand had captured the attention of the world's press.

Janice McLaughlin argues that 'Avila was the new church for a new society, changing Church-State relations irrevocably' (1995: 101). From her perspective Avila was not a new church because of relations with the local people but because events there brought about Bishop Lamont's historic decision that the Church should aid guerrillas. The mission hence-forth became emblematic both to the Rhodesian government and the liberation movement. For the government and its security forces, Avila's stand indicated that the '"cordial relations" which had existed between the Church and the State since 1890 were extinguished. The Catholic Church and the State were now on opposite sides of the fence' (Ibid.: 100). And this changed perception was made concrete by the arrest and torture of Avila's priests and the constant assault and harassment of other mission staff (Ibid.: 95–6, 100). Conversely, Avila's harsh treatment at the hands of the security forces convinced guerrilla leaders that they had gained a new source of support. In consequence 'some ZIPA leaders revised their attitude to religion in general and Catholic missions in particular' (Ibid.: 101).

McLaughlin's argument is important and may well be true. Nevertheless, from the perspective of local politics, Avila was more exposed to guerrilla distrust and local apathy than either Elim or Regina Coeli. As chapters 3 and 4 illustrate, Avila priests, from the late 1950s onwards, made no use of the powerful and long-established rituals and traditions of Manyika folk Catholicism – the scapulars and rosaries, pilgrimages and holy places – which earlier missionaries used to create Catholic communities and resacralise the landscape. The new missionaries' Catholicism was intellectual and abstract with little popular appeal. Thus, as we shall see, the area's *mhondoro* cult remained powerful, and the mission's leaders, unlike those at Elim, were unable to exert the necessary influence over the people to safeguard the station's property. Window and door frames, and roofing were removed from buildings. Only Peter Egan's architectural masterpiece – the round thatched church in Hwesa-style – remained untouched. Whilst the events of the war did empower African nuns, who conducted services, taught the faith, and ran the institution in the absence of black and white priests, popular Christianity around the mission remained weak.

By contrast, Regina Coeli did have elements of a folk Catholicism which influenced its relations with guerrillas. The mission was situated in a fertile valley of the Nyamaropa reserve adjacent to a large irrigation project, inhabited by Manyika Master farmers on their six-acre plots.[40] As Chapter 4 illustrated, those Manyika evicted from the Carmelite mission at Triashill retained the rituals and symbols of a vital, popular Catholicism and demanded the mission facilities they were used to in the south.[41] Like the Manyika around Elim mission they formed alliances with the local missionaries, and were instrumental in protecting the station during the war. Moreover the priests, Father Muzungu and Father Martin, actively helped the guerrillas. At one stage Muzungu mediated between ZANLA and Red Cross officials after Red Cross workers had been killed near the mission. He later crossed the border in September 1979 and joined the ZANLA base in Tete. Father Martin remained at the mission throughout most of the war.

Again, some mission property was taken but a small Christian community continued to function throughout the whole period of the war.

## DIKI RUKADZA, THE CULT OF NYAWADA, AND GUERRILLA MOBILISATION

The other religious institution guerrillas used for popular mobilisation was *mhondoro* cults. Some Katerere mediums played a significant role in facilitating popular support for ZANLA/ZIPA forces entering the area during the war. But the capacity of individual mediums to respond to the exigencies of the war was determined, not only by their own creative ability, but also by their geographic location, by the relative strength of popular religion, and by their spirit ward's ethnic make-up.

Accounts of peasants and ex-combatants regarding the traditional religious input into the war, were centred on the Katerere dynasty's most senior medium – Diki Rukadza, host of Nyawada. Rukadza was an outstanding figure, unrivalled by other Katerere mediums in his ability to manipulate legend, genealogy and 'tradition'. Through his remarkable capacity to reimagine Hwesa history, he provided the mythic basis for the alliance between the people and guerrillas. The basis in question was an oral tradition, considered in Chapter 1, describing a period of pre-colonial factional warfare amongst the Hwesa. The specific legend recounted the murder and ghastly roasting of the body of Chief Gambiza and the flight of his family to Mozambique (see Appendix 4). In the story's *dénouement* the heroic spirit, Nyawada, organised resistance and, in alliance with other *mhondoro* angry at the transgressing of their spiritual order, he wreaked revenge upon the murderous Chifodya faction. The story finishes with the safe return of Gambiza's kin to power. As the following chapter will show, the legend is recounted in times of peace by the ruling Mbudzi faction as part of their claim to succession. In time of war it was told by Rukadza as a statement of the revolutionary credentials of the guerrillas, who likewise came from Mozambique to restore spiritual order – this time by promising to hand back to the spirits control of the land and its ecology, seized from them by the Rhodesian state. Thus, by means of analogy Rukadza transformed this multi-purpose Hwesa story from an establishment charter into a manifesto for resistance.

Rukadza also offered the comrades the protection of nature, over which his spirit ruled. Birds and animals led the guerrillas and warned them of danger. According to Rukadza:

> The spirits feared that if the snakes were harmful it would be a war on two fronts which would make it difficult for the freedom fighters to win. They worked in the snakes and called them to be harmless so that they could concentrate on the enemy. Nature and the spirits

5.1 Diki Rukadza, Medium of Nyawada

5.2 Razau Kaerezi, Medium of Chikumbirike

were very faithful to the freedom fighters and tried to make it easy for them.[42]

He provided the comrades with protective charms and, as we shall see in Chapter 7, on the war's cessation, he helped heal them from the traumas of combat and killing.[43]

In doing this, Rukadza stood within a well-established tradition of resistance and symbolic innovation by Hwesa mediums, explored at the beginning of this study. Chapter 1 illustrated a tradition of medium-led resistance in the heroic legends of factional and inter-dynastic warfare in the latter half of the nineteenth century, and outlined the key role mediums played in the 1902 Makombe uprising and the 1904 unrest. In addition, it was established that mediums played an overtly political role as leaders of factions and as mediators for outsiders.

Furthermore, Chapter 2 illustrated that a discourse about a 'protective nature' existed long before peasants and guerrillas were to experience it in the liberation war. This discourse represented Katerere *mhondoro* cults' continued concern to exercise legitimising control over other religious institutions and movements entering the area (see Schoffeleers, 1979: 7). It became more important from the early twentieth century onwards as mediums were forced out of their public role in response to state repression of 'witch doctors' and itinerant holy men. We have seen how the idea of a protective nature was vividly invoked to explain the strange events of 1924–5, when the mendicant preacher from Triashill, Brother Zacharias, was badly mauled by a leopard, rapidly ending the first attempt to missionise Katerere. The *mhondoro* spirits unleashed the forces of nature against unwanted aliens but deployed them in the favour of those who paid them respect.

*Mhondoro* cults in Katerere reached a low point, in terms of numbers of adherents, in the 1950s, due to the successful penetration of mission Christianity. But increased state intervention in peasant agriculture ultimately enabled mediums to regain influence, by formulating a popular critique of state intervention in terms of 'traditional' religion. In the early 1970s Rukadza supplied the ethnographer Michael Gelfand with an excellent example of this critique in relation to state-directed agriculture. Gelfand reported:

> According to Diki Rukadza, his spirit disapproves of certain developments introduced in modern days. For instance, it does not care for contour ridging because it causes too much work and has introduced features which were not in the landscape in former days. His spirit declares that there is no pleasure in walking in the fields or bush as the contours make the movement difficult. This innovation makes the tribal spirits angry (*kushatirwa*) and as a result people are short of food

... The tribal spirits gave people soil on which to grow their crops and enough water to enable them to flourish. But nowadays they are being told to plough here and not there, only in particular places, unlike the instructions of the tribal spirit, which were merely to plant and water would be provided.[44]

Some Katerere mediums retained enough influence to be able to bestow legitimacy on the guerrillas who entered the area from 1976.

Despite the recovery of some *mhondoro* cults, spirit mediums did not mobilise every section of Hwesa society. As we have seen, the movement of great numbers of women, youth and some returning labour migrants into the church from the 1950s onwards, brought about the first effective challenge to the ideological hegemony of local eco-religion (*mhondoro* cults). These Christian youth and women's movements were an alternative to the patriarchal social order legitimated by male-dominated ancestor religion. Like other peasant institutions, *mhondoro* cults too must be disaggregated in terms of the categories of society subscribing to them.

## EXTENDING THE FOCUS:
## THE EXTENT OF SUBSCRIPTION TO WARTIME
## MHONDORO CULTS

Rukadza's mediumship will be considered in greater detail in Chapter 6; here we outline the extent of his influence. Crucial to his high standing was his alliance with the ruling Mbudzi house. In his symbiosis with this dominant faction Rukadza legitimated their claims to succession and, in return, derived authority for his public pronouncements. Through this alliance and other creative strategies, he achieved a degree of success in centralising a Katerere *mhondoro* cult upon his spirit, Nyawada. Rukadza was recognised as the leading Hwesa intellectual by numerous commoners, outsiders, 'big men' from adjacent dynasties, and even by the medium representing the rival Chifodya house.[45]

It is not surprising then, that Rukadza's account of the war resonated widely throughout Katerere. Hwesa peasants identified with his character- isation of Nyawada as a heroic resistance leader. Even Madzeku Chifodya was prepared to admit: 'Nyawada [Rukadza] is famous and the most radical and active medium because he does not fear war.'[46] In a less elaborate way, many of the Hwesa peasantry and other mediums shared ideas and idioms similar to Rukadza's, which made it easy for his pronouncements to resonate widely. In this way folk-tale elements entered into the popular discourse of the war to dramatise the belief that nature was on the side of the comrades, and that animals were communicating with people. For example, a flock of Bateleur Eagles – *zvapungu*[47] – were said to have attacked a security force helicopter when it flew over a holy mountain.[48] A particularly widely told and vivid wartime story of this genre was of a white baboon who flagged down a bus and engaged the driver in conversation.[49] Both these signs from nature, and the burial of fallen comrades in sacred hills and royal graves, were strong expressions of the legitimacy the *mhondoro* had bestowed upon the guerrillas.

According to David Lan (1985: 160–3), taboos were an important means of legitimising guerrillas. The taboos originated from the mediums and people themselves, although of course many of the guerrillas shared them, as they were also from a peasant background. If we 'start with the explanations and commentaries which … informants *themselves* offer about their symbols' we see that they were popularly understood in a number of different ways, the first being as sets of analogies (Lewis, 1976: 112). A few examples will serve to illustrate how these analogies worked. The general taboo on washing sooty cooking pots in wells is to be explained by their association with fire: the well would dry up.[50] This principle worked in the same way for the guerrillas. The daughter of a medium explained that the comrades avoided pregnant women because women have problems and pains which would have been transferred onto the freedom fighters. *Muboora* – pumpkin leaves – were avoided in diet because they stretch; the war would become unnecessarily long.[51]

Some taboos, like those on sex and certain types of food, were a popular means of associating ZANLA/ZIPA forces with both hunters and ancestors (Lan, 1985: 160–6). For example, hunters never had sex on the night before a hunt, and never ate *derere* – okra.[52] Lastly, as Lan also notes, there were 'common sense' explanations of the taboos.[53] These were offered by more educated comrades who, for instance, recognised that unwanted pregnancies would be detrimental to their cause.

Having established that there are resonances here with Rukadza's description of his wartime *mhondoro* cult of resistance, it is necessary to ask a number of subsequent clarifying questions in order to 'make it clear precisely which people' perceived this cult as a means of popular mobilisation (Bourdillon, 1987b: 273). Accounts of spirit mediums as coordinators of wartime resistance came from certain categories of Hwesa society: members of royal lineages and other 'leading houses', elderly men and women, and certain mediums and their families along with their acolytes and other ritual accomplices.[54] These groups had a vested interest in *mhondoro* cults as a means of gaining status through participation in their rituals, or as a source of legitimacy in local factional politics. Mediums acted in the war to safeguard the interests of these social categories from which they derived their following. Together, mediums and their followers reproduced the taboos placed on the comrades, to restrict their access to young women and limit the spilling of innocent blood. Both actively responded to guerrilla promises to restore to them control over the land.

However, although these social categories subscribed in a general manner to much of what Rukadza said, as Michael Bourdillon suggests (1987b: 273), they were far less interested in 'cognitive coherence' and 'consistency'. Much of Rukadza's charisma sprang from his ability to tell a convincing story, or provide a coherent account of his religion. His embellishments were important as a means of inspiring his followers, but few were able to reproduce them with such compelling accuracy.

Considering that a large portion of young adult men would have been absent, working in the migrant labour economy, those who subscribed to a wartime *mhondoro* cult formed a sizable proportion of the Hwesa peasantry. However, many youth and women did not actively subscribe. *Mhondoro* cults are the province of post-menopausal women, middle-aged and elderly men. As stated earlier, younger married women and youth, excluded by their 'physiology' and age respectively, were rapidly drawn to the new mission churches in the 1950s, and to the new spirit churches in the 1980s. Women and youth engaged with the war for reasons other than religious ones.

As Kriger found in Mtoko, youth, especially males, cooperated closely with guerrillas because such an alliance provided them with a new sense of freedom and power, particularly over elders (Kriger, 1992: 179–86). One *mujiba* explained:

> We used to beat old people who did not respond to the word preached by the boys [guerrillas] ... those we thought were sellouts – we were responsible for telling the boys of such people ... that person was ... sometimes beaten or even shot to death ... Since we were young boys we would go with girls and if we found that their father was refusing his daughter to go with us that's the very time we would find ways of creating enmity between that man and the boys ...[55]

The war also provided youth with the opportunity to get even with the rich, and give vent to their ethnic prejudices. Thus Gande village which comprised outsiders of Jindwe origin, who were particularly socially mobile by virtue of their proximity to Elim mission, was subject to constant harassment by *mujiba* who beat and stole from its inhabitants.[56] Youth became so powerful that the comrades were forced to take steps to assert control over the war's agenda. One comrade described what happened:

> Children took advantage of the comrades and went out of control. Parents came to tell us that they could not control their children. We called the children and the parents and cross-examined them and disciplined the children.[57]

Some young men also seemed to find the violence of the war seductive. Their written accounts described gruesome acts of violence in glorifying terms.[58] There is no denying, of course, that they were 'traumatised' by their wartime experiences. Youth were to bear the greatest emotional scars from the struggle (see Reynolds, 1990).

In a similar manner, some young girls seized the opportunity of the war to escape the drudgery of domestic chores and replace them with the attentions of 'heroic' young men with guns.[59] Some actively aided guerrillas by laying landmines and carrying ammunition, or even left their homes to join them in Mozambique.[60] Other women resented guerrilla demands and feared for their chastity.[61] Although youth, both male and female, believed in *mhondoro*, the fact that they actively broke their mediums' taboos, for example, on the spilling of innocent blood and extramarital sex, showed that they had little interest in, or desire for, a religious legitimacy. Instead youth exploited the comrades' need for zealous, unswervingly devoted helpers.

Finally some church groups like the Apostles – *Vapostori* – of Johanna Marange did not respond to guerrilla mobilisation at all. Adopting a pacifist stance, they were humiliated by guerrillas who forced them to break their own taboos on drinking beer, smoking and shaving.[62] Thus, while some adherents of independent churches offered no support to the comrades, youth and women had their own reasons for cooperating with them. Only specific elements of the Hwesa peasantry adhered to *mhondoro* cults and accepted the political legitimacy they conferred upon guerrillas.

### DIFFERING MEDIUM RESPONSES TO MOBILISATION

When the guerrillas appealed to the Hwesa through their mediums it could be argued that they were attempting to revive the Zambezi-wide network of religion, which had facilitated mobilisation against the Portuguese at the turn of the century (see Chapter 1). This guerrilla strategy, already compromised by the piecemeal response of various social groups in Katerere to *mhondoro*-led mobilisation, was further limited by the response of the religious leaders themselves. Not all Katerere mediums willingly bestowed religious legitimacy on the comrades, nor indeed were all mediums in the position to do so. In comparison with Rukadza, some mediums offered support to the comrades only reluctantly, whilst others were unable, or unwilling, to transform their cults into radical wartime movements. Their response to guerrillas was determined by the geographic location and social base of their wards, by their personal inclinations and by their particular experience of the war.

Rukadza was in a prime position both to articulate a discourse of resistance and authorise it because of his alliance with the dominant royal faction. He also enjoyed the advantage of proximity to the sympathetic Roman Catholic mission at Avila. Here, as we have seen, the priests made no use of the elements of Manyika popular Catholicism by which their predecessors in the south had seized hold of the landscape. Instead, they emphasised inculturation – a process which had not gone very deep by the outbreak of the war. Thus, Rukadza was tolerated and allowed to articulate the needs of the people and the land.

Around Elim mission things were very different. In chapters 3 and 4 we saw how the Pentecostals had their own unique way of sacralising the land through contestation. Those people possessed by evil spirits were exorcised, charms and bracelets were burnt, and 'traditional' medicines destroyed. Local spiritual power relations were altered considerably. Drums used to appease the ancestors fell silent and Razau Kaerezi, the medium living just outside the mission, was completely undermined. During the armed struggle, the comrades came and moved him to a distant and isolated village, still in his ward, where he would be of more help to them.[63] Around Elim, the Pentecostals held spiritual sway. Black Pentecostals had authority enough to be able to construct their own networks of information and supply with the guerrillas, and thus avoid the dangers involved in working with over-zealous *mujiba*.[64] One ex-platoon commander and political commissar succinctly summed up the situation, showing how remarkably aware ZANLA were of the dynamics of zones of popular Christianity: 'The people around Avila believed in both the spirits and Christianity while the Pentecostals did not accept the spirit mediums and Kaerezi's popularity was going down.'[65]

Rukadza, the key medium in the war, also lived close to the Mozambican border. Both the accounts of ex-combatants and local people make it clear that it was those mediums who lived in this mountainous region who offered most assistance to the guerrillas. There is evidence too that they worked closely with Barwe mediums from Makombe and Samanyanga, who lived just on the Zimbabwean side of the border but retained contacts with Mozambique.[66] These mediums on the border had the most chance of initiating the comrades into the secrets of the area and conducting vital rituals of possession safe from the public glare and the threat of a security force raid. It is not surprising that the comrades moved some other mediums to the remote border areas.

As Pamela Reynolds discovered (1990: 10, 13), not all mediums actively aided guerrillas. One medium, Taimo Kapomba, the host of Chimucheka, had been a reluctant convert to the guerrilla course. When asked why the spirits helped the comrades he responded: 'The people and the *mhondoro* helped them out of fear because they were armed'. The discussion continued:

Q. Why were the spirits so powerful in the war?
A. It was out of fear.
Q. Even the spirits were fearful? Why did they fear?
A. They feared the war.

It was clear that Kapomba only aided ZANLA/ZIPA out of a sense of self-preservation. He recounted with great horror the vulnerability of his position, caught between guerrillas and the security forces.[67]

There were other reasons for Kapomba's limited response. First, his homestead was only a few metres from the road, and in an area which saw a good deal of fighting between guerrillas and security forces in the early stages of the war.[68] Secondly, his constituency was far weaker than Rukadza's. He was allied to a small royal house which lacked both a territorial and material base for power. He thus did not have the status that Rukadza had derived from his alliance with the ruling house. Rukadza's ward contained ex-refugees from Barwe in Mozambique who were sympathetic to local mediums, whilst Kapomba's contained numerous Manyika Christians who had dissociated themselves from 'traditional' religion.

The increased plurality of Katerere's religious field from the 1950s onwards meant that it was too late for guerrillas to revive the Zambezi-wide network of African religion which had aided multi-ethnic mobilisation against the Portuguese. *Mhondoro* cults were no longer as dominant.

### DIFFERING RESPONSES WITHIN GUERRILLA ARMIES TOWARDS MOBILISATION

Like the peasantry, the guerrilla armies were not an undifferentiated whole. There was a great deal of variation both within and between platoons in terms of strategies for mobilisation. Recent work has deepened our understanding of the guerrillas. Janice McLaughlin has alerted us to the ideological struggles that took place within ZANU forces, particularly in relation to the role of religion as a factor in mobilisation (1991: chapter 11), whilst David Moore's research (1995) provides us with a wider periodisation for shifts in ideology.

There were a number of other sources of difference and contestation. First, there were differences in recruitment patterns and ethnic composition. The first ZANLA recruits were predominantly Korekore because the Zambezi escarpment was the first ZANLA operational zone in the armed struggle. This location has experienced relatively little missionisation or state penetration with its rationalist interpretation of ecology. As Lan has shown (1985: chapter 3), *mhondoro* cults remained influential there. Consequently, this first generation of guerrillas were more disposed to use *mhondoro* mediums in comparison, for instance, with later intakes of Manyika recruits. There were also differences in type, origin and duration of training. Early recruits taken from Zambia could be sent for extensive military and political education in Tanzania, or China, whilst those who joined in the later stages of the war were given a few weeks arms training in Mozambique. Thus, the different strategies of mobilisation used by ZANLA/ZIPA cannot simply be explained as a response to local factors. They were also a product of differing guerrilla aspirations.[69]

There was also a distinction between the literate guerrilla élites and the less educated rank-and-file, in their reaction to spirit mediums. The élites, who were usually mission-educated, were often sympathetic to rural Christians. As we have seen, mission leaders sought to court these guerrilla élites, who in turn recognised the importance of capturing church-based constituencies and used Christian songs and symbols as means of mobilisation. Conversely, the rank-and-file tended to seek out mediums for self-affirmation in a period of great personal upheaval.[70] There were also differences between platoons. Whilst one platoon would devote considerable energy courting white missionaries and black Christian élites, another would be particularly threatening to the church.[71]

Finally, there was great variation in guerrilla response to witchcraft and the use of 'medicines'. Lan perceives a structural opposition between *mhondoro* and witch. The first is altruistic and benevolent, the second antisocial. As guerrillas and the nationalist cause became identified with the ancestors, so sell-outs, characterised by their selfish and individualistic nature, became identified with witches. Lan claims (1985: 167–70) that the comrades dissociated themselves from witchcraft and killed sell-outs as witches. However, in practice, it does seem that some guerrillas sought out *n'ganga* – traditional healer[s] – for magical aid.

In 1976 a witchcraft eradication movement, led by a man called Makombe, traversed the north-east. It bore great resemblance to the Mchape movement of the 1930s described in Chapter 2. Makombe compelled local people to surrender their horns and charms for destruction. *N'ganga* were compelled to display their range of medicines, and a distinction was made between medicines which were antisocial and those which had healing qualities. The former were destroyed. Makombe was eventually assassinated by guerrillas.

The reasons for his death are complex. Some informants spoke of Makombe using his magical powers for the benefit of the Rhodesia Front, whilst others explained it as a result of his destruction of potential magic for use by guerrillas.[72] An ex-combatant, who sat on the tribunal convened to try Makombe, mentioned both of these factors. However, it seems that the major reason was that his enormous success undermined the comrades' own legitimacy as witchcraft eradicators. Whilst they killed witches, he successfully reintegrated them into society. When detained by the comrades, Makombe complained that they were too young to question him and taunted them, claiming that their guns could not kill him. The frightened comrades finally shot him in the back with a bazooka.[73] The story undermines a simplistic analysis equating guerrillas with pure ancestral religion and witchcraft eradication, and the state with witches and the use of antisocial magic. As with the case of the peasantry it is essential to differentiate precisely which groups of guerrillas interacted with *mhondoro* mediums and traditional healers.

## CHANGES IN GUERRILLA STRATEGY OVER TIME

Not only were there variations in strategies of mobilisation within and between platoons but also variations over time. In 1976, when ZIPA guerrillas first entered the Katerere area, they were unfamiliar with the terrain and the people, and insecure in their status. At this early stage in the war they were willing to respect the taboos laid down by the mediums. The fact that they were ZIPA and *not* ZANLA may also explain their greater willingness to interact with local political agendas (D. Moore, 1993). However, as the guerrilla rank-and-file became established, a willingness to break taboos became more apparent. This tendency was compounded by the decrease in the length of their training in 1978 as emphasis was placed on the final 'big push' to overthrow the settler state. By the end of that year the taboos were being broken regularly.[74] The comrades found it far easier to keep those taboos concerning certain types of food than the one prohibiting sex with local women.[75] Guerrilla relations with young women caused widespread resentment.[76]

The narrative of this chapter also reveals shifts in political initiative as the war progressed. Initially, the guerrillas mobilised groups of socially mobile and more politically sophisticated outsiders such as the Manyika and mission élites. As they subsequently turned to court the autochthonous Hwesa, so ethnic conflict emerged. Villages of outsiders were allowed to be harassed by *mujiba*, or were subject to punishment by specific guerrilla platoons. The final shift in agency was from youth to guerrillas and elders. The comrades moved to restrain over-zealous *mujiba* in an attempt to appease their parents.

Crucial to this reassertion of male gerontocratic power was the rehabilitation of Chief Njanji Katerere. An ex-native department messenger and member of the Chiefs' Council, Njanji Katerere was met with considerable suspicion by a powerful platoon, who objected to his circum-spect behaviour towards the comrades. He was replaced by a Samanyanga outsider from Barwe in Mozambique. The story is one of great irony. The new man became too powerful and was assassinated by his makers whilst his predecessor remained popular with many of his people. Njanji Katerere, like many African chiefs, had remarkable skills in political survival, learnt from the experience of mediation between the conflicting interests of his people and the state (see Van Rouveroy van Nieuwaal, 1987: 24). Foreseeing his successor's imminent assassination, the Hwesa chief even tried to save him by creating a place for him on the ruling council.[77]

Ironically, as Hwesa territory became freer from security force incursions, relations between guerrillas and people grew more strained. By 1979 the comrades felt so secure in Katerere that some were literally living in houses. In especially secure semi-liberated zones like the Kambudzi area, there were such large numbers of guerrillas that the population had difficulty supplying their needs.[78] These difficulties were compounded by the severe drought of 1979. In such stressful circumstances some comrades began to commit spontaneous acts of violence against civilians. They also made what peasants perceived to be arbitrary demands. One informant complained bitterly about being sent miles in order to purchase *mbanje* – cannabis – for the comrades. He proceeded to remark: '1979 was a terrible year. They [the guerrillas] were so bad. We wanted the war to end.'[79] Instead of using the freedom and legitimacy they possessed at the beginning of 1979 to transform the structures of rural society, the guerrillas were content to bide their time until the war's cessation. The influx of poorly trained recruits in 1978 diluted any ideological resolve the comrades had. Their Shona cultural nationalism had great rhetorical effect against the white settler state, especially amongst the Manyika. But once the threat of the state subsided, the guerrillas were at a loss for a clear-cut political programme.[80] As indicated at the beginning of this chapter, alternative institutions did emerge in embryonic form, but they were never given the chance to mature. The local committees simply continued to function at the level of servicing the guerrillas' material needs. It is hardly surprising that due to a combination of coercion and lack of strategy the guerrillas suffered a 'crisis of legitimacy' in 1979.[81]

## DEBATES ON WARTIME MOBILISATION: A REAPPRAISAL

In *Peasant Consciousness* Terence Ranger argues that, by the outbreak of the liberation war, the peasants of Makoni district had a revolutionary consciousness. This had emerged out of a set of grievances against the settler state which had consistently legislated against peasant production. The implementation of the Land Apportionment Act, followed by the Native Land Husbandry Act in 1951, fuelled this peasant consciousness which 'at its highest stage of development ... proved potent enough to allow the spread of ZANLA's guerrilla action across two-thirds of the country in the 1970s' (1985: 137). Moreover, Ranger argues that: 'Peasant religion formed an indispensable part of the composite ideology of the war' (Ibid.: 188). Through this ideology, spirit mediums offered peasants some conceptual control over the war. This was because 'above any other possible religious form the mediums symbolised peasant right to the land and their right to work it as they chose' (Ibid.: 189). As the people's royal ancestors, *mhondoro* spirits were the true owners of the land. (Ibid.: 197)

Thus, for the purposes of mobilisation, ZANLA found it unnecessary to 'transform peasant consciousness'; rather, they merely sought to 'intensify' rural resentment (Ibid.: 177–8). The composite peasant/guerrilla ideology sought to reconstitute the peasant option, whereby peasants conceived of a 'transformed state' which would not just give them a free hand in production, but also back black farming against white (Ibid.: 177).

According to Ranger, mediums were able to perform the vital function of bringing peasant elders, who had hitherto held sway in rural society, together with young 'stranger' guerrillas, who came into each district with guns, seeking to construct a new revolutionary order. Mediums also performed rituals which gave guerrillas access to Makoni district's holy places – burial caves and sacred mountains – whose secrets had previously only been known by the elders and headmen. Such rituals did not just provide the fighters with excellent hide-outs but also bestowed upon them the legitimacy of the past (Ibid.: 189, 208–9).

In an auto-critique of *Peasant Consciousness*, Ranger admits to a neglect of the theme of nationalist mobilisation. He 'focused on the junction of peasant experience and aspirations with guerrillas almost to the exclusion of the history of nationalist parties' (Ranger, 1990). The material presented here on the Manyika is a case in point. Their ethnic radicalism, founded by labour migrants politicised in the cities of Southern Rhodesia and South Africa, and articulated by the Manyika Society in the 1950s, was compatible with nationalism. This was demonstrated by their high level of support for the NDP.

Admittedly in Makoni district, some Manyika still recognised the authority of their autochthonous ancestors and thus the comrades were able to mobilise them through the idiom of *mhondoro* cults. However in Katerere the guerrillas had no use for a composite ideology with a traditional religious factor, when interacting with the Manyika. The Manyika were a long way from their ancestral lands. The guerrillas addressed and initially won them, through the rhetoric of cultural nationalism.

In *Guns and Rain*, David Lan comes to many of the same conclusions as Ranger concerning the function and contribution of spirit mediums in Zimbabwe's liberation war. Both, for instance, have constructed an argument which hinges on a perceived dichotomy between chief and medium, which will be considered in the following chapter. However, as an anthropologist, Lan arrives at his conclusions through a very different methodology. The focus of his study is the change in meaning of the dominant symbols and culture of the Korekore people in Dande in north-east Zimbabwe. Through ingenious analysis of myth and taboo Lan shows how popular understanding of tradition moves to allow strangers/guerrillas to be assimilated into a Korekore world view. Lan's analysis, which works in the form of a great anthropological drama, closes with a grand finale. The final 'movement' of the signifying process ends when the guerrillas become like the dry, brittle autochthonous ancestors – owners of the land (Lan, 1985: 94–7, 161–2). Lan writes:

> By observing the ancestral prohibitions the guerrillas were trans-
> formed from 'strangers' into 'royals', from members of lineages

resident in other parts of Zimbabwe, into descendants of the local *mhondoro* with rights to the land. They had become at home in Dande. (Ibid.: 164)

Lan's account of the liberation war centres upon the workings of a grand Korekore cosmological system as it transforms itself to assimilate ZANLA guerrillas. Anything that conflicts with the smooth functioning of the system is ignored or lightly dismissed by Lan. When writing on the restrictions imposed by the mediums, Lan does admittedly pause for a page, both to acknowledge that such taboos often were not kept, and that there were other more common-sense explanations for them. Yet such a small digression seems odd considering that so much of his analysis hinges on what he describes as the 'symbolic power' of the restrictions (Ibid.: 163). It seems reasonable to demand that any argument about the pervasiveness of a discourse must be backed by an enquiry into *who* it resonates with, and its effectiveness. The absence of such an investigation leaves the anthropologist vulnerable to the suggestion that he, or she, is simply reproducing the views of a few 'unusually perceptive and creative thinker[s]' or even exploring the deep unconscious structures of his, or her, own mind. (Bourdillon, 1987b: 273)

Admittedly there are significant epistemological differences between this study's approach and Lan's, whose structuralist methodology is accompanied by the assumption that daily life is mystified, needing to be decoded and set within a wider structure of meaning. Yet at times Lan does seem to get carried away by the force of his own analysis, which is both highly imaginative and compelling. For instance, he writes: 'By their very nature the *mhondoro* are conquerors, warriors, killers' (Lan, 1985: 152). They can perhaps be depicted as heroes, albeit often in the tragic sense, but are certainly not all 'conquerors, warriors, killers'. One must stop to consider the actual content of chiefly oral traditions. As Chapter 1 illustrated, there is the Hwesa tradition about Chimucheka, the spirit possessing the reluctant Kapomba, who was killed along with his son, their bodies left stripped naked; and the story of unfortunate Gambiza who was murdered and then roasted (see Appendix 4). Lan has forgotten the losers.

The final contribution to the debate on wartime mobilisation is Norma Kriger's *Zimbabwe's Guerrilla War: Peasant Voices*. This monograph takes a very wide perspective, seeking to make a contribution to the theory and method of study of peasant revolutions through a case study on Zimbabwe's liberation war. Kriger makes substantial and detailed criticisms of both Ranger and Lan for their failure to pay attention to struggles internal to the peasantry. By differentiating rural society along lines of gender, wealth, lineage and age, she brings new dimensions to the study of guerrilla wars. Kriger writes:

> Oppressed peasants saw the breakdown of law and order during the war as an unprecedented opportunity to transform oppressive village structures. While guerrillas were persuading and coercing peasants ... oppressed peasants were forging alliances with guerrillas to try and restructure village relations. Unmarried peasant children challenged their elders, women battled their husbands ... and the least advantaged attacked the better off. (Kriger, 1992: 8)

Kriger further argues that because guerrillas were unable to diminish the power of the state, or make utilitarian appeals to peasants, they were forced to rely on cultural nationalist appeals, and more particularly on coercion, to mobilise the peasantry (Ibid.: 109–15). Sifting through Lan and Ranger's sources she argues that their case for popular support for the armed struggle is very weak. She maintains that it is essential for researchers working on the war to consider, as peasants did, the costs of their exchange relations with guerrillas, 'of compliance coercion and of inconsistent appeals' (Ibid.: 160). Such a utilitarian explanation obviously down-plays the role of religious ideology in mobilisation.

In contrast to Kriger, this study has shown that some peasants' support for ZANLA did spring from genuine ideological motivation. Thus, the amount of stress she places on the linkage of peasant motivation to material gain or 'individuals' calculus' is too cynical (Ibid.: 160–2). Here it would have helped if Kriger had listened to a few more 'guerrilla' voices. Ex-combatants were well aware that the people could use them to settle their own scores, and often took steps to limit the destructiveness of such internal struggles.[82]

Moreover, Kriger has not questioned enough the peculiarities of her fieldwork location. For instance, her own material often betrays a high level of coercion relative to other districts (Kriger, 1992: 164). Mtoko presented specific difficulties to guerrillas due to its proximity to the capital, the presence of a wide tarred road through the district facilitating rapid access for the security forces, and the prevalence of keeps (protective villages) in the area. In such circumstances the guerrillas would have had little opportunity to win the hearts and minds of the people.[83]

Kriger could no doubt take her fine-tooth comb to sources used in this chapter to highlight the instances of guerrilla coercion they certainly reveal. However, the argument here is not that there was no coercion in Katerere, but that there was simply less of it. The beginning of this chapter described how ZANLA/ZIPA were able to establish semi-liberated zones there. Although they were vulnerable to random punitive sorties from the air, the comrades remained, more or less, in control. The mountainous terrain provided easy access across the border with Mozambique and natural hide-outs. Further-more, there was no tarred road in the vicinity nor any keeps. Nor did Muzorewa's auxiliaries make their presence felt. In contrast to Mtoko, guerrilla coercion in Katerere occurred not when the comrades felt insecure but when they became too self-assured.

Nevertheless, the particularity of Kriger's district of study does not undermine her conclusions, 'only the ability to generalise them without modification'.[84] Although the specific details of this case study, such as guerrilla preference for migrant and mission élites, differ from her own findings, we have arrived at such conclusions by adopting her method. Kriger's more general contention that one can only understand the intricacies of guerrilla mobilisation, or indeed the dynamics of rural society, by disaggregating the peasantry, is a very important one. This chapter, indeed the whole study, simply shows that the aggregates are more diverse and complex than she realised.

## CONCLUSION

This chapter has traced intricate patterns of guerrilla–peasant interaction. These strategies were a product both of Katerere's remoteness and its social complexity, and resulted in a diverse range of 'mobilisation'. Guerrillas worked out locally specific strategies to respond to the differing agendas they perceived amongst the peasantry. These varied not only in relation to gender, generation, ethnicity and social stratification, but also with geographical location. The comrades were acutely aware of the existence of zones of popular religion – 'traditional' and Christian – and of the varied ability of the holy men who controlled them to act both as peasant leaders and as agents capable of bestowing political legitimacy upon them. Throughout the period of the war, local politics and religious belief were more prominent than guerrilla ideology.

The guerrillas had to fall back on local agendas because they lacked an ideology with a wide enough appeal. The plurality of Katerere's religious field meant that it was too late to revive traditional religious mobilisation through a regional network of *mhondoro* cults, whilst it was still too early to achieve a territorial nationalist mobilisation, even with the help of the Manyika.

However, the key to understanding popular mobilisation in Katerere lies not only in disaggregating its rural society. ZANLA itself was by no means monolithic. The guerrillas were differentiated in terms of élites and rank and file, ethnic origin and year of recruitment. Their conceptualisation of strategy varied over time.

There were shifts in control of the local political agenda as political ascendancy moved from one category of society to another, and eventually to the comrades themselves. However, in 1979, when the guerrillas were well established in Katerere, their concern for legitimacy began to subside. They deferred instituting a political programme which would transform the structures of rural society. Instead they were content to bide their time, living off the resources generated for them by the local committees. When such supplies failed they resorted to coercion, bringing about a crisis of legitimacy.

The war was a great engine of change for rural churches. Whilst many Christians did turn their backs on the church during the violence others retained their faith and were empowered in the process. As missionaries were killed or withdrew to towns or their home countries, church leadership was rapidly Africanised. At independence many churches were revived by a core of faithful empowered by their defence of the faith during the war.

Similar experiences of empowerment were to be found in wider society. The local support committees survived the war in their embryonic form, producing the first generation of local ZANU/PF party officials. However, those categories of society such as women and youth, who were empowered by their participation in the war, secured few permanent gains. The record of Katerere's first meeting with a state official in 1980 portrays an assertive peasantry demanding new resources to bolster agricultural production. Among those peasants were women, insisting on improved health facilities, women's organisations and adult education, and youth demanding access to schooling.[85] Yet because those shifts in local power relations, which brought women and youth to the fore, were never institutionalised, their new-found status was short-lived.

The following two chapters will illustrate how in the latter years of the 1980s there was a revival of rural patriarchy with increased subsidies for chiefs and the reconstitution of traditional courts (see Alexander, 1995). Moreover, they will also show how restored hierarchies within both the church and state clawed back power to the centre, away from local people. Guerrillas did initially secure local legitimacy, but their lack of a concrete political programme meant that they lost the opportunity to bring about lasting change in rural areas.

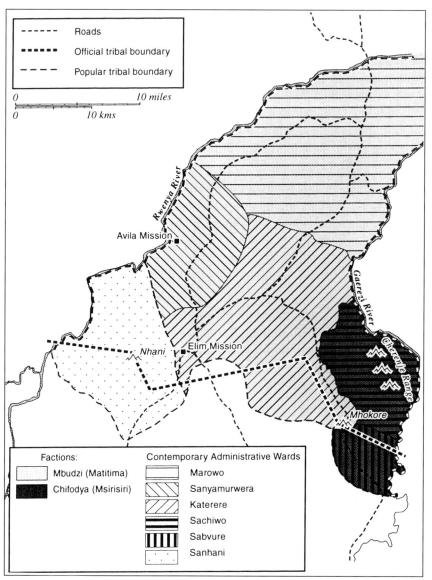

Map 6.1 The Territorial Basis of Contemporary Factional Politics

# 6

# THE ROASTING OF CHIEF GAMBIZA: THE RETURN OF CHIEFS IN ALLIANCE WITH THEIR ANCESTORS SINCE INDEPENDENCE

## INTRODUCTION

The previous chapter explored political struggles between various social categories in Katerere during the liberation war. This chapter narrows the focus by investigating a contemporary struggle within one social group: the male gerontocratic élites who hold power in Hwesa factions. The concern with factional politics represents a return to one of the opening themes of this study. At the same time its contemporary nature prompts a very different set of questions. In pre-colonial times, the outcomes of factional struggles were influenced by the intervention of adjacent polities. This chapter inquires how, in the contemporary context, factional politics are mediated by the state, local party, and civic associations.

The chapter also establishes another continuity. In their present struggle, traditional leaders draw upon Hwesa oral traditions about pre-colonial factional warfare in order to make arguments of legitimacy. Chapter 5 illustrated how one influential spirit medium fashioned these local cultural idioms into a manifesto for resistance to mobilise Hwesa people during the liberation war. This chapter investigates their meaning as sets of political arguments in contemporary factional struggles. Two scholars, Terence Ranger and David Lan, have contended that the influence of chiefs and headmen has diminished in independent Zimbabwe. Briefly, their argument hinges on a perceived dichotomy between chiefs and mediums. The former, they argue, were stigmatised through their association with the colonial regime. This has caused them to be replaced by the local party, and eclipsed by spirit mediums who had a more illustrious record of resistance to the settler state. (Ranger, 1982c: 38–9; see also 1985: chapter 5; Lan, 1985: chapters 8 and 9)

However, it will be argued below that traditional leaders, in alliance with *mhondoro* mediums, hold great power in contemporary Zimbabwe. In response to their growing influence there has been a reimagination of 'tradition' in a number of different and often contradictory ways by the government, the local bureaucracy and the traditional leaders themselves. All these various interest groups seek political legitimacy by means of making appeals to authenticity. Furthermore, chiefs, with the aid of mediums, have regained power as both effective populist leaders and patriarchs, by filling the vacuum left by the collapse of the ruling party at the local level. In line with a growing trend across Central Africa (see, for instance, Van Binsbergen, 1987), their revival as political leaders has caused them to be courted by both local and national party politicians, and civil servants.

These large and general propositions will be substantiated through a case-study of one particular and local series of events in Katerere: its recent succession dispute. This account of the competition between factions for the office of chief will bear out a number of assertions. We begin with propositions about chieftainship itself. First, the very ferocity of the dispute indicates that chieftainship has far from lost its significance in Katerere. Secondly, a comparison of the contemporary contest with previous chiefly successions strongly suggests that the current debate is *more* complex and critical than any of the earlier twentieth-century successions: chieftainship is not only still significant in Katerere but *more* significant, because in independent Zimbabwe the political structure is more open and allows the participation of many more players. Thirdly, an analysis of the advantages – economic, educational, ideological – possessed by the dominant faction illustrates that chieftaincy is far from merely a source of status or prestige: the office of chief is linked with, and is the product and perhaps the source of social, economic and political influence. Fourthly, the study of the dynamics of Katerere 'lineage politics' reveals how ideological 'hegemony' is achieved within them. Thus, no matter what conclusions may be drawn about the interaction of chiefs with 'party' politics, there can be no doubt that chieftaincy is at the centre of its own very dynamic system of political ideology and action.

The study of the Katerere succession dispute also generates a number of propositions about the interaction of chiefs and mediums. Mediums will be seen to be deeply involved in the contest: each house has its own mediums or medium, and the administration is unwilling to approve a candidate not backed by the 'spirits'. So, far from separating himself from the chiefly political system, the medium who worked most closely with the guerrillas during the liberation war, and who put the ancestral myths most closely at their disposal, became the most effective player in lineage ideological politics; the trump card in the hand of the dominant faction. The ideology is based on the assumption that the well-being of the society and land depends upon close collaboration between the chief and the ancestors as embodied in the mediums. Thus, in Katerere, mediums do not occupy their own distinct, ideological and political sphere; they too are playing the game of 'lineage politics'. As with the chiefs, it is possible to attempt a historical reconstruction of the role of mediums in Katerere over the last 100 years. At present mediums are more actively, imaginatively and competitively involved than they have been since the nineteenth century.

Thus the reconstruction of the Katerere succession dispute will substantiate propositions about both chiefs and mediums in the game of 'lineage politics', and about 'lineage politics' as 'political' in the full sense. From this case-study it will be argued that the revival or increased intensity of 'lineage politics' also has an importance in the domain of 'party' politics as these are constituted in Katerere. The chapter ends with a consideration of what modifications the case-study suggests to recent historiography on chiefs.

## THE NEW ORDER: THE ARRIVAL OF THE RULING PARTY

Before considering the succession dispute it is necessary to sketch the post-Independence party political context. ZANU/PF swept to power in April 1980 winning 57 out of a possible 80 parliamentary seats and 63 per cent of the votes cast. Its victory was a shock to many external observers but not to rural Zimbabweans who had experienced the extent of ZANU/PF control of the communal lands. The new government quickly constructed a new system of rural local administration which excluded traditional leaders. At a rhetorical level ZANU/PF advocated social transformation on an international socialist model. It had little time for 'patriarchal' authorities which had collaborated with the colonial regime. Moreover, in practice, guerrilla support committees and party committees had emerged as representatives of the local will in many rural communities.

Hence the new regime removed chiefs' judicial and political powers. Chiefs and headmen were simply to act as 'guardians of traditional culture'. The ruling party usurped the power of traditional leaders. Organised from the most elementary level of the village, through branch and district to the province and nation the party was deemed to represent the will of the people. Alternative institutions were also created for the purpose of fostering development at a local level. Village development committees (VIDCOs) created out of every 100 households were established in 1984.

But government policy towards chiefs was contradictory. Chiefs sat as ex-officio members of the new councils, and along with headmen retained their salaries. Some key ZANU/PF politicians and officials publicly defended the continued recognition of chiefs in terms of the government's policy of reconciliation and its desire to preserve culture. Like politicians of the Rhodesia Front era, Prime Minister Mugabe held a course of *indaba* – meetings – with chiefs in 1980 (Alexander, 1993: 169–71). Thus, whilst traditional leaders were initially swept aside, the stage remained set for their come-back.

## PATRIARCHS AND MEDIUMS IN LINEAGE POLITICS[1]

I met Njanji, the late chief of Katerere and leader of the Mbudzi faction, only once, in June 1988. The meeting was a rather disappointing event. I had hoped to meet some splendid charismatic figure adorned in traditional garb.

6.1 Interview with Chief Njanji Katerere

6.2 Langton Muromowenyoka in his field, with his son, Onias

Instead I encountered the pathetic figure of a decrepit old man in a badly kept homestead. His words did nothing to reassure me. As I sat in the dust at his feet, clapping in respect, he thanked me for coming to see him and complained that few others seemed to bother. The interview was brief and we left after presenting him with a gift of money and some vitamin pills. He was very grateful.[2] The following March Njanji died, and much to my amazement the chiefdom was gripped by a succession dispute.

I discovered later that due to Njanji's infirmity, the chiefdom had been run by deputy chiefs since 1981. The first was Marisani Katerere, who acted until June 1987. Later came Njanji's own son, Eric. Popular interest in chieftainship was more in the office itself than in the particular individual who filled it. For a period between June 1987 and January 1989, after which Eric was appointed, the chiefdom had no acting chief. Nevertheless the ruling Mbudzi faction appeared to run it informally and saw little need to have Eric officially recognised.[3]

The contest to find Chief Njanji Katerere's successor became a giant drama stretching across the mountains and plains of Katerere – a story with rumours of murder, intrigue and corruption that would outstrip any modern-day soap opera. The drama unfolded with ever-increasing twists of irony. The actors held a variety of positions within local politics but all came from the same social category. They were best described as 'patrilineal clusters': groups of senior men claiming a common ancestry, who convene to handle domestic and economic affairs (Scoones and Wilson, 1988: 31). However, although these central figures cast their political manoeuvres in a patrilineal idiom, their politics actually concerned the mobilisation of territorially based factions which, as argued in Chapter 1, were *not* lineages,[4] but may be composed of nearby kin and their affines as allies, as well as powerful outsiders and commoners. The male gerontocratic élites at the centre of the intrigue also claimed royal descent. The bulk of the faction was excluded on the grounds of status, ethnicity, age and gender. However, this wider political community (Bailey, 1969: 23–4) still possessed a range of sympathies and loyalties which were mobilised at appropriate moments.

Three royal factions or houses were involved in the struggle for the chieftainship. These were the Mbudzi house (of which the late chief was a member), whose candidate was Patrick Tsodza; the Chifodya house, whose candidate was Matambo Chifodya; and the Chirimunyati (Nyaurimbo) house, whose candidate was the late Langton Muromowenyoka. In reality the territory was divided between two factions, Mbudzi and Chifodya, with the Chirimunyati house acting as an important make-weight (see Map 6.1).

In succession politics there is no rule on the number of houses that can compete. Houses define themselves by tracing their descent from a common ancestor and are consequently fissile in nature. New houses form by tracing their descent from a younger ancestor. Others appear claiming a more senior, but neglected, ancestor as their progenitor.[5] However, as this case-study will show, factions needed to control certain human and material resources in order to launch an effective campaign for the chieftainship. Hence each house also had allied mediums: the Mbudzi house, Diki Rukadza host of Nyawada and Razau Kaerezi host of Chikumbirike; the Chifodya house, Aluwizi Sanyamahwe host of Nyamande; the Chirimunyati house, Taimo Kapomba host of Chimucheka. As illustrated in Chapter 2, the mediums were often joined to factions through marriage.

Other major actors in the drama were members of leading families who had no claim to the chieftaincy but held important ritual functions within it. Like the royal house leaders, these too were elderly men.

Table 6.1 Key Players in Katerere's Factional Politics

| House | Leader | Medium/s | Ancestor Spirit |
|-------|--------|----------|-----------------|
| Mbudzi | Patrick Tsodza | Diki Rukadza Razau Kaerezi | Nyawada Chikumbirike |
| Chifodya | Matambo Chifodya | Aluwizi Sanyamahwe | Nyamande |
| Chirimunyati | Langton Muromowenyoka | (Taimo Kapomba) | (Chimucheka) |

The contest took the form of 'lineage politics' which worked in the idiom of 'tradition' and used a variety of forms involving the manipulation of legends, genealogies, procedures for chiefly installation, and the construction of slanders against enemy houses.

## LEGENDS

Chapter 1 interpreted Hwesa legends (see Appendix 4) as a series of recurrent events in Katerere's pre-colonial past such as battles, migrations and assassinations. Some legends included mythic elements whilst others merged with narrative history proper. By using genealogies, and corroborating accounts from adventurers who travelled through Katerere in the latter half of the nineteenth century, a narrative of Hwesa history during its period of intense factional warfare was reconstructed. These legends were filled with new meaning in the context of the late twentieth century, taking the form of political arguments which make claims to power and legitimacy.

The most significant story was the legend of the hitherto dominant Mbudzi faction. As we have already seen in this study, the story was about the assassination of an Mbudzi house leader, Gambiza, by the Chifodyas, followed by the gruesome destruction of his body. In its dénouement, the heroic spirit Nyawada restored the Mbudzi faction to power and punished the Chifodyas. The legend was recounted to me several times by its greatest proponent, Diki Rukadza, medium of Nyawada, from the Mbudzi faction. On the first occasion, prior to Njanji's death, he gave it as a justification for his well-known support of ZANLA guerrillas during the liberation war. On the following three occasions he recounted the legend to me in the context of the succession dispute. What had been a discourse of resistance was transformed into an establishment charter.[6]

In the context of the succession dispute, the Gambiza legend worked as a legitimating charter (in the Malinowskian sense) in the Mbudzi house's claims to the chieftainship (see Young, 1979: 237–90). Rukadza's exegesis of the legend asserted that the Hwesa had a moral economy when it came to succession disputes which was summarised as: *imhoni dzarumana*, meaning, literally, 'the field mice have bitten each other'. The field mouse was the Hwesa totem. It was acceptable in the past for factions to assassinate chiefs to gain political power but in roasting Gambiza the Chifodyas went too far! Thus: 'The Chifodyas were declared outcasts and forbidden from inheriting the chiefdom forever. The clan spirits punished them in this way because they had angered them by preventing a dead chief from being buried in the appropriate manner.' Rukadza finished his exegesis by stating that the whites were informed that the Chifodyas had been banned, in perpetuity, from succeeding.[7]

All this was an ingenious justification for the fact that one Hwesa house – Mbudzi – monopolised the chieftainship for well over 100 years. Under the normative rules of election, established by the Native Department, it was believed that it had been 'customary' for Shona dynasties to follow the system of collateral succession between the founder's sons, before any of his grandsons became chief, thus ensuring that no one house came to dominate (Bourdillon, 1987a: 106). In Katerere the official genealogies of the Native Department changed very little until the mid 1960s, being typical 'Mbudzi style'.[8] The only official record of challenge for the chieftainship came from within the Mbudzi house, where a sub-faction tracing its descent from a younger ancestor, challenged the appointment.[9] As Chapter 2 illustrated, the Mbudzi faction manipulated the state to maintain its political dominance.

The Mbudzi faction's Gambiza legend set the agenda for the succession dispute. It was assertive in flavour and centred on the figure of the spirit Nyawada who settled the original disorder and imposed his authority. In contrast, the other two legends concerned with the dispute were little known and varied greatly between informants; the Gambiza story was common currency, accurately reproduced by all, and most widely accepted as the true version of events. Thus the Mbudzi's story was the dominant discourse.

Myths and legends do not just have to serve the function of legitimating charters. Their accessibility means that they allow wide participation in their making and transmission, and their density as a medium of expression makes them adaptable both to absorb and to communicate discontent

(Schoffeleers, 1979: 11, 14). In periods of disorder, particularly those involving efforts to impose new centralised authorities, legends acting as counter discourses can appear (Berger, 1981: 90). Thus, amidst the political uncertainty caused by the death of Chief Njanji, there was a swift development in the rhetoric of legend, genealogy and slander of the two royal houses contesting the Mbudzi monopoly of succession (see Appendices 3 and 4).

When I visited the late chief, I had asked him which *mhondoro* was the most important. His answer was predictably measured. He told me that they all were important.[10] On the same day, I conducted my first interview with Langton, the contender for the Chirimunyati house. He gave me a half-hearted genealogy, told me nothing of his faction's story of the murder of Chimucheka, and made no mention of his claims upon the chieftainship. One and half years later, he provided me with an impressive account of Hwesa history 'Chirimunyati style' and a well-argued case for his own succession fashioned upon legend, genealogy and the manipulation of 'tradition'.[11]

The two other stories that figured in the argument between the three Hwesa factions about rights to the chieftainship emanate from the Chifodya and Chirimunyati houses. Chapter 1 discussed a number of common themes present in the legends and used them for the purpose of historical reconstruction. But other themes were more concerned with the current moral debate about the rights to succession. One fascinating structural similarity was the disrespect shown by assassins for the bodies of chiefs. Thus Chief Nyamande was 'chopped', 'speared' and pillaged; his wife, Njesera, had her legs cut off; whilst Chief Chimucheka and his son Hokoyo were 'stripped … of their clothes and left … bare and naked' (see Appendix 4).

The Nyamande story from the Chifodya faction can also be read as a direct subversion of the Mbudzi account. Much of it was straight polemic against the treacherous, cowardly Gambiza who 'was not a chief but a chief's servant'. But in contrast to the triumphalism of the Mbudzi story, the Chifodya legend and the Chirimunyati legend exhibited a strong fatalism in which relatives betray the faction, and the chiefs, in acts of suicide, offer advice or encouragement to their assassins. Thus in the Chirimunyati legend Chief Chimucheka told his assailants: '"You first kill my son and then kill me".' The Chifodyas lost the drum and thus symbolic control of the chieftainship whilst the Chirimunyatis were paid off with cattle.

## GENEALOGIES

All the informants closely related to the contenders[12] offered genealogies. Some were elaborate family trees with names of wives and princes, others were just lists of chiefs. Initially I set out to reconstruct the 'authentic' genealogy, but quickly realised that what I was being given was not so much fact, as political statements about the present. Informants manipulated genealogies to their political advantage in a number of ways. First, they claimed seniority for their progenitor. Secondly, they omitted the ancestors of competing royal houses or, more specifically, they omitted the ancestors possessing competing factions' mediums. When Michael Gelfand collected a number of Hwesa genealogies during the 1970s, he appears not to have been cognisant of their politics. His uncritical approach, combined with a lack of synthesis, meant that within the space of two pages of his book *The Spiritual Beliefs of the Shona* (1982: 134–5), he listed three different figures as founding chief.

The first tactic, of placing the founding ancestor as high up the list as possible to imbue him with greater seniority and legitimating power, was used by all contenders. But the omission of enemy houses' ancestors proved to be the most effective strategy when questioned by an interested outsider, whether they were a researcher or a Native Department civil servant.[13]

The reconstruction of pre-colonial Hwesa history in Chapter 1 suggested that some of those chiefs mentioned may have ruled at the same time in different parts of the chiefdom. It is probable that a number of those mentioned in the lists were not past chiefs at all but *machinda* – princes. Figures like Gambiza, Kondo and Tsarumunda were often included even though they were said not to have ruled long enough to undergo *kushawara*: the ritual process which turns a chief into a *mhondoro* after death. Nevertheless, the extra names acted as embellishments to enhance each house's claim to past influence.

Finally, nearly all of those who offered genealogies made short work of their genesis element. In one sentence they explained that the Hwesa originated from the mythical Mbire and arrived in Katerere having broken away from Makombe in Mozambique. Only Rukadza, medium of Nyawada, from the Mbudzi house, premised his genealogy with an elaborate genesis myth, telling me that the founding chief received the land from the High God, Karuva, who parcelled it to all the surrounding dynasties.[14] The effect was to furnish his list with a divinely instituted foundation.

## SLANDERS

Another feature of 'lineage politics' was the game of slander and 'one-upmanship' played through the idiom of 'tradition'. The slanders took a number of different forms. The first was to claim that enemy houses were in fact outsiders and hence had no right to succeed. Other derogatory accusations were that enemy factions' ancestors had been bad rulers when chiefs, or that they had never been installed or crowned properly. Present-day candidates were also open to slanders, which could range from their youth or westernisation to a poor physical constitution.

Slanders were also necessary to explain various anomalies. The most pressing one was why the spirit Chikumbirike, the progenitor of the

Chifodya line, sided with the Mbudzi house and why his junior, Nyawada, exerted more influence. The Mbudzi house's explanation for this was that Chikumbirike was chased away by his Chifodya offspring when he disapproved of their killing of Gambiza, and that he had been eclipsed by Nyawada because, when he was chief, he behaved like a witch, listening to rumour and not giving enough attention to his ritual obligations. The Chifodyas agreed that he was a witch, and used this to explain his banishment. They maintained that he remains aligned to the Mbudzi house because he has been bribed. The accusation of bribery was widely used by all.

The overwhelming impression gained from the 'lineage politics' was that Rukadza was not only attempting to maintain the Mbudzi monopoly of succession, but also seeking to centralise Katerere *mhondoro* cults upon his spirit Nyawada. It is possible that in the past, other entrepreneurial mediums within the dynasty have attempted to do the same, but a reconstruction of the cults in the late nineteenth and early twentieth century produced a decentralised pattern of royal factions on mountains with allied mediums, competing for power. Thus, Rukadza's attempts at centralisation were fiercely resisted by the other mediums. While he offered me a detailed breakdown of spirit wards within Katerere, taking the 'lion's' share for himself, his opponents contested this, arguing for a more 'free market' pattern of clientage.

## AN UNWRITTEN CONSTITUTION

The last area of 'lineage politics' concerns what could be best described as the Hwesa's unwritten constitution. There was a struggle between the royal houses to define what the normative rules for succession were. Official records of the rituals of the installation, crowning and burial of Hwesa chiefs were scant and dated only from the period of ultra-traditionalist policy towards chiefs, pioneered by the Rhodesia Front government in the late 1960s and 1970s. Hence, with much room for contestation, elders continually described their versions of these rituals. In these accounts they detailed the specific functions carried out by the senior male elders of other leading families, usually sub-chiefs and headmen.[15] The two most important families were those of Sanhani and Sachiwo, whose senior male elders were the chiefdom's two headmen, commonly known as sub-chiefs.

Two leading Sanhani elders feigned ignorance of the current succession dispute and instead gave a detailed account of their own faction's history. They explained that it was only their task to perform ritual functions.[16] As argued in Chapter 1, the Sanhanis comprise a distinct faction on their own, often removed from the political struggles that entangle the rest of the chiefdom (see Map 6.1). It was suggested that their autonomy may be explained by the fact that Sanhani was the former centre of the polity from which larger factions subsequently emerged, establishing a new centre of gravity.

In contrast, when I interviewed a leading elder from the Sachiwo family, located in the heart of Katerere (see Map 6.1), it rapidly became apparent that their loyalties were split between the Mbudzi house and the Chifodya house, with my informant siding with the former. He explained that the sub-chief, Petros, and his younger brothers had been persuaded by the Chifodyas to block the Mbudzi succession and install Matambo Chifodya as chief, in return for greater power under the new regime.[17] This alliance was indeed feasible in that both big families inhabited the same ridge of the Cherenje range on the Mozambique border. From the minutes of a meeting convened by the Assistant District Administrator it appears that Petros did initially ally with the Chifodyas but subsequently got cold feet and fled.[18] He left the area fearing that he would be axed to death by his younger brothers acting in the guise of RENAMO bandits.[19] When asked about this the Chifodyas argued that it was the function of the Sachiwo sub-chief to arbitrate in such cases, and that the Sanhani silence over the succession had been bought with an Mbudzi bribe. Conversely, the Mbudzi house argued for a separation of powers.

Obviously, the key figure in the dispute was the one awarded the title of chief-maker. The Mbudzi house claimed that it was one of their mediums who bore this responsibility; both Rukadza and Kapomba argued that they held the relevant office: *Samatswaka*. The Chifodyas argued that the final arbiter was *Zibaba* Sachiwo (literally 'big father'). It was clear from the 1960 election that sub-chief Sachiwo 'clothed' Katerere[20] but the responsibilities of *Zibaba*, or indeed whoever this person was, were far from clear. As we shall see, the rapid evolution of the *Zibaba* role was a crucial factor in influencing the District Administration.

## MEETINGS

On a number of occasions the three houses came together at public events, and the strong antagonism between them manifested itself in very vivid ways. Generally it was clear that much of the violent rhetoric uttered by members of the various factions was no more than posturing in the competition for political advantage. Most of the dispute does seem to have been a game played to understood rules. Yet, the very longevity of the struggle and the themes of violence that pervaded its central debates meant that, at times, it spilt out beyond the established norms. At moments in the contest, actors feared or fled for their lives.

At the late Chief Njanji's funeral, a Chifodya arrived with a gun and threatened war if a member of his family (Matambo Chifodya) was not elected as next chief. On 7 July 1989, the Assistant District Administrator, J. C. Masuka, convened a meeting in Katerere. When he enquired why there was no record of the Chifodya house on the official chiefly genealogy, Langton, the contender from the rival Chirimunyati house, proceeded to tell of Gambiza's roasting. 'Heated arguments' ensued.[21] By 4 January 1991, feelings were running high as all three houses turned out *en masse* for a meeting along with their *tetes* (aunts, female support) and local 'kraal' heads. Its events were recounted to me by numerous people and vividly recorded by James Gabaza, Assistant District Administrator for Makoni District, who was brought in especially for the occasion.

In front of such a large audience the houses and their mediums competed to seize ritual and dramatic initiative. The Chifodyas had already declared their candidate, Matambo, chief and danced *mapfuwe* – a traditional dance – around him as a sign of respect. For their part the mediums Rukadza, Kaerezi and Kapomba, of the Mbudzi and Chirimunyati houses, refused to allow Sanyamahwe, the Chifodya medium, to sit with them, or be part of their closed sessions. The usual arguments were reproduced – Rukadza/ Nyawada from the Mbudzi house retold the Gambiza story, whilst Sanyamahwe/Nyamande from the Chifodyas argued it was time to rotate the chieftainship between the three houses. Once again the Chifodyas tried to seize the initiative only to be outmanoeuvred by the Mbudzi mediums. James Gabaza described what happened:

> At this point, two men from the Chifodya House presented a wooden plate with a mound of snuff the size of a football to Aluwizi to present to the other mediums as a token to the spirits that they accept the Chifodya House as next successor. Diki and Razawa flatly refused this gift and without touching it went on to ask Tsodza to stand up so all could see who the next chief was. Again there was cheering from those who supported the Mbudzi House and boos from the Chifodya House.
>
> Then the scene degenerated into a war of words with each side threatening physical confrontation. Someone stood up and said this was indeed a shameful show of indiscipline in front of the District Administrator. The people then became quiet.[22]

To summarise, although three factions were involved in the continuing Katerere succession dispute, there were only two plausible outcomes: the election of a Mbudzi or Chifodya candidate. The significance of the Chirimunyati faction was that they had the potential to tip the balance one way or the other. In 1991 the Mbudzi house had the upper hand, at least in popular perceptions. Not only did they set the agenda but they still had the drum symbolising control of the chiefdom. Moreover by the end of that meeting on 7 March they had three mediums allied to their house. For perhaps the most significant event of the meeting was the defection of Taimo Kapomba, medium of Chimucheka, from the Chirimunyati faction to the Mbudzi side. Kapomba's change of loyalties will be considered later. First it is necessary to account for the Mbudzi faction's hold over the chiefdom.

## DIKI RUKADZA, PEASANT INTELLECTUAL;
## MICHAEL GELFAND, INNOCENT ETHNOGRAPHER

The previous chapter described how Diki Rukadza, medium of Nyawada, emerged as an important resistance leader during the liberation war, offering prophetic advice to the comrades and placing taboos on them to protect local people. After independence he retained this legitimacy through acts of post-war healing (as illustrated in the next chapter), and also as a rain maker. In the late 1980s he was in the prime position to act as the trump card in the hand of the dominant Mbudzi faction in the succession dispute.

Rukadza had a great sense of the moment. He was the only informant I met who went out of his way to court me, giving me a totem – *malunga* – dove. His conversation was full of proverbs and metaphor which enhanced his enigmatic persona. He relished the interview situation and was well able to deal with the cunning researcher. The accounts of Hwesa history and politics provided by mediums and royal house heads were, of course, heavily loaded. I tried to use this to my advantage by playing one informant off against another in order to provoke further disclosure. At times I caught my informants off-guard, but Rukadza would see me coming and refuse to take the bait. I would recount with great gusto the sayings and actions of enemy houses only to be crushed by Rukadza's combination of wit and sense of timing:

> Q. Langton Muromowenyoka told me that Chirimunyati was the brother of Chimucheka and that Chimucheka and his son Hokoyo were killed by Mbudzi.
> A. Lies!
> Q. I was told that the Chifodyas had already made Matambo chief and were dancing *mapfuwe* around him.
> A. Stealing![23]

At this point those present would erupt into fits of laughter.

Rukadza was also imbued with a sense of his own heroic mission. He was persistent in his strong conviction of the justice of his cause, and as we talked of the enemy Chifodya faction, he would often pause to point his long quivering bony finger in the direction of their home on Cherenje mountain. Before my third interview had formally started he was telling me of the evils of the Chifodyas, and continued to do so even as I was leaving. Moreover, there was also something outstanding about the quality of Rukadza's discourse on the nature of the relationship between nature, political order, and religious and moral conduct, which he was able to synthesise into a cultic pattern. He was the only medium able to provide me with an elaborate theology of a High God figure – in this case, Karuva. But, most fascinating of all was Rukadza's relationship with the ethnographer Michael Gelfand.

The over-reliance of scholars on entrepreneurial mediums is a well-established fact. For instance, David Lan has been criticised by Michael Bourdillon (1987b) for the weight he placed on the Chiwawa/Pondai medium's account of Korekore cosmology. More importantly here, Terence Ranger (1982b) has highlighted the seduction of Abraham, Paul Berliner and Gelfand by Muchetera, the medium of Chaminuka. In 1959 Gelfand published a monograph which had relied heavily on Muchetera as an informant. Ranger writes:

> The coherence in *Shona Ritual* came mostly from Muchetera, who offered a centralised hierarchical model of Shona religion, with the Chaminuka spirit at the top; who offered a centralised imperial vision of the past, with the Chaminuka spirit crucially involved; and who offered finally, a triumphalist account of his own dominant influence in Makoni district and throughout Mashonaland. (1982b: 352)

Ranger's own analysis of dynastic politics in Makoni district shows that Muchetera's account was far from true (Ibid.). Eleven years later Gelfand arrived in Katerere, and was hoodwinked again, this time by Rukadza.

The first time I met Rukadza he was reluctant to speak to me. Fortunately, I was accompanied by an ex-combatant who had operated in the area during the war and knew him. We talked about former battles and his late son, Comrade Saigon, whom my companion knew. We argued the importance of recording Hwesa history. Slowly he came round. Finally we showed him a copy of Gelfand's book containing numerous pictures of himself. His eyes lit up and he was willing to talk. It was well-known that Gelfand was fond of Rukadza, referring to him as 'my friend';[24] through this friendship the latter was able to supply the innocent ethnographer with an account of the Hwesa *mhondoro* cult, again centralised and hierarchical, but this time with the spirit of Nyawada at the top. (Gelfand, 1982: 132; 1974: 69, 71)

But the story does not end there. On 7 March, when James Gabaza, Assistant DA for Makoni district, was asked to come and assess the succession dispute in Katerere, he brought with him copies of NADA which he described as: 'An old annual publication found in most District Administrators' offices which contains valuable information on traditional customs and Chieftainships'.[25] He found useful a particular copy which contained Gelfand's account (1974) of his research amongst the Hwesa. Excited to recognise Rukadza from the pictures, he referred to Gelfand in his final report, hence endorsing the medium of Nyawada's own account of his spirit made 20 years earlier. He wrote: 'The *senior* spirit Nyawada *is* supposed to name someone from any of the three contesting houses which should reign in turn. The other spirits *should* concur' (my emphasis).[26] Thus the influence of Rukadza, the Mbudzi house's trump card, even penetrated the state bureaucracy.

There is, of course a danger of exaggerating Rukadza's importance in Hwesa politics. His was but one version of Hwesa history and politics. Nevertheless, he *was* important. My judgement that Rukadza was the leading Hwesa organic intellectual was no different from the perception of the vast majority of commoners, outsiders and 'big men' from adjacent ethnic groups.[27] Unlike Muchetera, whom Ranger (1982b) was able to show had little local influence in Makoni district, Rukadza did have a large popular following.

It has been demonstrated for other Shona dynasties that the influence of a *mhondoro* cult is linked to the qualities of its mediums (Bourdillon, 1979: 239). In Rukadza's case, he possessed a charismatic[28] quality which other mediums lacked. Rukadza's ability becomes more apparent when contrasted with the Chirimunyati faction medium. Such a comparison is made later below. First, it is necessary to consider the material and social bases of factional power in Katerere.

## THE SOCIAL AND MATERIAL BASES OF FACTIONAL POWER[29]

Rukadza's success cannot be divorced from the material and social basis of the Mbudzi faction. It is essential to consider the wealth and social status of the members of the competing factions to fully account for their differing success at gaining and retaining chieftainship this century.

Chapter 2 illustrated how the ruling house at the time of the Occupation exploited both Katerere's marginality, and its own immediate advantage of access to state officials, to gain a monopoly over succession. Whilst the Mbudzis moved from the mountains to control large tracts of land between Cherenje and Raungwe ranges, the Chifodya faction remained isolated in the Cherenje range. The Native Administration was unaware of their claims to succession because of its dependence for intelligence on Njanji, a native messenger from the Mbudzi house. The Chifodyas were excluded from competing at the only two key moments this century when the Mbudzi monopoly of succession could have been threatened. First, in 1932, when Chief Chikata was elected, the Chifodyas claimed that they were unaware of the Native Commissioner's visit to Katerere to ensure a popular appointment and complained that the Mbudzis told the NC that they had migrated to Mozambique.[30] The second possible opportunity for challenge came with the election of Njanji in 1960. Here, as the Chifodyas contend, there does seem to have been some collusion over succession between the Native Administration and the Mbudzis. The succession was timed to coincide with Njanji's retirement as a ruthlessly efficient Native Department messenger.[31]

Once established, the Mbudzi faction was also able to use the office of chief as a source of social and economic influence. Whilst Mbudzi territory has some chance of viable agriculture, even cash crop production, Chifodya territory lies in the rain shadow of Cherenje range and is traversed by numerous dry valleys. It offers very little opportunity for successful agriculture in any of its major crops: sorghum, millet or rapoko (Mazambani, 1990: 62–72). A larger proportion of Chifodya males are forced to enter the migrant labour economy, but the remoteness of their territory affected the ability of the men to be successful in the money economy. Mbudzi territory lies between the Roman Catholic Avila mission and the Elim mission. Thus, the incumbent house was in a ripe position to court and be courted by both sets of missionaries, becoming members of the local mission élites discussed in Chapter 4. More generally, the Mbudzi faction's close vicinity to the missions and the consequent opportunity of literacy has offered them greater chance of social mobility. Thus for instance, whilst 30.6 per cent of migrant workers from Gande village near Elim mission, in Mbudzi territory, were white-collar workers, only 9.3 per cent from Chiwarira village, in Chifodya territory, had such status.[32]

The Mbudzi house was richer, more numerous, and more educated than the Chifodya house, and this was an important contributory factor to their retention of chieftainship. Those who succeeded in the money economy were not only able to become local employers through use of their remittances; they also gained considerable prestige through their acquisition of consumer goods.[33] And if bribes were a significant part of 'lineage politics', then this again was an important explanation of Mbudzi success. It may be that the gift of cattle to the Chimucheka medium of the Chirimunyati faction, on the election of the Mbudzi house, had less to do with appeasing an angry lion spirit than buying off his host.[34] Likewise, the realignment of the Chifodya *mhondoro* (progenitor), Chikumbirike, with the Mbudzi's may have had more to do with the last two mediums' marriage into the Mbudzi house than with the chasing away of the spirit by the Chifodyas.[35] Steven Feierman writes: 'One of the ways a group rising to dominance establishes the legitimacy of its position is by conquering and assimilating pre-existing intellectuals'. (1990: 105)

The reality of Chifodya faction's marginalisation was made plain in a number of ways. Chifodya territory was a very different Zimbabwe from that which even the majority of rural people are used to. It was very remote. Here the elderly still stopped and offered lengthy greetings when met on the path. Those living on the Gaerezi side of the Cherenje range still relied on fishing and hunting and many of the younger children did go to the school on the Zimbabwe side of the mountain. Here Matambo Chifodya, the senior faction elder, *was* chief, no matter who was officially elected, and his people greeted him as such. Patrick Tsodza, candidate for the Mbudzi faction, would never drink beer in the Cherenje area or travel to Inyanga via its road, for if the Chifodyas came across him he would be killed.[36]

## THE RISE AND FALL OF THE CHIRIMUNYATIS[37]

The importance of both material and intellectual resources for a faction mounting a campaign for chieftainship became apparent in the case of the Chirimunyatis. The family had long nurtured aspirations for the chieftaincy. In the 1940s a senior elder in the faction, named House Mazambani, began to work to that end, marrying wives and buying magic. However, his neighbours began to fear the power of the vast number of horns and charms he was amassing, and forced him and his family to relocate to Ruangwe. By the 1980s Langton was the senior elder interested in succeeding. Two other possible candidates had moved away, one to Tanda in Makoni district, the other to Botswana.

Although his faction was a make-weight in the struggle for the chiefly office, Langton was helped by a span of connections and relations which secured him influence in the local party and influential organisations. These came through his relation to the Mazambanis – a particularly successful and influential Hwesa family. Todd Mazambani was a local ZANU/PF councillor, whilst his younger brother, David, was perhaps the most highly educated Hwesa to date. He had obtained a doctorate from Clarke University in Canada and worked for a foreign NGO in Zimbabwe. Together, Todd and David were influential figures in the Nyanga North Residents Association, a collection of people from Katerere working in Harare but seeking to foster development in their former home area. Another brother, Amos, had secured well-paid work on the South African mines, and was now the Elim hospital driver. Moreover, like Chief Njanji, Langton had been a Native Messenger and was also Court Assessor for Matizi ward. He also had 'traditional' sources of prestige. He had five wives and children, and it was rumoured that he had strong magic. Langton was second only to Rukadza in his ability to deploy an argument based on 'tradition'. After the death of Njanji, a *nhango* – a family meeting – was held, and Fansika and Katoya, the senior women in the Chirimunyati house, were called in to remind those assembled of their claim to the chieftaincy. On 26 June 1989, Langton made the journey to Inyanga to inform the DA of the past error of the Mbudzi monopoly and the possibility of claims from other houses.[38]

One crucial factor for competing factions was the support of a medium. The Chirimunyatis found theirs in Taimo Kapomba, medium of Chimucheka. On the late chief's burial Kapomba secretly summoned Chirimunyati elders to a meeting. There, speaking through his spirit, Chimucheka, Kapomba told those present that he was sick of the Mbudzi family and wanted to see his own family as chiefs. He told them to boycott Mbudzi-led rituals and that he would do what he could. He warned them not to tell anyone of the meeting. Langton and his family had been brewing beer for the Chimucheka for a long time before Njanji's death. Henceforth, Langton and Kapomba attended public gatherings and beer drinks together. The alliance seemed complete.

However, the Chirimunyati campaign had two major weaknesses. First, Langton had a weak material and territorial base. The faction had only a small number of families in comparison to the other two and these were dispersed throughout the chiefdom.[39] The one particularly successful and influential family, the Mazambanis, lived in Ruangwe, some distance away. Furthermore, a number of the faction were evangelical Christians. Although they wished to see justice for their faction, they were reluctant to attend traditional ceremonies and had an ambivalent attitude towards chieftainship, in that it was ritually supported, and legitimated by spirits which they considered evil. Langton's second problem was that in Kapomba, he had a weak and ineffective medium.

## MEDIUMS AND POSSESSION

I interviewed spirit mediums on the basis that they were either aware of what they were saying when possessed, or had been informed of their utterances subsequently. I asked to speak to all mediums *munhu chete* (person only), rather than *kubatwa* (possessed). This provoked a variety of reactions from mediums. Those with a good popular standing and allied to a powerful faction were willing to talk, whilst those with a weak standing and weak faction tried to steer a more difficult path through the interview. It seemed that in 'lineage politics', a medium's need to be possessed was a statement about both his own and his house's standing in the wider political community. This is argued on the basis of two propositions. First, possession provides cover for the making of subversive statements about enemies, and potentially more powerful factions. Secondly, the act of possession and the supplication of those participating in the seance was a means whereby the medium gained legitimacy.

The first proposition, concerning the medium's cognisance of his utterances made in trance, was confirmed in two ways. The first was by interviewing some mediums on several different occasions. I was then able to hear them reveal things that they had previously said only the spirit could divulge. The second confirmation came in instances when what was being discussed was so much in the medium's interest that he was forced to break his cover. For instance, when I met with Sanyamahwe, the Chifodya medium, he explained that he could not say much when not possessed and so he had brought along one of his attendants, Advice Chifodya, to speak for him. At a crucial point in the interview it was plain that Chifodya was getting the details of the murder of Nyamande wrong. Sanyamahwe stopped him, made a lengthy correction, and participated in the rest of the interview.[40]

My proposition about a medium's varying need to be possessed was confirmed when I attempted to interview Charles Madakwenda, a medium of the Sachiwo sub-chieftaincy. For well over two decades he had been outmanoeuvred and marginalised by a far more charismatic medium called

Bracho, who had kept the ear of the sub-chiefs. Madakwenda complained bitterly about the lack of respect his spirit got and insisted we brought a member of Sachiwo family with us; we had to clap to his spirit before he would talk to us.[41] In a similar way Kapomba would often claim to be 'only a servant' and thus have no answer for my questions, when not in seance. He continually denied any links with the Chirimunyati house. In contrast, Rukadza of the Mbudzi house (and to a lesser extent his colleague Kaerezi), speaking from a position of relative security, was more than happy to speak for his *sekuru* (spirit, literally 'grandfather') and at times the two appeared synonymous.

Kapomba was simply not a good medium. Clients complained that he was often unable to enter into a state of possession. His colleagues cultivated an aloofness, an air of detachment from their people, living in remote locations which meant passing through a cultural minefield of explanations and appropriate procedures to gain access to them, but he lived right next to the road. Other mediums seemed to relish the more probing questions but he was positively irritated by them. Thus, at some later stage in the succession dispute, Kapomba decided to defect to the Mbudzi side, without telling his former ally. James Gabaza vividly described the scene as this became apparent at the meeting of 4 January 1991 referred to above:

> At this point, Langton, the contestant from the Nyaurimbo (Chirimunyati) House arrived. There was no formal recognition of his arrival and no formal greeting by clapping of hands which was always the case when respected latecomers arrived. Langton went to sit close to the medium of Chimucheka, Taimo, who had not spoken since the proceedings began. The two talked privately for a few minutes and then Taimo, Diki and Razawa went into closed session. Soon afterwards they addressed the crowd again, Razawa … announced that a third contestant in the name of Langton had arrived. He and the other mediums had consulted the spirits and had been told that this Nyaurimbo House was unknown to them, therefore it was an imposter … The mediums insisted that they had never heard of Nyaurimbo before. It is interesting to note that Taimo who was supposed to stand for Langton and had not spoken since began to argue too but in favour of Tsodza. A very disappointed Langton sat brooding, having been disowned by the very spirit he had hoped would support him.[42]

In concluding his report, Gabaza wrote: 'Our observation is that although Nyaurimbo [Chirimunyati house] is still interested, it appears that the contestant is a lone ranger. He has no following and seems to be unknown to the people of the area.'[43]

Sadly the story did not end there. One night in late March 1991, Langton – who persisted in his struggle for recognition – fell strangely silent. The following morning he was found unconscious in his field seemingly struck dumb. He died without uttering a single word. The medical explanation for his death was that it had resulted from a combination of pneumonia and malaria, but other senior elders in his house were not so sure. The Chifodyas were quick to claim that they, the Chifodyas, had 'fixed him' and no one emerged to take his place.

### PUTTING THE HOUSE IN ORDER:
### THE BUREAUCRATIC RESPONSE

On occasions officers from the District Administration were called upon to offer advice or arbitrate in the succession dispute. And it was with them that the decision for the official state appointment lay. What was striking about their initial interactions with the Katerere dynasty was their tendency to view it as a monolithic institution and not as a collection of competing factions, each with its own version of the past. In the meeting of 7 July 1989 Assistant DA Masuka, frustrated by the 'heated arguments' between factions, closed the meeting advising *all* three houses present to: 'clean their own house first'[44] – an unfortunate remark in the circumstances.

Assistant DA Makoni ended the meeting of 7 March 1991 by telling all assembled to meet again after 'more research on their history so that they may come up with one candidate'.[45] The same approach of aggregating the highly contested accounts of the past given by different factions was seen in the official construction of genealogies. This bureaucratic response was reminiscent of the late 1960s and 1970s when the Rhodesia Front Government, in its attempts to bolster 'tradition' against the nationalist movement, sent out its black administrative cadets into the countryside to research 'traditional' history and culture. This continuity of approach to 'tradition', seen most vividly in bureaucratic use of the same administrative files, is easily explained by the fact that many of those cadets are now Assistant DAs (see also Alexander, 1993: 169–73). Assistant DA Makoni's final Katerere genealogy bore great resemblance to the 1965 delineation report for Katerere.[46] This process of delineation was a nationwide exercise to establish the authentic version of local tribal cultures.

Indeed it was with Assistant DA Makoni that the 'official' response to the conflict lay. Although other officials like Gabaza submitted lengthy and impressive assessments of the succession dispute, the responsibility for its resolution increasingly passed to Makoni, who represented an administrative continuity between changing DAs. Although his grasp of the issues became more sophisticated over time it is clear that he was never fully aware of the scale of contestation and intrigue the succession dispute involved. His final decision, made on 3 April 1992, in favour of Matambo Chifodya, appears to have been influenced by a number of factors: irritation at Mbudzi methods; a sense of fair play; and Chifodya skill at manipulating tradition.

While the Mbudzi faction effectively controlled the chiefdom and had a great popular following, its leaders made a number of tactical blunders when it came to dealing with state officials. Whether it was through over-confidence, or fear that the District Administration would finally decide to appoint a chief on the basis of the rotation of houses, as happened elsewhere in Zimbabwe, they cultivated an aloofness from officialdom, stressing with a finality that theirs was the traditionally legitimate candidate. In their first meeting with Makoni on 23 November 1989 they informed him that Tsodza had already been appointed.[47] They boycotted the following combined meeting of houses the next March[48] and only sent an observer delegation to a number of other meetings. Such disdain for bureaucratic process did nothing to endear the Mbudzi faction to District Administration which was keen to stamp its authority on communal lands, and Makoni chose to read it as 'a sign of acceptance of defeat'.[49]

Moreover, Mbudzi failure to mobilise for meetings undermined the popular support they had. Only at the last meeting, of 3 April 1992, did they make a true show of force, mustering 110 men and 125 women in comparison with the Chifodya showing of 59 men and 91 women. But by then, of course, it was too late; Chifodya was pronounced chief. Whilst his followers sang and threw dusty soil into the air the larger Mbudzi faction left shouting 'inaudible comments'.[50] Indeed, Makoni did rightly gauge a disorganisation in the Mbudzi camp, an inability to press their case in a convincing manner.[51] Much of the problem lay in their choice of a candidate, Patrick Tsodza, who embodied perhaps the strongest irony of the whole drama. After all the creative energy expended by his Mbudzi house and allied mediums, Tzodza initially had no wish to be chief. When the faction's *mhondoro* announced him as their candidate at an early meeting, he was not present and had to be sent for. On hearing the news Tsodza fled to Mutare, to consult the Catholic Bishop, Patrick Mutume. Mutume told him, that like King Saul of the Israelites, he could not resist his own destiny.[52]

Finally, in 1994, Diki Rukadza died after a period of illness. The famous Nyawada medium had helped to galvanise popular support around the Mbudzi faction even into his 90s. His illness came at a moment when his charisma would have done much to impress district officials.

The Chifodya house had been planning its campaign for a long time. It recognised the importance of the District Administration in the dispute and acted in a way which legitimated the bureaucratic role. The Chifodyas made a standard case for the rotation of houses, mobilised for all the public meetings, travelled to Inyanga to lobby the DA on a number of occasions, and made a number of written submissions which became evidence. Meanwhile they had cemented what turned out to be a crucial alliance with leading elders in the Sachiwo faction.

Faced with a bewildering array of claims *all* based in the idiom of tradition, Makoni was left to decide for himself which normative rules to accept and which ones to ignore. In a fairly arbitrary manner he appears to have accepted Chifodya claims as more authentic. His written submission justifying his decision was a fascinating collage of evidence citing genealogies, oral traditions, accounts of meetings, appendices of correspondence. The Chirimunyati claim was quickly dealt with by means of reference to a letter from Langton's son stating that his house had withdrawn for the present.[53] On the burning issue of the destruction of Gambiza's body, Makoni dodged the question of profanity, seeking instead to square this act with the retaliatory violence meted out against Nyamande and his wife by the Mbudzi faction.[54]

But the key influence on Makoni was the supposed role of the Sachiwos as chiefmaker. Ignoring Gabaza's exaltation of Rukadza as chiefmaker, or *Samatswaka*, he chose instead to accept the Chifodyas' account of a figure called *Zibaba* Sachiwo who arbitrated between claimants. But here a remarkable slippage occurred as the role and identity of the *Zibaba* evolved under the Assistant DA's nose. The administrative account of the election of Chief Njanji Katerere in 1960 has no mention of such an office. Headman Sachiwo convened a meeting of the relevant villages and five mediums deliberated in front of those present. The headman subsequently 'enrobed' the selected candidate as chief. However, at a key meeting held on 8 December 1989, which was poorly attended by Mbudzi supporters, the Chifodyas made a foundational statement about the *Zibaba* role. The *Zibaba* was to convene a meeting of spirit mediums, ask the *mhondoro* to nominate and deal with anomalies. In this case the chiefmaker was the *mhondoro* medium, Bracho Chiwenga, host of the Sachiwo ancestral spirit, Dzihambo.[55]

But Dzihambo's voice was never heard throughout the whole dispute. His host, Bracho, died in 1990, and a new medium was not forthcoming. Prior to Bracho's death, Dzihambo's sentiments were supposedly voiced by a Sachiwo elder called Choto Chabundo.[56] After Bracho's death, Chabundo slowly became the *Zibaba*. In a submission to the Provincial Administrator, Manicaland, in April 1990, Makoni wrote '*Zibaba* Sachiwo [Choto Chabundo] is not aware of the fact that a successor [Patrick Tsodza] has been appointed.'[57] At the final meeting of 3 April 1992 all mention of the *mhondoro* Dzihambo had disappeared and *Zibaba* Sachiwo *was* Chabundo.[58] The first meeting convened by Chabundo ended in chaos, and subsequent Mbudzi refusal to have anything to do with *Zibaba* led him to pen a letter to the DA in support of Matambo. Great weight was placed on this letter by Makoni in his final summation.[59]

Chabundo himself had no great distinction apart from being a Sachiwo elder with a somewhat forceful personality. Lacking any spiritual legiti-mation for his new-found role, he had cultivated relations with non-Hwesa mediums from Barwe living in Katerere. In local politics, Chabundo, along

6.3 'Official' Chief, Matambo Chifodya

6.4 Matambo Chifodya (right) and his Council

6.5 Patrick Tsodza (standing right) and Members of his Council (Medium Taimo Kapomba is seated on the right)

6.6 Patrick Tsodza presiding over a First Fruits Ceremony, as 'Popular' Chief

with Fani and Champion Sachiwo, was part of the Sachiwo faction strongly allied to the Chifodyas and which appeared to run the sub-chiefdom in the absence of the elected candidate, Petros.[60] Thus, so successful were the Chifodyas at manipulating official understandings of tradition that they managed to make the whole process of chiefly election hinge around one man: their man – Choto Chabundo.

## ONE CHIEFTAINCY, TWO CHIEFS

On 6 April 1992, Assistant DA Makoni wrote to the Provincial Administrator requesting the election of Matambo Chifodya as chief. The following March, President Mugabe made the appointment.[61] But the struggle between the Mbudzi and Chifodya factions did not end. On 3 February 1994, Acting DA Makoni conveyed the following information to Ruangwe's local police inspector:

> Reports [have been] received that Mr P Tsodza who is a school teacher …
>
> (i) has claimed succession to the Katerere Chieftainship.
> (ii) is collecting … cash for the purpose of hosting an installation ceremony.
> (iii) has divided the Chief's area into two (a section is 'ruled' by him and another is 'ruled' by Mr Matambo Chifodya who is currently recognised by this office as chief).
> without the approval of this office.[62]

Tsodza was duly summoned to the police station and told not to act as chief. But in his response to the District Administration the Inspector noted that: 'Some investigations made indicated that most of the people wanted him to be made chief and he had objected to this, however I am made to understand that there are some spirit mediums who asked him to stand as chief.'[63] Two years later the District Administration sent a Katerere councillor, Nyamupondo, a curt note entitled 'ADDRESSING Mr Tsodza as Chief Katerere instead of Mr Matambo Chifodya who is the substantive Chief', expressing its displeasure with his introduction of Patrick Tsodza as chief to a local leadership workshop.[64]

In Katerere, the reality was not so much a territorially divided chiefdom but two conflicting notions of authority. There was a state-appointed chief with administrative responsibilities but a small following, and a 'traditionally legitimate chief' controlling most of the territory but lacking official recognition. Kraal heads and elders often boycotted meetings Chifodya attended, and many Hwesa brought their problems to Tsodza. Chifodya had the tin badge of office given him by the state but the Mbudzi faction refused to hand over the drum, staff and cloth used in a 'traditional' coronation. My last visit to Chifodya's homestead coincided with a meeting of his *dare* – council. Rather than appearing the nerve centre of the chiefdom his village seemed more as if it was under siege. Despite the presence of his councillors, Chifodya sought to flee when my research assistant entered his hut, even though my colleague was well-known to him. His council, which was drawn from only two or three villages, were keen to emphasise state recognition of Matambo but complained bitterly about Mbudzi retention of the drum, warning that it would soon become an irrelevant archaism if it was not handed over. They requested that I photograph Chifodya wearing his badge of office and spent a long time grooming him for the picture.[65]

In contrast, Tsodza retained the support of important leaders like sub-Chief Sanhani and headman Maroo, and his *dare* drew elders from across the territory. Tsodza was a changed man. Energised by his house's official exclusion from power he had now begun to take his calling seriously, convening his own ceremonies for sowing and first fruits. When asked about Chifodya's election he dismissed it as a product of 'whiteman's rules', alien to Hwesa culture.[66]

A fascinating reversal in Hwesa politics had taken place. For a century the Mbudzi faction had colluded with the state in order to enhance its social, economic and political influence though control of the chiefdom. In so doing it had run roughshod over 'traditional' notions about succession. Now excluded from alliance with the state, the Mbudzi faction protested in idioms of tradition it had previously ignored. Meanwhile the Chifodya faction which had always made traditional claims to office now found that the state's support was their strongest card. Bitter at his rejection by large numbers of Hwesa, Matambo Chifodya talked of exploiting his control of aid and development money to secure loyalty. Only time will tell whether the Chifodyas will be as successful as the Mbudzi faction in using the office of chief as a source of political and economic leverage. A century of rule has given the latter a good head start.

## MODERNITY AND TRADITION: COLLAPSING DICHOTOMIES

It is apparent that the idea of 'tradition' meant very different things for the various parties involved in the Hwesa succession dispute. For the bureaucrats in the District Administration it was a fixed set of normative rules delineating what they, and the chiefs, could and could not do. For the government, as shown below, it was a rhetorical device for gaining legitimacy in the face of failed development strategies and an increasing inability to mobilise the rural constituency. Finally traditional leaders used 'tradition' as a set of strategies which enabled them to enhance their own social, economic and political influence (see Ranger 1982c: 24). But theirs was not a fixed model of the tradition. Chifodya attempts to make the drum and other symbols of legitimate chieftainship redundant, and their innovation with the *Zibaba* figure illustrate how arguments changed as old strategies were replaced by new ones. And, as in the case of the imagination of customary law, discussed in Chapter 2, those successful in persuading the state to adopt their version of the past, were often those who made the first statement.

It was the traditional leaders' version of 'tradition' that local party politicians and civil servants most desired to learn. When I first interviewed Todd Mazambani, the local councillor for Ruangwe, in early 1988, he made no mention of 'lineage politics' and knew little about *mhondoro* cults. His interest in the succession dispute grew when he realised that his own Chirimunyati house was involved. He then acted as spokesman for his house at meetings with the DA. A literate man and a successful politician, Mazambani was uneasy with genealogies and stories, and had written them down. His family tree, Chirimunyati style, was read to DA Makoni and subsequently inserted into the Katerere Chief's File kept at Inyanga.[67] The Mbudzi house candidate, Patrick Tsodza, also demonstrated an unease with this rhetoric. He too had initially written notes and met regularly with his house's mediums for lessons.

Traditional leaders could best be described as claiming authority by 'right of their position as autochthonous owners of the land' and their 'access to a body of knowledge which derives from their position as living representatives of the ancestors' (Alexander, 1990: 2). However, in order to further their agendas, these leaders drew on other sources of legitimacy such as access to technical or scientific knowledge, or a good record of wartime resistance and party membership (Ibid.). Thus, Langton's confident bid for the chieftaincy was not simply based on his standing as the Chirimunyati house leader, but also upon his connections, through relatives, with the local party, and an influential urban-based association. Likewise, Rukadza's great popularity had much to do with his standing as a wartime leader. When the Shona popular weekly, *Kwayedza*, covered the story of the Katerere succession dispute in December 1995, Mbudzi faction leaders made great play of Tsodza's education: 'Because of Mr Chifodya's old age … what improvements do you think he will effect? He is lagging behind the time but Tsodza is educated and he is still young.'[68] Indeed the ancestor spirits had proven thoroughly pragmatic in their choice of candidate. Tsodza was a literate school teacher, fluent in English, and proud of his Catholicism and church wedding. His wife had refused to brew beer for the *mhondoro*, but they were impressively conciliatory. Other women could be brought in to do this task.[69]

Mutually beneficial alliances between traditionalists and modernisers were formed. When Langton needed to understand the machinery of the local bureaucracy or the party, he consulted his Christian 'brother', Todd Mazambani, the councillor for Ruangwe. As chairman of the district council, Mazambani was keen to have a relative as chief because this would mean that councillors representing other Katerere wards would feel more obliged to side with him when voting. Likewise, councillor Nyamupondo's public introduction of Tsodza as chief was a logical recognition of the Mbudzi faction's local influence. Traditional leaders were not merely attempting to build an encapsulated political structure – a traditional enclave within the contemporary state; their reimagination of tradition sought to gain them influence within wider, local and national, political processes. That councillors courted faction leaders for secular political purposes was a strong indication of their growing political influence.

## THE REVIVAL OF MALE GERONTOCRATIC POWER AND THE COLLAPSE OF THE PARTY AT LOCAL LEVEL

During the late 1980s Katerere's male gerontocratic élites reasserted themselves in two senses: the first more specific, a counter-reaction to the decline of patriarchal influence during the war; the second more general, a repetitive process occurring in the trajectory of succession.

Male elders' loss of power to women and youth during the war was described in the previous chapter. Commenting on the political position of Chief Njanji Katerere in early 1980, the outgoing District Commissioner wrote: 'He was subject, along with all his followers to the control of *mujibas* and terrorists. This included their judicial and financial movement systems.'[70] But old men clawed back power. Not only did *their* sphere, 'traditional' politics, become more significant, but they also came to dominate party politics. By the end of the 1980s the local party was controlled by kraal heads, faction leaders and elderly, who may also have been successful builders, store owners or farmers. In a sense party politics were localised to reflect local patterns of gerontocratic authority. As we shall see this process occurred elsewhere within Zimbabwe.

But there was also a cyclical revival of rural patriarchy. Implicit in Shona society is a strong duality between youth and elders. Young men and women have always expressed a disinterest or antagonism towards the religious beliefs and practices of their parents and grandparents. As this study has shown, and will further illustrate in the final chapter, this generational conflict has often expressed itself in changed patterns of religious adherence, particularly conversion to Christianity. Nevertheless, youth eventually become old men and women themselves. And some, but by no means all elders, accommodate traditional practices, or revert back to them wholesale in order to come to terms with ageing and bolster their authority within the household. Men in their 40s and 50s continually talked of their recent knowledge of the traditions of their faction. It would seem that succession disputes represent a rare but cyclical opportunity to initiate them into the key significance of the patriarchal myth.

Thus the politics described in this chapter were dominated by senior male elders. This impression was continually confirmed during field work. As I conducted interviews in fields, under shady trees, or in homesteads, older men passing by would come and sit and listen intently, often offering their own opinions. The interview over, I would be referred to other 'knowledgeable' men to talk to. Only when I persisted would the names of one or two women be given.

Nevertheless I did grow increasingly aware of very aged women acting as prompts in interviews. These were *nyakwawa*[71] – Hwesa women, in this case the elderly sisters of faction leaders – who had either returned home on the death of their husbands or were called back for important family and public meetings. These women acted as guardians of the family history, of legends and genealogies. Because these women were post-menopausal, they were considered ritually clean and were allowed to participate in spirit medium rituals. Moreover their marriage to outsiders, and networks of gossip based on meetings of sisters were the very stuff the factions were made of.

But these elderly *nyakwawa* helped to reproduce the patriarchal social order, repeating the common male slanders about younger women: that they were prostitutes, liars, unreliable and impure. They derived their high status not so much from their gender as from their age, which they went to great lengths to emphasise.[72] Generally the vast majority of women did not publicly participate in factional politics; first, due to exogamy which made them outsiders, and secondly because of their ritual and symbolic exclusion from the *mhondoro* cults from which faction leaders drew legitimacy. As the following chapter will show, the reassertion of male gerontocratic power has produced a counter-reaction – a second Christian movement of women and youth into a new wave of Pentecostal churches.

The vast amounts of intellectual and emotional energy which faction leaders and their allies invested in the struggle for the Katerere chieftainship epitomised the revival of male gerontocratic power. For chieftainship is the ideal patriarchal system. The chief is the senior member of the dominant faction within the dynasty. He is referred to by his people as *baba* – father – and calls them his children. He exercises authority over his subjects as a father would over his children. (Bourdillon, 1987a: 114)

The growing influence of traditional leaders in local struggles for resources in Katerere has led to a sharpening of ethnicity. Chapter 4 described how members of the Nyamhute family had returned north to Katerere in the 1950s after their flight during a period of pre-colonial factional warfare. Seeing no benefit to be gained from claiming Hwesa ethnicity, they continued to closely identify themselves with the Manyika élites with whom they were evicted northwards. However in the present climate it pays to claim the Katerere totem, and certain members of the Nyamhute family now style themselves as Hwesa.

The return of chiefs was inseparable from another process in rural politics in the 1980s and 1990s, the decline of the ruling party at a local level. In Katerere, there was little evidence of (vibrant) councils or advisory boards prior to independence.[73] The first real opportunity for popular participation in politics came with the revolutionary committees established in the war. Out of these often emerged the first wave of ZANU/PF branch officials.[74] Yet the rural dynamism which characterised local politics in the early 1980s (see Chapter 5) slowly vanished. Party structures, such as village development committees (VIDCOS), arbitrary collections comprising 100 villages, were imposed from above, replacing 'previous communities and affiliations' (Alexander, 1995: 183–4). Local control over development diminished as authority was transferred further up the party hierarchy from village to ward level.[75] As elderly males consolidated their control of the branches, popular participation declined. The local turn-out for rallies and branch-level independence celebrations steadily decreased in the latter years of the 1980s, and only male elders, local dignitaries and missionaries were invited to the sumptuous meals which often followed such events.

Judith de Wolf's 1996 study of the practices of local government in Katerere and, more broadly, Nyanga district paints an even grimmer picture of centralisation by both the ruling party and district level bureaucrats. On VIDCOS she found '[they] do not seem to function as independent local government institutions in Ru[w]angwe ward. They exist more on paper and in official government records ...' (De Wolf, 196: 66). WADCO (Ward Development Committee) meetings in Ruangwe were primarily

> an opportunity for the councillor (and ministries) to inform people on government policies. Regularly local government issues are mixed with ZANU(PF) issues ... the councillor acts as a representative of the government, 'selling' policy to the people rather, than representing the people at the grassroots in the RDC [Rural District Council]. (Ibid: 84)

Worse still, communal councillors deferred to bureaucrats, who despite claims to the contrary, formulated 'most of the policy' (Ibid: 51). In the same way that the guerrilla war failed to bring about a revolutionary trans-formation of the state bureaucracy, so too local revolutionary committees failed to bring about a permanent transformation of rural politics.

The shift in authority away from grassroots was compounded by a decline in the Zimbabwean economy. By 1988 many adults talked nostalgically about '*makore eSmith*' – 'the years of Smith' – when money had value and a secondary-school education would almost certainly lead to employment. And the majority of Katerere youth supported the newly formed opposition party, the Zimbabwe Unity Movement. By 1996 De Wolf found that most of Ruwangwe ward 'display[ed] apathy towards everything concerning ZANU(PF)' (Ibid.: 64).[76]

Into the gap created by the local party's demise came traditional leaders who, through their revival of 'tradition', were able to create a constituency from those alienated by aspects of the government's new legal and agricultural policies. Traditional leaders' attack on specific features of 'modernisation' was well conceived because authoritarian implementation of certain development policies was a threat to their own autonomy and social standing (Alexander, 1995: 6–16). Reflecting on the demise of the local party, Jocelyn Alexander writes:

> Though guerrilla mobilization in the rural areas successfully sustained the war and set in motion radical challenges to existing power structures, it failed to produce new political organizations able to resist the manipulations of powerful bureaucracies. The government was thus able to 'demobilise' the local level political party by excluding it from policy decisions and starving it of resources. (Ibid.: 1)

The minutes of the Provincial Council of Chiefs for Manicaland extends the pattern of revival of traditional leaders beyond Katerere. Once the chiefs perceived the authoritarian direction of local government, they moved speedily to add their own critique. In December 1986, they complained of councillor selection by civil servants, and of council favouritism in the distribution of land, claiming the right to allocate for themselves. In September 1987, Nyanga district chiefs and headmen criticised the confusion over the roles of headmen, VIDCOs, kraal heads and councillors in land distribution. Again chiefs suggested that they should be involved in controlling the influx of outsiders because of the overcrowding they were causing.[77] Chiefs turned land into a populist issue. The following year, they invoked memories of the liberation struggle and demanded land owned by white commercial farmers.[78]

Of course, the rhetoric of chiefs and other traditional leaders is fundamentally self-interested. Chiefs' struggle to gain 'official' control over land allocation also represents their local struggle for authority. In their search for popular followings, traditional leaders have worked out very local strategies for success. Elsewhere, outside Katerere, chiefs threatened by VIDCO land allocation have sided with land-hungry outsiders in order to create new constituencies of support.[79] Chiefs' desire to restore the old patriarchal social order has shown itself most clearly in the sphere of law. In February 1984, the Manicaland chief, Mutambara, spoke strongly against the disrespect youth showed to elders, and of chiefs' inability to punish them. He wanted an end to community courts. In 1989, Chief Makoni proposed the repeal of the Age of Majority Act, which allowed young couples to marry without the consent of their in-laws. Other chiefs added that it led to a high divorce rate, baby dumping and disputes upon the occasion of the wife's death.[80] The law had weakened the power of fathers over children and for the first time

African women had the right to enter into legal contracts. (Folbre, 1988: 74–5)

In the late 1980s there was a significant shift in the government's attitude towards traditional leaders which culminated in the return of their judicial powers and in guarantees that they would be involved in the process of land allocation.[81] The explanation for their official recognition as popular leaders is directly linked to the weakening rural base of the ruling party. During the late 1980s the level of popular support in the ZANU/PF government steadily declined. Senior ministers were convicted on charges of corruption, and there was much public disaffection over rising unemployment, inflation, and the slowness of development. The ruling party's search for legitimacy brought it to the feet of the chiefs and revived its interest in tradition.

In 1989 the Provincial Administrator for Manicaland sent a minute to all district offices complaining that some chiefs and headmen had not been properly installed and that no action seemed to be planned to improve the situation.[82] Other circulars devoted much attention to traditional leaders having the correct regalia: state-invented symbols of chiefly authority. Such administrative attention to the status of chiefs, the amount of time and energy high-ranking officers of the District Administration have spent in Katerere in order to secure the speedy and popular election of the two headmen and the chief, and its dismay at the poor reception of Chief Chifodya Katerere, suggests an official concern that chiefs do not become marginalised as radical opposition leaders. A closely monitored election and the official recognition of the successful candidate are the best means the state can use to co-opt chiefs as allies in local government. As one rural district council bureaucrat commented, 'it is good that they are in the council, because sometimes they accuse the government and now they are part of government' (De Wolf, 1996: 319). The co-option of chiefs has become increasingly important because these traditional leaders in alliance with *mhondoro* mediums have significant local followings.

## MEDIUMS AS POPULISTS AND PATRIARCHS

In his book *Guns and Rain*, based on research in the Dande region of Zimbabwe, David Lan cited evidence (1985: 210) of occasions when mediums made their presence felt at local party committee meetings, and of occasions when some were elected as councillors in the Dande region. In Nyanga there were no examples of spirit medium involvement in local party politics; rather, there was evidence of exclusion at district level. Early in the 1980s it was suggested at a district level meeting that ancestors should be honoured before commencing with business. Christian councillors spoke strongly against it, arguing that religion and politics should not mix. The traditionalists were defeated.[83]

In Katerere, mediums, like chiefs, experienced a rapid marginalisation after Independence.[84] In my first meeting with Rukadza, I asked him about the government; he looked away in disgust. He told me: 'The government does not respect the ancestor spirits. They have taken part of their power for their own. The spirits can no longer give judgements through the chief.'[85] Other mediums felt that the government owed them a debt for the help they had provided during the armed struggle. They argued that members of the local party should come and present them with gifts, such as cloth and hoes, as tokens of respect. They were quick to make populist statements about slowness of development. The drought of the 1980s provided ample ammunition for criticism. The wife of one medium commented:

> When people come to ask why there is so little rain the *mhondoro* says it is not your problem it is because of President Mugabe. And also it seems that they are losing their role. Most of the chiefs are not hearing cases. They had been judges but other ZANU/PF members have been selected to hear cases. As a result chiefs feel that their authority has been taken and not many people are recognising their authority.[86]

Mediums like Rukadza used the idiom of tradition to depict community courts as alien:

> Community courts are misplaced because they are operating in land which belongs to the chief. Since the chief is the owner of the land he should try the case. The job of the community courts is taking place in the forests because the land is not theirs, it is the chief's land.
> Q. What do you mean taking place in the forests?
> A. It is because what the government did is unlawful. The acts of the community courts are just wild.[87]

Their public proclamations were well placed. Many people *did* complain about the inability of community courts to dispense quick and effective justice. By the late 1980s the inhabitants of northern Nyanga had become increasingly outspoken over the slow pace of development in their meetings with their Member of Parliament, Comrade Masaya.[88] In the 1990 elections, those in Ruangwe ward attempted to put up their own candidate for party selection. Plans for villagisation were very unpopular, seemingly imposed in an authoritarian manner, and involving expensive dislocation. They were particularly resented by younger men and women who had built brick houses, especially when the lines along which the villages were planned went straight through the homesteads of local party officials. Under such schemes, the new portions of land were said to be too small and the closer proximity of homesteads to each other was deemed to encourage witchcraft accusation. Mediums also skilfully exploited public opposition to dams, which again involved displacement of people.[89]

But like chiefs, mediums' utterances were both populist and patriarchal.

Their 'traditional' ideological critique of modernisation was double-edged. Specific development projects such as villagisation and dams were condemned because they undermined the control of land by senior males. Medium opposition to more popular schemes like irrigation projects can be seen as attempts by them to impose their own authority (Alexander, 1995: 13). But in this latter context, mediums' public statements were more subtle, simply saying that the correct procedures for obtaining permission from the spiritual owners of the land must be followed.[90] Less discerning mediums, whose *mhondoro* spirits have opposed the use of fertiliser because it contains salt, or sunflowers because they are too bright, found their utterances dismissed as mere rhetoric by more entrepreneurial farmers who adopted the practices of Agritex officers.[91]

Mediums also opposed community courts out of a sense of patriarchal self-interest. The chief's court offered the best hope of enforcing conservationist taboos (Daneel, 1991: 4). Furthermore, as Andrew Ladley notes, community courts were popularly perceived as 'women's courts', used to chase men for the maintenance of children born outside marriage. Women could thus potentially replace their dependency on men with a dependency upon the state, destroying the whole basis of marriage as a union of kinship groups. Ladley writes: 'With the *traditional* system of descent and lineage threatened, it is small wonder that the ancestors objected ... They are losing their children.'[92] When the medium Rukadza spoke of his opposition to community courts he premised his remarks with the words: 'It is impossible to have two cocks in one fowl run. The two fight for the hen.'[93] In this context, his use of gender-laden imagery was striking.[94]

## CHIEFS IN ALLIANCE WITH THEIR ANCESTORS: A REAPPRAISAL OF THE DEBATE

As noted in the introduction to this chapter, two influential scholars, Terence Ranger and David Lan, who conducted research in the wake of the liberation war, perceived a dichotomy between chiefs and mediums. Both argued, from their respective case studies on Makoni district and Dande, that chiefs became increasingly associated with the white settler state, particularly with its unpopular agrarian policies, which they were expected to administer as local agents. With the Rhodesia Front's rise to power in the 1960s, their popularity further declined, for the state increasingly sought to use them to bolster 'tradition' as a means of countering the nationalist movement. Thus in the war, many chiefs and headmen were killed by guerrillas, and new administrative structures run by party committees were set up in their place. In a paper entitled 'Tradition and Travesty: Chiefs and the Administration in Makoni District, Zimbabwe, 1960–1980' Ranger argued:

It is not possible, of course to make a complete distinction between chiefs and mediums ... Nevertheless, the distinction *is* important and its consequences can be seen today. The chiefs [even Muzanenamo Makoni] are in eclipse ... In replacing chiefs with ZANU village and district committees the Government commands the politics of the present. (1982c: 38–9)

Whilst Lan contended:

Of the chairman of the branch committees it is said, *ndimambo zvino*, he is now chief. This does not mean that he is like a chief, or that he is acting as or for the chief. The word *mambo* is applied to anyone who acts with the authority of the ancestors. The old chiefs no longer have this authority. As branch chairmen do, they are the *mambo* of today. (Lan, 1985: 211)

In contrast to chiefs, mediums as hosts of *mhondoro* represented a tradition of resistance. They embodied an age of past chiefs, who were heroes and conquerors at a time of African pre-colonial autonomy, hence they dissociated themselves from patterns of rural land use and conservation which contemporary chiefs were obliged to enforce. Mediums rose in significance to become 'the focus of political action' in Dande. During the war they transferred the legitimating power of their spirits away from their royal descendants onto the guerrillas, who offered a means of return to a more glorious age (Lan, 1985: 136–8; see also Ranger, 1985: 200–2). An alliance was formed between guerrillas and mediums and, as in Makoni, mediums delivered peasant support to guerrillas, believing that a victorious outcome to the armed struggle would mean an end to all discriminatory legislation affecting peasant agriculture and independence. (Lan, 1985: 148)

One obvious explanation for Lan and Ranger's conclusions on the demise of chiefs is their neglect of chiefs who operated as wartime resistance leaders, or mediums who had little sympathy for the nationalist cause (Alexander, 1995: 13). This study has shown that only certain Hwesa mediums delivered the legitimating potential of their cults to the guerrillas. It has also demonstrated that the comrades took an ambiguous stance towards the Hwesa chief, realising, as they did elsewhere, the difficult and compromised position many traditional leaders found themselves in (Daneel, 1991: 15). Nevertheless, guerrillas did make a distinction between traditional leaders and mediums in Katerere. The chief and his headmen were deposed, and mediums like Rukadza were held in great esteem. A dichotomy between chief and medium did exist in the guerrillas' minds, but it was not as totalising as Lan and Ranger contended.

More importantly, this study has shown the need for a reassessment of chieftainship during the colonial period. It is apparent that the stigmatising of chiefs was only a partial reality. Chapter 2 illustrated that chiefs found new sources of power and prestige during the colonial period. One such source was their role in the maintenance of the peasant option against the settler state. Another was their position as representatives and architects of a patriarchal social order which exerted control over women, young men and youth.

But there are other explanations for the different conclusions reached by Lan and Ranger, and this study. In Lan's case there is an important difference of context. In Dande, the prior reality of weak chiefs before the colonial occupation gave him greater cause to argue for a dichotomy between them and mediums (Lan, 1985: chapter 8, esp. 144–5 and 152). There is also the issue of scale. Lan and Ranger both refer to super-tribal spirits such as Mutota, Nehanda and Chaminuka, whilst those in Katerere have a local clientage, and are more entangled in the affairs of the chieftainship. Hwesa *mhondoro* have a strong interest in the chief, acting as his benign ancestors. Once installed he acts as their personally appointed descendant, through whom they exert influence. The idea that the chief and the *mhondoro* are kin is an important one, signified by the fact that when someone becomes a medium the chief pays his father a sum of money, because it is the chief who is now responsible for him. On the medium's death, it is the chief and not the father who is responsible for the burial. Again, it is the chief who supplies the mediums with their ritual para-phernalia. (Gelfand, 1974: 71, 73)

Mediums and their allies continually stressed that chiefs and *mhondoro* worked together. The *mhondoro* passed judgement through the chief. The ancestors informed the chiefs of laws and taboos, and together they made sure that they were enforced. The chief consulted the royal ancestors, because as past chiefs they possessed fecundity and wisdom. Out of respect the chief also convened the appropriate rituals for them. Chiefs and mediums hold together a balanced cosmos. As past and present guardians of the land, chiefs and mediums maintain the trio of morality, just rule, nature and fertility (see Van Binsbergen, 1987: 189). They must, therefore, be in harmony if this dynamic relationship is to be maintained.

The image of maintenance was *kutonhodza pasi* – the cooling of the earth. It was invoked by elders when discussing both the past and present well-being of the chiefdom. In the war, the High God, Karuva, sent birds as signs of danger to the people and the comrades, so that they would not die. The earth was cooled. Immediately after the war the ancestor spirits sent heavy rains. The earth was cooled. When beer was brewed for the *mhondoro* so that they could eat the first fruits of the harvests, the earth was cooled. When a chief was crowned the earth was cooled. Thus together chiefs and mediums bring about a 'cool damp environment', able to sustain good crops, raise livestock and promote human growth. *Chishava* which means 'blood shed' is the opposite of this cooling effect.

To summarise, the oppositional relationship between chief and medium, perceived by Lan and Ranger, is illuminating, but more clarification is needed on its utility. A polarisation between the two is least useful when argued as a process; i.e., on one side of the opposition the mediums gain in authority and legitimacy, and on the other side, the chiefs are stigmatised by their association with the colonial regime. Such a dichotomy is flawed, as the numerous examples of chiefs as wartime resistors and collaborator mediums show. The argument is also called into question by ethnographic evidence from dynasties other than the unique case of the Korekore, where it is possible to create a dichotomy between some *mhondoro*, as symbolic invaders, and chiefs as collaborators. Elsewhere, as in the case of Katerere, it is possible to characterise *mhondoro* as benign ancestors. Here, one can point to the existence of long-standing factions built through the alliance of families of mediums with the incumbent house. Mediums like Rukadza were able to derive authority from such alliances.

The dichotomy between chief and medium does work, however, on the conceptual level, where there are tensions between a medium's transcendental power and a chief's contemporary secular power, and between a higher moral authority of the past and the compromised authority of the present. Incumbent chiefs, like all political leaders, will always be subject to criticism, and where in the past they over-stepped the mark, actively cooperating with the settler state in locations like Dande and Makoni, so mediums made greater dissociative noise.[95]

## CONCLUSION

This chapter has highlighted fascinating sets of continuities and changes in Katerere's contemporary local politics. First, the struggle between male gerontocratic élites is an important internal dynamic in Hwesa social history but one mediated by changing political contexts. In the pre-colonial period, faction leaders' success in part depended on their ability to ally with the leaders of adjacent polities. In contemporary Zimbabwe, a successful faction leader needs to understand bureaucratic power and make connections with local and national party leaders, and civic associations.

Secondly, the chapter highlights the continued importance of local cultural idioms as a means by which Hwesa people conceptualise social and political change. But it is apparent that in their present meaning such idioms have been localised. Whereas, in the past, they were deployed in a territory-wide religious movement of popular mobilisation during the liberation war, they are now involved in a local ethnically based struggle. The exclusive nature of the reassertion of power by Hwesa traditional leaders also further sharpens Hwesa ethnicity.

Thirdly, the pivotal role of mediums in the succession dispute, and other local struggles, represents another continuity or revival. It signals their movement back to the political centre where they were 100 years ago. Of course, the presence of the Zimbabwean state complicates the relationship between chief and medium, but that calls forth another historic function of mediums. In the absence of a chief, the medium mediates between the state and the people. When investigating a succession dispute the District Administration immediately seeks out the legitimating presence of a spirit medium.[96]

However, the succession dispute is not simply about local struggles. Those who operate in the realm of party politics at local, regional and national level have joined the enterprise of reimagining and redefining 'tradition'. In response to the collapse of the party at local level, chiefs, mediums and factional heads have emerged as popular leaders, and local and national leaders court them to safeguard their projects in rural areas, and retain legitimacy.

Finally, one cannot but feel sympathy for the District Administrators, who have to settle succession disputes, hampered with a sense of fair play, and a 'wooden' definition of tradition. For as this study has shown, normative rules of succession along with a ritually supported chief are a construction of the colonial period. In the nineteenth century, 'big men' both gained and retained power through a variety of strategies such as intrigue, magic, connivance with outsiders and use of force, as in the instance of the roasting of Chief Gambiza.

# WITCHES, PROPHETS AND AVENGING SPIRITS: THE SECOND CHRISTIAN MOVEMENT IN KATERERE

## INTRODUCTION

The previous chapter focused on the dynamics of a central feature of the traditional religious system: *mhondoro* cults. It explained their movement back to the centre of the political stage in their current interactions with the Katerere chieftainship, and more widely with the Zimbabwean state. This chapter[1] sets this development of the traditional religious system within a broader context by surveying the dynamics of the wider religious field in Katerere since independence in 1980. In doing so, it shifts the focus onto religious change within Christianity where there has emerged a new sequence of Pentecostal churches which has challenged and transformed not only older churches but also various forms of traditional religion.

In a recent article on religion and witchcraft in everyday life in Zimbabwe, Terence Ranger observed that there has been a tendency to explain contemporary religious phenomena, such as Katerere's new spate of Pentecostal churches, as legacies created by the liberation war. While acknowledging that there was some validity in this position, he argued that new tendencies in Zimbabwean religion needed to be analysed from two further perspectives: first, as the effect of long-term and persistent tensions within rural society; secondly, as responses to the rapid transformations in Zimbabwean rural society since independence (Ranger, 1991b: 155). This chapter takes Ranger's explanatory model as its starting point. By adopting this broader perspective, it illustrates the patterned nature of religious change amongst the Hwesa and their neighbours. As in Central Africa (De Craemer et al., 1976), so in north-east Zimbabwe, Shona religion, both traditional and Christian, is animated by a series of waves of enthusiasm with recurring characteristics. The recent upsurge in Pentecostal activity is the second such movement in recent Hwesa religious history. And both these movements themselves must be located within a trajectory of cyclical religious renewal which, in accordance with De Craemer, Vansina and Fox's classic statement, aims to 'prevent misfortune and maximize good fortune'. (Ibid.: 460)

The chapter illustrates how Katerere's inhabitants have, once again, seized upon Christian beliefs and practices, in response to locally specific conditions, and in the process transformed their own pre-existing religious

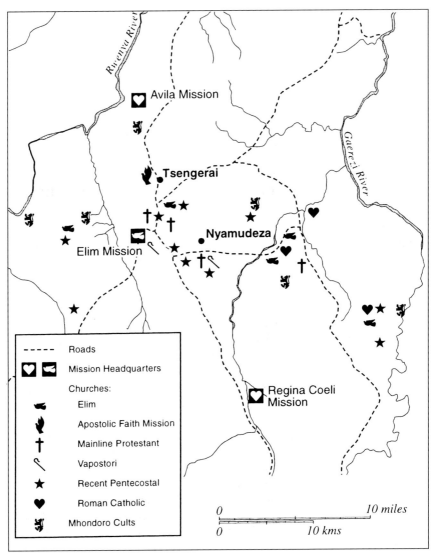

Map 7.1 The Distribution of Churches and *Mhondoro* Cults in Katerere in the late 1980s and 1990s

system. Christian exorcism and demonisation have provided a new means of contesting the authority of patriarchal ancestor religion. Witchcraft eradication movements have been Christianised, and more recently undercut through witch cleansing in Pentecostal churches. Finally, the persistence of Pentecostalism since the 1940s has led to a redefinition of the meaning of possession by abolishing the dichotomy between central and peripheral cults, and created new means of healing in post-war society. These local sources of renewal are all the more important in light of the state's failure to deliver its benefits of independence promised in 1980.

## THE HISTORICAL CONTEXT OF THE SECOND CHRISTIAN MOVEMENT WITH PARTICULAR REFERENCE TO THE POST-WAR DECLINE OF MISSION CHRISTIANITY

This study has demonstrated that the Hwesa religious system was neither static nor closed. Chapter 2 introduced the territory-wide witchcraft eradication movement, Mchape, which swept through the north-east in 1933. Mchape was the first documented instance of renewal in Katerere. To illustrate what they mean by renewal De Craemer, Vansina and Fox list a variable range of goals and values indicative of this collective pursuit of harmony or 'good life': fertility of women; successful hunt; abundant harvest; material wealth and prosperity; to become like a European, to replace Europeans (fight them, expel them); salvation; protection against evil, sorcery or witchcraft. (Ibid.: 467–8)

In 1946 a small group of labour migrants opened up the religious field to new sources of renewal by founding a branch of the Apostolic Faith Mission, a Pentecostal church of western origin, in their village. Five years later these local agents of Christianity facilitated the arrival of Elim Pentecostal missionaries from Ulster. Chapters 3 and 4 illustrated how the founding of Elim mission in 1951 supplanted the village-based Apostolic Faith Movement and brought about the immediate expansion of the zone of popular Pentecostalism in Katerere. Groups comprising, in particular, women, youth, and labour migrants, in alliance with missionaries, destroyed charms and magic and castigated their non-Christian neighbours for their paganism. Rural Pentecostalism had a totalising effect on its adherents. Members of Pentecostal gatherings were encouraged to erect firm boundaries between themselves and the world by abstaining from traditional rituals and practices. Pentecostals were also urged to avoid witchcraft, alcohol, tobacco and crime and many relocated in the vicinity of the mission. Religious polarisation was particularly marked because Pentecostalism 'demonised' the traditional religious opposition. Throughout the 1950s and early 1960s there was an influx of Elim missionaries to staff the mission's growing hospital, schools and churches. But a decade after its founding, Elim had lost its Pentecostal practice: exorcisms and divine healing declined.

In 1962, a Pentecostal church of the indigenous prophetic type, known as the *Vapostori* or Apostles of Johana Marange, established itself in Katerere. It immediately attracted large numbers of adherents due to its willingness to engage in divine healing and exorcism. Although Pentecostals with a clearer descent from First World Pentecostalism contest the *Vapostori's* Pentecostal pedigree, its development from an ambience of missionary Pentecostalism and Methodist revivalism is clear. (Ranger, 1987a: 34; Daneel, 1971: 321, 344)

The emergence of the *Vapostori* reinvigorated Elim's hardened Pentecostal arteries. In the 1970s a young evangelist of *Vapostori* origins, employed by Elim, briefly led a campaign of exorcism amongst church members, whom he contended had lapsed back into the world of the traditional spirits.[2] Yet it appears that even the *Vapostori* lost their Pentecostal vigour. It was no match for a witchcraft eradication movement which swept the north-east in 1976. The mass consumption of anti-witchcraft medicine was accompanied by the widespread popular destruction of ritual objects associated with the practice of sorcery.

From 1976 onwards the north-east was caught up in Zimbabwe's war of liberation. One remarkable and widely documented religious feature of the war was the resacralisation of the ancestors described in Chapter 5. It is this rehabilitation of Katerere's *mhondoro* cults which forms part of the backdrop to the area's second Christian movement, characterised by the proliferation of new Pentecostal churches.

The second immediate background factor influencing the rise of new Pentecostalism was the post-war condition of mission Christianity. The war had been double-edged for missions. The flight and death of expatriate priests and missionaries had brought about brief de-institutionalisation of the rural church and thrown local Christian communities onto their own resources. Some had failed, but those black élites running mission infra-structure maintained a public confession of their faith and found themselves in charge of the stations at the end of the war. In the Catholic case their new-found freedom was short-lived. The state's centralisation, discussed in the previous chapter, was matched by a similar process within the established church. Urban clerics who controlled the ecclesiastical hierarchies seized back both the structure of the church and religious authority from the grass roots (McLaughlin, 1991: Chapter 8). The dynamism exhibited by the local established churches during the war withered away. (Linden, 1991: 4–6)

The rapid Africanisation of mission church leadership also had its down-side with the unexpected outcome of drawing African Christian leaders away from the people. The new zanu/pf government immediately sought to increase black access to health care and education. The missions were to be key players in this strategy and quickly had to crank up services which had either ceased or deteriorated during the war. The widespread suspicion, fed by Zimbabwean nationalism, that mission Christianity had too easily collaborated with colonialism, left black church leaders at a moral disadvantage and gave them little room to contest the ruling party's ideology of development. Avila and Elim's secondary schools had closed down and their hospitals were operating at the level of clinics.[3] Thus, Avila's black nuns and priests and Elim's pastors found themselves, like the missionaries before them, running large institutions with little time to devote to evangelism. The rapid Africanisation of mission leadership also contributed to rural class formation, again leading to the distancing of leaders from their flocks. New responsibilities brought rewards of bigger houses – those vacated by missionaries – access to cars and trucks and larger salaries. Mission pastors and priests, headmasters and teachers, nurses and technical staff joined policemen, store keepers and Agritex workers as members of a rapidly forming rural middle class. Members of this new class often lived in compounds and invested their savings in their homesteads in communal areas, fencing their fields and building brick houses with zinc or asbestos roofs.

Finally, the need to indigenise too rapidly led to costly and time-consuming power struggles. Both Elim and Avila appointed able, but corrupt, men into positions of responsibility, who proved more committed to accumulating at their institutions' expense. Elim's new recruit sought to sell off church property and redirect aid money, and Avila's concentrated on gold panning. Elim's attempts to rectify the situation led to a protracted dispute when Mutare-based MP, Edgar Tekere, and the Provincial Governor, Bishop Dube, were gulled into intervening on the new man's behalf. Aided by the legal advocacy of a former secondary school pupil, the Elim executive resisted party interference and settled the matter through civil action.[4] The rapid untying of missionary 'apron strings'[5] left African mission personnel initially ill-prepared for the exigencies of the 1980s. Nevertheless, the stage was set for a revival of mission Christianity. The vast educational and health infrastructures, which appeared an encumbrance to black mission élites in the early 1980s, increasingly became an asset in the context of declining state provision at the end of the first decade of independence.

## NEW WAVE PENTECOSTALS: A TYPOLOGY

The new Pentecostal churches which appeared in Katerere in the 1980s are: ZAOGA (Zimbabwe Assemblies of God Africa) Mugodhi, Torpiya, Zviratidzo, Rujeko, Borngaes-Njenje and Samanga. A number of the movements have existed for three or more decades but all are new in the sense that they appeared in Katerere after independence. Their memberships describe themselves as Pentecostal. All save Torpiya, whose origins remain uncertain, have clear lines of descent from the western-derived Pentecostal church, the Apostolic Faith Mission.

ZAOGA is markedly different from the other churches and needs to be dealt with separately. It seceded from the Apostolic Faith Mission in 1959 when a zealous band of young men and women centred around Ezekiel Guti, Abel Sande Joseph Choto and Raphael Kupara, fell out with missionaries and an African leadership of elders. The breakaway faction, based in the township of Highfields, subsequently cultivated links with the South African Assemblies of God of Nicholas Bhengu before founding its own constitution in 1967. It modernised through contact with American Pentecostalism in the 1970s and expanded into surrounding African countries. In 1986 ZAOGA movement embarked on a programme of evangelism in Britain. ZAOGA maintains that it is the largest church in Zimbabwe, claiming one million members. More recently ZAOGA expanded into the countryside. In 1989 it was brought to Katerere by labour migrants, working in Harare, who subsequently cooperated with evangelistic teams from the capital in order to expand the movement.[6] In rural locations ZAOGA took on many of the religious forms present in other new wave Pentecostal churches. A striking example of this process of localisation is its evangelistic campaigns. These are accompanied by characteristic deliverances from witches and demonic spirits, and by the destruction of charms and magical substances.

It is possible to generalise about the remaining new wave of Pentecostal churches. Their origins were difficult to discern through fieldwork because their local leaders and members are often extremely vague about, or appear little interested in, questions of their own church history.[7] The Mugodi Apostolic Faith Mission of Kruger was founded in the 1940s after its leader Elijah Mugodi was expelled from the Apostolic Faith Mission for taking a second wife. The inclusion of Kruger in the new church's name was an assertion of authenticity. L. L. Kruger was one of the church's first and most remembered missionaries.[8] The Mugodhi church headquarters are in Wedza in eastern Zimbabwe. Samanga was a village-based gathering founded by a local man who broke away from the Apostolic Faith Mission in 1980. The Samanga church had collapsed by 1989.

Borngaes-Njenje, centred in Murewa in the north-east, is a breakaway movement from Mugodhi founded by a 'prophet' called Njenje. Rujeko was a very local village-based succession from Mugodhi which lasted for just two years, 1990–2. Neither Mugodhi nor Borngaes-Njenje have been able to turn themselves into a bureaucratic urban-based Pentecostal church with international linkages like ZAOGA, and remain regional and predominantly rural. Zviradtidzo and Torpiya are based in the north-east with small gatherings in the capital. Research so far suggests that the former broke away from the '*Vapostori*' (particular movement not specified), whose leaders themselves had connections with the Apostolic Faith Mission (see Chapter 2). Torpiya is said to have come from a 'Methodist Church' (unspecified).[9]

Despite the modest size of much of this new collection of Pentecostal churches in Katerere, they are nevertheless representative of what is commonly called Christian Independency.[10] As Hastings observes: 'if a few larger churches are those most noted by the historian, it is the multitude of tiny groups, breaking off from one another, often with a minimum of knowledge, that continue to dominate the scene in so many places'. (1994a: 534)

The new Pentecostal movement's lack of interest in history has a number of explanations. One is a characteristic of all Pentecostal churches, namely their desire to jump back over history to New Testament times in order to bolster their claims to be truly apostolic. Another explanation is the new Pentecostals' concern to appear authentically African, causing them to de-emphasise links with western movements (Daneel, 1971: 321). This is often combined with a strategy for self-legitimation by means of a spiritualised or mythical story of origin.[11] The desire to indigenise may be but the first part of an ageing process which gradually shifts to an assertion of universal credentials (Hastings, 1994b: 197). Today, ZAOGA, which is one of the older movements, is keen to demonstrate its international standing. A further complicating factor results from the fact that the *Vapostori* perceive these new churches as a great threat. Hence *Vapostori* leaders, like traditional leaders described in the previous chapter, construct myths which claim that all their main rivals are descended from them. The fissions are attributed to the design of the corrupt seceding leader, thus portraying the *Vapostori* as the only legitimate Pentecostal church.[12]

The most important explanation, however, for the Pentecostals' vagueness about the origins of these new movements is that in Katerere the churches are both autonomous and localised. Leaders and a few adherents may travel to a yearly convention, or *pasca*, and evangelistic teams may occasionally visit to lead a campaign, accompanied by Bishops or church dignitaries, who baptise the newly converted, but on the whole the local churches are mostly left to their own devices. All the churches are restricted to one or two villages, like the local founding of the Apostolic Faith Mission in Tsengerai village in 1946.

The localised origins of the new wave of Pentecostal churches are not surprising in light of their continuity with previous patterns of Christianisation in Katerere. Although the *Vapostori* also possess links throughout central and southern Africa, the movement is known in Katerere as the 'Masamvu People', after the local founder, Moses Masamvu. Masamvu was a successful entrepreneur who would marry and then leave the new wife in charge of a store which would become a place of meeting for the church. This study has already shown that, even in its mission form, Pentecostalism was rapidly localised in Katerere.

The process of localisation becomes clearer when it is noted that many of the latest movements were located in, or originated from, the well-established zone of popular Pentecostalism in Katerere. New movements found a fruitful environment there and were rapidly indigenised in a process of cross-fertilisation by new adherents leaving older Pentecostal churches.

In sum, the latest sequence of Pentecostal churches to arrive in Katerere takes on a very different form from the urban Pentecostalism highlighted in work by Paul Gifford (1991, 1994a) and Ruth Marshall (1993). As predominantly rural movements, they are all autonomous, localised and charismatic, usually collected around one or two younger males. By contrast, middle-class[13] urban Pentecostalism is bureaucratic and international (D. Martin, 1993). Whilst middle-class urban Pentecostals exhibit a strong sense of fraternity, perceiving themselves as part of an international community of born-again Christians (Marshall, 1993: 218), rural Pentecostals are fiercely competitive in their struggle for territory, adherents and legitimacy. The countryside is fragmented into segments controlled by rival churches. (D. Martin, 1990: 262)

As a movement, the proliferation of Pentecostal churches proves extremely difficult to quantify. Accurate population figures for Katerere do not exist and it is difficult to arrive at a figure of those absent in the cities. Nevertheless research[14] conducted in April and May 1993 in the area between Avila and Elim missions found that the new Pentecostal churches comprised about 16 per cent of total church membership. However, of the remaining 84 per cent which represented churches established prior to 1980, as much as 52 per cent belonged to older Pentecostal churches, predominantly Elim, but also the Apostolic Faith Mission, Church of Christ and the *Vapostori*. But the above survey can only be used to illustrate broad trends. It was difficult to ascertain figures of church membership which allow for comparison between churches. Whilst the established churches had membership cards and kept baptismal and attendance registers, these may well not have represented the actual number of regular adherents. In contrast, a simple head count at a weekly service, the only option for the new churches, was likely to be more representative of actual membership. The material benefits offered by the area's two mission churches may also have exaggerated the level of their membership by committed adherents.

The problem of measuring the strength of the new Pentecostal movement is further compounded by the rapidly changing fortunes of the churches. Membership can fluctuate quite dramatically, and congregations can rise and fall in a matter of a few years. Thus the figures given above for membership of the new churches do not include Samanga and Rujeko, both of which grew to a considerable size before collapsing in 1989 and 1992 respectively. The fluidity of the movements is well illustrated by a young (Catholic) female student's account of another Pentecostal church which established itself just south of Katerere:

> Many churches were introduced after independence which elders joined. The most well known was called *Matenga Zvakazvarurwa*

(Heavens are Opened). When this started there was an influx of young and older people. The leader of the church pretended to perform miracles, and he even said that he could heal the blind, lame and deaf. Hearing this, many people went to him giving him cattle and large sums of money. He only pretended to do some miracles, but none was healed. The way they danced and sang were real pulling factors especially to young people.

After deceiving people he just disappeared and the people remained with their great anger. The church then split and joined other churches.[15]

Indeed, fluidity seems to be a defining characteristic of the new Pentecostal movement. The churches have no central place of worship, gathering at a number of sites, usually under shady trees in the vicinity of the leader's or his members' village. The imagery of a people on pilgrimage is central to the adherent's identity. The taboos or Levitical-style purity laws which give the movement its distinctive flavour find their biblical basis in a series of commands attributed to Israelites during their wilderness experience. Doubtless the churches have the same function of providing Pentecostals with an identity among alien – pagan – peoples.[16]

Despite the modest figures of adherence for new wave Pentecostals recorded in a snap-shot head count, it will be argued that their impact far exceeds their numerical size. Numerous people outside the movement have come into contact with it through curiosity, witnessing its night dances or vigils, or experiencing its aggressive style of evangelism. Moreover, although its numerical size is currently small, the movement is expanding, and more new churches have appeared than disappeared since 1988. However, the best measure of its impact is not figures of church adherence but the sheer intensity of the debates which it creates in schools, churches, and amongst elders participating in 'traditional' religion, particularly *mhondoro* cults. The core of this debate is new wave Pentecostalism's critique both of traditional religion and of other forms of Christianity.

The first wave of scholarship explaining rural Pentecostalism (Christian Independency), dismissed it as syncretistic, a mixing of Christian and tradi-tional religion.[17] For instance, scholars pointed to the similarity between a Christian prophet's use of sanctified objects, symbolic of God's protective powers, and a traditional healer's charms. However, such interpretations of these Pentecostal churches confuse their origins – First World counter-establishment Christianity – with their appeal, and their form with their content. Pentecostal churches may borrow from traditional practices, but their borrowing is recoded when located within a Christian system of ideas, and hence it takes on a new form and significance.

Fundamentally, Pentecostalism and traditional religion are at odds with each other. Conversion to Pentecostal Christianity is followed by a total immersion baptism, symbolising rebirth. Furthermore it is often associated with the destruction of things 'traditional'. Traditional religious leaders are more vitriolic about Pentecostal churches than any other type.

If the concept of syncretism is to have any value at all, then it must first be extended to all the elements within the religious field. There is movement and borrowing between them all. For example, we have noted in Chapter 1 how the medium, Rukadza, appears to have embellished his account of the High God, Karuwa, by borrowing Judaeo-Christian concepts of God gleaned from a nearby mission. We have also seen Elim drawing inspiration for revival from the *Vapostori*. But even within Katerere, religious movements and institutions engage in heated debate concerning religious hybridity from the standpoint of syncretism or anti-syncretism. It is more productive to view these local contestations, and the first wave of scholarship on African Pentecostalism which likewise emanated from a committed religious position,[18] as a form of cultural politics.[19] But syncretism does not explain the origins of these new movements, and explanation for them must be sought elsewhere. The first place to enquire is in past continuities.

## NEW PENTECOSTAL CHURCHES AND THE REVIVAL OF OLD TENSIONS

The first means of explaining the rise of new Pentecostal churches is in terms of continuities. They are a perpetuation of gender, generational and ethnic struggles which have raged in Katerere throughout this century, and which were first made explicit to the Hwesa with the arrival of the Apostolic Faith Mission in the 1940s. The new churches are also the Christian heirs of older witchcraft eradication movements. These assertions rest on a number of propositions implicit in the initial narrative section of this chapter. The first proposition derives from the observation that the Christian movement in Africa often began as youth and/or women's movements (Sundkler, 1987: 83). This is because Christianity represented a better option for them. To young men it provided the opportunity to break free from traditional commensality (Schoffeleers, 1985: 33) and set up their own household; for women and youth the church offered a domain where they were relatively free from the tutelage of elder males. This is not, for one moment, to contend that *all* members of the same social category acted in unison or had an identical set of interests. This study has clearly shown that individuals had multiple identities of status, gender, ethnicity, and moved between different institutions and ideologies. The proposition merely asserts that Christianity offered members of these social categories the opportunity to reformulate social relationships in ways that were more conducive to their interests. Moreover, the potentiality of Pentecostal Christianity for women and youth exceeded that of other Christian movements. This was because it fundamentally challenged patriarchal religion through the idiom of exorcism which is elevated to a central position in Pentecostal practice.[20]

The second proposition is that Pentecostal churches can lose their Pentecostal vigour. In a similar manner to the way established and non-conformist churches experience charismatic renewal, the process can be reversed. This occurs for three interrelated reasons. First, churches are vulnerable to bureaucratisation. As inspirational movements, they 'lose their ecstatic fervour and harden into ecclesiastical establishments' (Lewis, 1989: 156) where legitimacy is no longer a matter of possessing the charismatic authority of the Holy Spirit, but is based on ritual and dogma.[21] Secondly, Pentecostal churches are particularly affected by the process of 'ageing' (Iliffe, 1979: 359). The young men who often found and comprise the core of Pentecostal churches eventually become elders themselves. Now ironically threatened by Pentecostalism's egalitarian potential, whereby revelation through the Holy Spirit is universal, they introduce authoritarian and hierarchical government into their churches. As such, they resurrect and reconstruct pre-Christian patterns of male gerontocratic authority (D. Martin, 1990: 231). Third, Pentecostals gradually adapt to the fact that their brethren have remained in idolatry and the church goes cold. A sequence of Pentecostal churches emerges as older bureaucratic or gerontocratic gatherings are challenged by newer more vigorous Pentecostal movements.

The stage was set for a second Christian movement on the dawn of independence. Elim had already bureaucratised in the 1960s, and the brief revival in the early 1970s indicated that many church members had returned to idolatry. Moreover the liberation war had closed off five of the mission's out-stations leaving space for new movements. The war had left a new African leadership but they were now patriarchs in their own right, albeit Christian ones. They discouraged renewal, fearing that they would lose control. Theirs was a logical response to the universalising of authority which can accompany such movements (Ter Haar, 1992: 196). Elim's loss of Pentecost was popularly characterised in a number of ways: some claimed that the deacons did not have the Holy Spirit, whilst others said that the demons cast out by Elim in its early days were now returning. The issue was widely discussed in Elim's conventions, its schools and churches. The other main Pentecostal force in Katerere, the *Vapostori* of Marange, also became dominated by an elder male faction who had drawn from its entrepreneurial ethic and thrived as local businessmen. Although it did not lose its pentecost – signs and wonders continued – its potentiality for women and youth could no longer be realised. In response to the emergence of Christian patriarchs, and a more widespread post-war revival of rural patriarchy, as discussed in the last chapter, groups comprising women and the next generation of young men founded the latest sequence of Pentecostal churches.

Pentecostal churches are popularly perceived as being churches of women and youth. But such a perception appears to have little to do with the proportion of these social categories attending the churches relative to other groups such as elder men and women. The first reason for the strong association of women and youth with the new Pentecostal movement is that members of these social categories were its founders. Women and youth had less of a stake in the old order and were more willing to break away and challenge it.

The second reason is the Pentecostals' explicit challenge to patriarchal religion. Their contest with male-dominated ancestor cults occurs in graphic ways. Not only are all traditional spirits demonised, but a struggle takes place for control of the spiritual landscape. The contest usually concerns holy mountains.[22] For traditionalists, these are associated with *mhondoro* spirits as they are the burial sites of past chiefs. For Pentecostals they are a place of pilgrimage, fasting and prayer. The brash young leader of Mugodhi explained: 'We go there to challenge them. Suppose they say "that mountain is holy" and we don't go, they will be challenging. We go to the mountain to prove them wrong and demand they repent.'[23] The traditional response is condemnation. Katerere's leading *mhondoro* medium, Rukadza, announced: 'It seems as if they have no rules at all. They just climb mountains as if they are mad people ... They have a quarrelsome disposition and even live where they are prohibited ...'[24] The medium's remarks mark a struggle between young men and elders for land and political power.

The success of Pentecostals in founding zones of popular Christianity is illustrated by the changing nature of power relations between them and traditional religious authorities over the last 40 years (see Maps 4.1 and 7.1). Whilst a number of *mhondoro* cults active in the liberation war have success-fully responded to their post-war demobilisation through participation with royal factions in local politics, they *have*, nonetheless, experienced a decline relative to Christianity. The decrease of *mhondoro* cults can be explained by the diminishing appeal of an existence tied to the land or state assumption of resource management. But the steps taken by guerrillas to move mediums out of zones of popular Christianity during the war (see Chapter 5) suggest that there was a perception shared by peasants and freedom fighters alike of the efficacy of Pentecostalism in providing good fortune and doing away with witchcraft and affliction, and hence undercutting cults of the land. Today the most active *mhondoro* cults operate in the marginal areas of Katerere, and in zones of Catholic missionisation where they are allowed to co-exist with Catholics.

New Pentecostalism also engenders intense generational struggles within the household. Children accuse parents of bringing bad spirits into the home and relocate without permission. Pentecostal night dances, which cause youth to remain away from home all night, are a further challenge to adult authority. Along with the traditionalists, the established churches condemn the new Pentecostal churches for engendering 'mischievousness' in youth.[25] In this light, the new Pentecostal churches' taboos on beer and tobacco are as much an assault on symbols of elder male spirituality as they are a positive affirmation of abstinence.

Women and youth benefit from this contest with male ancestor religion. In Pentecostal churches, possession by the Holy Spirit is open to all members. Although the leaders are young married males, they have no monopoly on revelation.[26] Women and youth can prophesy, heal and testify within the loosely structured framework of the service. The status and sense of empowerment in healing, and the struggle against witchcraft and affliction gained by some adherents of the new Pentecostal churches, spilled over into Elim mission, bringing with it a desire for revival as well as concern from church leaders regarding the activities of schoolboy prophets.

Although the new Pentecostal gatherings are characterised as places of debauchery and sexual immorality by the elders in neighbouring churches, new Pentecostal adherents profess to have a highly structured set of rules which attempt to discipline their body and speech, and control their sexuality. As Schoffeleers observes (1985: 33), such codes of conduct are not so much decreed by the male leaders as demanded by the membership. Thus fidelity and sexual loyalty benefit women on the receiving end of a migrant labour system. In a similar vein, women and youth gain materially from the eradication of drunkenness in husbands and fathers. The church gathering, usually a tight local community, maintains itself in a state of purity. The rules are enforced by prophets with an ear to the ground, who compel backsliders to confess and repent. The collapse of the Samanga Church in 1989 occurred because the leader transgressed these codes of conduct. Pentecostalism's emphasis on the discipline of the body, of speech, and of sexuality is one of its most salient features. (Marshall, 1993)

The new Pentecostal churches also appeal to women as sources of witchcraft cleansing. As outsiders in a patrilineal society, women bear the brunt of witchcraft accusation. Instead of having to partake of the dangerous *muteyo* – poison – ordeal, or be shunned, they can confess, be exorcised and reintegrated into the community.

The issue of witchcraft eradication brings us to the last continuity which the new Pentecostal churches embody. In the final chapter of her book, *Zimbabwe's Guerrilla War. Peasant Voices*, Norma Kriger interprets the immediate post-war witchcraft eradication movement led by the Tanzanian 'witch finder', Mataka, as a product of 'short-lived, peasant divisions such as between those who contributed to guerrillas and those who fled the rural areas' (1992: 236). This interpretation has two flaws. First, it limits the potential of post-war healing and reconciliation, considered below. Secondly, Kriger tends to interpret witchcraft as a *purely* functional phenomenon, thus ignoring the real fear of witchcraft in local societies. Witchcraft is not merely an idiom through which members of a community negotiate social stress. Individuals *do* practise sorcery, buying medicines in order to gain an advantage over their relations or neighbours, or to gain protection from them. The cost of witchcraft accusation within a community can become too high. In such circumstances, public demand arises for an alternative means to redress fears of sorcery. Eradication movements are movements of absolution operating at communal level, and those who participate in the rituals, particularly the imbibing of a medicine, are cleansed of witchcraft.

This study has outlined a trajectory of witchcraft eradication movements which have traversed the north-east of Zimbabwe.[27] In 1976 a movement, which according to aged informants had many resonances of Mchape, swept the region. In this movement, led by a man called Makombe, individuals were compelled, on fear of sudden death, to bring out their horns and charms for destruction. The Mataka movement in Mutoko should also be located within this trajectory. Kriger, however, appears unaware of Mataka's antecedents, both of which operated in Mutoko.[28]

It is also possible to trace this trajectory of witchcraft eradication into the sequence of Pentecostal churches which have arisen since independence. Witchcraft eradication has increasingly become a Christian idiom. When the Mchape agents entered the north-east of Rhodesia in the 1930s, they found scant Christian tradition with which a more Christianised message could resonate.[29] This was not true for the second movement led by Makombe in the 1970s. Although informants stress that a good deal of the praise and adulation of Makombe's campaigns was directed at himself, hymns and prayers were also directed to God, especially intercessions for the sick.[30] Moreover, the spatial design of the service, a near complete circle, with an opening marked by the presence of two choirs, through which attendants had to pass, resembles the lay-out of certain Apostolic services such as their *penta* – communion.[31]

By tracing this trajectory of increasingly Christianised eradication movements into the 1980s and 1990s, Mugodhi and Torpiya can be interpreted as heirs of Makombe. They should be strictly characterised as *cleansing* rather than eradication movements because they deal with a multitude of individual cases and their cure is not collectively administered; however, they were certainly more communal in their founding stages when whole villages gathered together to witness a new spectacle. Nevertheless, as sources of witchcraft cleansing, their existence undercuts the possibility of witchcraft eradication movements. In Pentecostal services, women who have inherited witchcraft can be exorcised of evil spirits, and those who practise sorcery can bring their magic for destruction before being baptised. Accusations of, or conscious lapses into, witchcraft can be overcome through continued acts of confession.

## PENTECOSTALS AND SPIRIT POSSESSION

Although Pentecostalism overtly divided the religious field along gender, generational and ethnic lines, it only made explicit tensions which were already inherent in rural society (see also Schoffeleers, 1985: 38). Prior to the arrival of Christianity in Katerere in the 1940s, a large number of Hwesa and Barwe women were involved in *shave* possession cults. Since independence, many women have become involved in *ngozi* cults, and like those possessed by *shave* spirit (Lan, 1985: 38), they operate in a sphere distinct from ancestor religion. Much to the chagrin of ancestor spirits and their hosts, adherents of *ngozi* cults express their participation by hanging bright red cloths around their homestead.[32] However, since their arrival in Katerere in the 1940s, Pentecostal churches have become increasingly effective rivals with, and challenges to, possession cults in quotidian struggles against changing popular conceptions of evil. Much of Pentecostalism's appeal can be attributed to the manner in which it redefines the meaning of possession.

In his classic, *Ecstatic Religion*, Ioan Lewis distinguishes between two types of possession: central and peripheral. The former concerns spirits and hosts who are at the 'centre of the stage in the religious life of society and play a crucial, and direct role in sanctioning customary morality' (1989: 119). The cult leaders are usually the powerful elements within a society, i.e. elderly men. A *mhondoro* cult is a good example of a central possession cult in the Zimbabwean context. The second category of possession cults are peripheral in three senses: first, the spirits are not involved in upholding a hegemonic morality code; secondly, the spirits are not ancestors but outsider spirits; and lastly, the members are men, women and youth, peripheral to the centre of power in society (Ibid.: 27). Lewis argues that, because the possessed medium can behave anti-socially and make social statements with impunity (Ibid.: 105–6), peripheral possession cults as such can be interpreted as an indirect strategy of attack on male authority and male-dominated religion.

Lewis's model is open to substantial modifications, particularly in his conceptualisation of centrality and marginality. This study has shown that women are at the centre of the domestic sphere, exercising control over reproduction and labour. Moreover, elderly Hwesa women play a key role in the politics of the chieftainship, holding factions together through marriage alliances, and guarding their oral traditions. In another sense, David Martin has argued that whole societies or regions are marginal to political and religious establishments and take religious options, be they non-conformist or later Pentecostal, which both reflect and challenge that marginality (D. Martin, 1990: 275–7). Turning to possession itself, Richard Werbner's work on the Kalanga of southern Africa reveals a high incidence of demonic possession amongst élite women who, by virtue of their social position, are able to act, when possessed, as 'foci for strategic action in the management of intimacy and trust in kinship relations'. (Werbner, 1989: 81)

Although it can easily be demonstrated that those who Lewis would classify as marginal have status in their own sphere of influence (Boddy, 1989: 138–9), this does not completely rule out the interpretation of possession as a means of ameliorating an inferior social position. Despite her brilliant critique of Lewis's work, Janice Boddy still concedes that 'status may be a consideration' (Ibid.). Matthew Schoffeleers, who conducted research in a rural community similar to Katerere, identified (1985: 10) a steep increase in possession rituals in the period 1940–70, when cotton growing almost collapsed and labour migration was becoming one of the principal means of earning an income. This led to a serious deterioration in the position of women who became more dependent on their husbands' remittances as local sources of income, which offered greater financial independence from men, diminished. Schoffeleers concluded:

> Lewis may well have overstated his case ... it would be incorrect to see male dominance as the sole source of possession ... Even so, the increase of ... [a] husband-related type of possession during the 1940–1970 period was such that the conclusion we have arrived at seems to impose itself with some force. (Ibid.: 41–2, footnote 27)

It is clear that marginality is not fixed to specific social categories but is experienced by members of different social groups in different contexts. This study has highlighted the social and economic deterioration of the position of Hwesa women in north–east Zimbabwe, 1920–50, as their husbands were drawn into the migrant labour economy and the local subsistence economy declined, and has noted the high level of female adherence to *shave* possession cults in that period. We have also seen that since independence in 1980 many youth and women have become marginalised from the communal political process[33] as a male gerontocratic élite has reasserted itself. Pentecostalism appears to be another means to redress this experience of marginality.

The entrance of Pentecostal Christianity into Katerere in 1946 via labour migrants adhering to the Apostolic Faith Mission, followed by the arrival of Elim Pentecostal missionaries in 1951, brought about the swift movement into the new church of many women who had previously been possessed by *mashave* spirits. Their change of allegiance was marked by the destruction of religious paraphernalia associated with the cult, and its demonisation in a similar manner to the Pentecostal response to *mhondoro* cults. Katerere's second Christian movement is a similar response to marginality.

The similarities between possession cults and Pentecostal churches have been commented upon by numerous scholars of African religion. Both share a common appeal, seeking spiritual empowerment in order to combat evil. The similarities between the two religions have also been commented upon by scholars researching beyond Africa. Writing on the spread of Evangelical churches in South America, David Martin describes (1993: 114) how Pentecostalism 'takes fire among the tangled brushwood of innumerable cults of the spirits'.

Martin argues that South American possession cults 'embodied symbols of resistance to established religion and the wider social system, which Pentecostalism subsequently renews' (Ibid.). Thus where Catholicism became the new established religion in Mexico, supplanting a traditional one, Pentecostalism emerged as its critique. Numerous scholars have noted Pentecostalism's counter-establishment origins and its counter-cultural potential (Jean Comaroff, 1985: 177–84; Hollenweger, 1972: 457–61). But Martin's analysis is based on the Latin American context where Catholic religious monopolies are disintegrating. In Africa, Pentecostalism thrives in an environment of religious pluralism and can assume a variety of positions within the religious field. In Katerere it arrived *before* Catholicism and orthodox Protestant churches, and hence became, *in its mission form*, a local establishment religion.

It is more plausible to suggest that, rather than directly renewing the resistance potential of possession cults, Pentecostalism in this context redefines the meaning of possession.[34] Chapter 3 introduced Terence Ranger's persuasive argument that Pentecostal Christianity has redefined the meaning of local perceptions of disease by abolishing the dichotomy between diseases of man and diseases of God. In a similar vein, Pentecostalism has redefined the meaning of possession by abolishing the dichotomy between peripheral and central cults. Although Pentecostalism is peripheral in the sense that it empowers those on the margins of society, it is central because its adherents are possessed by a single universal spirit of primary importance – the Holy Spirit.

As a redefined form of possession, Pentecostalism poses an extremely effective challenge to 'traditional' possession cults, both central and peripheral. The demonising *mhondoro* cults have enabled certain young men to ignore their demands for traditional commensality, and decrees on where to live. Lewis himself observes the limitations of peripheral possession cults. He argues (1989: 114) that they only offer the host a temporary remission, rather than a lasting change in social relations. Indeed, possession can be costly. Two informants, both traditional healers possessed by the *ngozi* spirits, spoke with regret of the injury their spirits had caused them in the primary phase of possession, and of the fact that their husbands expected them to earn money as diviners.[35] Pentecostals have their own critique of possession cults. Some complained that they damaged the family, either through the physical injury they caused, or their ability to sow discord by apportioning blame for past events. Others disapproved of the financial drain brought about by the appeasement of the spirits.

Christian women in particular offered a set of criticisms which hinged on their experience of patrilocal exogamous marriage. This had brought them, as wives, into a spirit world with which they had no familiarity, and over which they had little control. They complained that the ancestor spirits that they had to brew beer for, were not 'their spirits'.[36] In contrast, possession by the Holy Spirit means that these women are no longer cosmologically represented as strangers or aliens but belong to a universal community. These Christian women also pointed out that the latest wave of possessing spirits which generally took women as hosts were usually the result of *male* violence and jealousy.[37] The appeasement of *ngozi* spirits was a particular grievance to women, because it often involved the gift of a young girl to the family of the murdered victim.[38]

Although a new form of possession, Pentecostalism's appeal is enhanced by the fact that it is able to resonate with the popular understanding of the mechanics of 'traditional' cults. This becomes apparent, for example, in Gerrie Ter Haar's account of the charismatic ministry of exorcism and healing of the Zambian prelate, Archbishop Milingo:

> In response to the oppression by evil which so many people experienced, Milingo introduced the Holy Spirit as a possessing spirit to replace evil ones: he literally tried to 'fill' people with the Holy Spirit. (Ter Haar, 1992: 129)

New wave Pentecostals in Katerere also used this imagery of filling and emptying when describing Christian exorcism.

The impact of Pentecostal and evangelical Christianity's synthesis with 'pre-Christian' (traditional) religion is seen in the redefinition of the latter. In Katerere, Pentecostalism's redefinition of possession cults has transformed the perceptions of many youth and second-generation Pentecostals. These groups can no longer distinguish between specific types of spirits, whether benign or malevolent, within Shona cosmology. All such spirits are now branded *mademoni* – demons – and must be exorcised. For these adherents, the idea of coming to terms with the spirit no longer appears an option.

As a new form of possession, Pentecostalism is not only safer and less costly, it also represents a more complete break with the traditional social setting (Lewis, 1989: 115). Because its recent proliferation is a threat to the religious establishment, both traditional and Christian, it is not surprising that the establishment's rejected religious officials discredit new Pentecostals. Established church leaders depict them as syncretistic and, together with traditional leaders, accuse them of corruption and sexual immorality. *Mhondoro* mediums, their acolytes and allies, seem to have been caught off-guard by the aggression of the new Pentecostals. One medium spoke of the confusion they caused,[39] another elder suggested that their arrival signalled the end of the world.[40] Such images of order being turned to chaos are reminiscent of those used by mediums to express their disapproval concerning the empowerment of youth during the liberation war.[41]

The advent of Pentecostal Christianity in Katerere in the 1940s led to an erosion of *mashave* cults. Today, the drums used to summon the spirit are rarely heard.[42] The decline of this cult was caused by the spate of exorcisms which accompanied the founding of a popular Pentecostalism. It is probably also accounted for by an indirect factor associated with missionisation. The arrival of western bio-medicine with the missions immediately led to a decrease in infant mortality. According to Boddy (1989: 156) this would cause women to have less need to seek solace in the 'counter reality' of possession. However, although *mashave* cults have declined, other cults of affliction have risen in prominence to replace them. As illustrated below, *chikwambo* and *ngozi* are particularly prevalent, and the new Pentecostalists devote much attention to combating them. The notion of exorcism has transformed the possibilities available for those living in rural Zimbabwe.

### PENTECOSTALISM AND THE LEGACIES OF THE LIBERATION WAR

A significant legacy of the war was the trauma caused by the memories and experiences of the war's violence. The most important work on the subject to date is Richard Werbner's *Tears of the Dead. The Social Biography of an African Family* (1991). Werbner focuses on the region of Matabeleland, which was not only affected by the liberation war, but also by a murderous civil war which only ended in December 1987. Werbner describes popular sentiment on the civil war's cessation:

> There was a widespread experience of senseless loss and anxious bereavement, often due to kin dying in atrocities without decent burial or wakes. It was well known that there were mass graves into which people had disappeared, leaving no trace for their kin. The need to be cleansed from wartime acts of violence was also widely felt ... (1991: 186–7)

Pamela Reynolds has shown that the popular demand for post-war healing, described by Werbner, is also present in the east.[43]

The definition of healing is problematic. Borrowing from Jean Comaroff, Schoffeleers provides a very wide definition: 'the totality of activities and ideas [meant] to reconstitute physical, social and spiritual order'.[44] In the context of discussion of post-war reconstruction, this definition has a dangerous potential. This chapter has illustrated that phenomena which male elders represent as disorder may represent social advancement for women and youth. Healing can mean the return of élites to power. It is wiser, at least in our context, to seek a more limited definition, such as 'the totality of activities and ideas which help both individuals and the wider community to come to terms with the experience of violence and bereavement caused by war, in a manner which allows them to continue their daily existence'. The recipients of such healing must pursue or accept it freely in order for it to work. Coercion will only cause further wounds. Although this latter definition avoids the restoration of the pre-war order, movements of healing can constitute a new order. The need for a diagnosis, and the pronouncement of a cure, puts the client in a subordinate power relation to the healer. The healer thus derives authority and power through his or her work. Hence it is hardly surprising that there is competition in and across the religious field in meeting popular demands for healing.

The range of post-war demands for healing was wide. Healers, both traditional and Christian, helped ex-combatants from both sides to come to terms with their memories of violence, and often with their sense of guilt. Parents were directed on how they were to mourn their children who had not returned from the fighting. (For more detail see Maxwell, 1994: 360–2)

But in the late 1980s and early 1990s, the greatest spiritual legacy amongst civilians occurs at an inter-family level. This is the crisis of *ngozi* – avenging spirits. Numerous informants described how, upon the war's cessation, their village was plagued by angry spirits of the dead who had been killed after being falsely accused by neighbours of being a witch or a sell-out:

> After the war many bad things started to happen ... There are avenging spirits of people who were murdered for no justifiable reason. Many people were killed during the war for no reason.
>
> Those unjustly killed [during the war] came out as spirits against those who had ordered the comrade to kill them ... There was much guilt after the war.[45]

*Ngozi* is the most feared of all spirits amongst the Shona. As the spirit of someone unjustly killed, improperly buried, or mistreated when alive, it is believed to kill members or descendants of the offending family before revealing its identity. Through a host in the offending family it demands that fines be paid to its kin in the form of money or cattle, and often a young girl (see Bourdillon, 1987a: 233–5). As noted above, coming to terms with an *ngozi* is costly, not only for the host, but also for the offending family. Hence many have sought an alternative option – its exorcism by one of the new wave Pentecostal churches.[46] Indeed, the Mugodhi Church, which emerged just after independence in Katerere, comes into its own in response to the crisis of *ngozi*. Its leader described the symptoms of many of his clients:

> Some men and women start crying alone, others act[ed] as if they are cooking sadza, others try to take things and run with them. They pretend to have guns implying that [the person with] that spirit died

whilst performing that act. Old women crawl like guerrillas when possessed ... by bad spirits and men have to restrain them ...[47]

He claimed to have exorcised numerous *ngozi*. The Torpiya church also appears to meet this need, and those with the ministry of casting out demons wear a white robe and red belt.[48]

It is important to stress that though leaders of churches like Torpiya and Mugodhi claim ability in this type of exorcism, the process is not always successful. Indeed, the avenging spirit can sometimes win in a power encounter with a Christian exorcist. Moreover, ordinary members of Torpiya and Mugodhi, and other new churches like Rujeko, claimed that someone could only join the church after having dealt with an *ngozi* in the appropriate traditional manner. Whilst exorcism increases the range of responses open to families visited by an avenging spirit, it is clear that many, even some older established Pentecostals, prefer the traditional means of redress. *Ngozi* cults memorialise the dead through the agency of the living, providing their families with the opportunity to grieve and mourn their loss. Often in the war the families of 'sell-outs' were unable publicly to attend to their dead for fear that they too would be cast as sell-outs.[49] Moreover, the *ngozi* host, along with a traditional healer, is in a prime position to mediate between the two families involved, and thus bring about reconciliation and restitution. Finally, many informants including Christians, expressed the view that fear of *ngozi* acted as a deterrent to those contemplating murder.

It is difficult to measure how widespread and effective post-war movements of healing have been, but it is important to emphasise that, just as there are limits to the Pentecostals' powers of healing, there are limits to the whole process itself. All informants involved in healing stressed the need for confession to make the process work. Often the perpetrators of past violence, or their families, are not in the community so direct restitution cannot work. Some tensions caused by the war still run deep in rural society, as victims of violence are forced to live with neighbours who have wronged them but have made no attempt at reconciliation. Many who have found no satisfaction have moved away, whilst others, having no opportunity to leave, remain with the tensions.

The war also left other more tangible legacies which explain the rise of new Pentecostal churches. We have seen that it was double-edged with respect to mission Christianity. Those who remained committed Christians experienced great empowerment, and on the war's cessation found new responsibilities. But the war also had many costs, leaving gaps in mission services. The running down of mission hospitals meant that, once again in Katerere, bio-medicine was a long way off. The new Pentecostal churches which practise divine healing, through the laying on of hands or the use of holy water, were an obvious compensation. Furthermore, the initial collapse of bio-medical care in rural areas after the war led to increases in infant mortality rates. The death of children remains one of the pretexts for witchcraft accusation (see Ranger, 1991b: 161). Below, it will be illustrated how the new Pentecostal churches can supplant the traditional healer in mediating such allegations.

### WITCHES AND PROPHETS: NEW WAVE PENTECOSTALISM AND SOCIAL TRANSFORMATION SINCE INDEPENDENCE

The proliferation of Pentecostal churches in Katerere must also be explained in terms of more contemporary social processes, in particular the popularly perceived rise in witchcraft accusation since 1980.

Having argued above that Kriger has been overly functionalist in her explanation of witchcraft, this does not mean that such a model of explanation has no utility. However, it is doubtful that the rise in witchcraft accusation, which continued throughout the 1980s, can be explained, as Kriger does (1992: chapter 6), in terms of short-term conflicts created by the war. Although tensions created by the war may be a consideration, the persistence of witchcraft accusation through the first decade of Zimbabwe's independence can be better explained by the rapid social transformations which the country has experienced.

Witchcraft accusation *can*, in part, be viewed functionally as an idiom through which members of tightly-knit societies mediate conflict. The incidence of accusation thus becomes a barometer of social stress. There is a danger, however, that such an approach does not reveal very much about rural societies besides the fact that they experience internal conflict. Thus witchcraft accusation needs to be historicised, and increases in its frequency explained in terms of the changing context of rural societies.

Since independence, Katerere has experienced a rapid increase in differentiation, as some families reaped the benefit of high urban income whilst others experienced unemployment, particularly the youth. This differential access to remittances also transformed the possibilities for pro-ductive farming, because the initial acquisition of livestock, grain, plough, etc. depended upon a cash income. New sources of differentiation also emerged within rural society itself. The expansion of health, educational and Agritex staff created a rural salariat (Scoones and Wilson, 1988: 34). The arrival of the party (ZANU/PF) also created new sources of power, status and patronage, or exaggerated existing power relations where recipients were already established rural patriarchs. (Alexander, 1993: chapter 9; De Wolf, 1996: 66, chapter 6 *passim*)

This social differentiation has led to an increase in witchcraft accusation. Informants spoke of a 'spirit of jealousy', elaborating how jealous neighbours and relatives have put spells on them. One man offered examples of how the spirit worked:

My relatives can become jealous when I have more wealth than them and they go get magic from the *n'ganga* and will later send bad spirits to me. The idea will be that of killing me or destroying my wealth ...
Q. Are there also bad spirits between neighbours?
A. Yes [for example] that man up there ... has a car. I do not have a car and a good house. I may hate him because he may seem to be proud and live luxuriously like a *murungu* [white man]. Consequently I may send spirits to such a neighbour.

Informants also often mentioned *chikwambo*, a spirit associated with unpaid debts.[50]

Martinus Daneel observes that the Marange church has never concentrated on the removal of medicine and horns from homesteads considered bewitched, unlike other Apostolic-type Pentecostal churches. Current *Vapostori* leaders explain this by the fact that the removal of horns may lead to direct accusations of witchcraft and the possibility of prosecution. Instead, like some of the new Pentecostal churches, they detect those who practise sorcery and offer confession to those who have inherited witchcraft. (Daneel, 1971: 325)

However, Pentecostal churches like Rujeko actively engage in witchcraft accusation. One member of this church was obsessed by fear of witchcraft. His six daughters remained unmarried causing him to believe that he was the victim of sorcery. In interview, he spoke of relatives who had sent horns of magic in the wind into his roof (see also Auslander, 1993: 178); he took a stick and scraped some small coins from the earth surrounding his hut. Fearing to touch them, he explained that they contained dangerous magic; he awaited a prophet who would come and remove them, and reveal who had put them there. In Mugodhi church a prophet, in similar manner to a traditional healer, will remove *zvitsinga* – bones or charms placed inside someone by a witch.[51]

The presence of the state in the countryside has indirectly stimulated the proliferation of new Pentecostal churches. Its piecemeal support for peasant agriculture and channelling of development money through a male gerontocratic élite has led some families to prosper whilst others have not benefited. Pentecostal churches have responded to the social effects of rural differentiation. However, the question arises: do the new Pentecostal churches have any direct relation to the state in terms of responding to its agendas?

The previous chapter showed how the ruling party, ZANU/PF, rapidly declined at local level in the 1980s, losing its ability to influence grassroots political processes. The government's recent attempt to court chiefs is part of a two-pronged strategy to secure allies willing to manage its development projects at local level, and to draw upon perceived powerful sources of 'traditional legitimacy'. More generally, the ruling party's widely discussed failure to guarantee human rights, deliver development, and steer clear of corruption,[52] has caused many Zimbabweans to lose faith in the ability of the state to bring about meaningful social and economic change. Recently such disillusionment has manifested itself in what one commentator describes as a nationwide 'nascent social movement for democratisation' (Werbner, 1993: 5). This movement comprises lawyers, students, trade unions and churches, and is accompanied by a rise in urban associational life. Self-consciously borrowing from a discourse emanating from Eastern Europe, Southern African intellectuals conceptualise this democratisation process in terms of civil society-state relations.[53] Local research on this theme in Zimbabwe has recognised the importance of the hierarchies of the established churches of mission descent, in 'constraining' and 'restraining' the state by means of their pastorals and human rights declarations (Mandaza, 1991: 2). The question arises: can the new Pentecostal churches described in this chapter, many of which established themselves in Katerere simultaneously with the emergence of popular demands for democratisation, be interpreted as part of this process?

If in any sense Pentecostal churches challenge the state, then it is in an indirect manner, through contesting the language and ideology of development. Sholto Cross has noted (1978: 312) that the independent African state is often 'jealous of its authority and is fearful of threats to its monopoly over the means of persuasion and coercion, and the function of prescribing national policy.' This is because the state is weak, holding together 'highly fragmented societies generally lacking a civic political culture' (Ibid.). Thus 'attempts to consolidate power are often legitimized in terms of development – a commitment towards economic and social goals ...' (Ibid.). Cross argues that when sects and small-scale religious groupings refuse to participate in modernisation, they are striking at the hegemonic ideology of the state.

Throughout Africa in the 1980s, the established churches adopted the state's language and priorities of development to such an extent that members of the All African Council of Churches began to speak of the NGOisation of the church.[54] And, in 1985, Zimbabwe's MOTO magazine, a popular Catholic monthly, argued that the nation's churches were so development orientated that they were nothing more than 'sub-contractors for the government'.[55] However, the Apostolic churches of Johana Marange (and Johana Masowe), have consistently resisted 'development'. Since 1980, the state, through its controlled media, has been at war with them over their rejection of schooling and bio-medicine.[56] Although development is obviously not bad *per se*, and one might not agree with the Apostolic's particular stance, their struggle with the government raises the important question of where the 'locus of moral authority lie[s]' (Cross, 1978: 313) – with the church or the state? The Zimbabwean state's desire to capture traditional leaders and utilise the rhetoric of 'tradition' (discussed in the previous chapter) stems from its recognition that chiefs and mediums, like the *Vapostori* churches, also possess an alternative moral discourse and language of development.

Notwithstanding Cross's perceptive analysis, a civil society-state focus for rural Pentecostalism obscures the major intentions of these churches. In line with the findings throughout this study, local struggles appear more salient than the national ones. The state is 'not the critical referent' for new wave Pentecostals (Marshall, 1993: 216). It is clear that their critique is directed first and foremost at other local forms of civil society, though not to the exclusion of the state's present regime. They are not just critical of 'traditional' religious institutions and associated male gerontocratic power, but also of mission Christianity. At independence, mission churches in Katerere were unable to provide the healing, liberation from locally perceived evil, and the sense of community that rural people require. The new Pentecostal churches have the ability to direct themselves 'at problems which are of immediate relevance to the faithful'. (Schoffeleers, 1985: 20)

Moreover, the intensely localised new Pentecostal churches in Katerere, characterised by their charismatic leadership and fissile tendencies, barely resemble the urbane, bureaucratised associations of bourgeois industrialised cultures from which the concept of civil society is derived. More accurately, they should be understood as *movements*. They embody a systematic attempt by young men, women and youth to restructure rural social relations in the face of the intransigence of male elders. And more generally, they represent the continuing search of the wider community for healing and liberation. As such, these rural Pentecostal churches seek a local rather than a national accountability. Where the state does impinge, it does so only in a secondary manner, in relation to the inequalities its policies have indirectly created or perpetuated.

For a brief moment in the early 1980s, however, the state *was* the focus of peasant attentions. During the liberation war in the 1970s women and youth did experience some empowerment through the mobilisation process. The record of Katerere's first meeting with a state official in 1980 portrays an assertive peasantry demanding new resources to bolster agricultural production. Among them were women insistent upon improved health facilities, women's organisations and adult education, and youth demanding access to schooling.[57] Yet because those shifts in local power relations, which brought women and youth to the fore, were never institutionalised, their new-found status was short-lived. As this study has shown, elder male 'traditional' leaders clawed back power. And those who placed their faith in the transformative potential of the local party were also to be dismayed. The state rapidly demobilised the party at local level, stripping it of its autonomy (see Chapter 6). Peasants soon encountered bureaucratic intransigence.

The record of peasant demands from the state on the immediate cessation of the war, mentioned above, provides a vivid illustration. In its margins, a bureaucrat had pencilled the following: 'If this is what they want they must get on and do something about it ... It's no good sitting down and saying *we want* and expect to be given everything on a plate.'[58] Although the demobilisation of the party was by no means a complete process, the revived fortunes of 'traditional leaders', and indeed their kinship links with leading elders within the party, point to the reality of its neutralisation.

The demands made of the state by Katerere peasantry after the war were by no means out of place. As numerous informants' accounts of the war suggest, it had a distinctly millennial flavour (see also Lan, 1985: 200–1). The guerrillas promised that the old order would be swept away,[59] and made outrageous predictions about the future (see also Alexander, 1993: 328–30). Blacks would have tractors. Blacks would live in whites' houses. Blacks would pay no taxes, and whites would be their servants. Obviously not everyone believed such promises, but many did. Their breaking was a common subject for discussion, and frequently referred to by informants.

The collapse of peasant expectations in the transformative capability of the state has led to their depoliticisation or, more accurately, to a change of focus back onto local struggles. Kriger notes (1992: 234) that after the war in Mutoko, 'Direct and open generational struggles seemed to lose significance quickly once the guerrillas departed from rural areas ... Similarly, the public attacks on wife-beaters seemed to subside ...'. Pentecostalism again became the idiom through which such struggles were fought out. This reascendancy of the Pentecostal church as an arena for local struggle is best illustrated by transformations in one of its key mediums of expression – Christian song. Chapter 5 described how, in the war, Christian guerrillas and rural Christians rewrote well-known hymns for the purposes of mobilisation. Since independence, the process has been inverted. Numerous *pungwe* songs have been transformed into Christian hymns. Thus:

> Boys,
> Boys, let's be courageous,
> Until we take Zimbabwe,
> Until we take it.

becomes:

> Boys,
> Boys, let's be courageous,
> Until we get to heaven,
> Until we get there.

Thus:

Heroes, heroes of Zimbabwe died at Chimoio,
Sit down heroes of Zimbabwe,
So that we may remember those who died for Zimbabwe.

becomes:

Heroes, heroes of the gospel, died on the cross,
Sit down heroes of the gospel
So that we may remember those who died on the cross.[60]

In yet another song, the figure of a sell-out called Nyathi is transformed into both Judas and the Devil. Mobilisation becomes evangelism as the struggle changes focus. Hence the Pentecostals of Katerere have heeded the words of the bureaucrat who suggested that they changed things themselves. They have returned to the more familiar idioms of religious movements in an attempt to bring about lasting social change.

## NEW PENTECOSTALISM, THE SHRINKING STATE, AND THE REVIVAL OF MISSION CHRISTIANITY

In 1991, President Mugabe assiduously attended the centenary celebrations of a number of the larger mission churches in Zimbabwe. In his public addresses on these occasions he requested that mission churches resume responsibility for primary education, and also that they help 'renew the moral fibre of the nation'.[61] A number of conclusions can be drawn from the President's religious itinerary. First, as the state's welfare and educational provision shrinks in the face of World Bank and International Monetary Fund ordained liberalisation policies[62] missions have become increasingly important for their resources. Moreover, as donor organisations grow suspicious of the state, so missions are seen to represent viable forms of civil society through which to channel aid money. In a sense, mission churches *have* become NGOised, but their power to influence definitions of human development has increased as the government's has diminished. President Mugabe's entreaty to the church to help renew the nation's moral fibre must also be taken as a comment on his own party's waning moral authority. Thus, like the institution of chieftainship, Christian missions have recovered from the nationalist slur that they were collaborators with colonialism. In contemporary Zimbabwe, as in colonial Rhodesia of the 1930s, they are viewed as stabilising influences, vicarious sources of political order for a ruling party increasingly insecure in its hold over the people.

But the mission churches' wealth and new-found importance has not necessarily made them 'worldly'. In Katerere it indirectly contributed to their renewal. In the face of growing unemployment, missions were a rare source of employment for local youth. Zealous young men and women returned to work as school teachers and pastors, renewed by their experience

7.1 Elim Women Dancing at a Wedding

of Pentecostal and charismatic Christianity they encountered at the University of Zimbabwe Christian Union or Harare bible colleges. Together with expatriate teachers and nurses from Britain, and a remarkable Ugandan Pentecostal called Tom Riyo, Elim's evangelical agenda was gradually pushed towards Pentecostalism in the early 1990s. New Pentecostal churches like ZAOGA, which had struggled to find rural pastors, were undercut and their numbers declined. Moreover, the Elim movement's ability to retain its hold over local youth was enhanced by its founding of churches in Mutare and Harare, creating networks along which people could move into the city.

Both Catholic and Elim missions have also managed to transcend a potentially deadening preoccupation with health and education by founding a variety of lay associations for men and youth to complement the historically vibrant women's *ruwadzano* groups. Here they have learnt a lesson from the successful urban Pentecostal churches like ZAOGA and the Family of God which promote a rich associational life catering for a large range of social categories.[63] Finally, Catholicism in northern Nyanga has been renewed by another Catholic holy man. The tragic Nyanga bus accident in 1991, which caused the death of over 90 students and teachers from Regina Coeli mission, led to the complete replacement of Zimbabwean and expatriate personnel on the station. A new priest, called Father Tom, arrived and immediately set about constructing church buildings throughout Katerere and organising local gatherings for mass. One black Pentecostal, impressed by the new priest's energy and charisma, confided that 'he [the Father] is just like us'. There is a sense in which religions under threat come to look like their adversaries. (see also Schoffeleers, 1985)

## CONCLUSION

This chapter has shown that Hwesa society is prone to periodic renewal. This process, which occurs every 20 to 30 years (see also De Craemer et al., 1976: 472), is a generational phenomenon. Although the process is cyclical its form and content has evolved. The meaning of good fortune and misfortune has changed in relation to locally generated conditions, and the means of renewal has become increasingly Christianised.

As a form of renewal, Pentecostalism has introduced new possibilities into the religious field. For women and youth it has a potential beyond other Christian movements. This is due to its overt challenge to patriarchal religion through the idiom of exorcism, which is central to Pentecostal practice, and because of Pentecostalism's capacity to reformulate social relationships. The notion of exorcism, and the associated idea of witch cleansing, trans-form the options for those accused of practising sorcery, or for those who have inherited the spirit of witchcraft. Moreover, although sharing the appeal of 'traditional' possession cults, Pentecostalism redefines the meaning of possession by abolishing the dichotomy between peripheral and central cults. These qualities are particularly pertinent for post-independence rural Zimbabwe, where possession by avenging spirits can prove costly, and witchcraft accusation is rife. With the collapse of expectation in the revolutionary capacity of the state, it is hardly surprising that new wave Pentecostalism should thrive, holding as it does the potential to transform the nature of local struggles.

# CONCLUSION

It was reported to me ... that Chief Katerere of Inyanga North, who is very, very old, had died, but enquiries revealed that the report was premature. He had been ill and sunk into a coma so deathlike that wives and relatives had gathered in his hut to bewail his passing, but their lamentations must have awakened him for he suddenly rose, wrathfully dismissed the mourners, and demanded I regret to say – a coca-cola.[1]

This wonderful tale narrated by the Native Commissioner, Inyanga, in 1958, further illustrates the gap between colonial perception and local realities. The image of an ancient coca-cola drinking chief suggests to us (but obviously not the shocked NC) the intricacies of Katerere's social history: local utilisation of global icons; the complexity of identity; the error of explaining religious and political processes in terms of crude dichotomies such as traditional and modern. This concluding section draws out the significance of these intricacies for the wider debate about religious and political change in rural African societies.

## DECONSTRUCTION AND THE RECOVERY OF MULTIPLE IDENTITIES

This study has shown the reductionism of standard social divisions in a number of different ways: in terms of individual social identity; with respect to the appeals of factional politics; and as explanatory tools for social change. It has shown that individuals do not always embody the ideas they *should* as stereotypical representatives of their categories. Rather, individuals can have multiple identities, move between different institutions and ideologies, and form links with others across categories. This point is best illustrated by both the diversity of the actors and their differing roles in the factional politics discussed in Chapter 6. One faction leader was a Catholic school teacher, and another, a committed polygamist, exploiting links with his Pentecostal relatives. The key medium had embellished his *mhondoro* cult by borrowing from Judaeo-Christian concepts of God. Elderly women, in alliance with their brothers, held the faction together through marriage and the preservation of family traditions. The danger in restricting social actors to one rigid identity is apparent in Norma Kriger's *Zimbabwe's Guerrilla War. Peasant Voices* (1992). Although Kriger should be praised for her path-breaking analysis of rural social differentiation in response to wartime political mobilisation, she could have disaggregated rural society still further. All too often her social actors are limited to one voice as 'women' or 'youth' or 'strangers' in a complex socio-political drama where roles continually changed and allegiances shifted.

Nor do the tensions between social categories provide adequate explana-tions for social change. The focus on competing religious ideologies and factional politics illustrates that there was as much conflict *within* the categories as between them. Finally, this study has explored agency in rural social change at a number of different levels which are usually ignored: the politicking of the charismatic medium, Rukadza; the penchant for witch cleansing in Pentecostal women and youth; the vigorous defence of mission Christianity and peasant agriculture by élites of migrant Manyika. These methodological advances in turn lead to new insights into processes of religious and political change in rural Zimbabwe.

## THE SALIENCE OF THE LOCAL

Although Katerere was never closed to political or religious movements operating at national level or, for that matter, to global forces such as Christianity or capitalist imperialism, localising forces were salient in a number of senses. First, local cultural idioms were resilient enough to enable Hwesa people to encounter national and international agendas and reinterpret them. State intervention in peasant agriculture under both the colonial and post-colonial regimes has met with a consistent popular critique couched in the ecological idioms of *mhondoro* cults. Similarly, those same mediums offered Hwesa people conceptual control over the nationalist movement during the liberation war by drawing upon a well-established tradition of resistance and symbolic innovation: a mixture of ritual, taboo and folk-tale.

The second form of localisation was the indigenisation of global cultural flows, particularly mission Christianities. Despite its global claims, Christianity, whether in the hands of returning labour migrants, missionaries, or Zimbabwean evangelists from the cities, has consistently legitimated itself in local terms, pitting itself against local demons, making links with indigenous concepts of illness, and resacralising the landscape through the creation of its own holy places. In localising Christianity in this way, its African agents have done what able and imaginative Christians have done throughout the centuries: adapted prevailing ideologies to the service of their faith, and their faith to the needs of their society. As Wendy James and Douglas Johnson's recent collection (1988) forcefully illustrates, there is no lived Christianity outside of vernacular Christianity. In this light, the appearance of the thesis that much of contemporary African Christianity replicates the ideology and practices of American imperialism (Gifford, 1991) represents an unfortunate rerun of the Christianity, Commerce and Civilisation debate when victory has already been awarded to African creativity.[2] Whether Christian movements operated on the principle of inclusivity or separation, both types, Hastings reminds us (1994a: 598–9), resulted in Africanisation. And the emerging Christian traditions *can* also be regarded as 'authentic' because 'people claim that these traditions are unique, and uniquely their (historical) possession'. (Shaw and Stewart, 1994: 7)

A final form of localisation took place when pre-colonial spheres of religious and political action were narrowed by the state, in collusion with local elders, in order to invent a traditional localism. Both the colonial and post-colonial states constructed themselves by forming links with local political institutions. In Katerere, as elsewhere, the state's local representatives consistently courted elderly male religious and political leaders, particularly those associated with the ruling Mbudzi faction. Their basic aim was simple: divide and rule through the creation of discrete ethnic units, each with its own official set of genealogies and traditions but dependent on administrative recognition from the state.

An interesting development stemming from this latter form of localisation has been the gradual culturalisation of Hwesa royal ancestral religion – *mhondoro* cults. While the process is by no means as complete as in the case of the Yoruba Orisa Cult (Peel, 1994: 162–3) – Hwesa *mhondoro* cults do retain some political functionality and the adherence of the elderly – it is possible to detect a narrowing of the meaning of religion to the spheres of heritage. This process of culturalisation is a means of reconciling 'two contradictory conditions: (1) the aptness of the … cults for the expression of communal and ethnic identity, and (2) the large-scale and growing adherence of the … [Hwesa] … to new and demanding forms of world religions' (Ibid.: 163). Thus when medium-led rituals are secularised so that they become normative procedures in the election of a chief or communal harvest festivals, even Pentecostals feel able to participate. They also become a form of cultural tourism for educated urban-based élites. In January 1991 Assistant DA Gabaza witnessed a Hwesa spirit medium ceremony central to the succession dispute. At the end of his lengthy and enthusiastic report he concluded: 'This indeed was a tour I enjoyed and benefitted from, learning more about traditional customs … I only wish we had a camera and tape recorder so that our experiences would be more vivid.'[3]

## THE PATTERNED NATURE OF RELIGIOUS CHANGE

It is evident from the broad sweep of Katerere's social history that Hwesa society is animated by a series of waves of enthusiasm which lead to its periodic renewal. While it is possible to link the religious movements which have spread across the region to the stresses of the colonial experience or modernisation, De Craemer, Fox and Vansina (1976: 467) are right to assert that they are *primarily* religious in nature. The meaning of good fortune and misfortune has changed with Katerere's evolving political economy but nevertheless the process of renewal occurs every 20 to 30 years with regularity. (Ibid.: 472)

The periodic process of societal cleansing is linked to the resurgence of sorcery and witchcraft and the revival of ancestor religion, but also to the ageing of Christian churches. As the first generation of church leaders grows old they become tired of the ceaseless battle against real and imagined spiritual enemies. They become reconciled to the fact that many have remained in idolatry and some begin to acquire magical substances themselves. This ageing process is often accompanied by a bureaucratisation of the church. Angered by the resultant loss of adversarial zeal and egalitarian potential the next generation of Christians embrace the new religious movement. In the case of Katerere the resacralisation of ancestor cults during the liberation war, and the ageing of the first generation of Pentecostal leaders, made conditions ripe for a second Christian movement in the late 1980s.

However, this study departs from De Craemer, Fox and Vansina's premise of a 'common Central African culture ... [of] rituals, symbols and beliefs' 'reshuffled' for each new wave of enthusiasm (Ibid.: 472–3). The Hwesa religious system is both dynamic and open to new ideas and practices, becoming more pluralist throughout the twentieth century. Thus, although the process of societal cleansing is cyclical it is also, at present, unidirectional. The means of renewal has increasingly been Christianised. Whereas the destruction of charms and other magical substances was carried out by Mchape acolytes in the 1930s, it was performed by church leaders and Christian prophets in the 1950s and late 1980s. Nevertheless, given the recurrence of Mchape in Malawi in 1994,[4] and the resilience of other traditional religious and ritual practice discussed in this study, it is perhaps too early to argue for the inevitable victory of the Christian idiom.

## RELIGION AND POLITICS

Religion and politics interacted at numerous levels in Hwesa society. At the most basic level the religions themselves had their own politics which generate power and flows of clients which are worth struggling for (Ranger, 1986b: 31). Within both Christianity and traditional religion, women fought for their own free space in which they could develop a sense of solidarity and autonomy. And within the church they allied with young men and missionaries to challenge the legitimacy of their husbands and fathers. There were also struggles both within and between the religions for control of holy places such as sacred pools and groves which often also involved conflict over valuable resources. Furthermore, as a recent study suggests (Shaw and Stewart, and Werbner: 1994), it is useful to view accusations of syncretism or anti-syncretism, which Katerere's Pentecostals and Catholics have been so fond of making, as religious polemic. Thus religious hybridity is politicised. Catholicism argues for a mix, and its Pentecostal opponents present themselves as pure or unmixed in heated debates about identity, and the moral high-ground of authenticity.

The examination of the total Hwesa religious complex as it interacted with local and territorial political institutions also helps us escape from often contradictory stereotyping of both Christianity and traditional religion as either forces of resistance or conservatism. Both have exhibited a capacity to oscillate from established religious institution to protest movement and back again. Thus whilst many often see African traditional religion as providing legitimacy for the pre-colonial establishment, Hwesa *mhondoro* cults displayed a considerable degree of independence from the political centre. Prior to colonialism, spirit mediums had links beyond the locality with the federative High God cult of Karuva operating at a regional level. Their military/ political activities were curtailed when the colonial state sought to privilege local institutional religion in the interests of stability and control. But in the liberation war, mediums once again became part of a territory-wide movement, their individual cults forming a network which provided guerrillas with access to secret caves and burial places within each spirit ward, and which legitimated them through association with royal ancestors.

Other scholars make equally unsatisfactory generalisations about Christianity depicting it '*tout court* as hegemonic and "paganism" as providing the essential discourse of resistance'.[5] The conclusions about the contradictory relationship between Christianity and indirect rule which Karen Fields has drawn for Central Africa work for Rhodesia as they do for other British colonies.[6] Although the Rhodesian state used missionaries as unofficial agents of its civilising mission, it nevertheless sought to construct itself at local level by drawing upon traditional religious legitimacy. Thus, in the hands of women and youth, Christianity could have a subversive influence, undermining male gerontocratic control. The language of conversion – 'coming forward', 'setting yourself apart' – was not merely a new source of identity but also provided 'legitimate grounds for denying formerly legitimate obligations' (Fields, 1985: 41, 46). It is no wonder that the state paid so much attention to the complaints of chiefs and headmen about religious movements which aimed at the destruction of things traditional: its own local existence was also under threat. Fundamentally, the colonial regime was a religious as well as a political complex.

## COLLAPSING DICHOTOMIES (AND TRICHOTOMIES)

The study of religious and political processes in African societies has been hindered by the tendency of scholars to explain these complex phenomena in terms of their own cosmology (MacGaffey, 1983: 19–21). In particular, historians and social scientists have built their explanatory models from sets of oppositions. Viewed though the lens of the local, many of their false dichotomies collapse.

Already we have seen the imbrication, rather than the separation, of religion and politics. In a similar manner, rural and urban, and tribal and territorial collapse into each other. What at first appears to be a locally constituted rural faction in reality draws upon patronage and knowledge of its urban-based kin. Whilst much religious activity in Katerere has focused on the locality, at times the Hwesa have looked outwards to embrace religious cults and witchcraft eradication movements operating at a national level.

The focus on the internal dynamics of Hwesa society also illustrate the dangers of viewing social change in terms of the trichotomy of the pre-colonial, colonial and post-colonial periods. Whilst this periodisation is useful, for example in highlighting the arrival and evolution of the state, it should not be used uncritically. Many of the struggles highlighted involved tensions which existed prior to colonialism and which did not disappear with its cessation. When the Hwesa did respond to the interventions of freedom fighters or state officials they did so by drawing upon idioms already available.

Implicit in many studies of Christianity in Africa is the perceived dichotomy between its rejection or acceptance. This model of religious change, often advanced by those with a stake in defending religious boundaries, stems from false assumptions about the nature of the religious encounter in the colonial period. Its premise is of an essential or ideal Christianity confronting an essential or ideal African religion – the religion of the invader confronting the religion of the autochthon.

But Christianity was not propagated as a monolithic entity encountering a homogeneous local society. Particular Christian ideas and practices were appropriated by specific ethnic groups, classes and social categories. New forms of vernacular Christianity or popular religions emerge out of processes of borrowing, gleaning and recoding. To label African Christianity 'syncretic' in a pejorative sense is to miss the point that all vernacular religion is a form of syncretism. (Shaw and Stewart, 1994: 'Introduction')

Finally we must reconsider the dichotomies: collaboration and resistance, modernity and tradition. A recent study by Jocelyn Alexander on local politics in two Zimbabwean districts has begun the process. On collaboration and resistance, she found: 'chiefs were able to negotiate for significant concessions from the government, mitigate the effects of unpopular policies, and make alliances with opposition movements. Strategies of collaboration and resistance could be employed to achieve the same goals' (Alexander, 1993: 372). Whilst on modernity and tradition she writes:

Holding a 'traditional' office did not preclude participation in 'modern' opposition politics, or resistance more generally. Indeed, chiefs and headmen adopted a wide range of political ideologies and strategies; they were not constrained to fulfil the determinism of a single sociological category or political office. (Ibid.: 4)

This study has no quarrel with such findings but further questions these sets of dichotomies by tracing the internal dynamics of Hwesa political systems throughout the last century. Thus the ruling Mbudzi faction oscillated between strategies of collaboration and resistance, whether confronted by surrounding dynasties, the Portuguese, the British, or even the post-colonial state. Likewise, we have seen that the institutions of the traditional sector are in fact fully modern: the inventions of the colonial and post-colonial state in collusion with local gerontocratic élites. And these elderly leaders themselves have used old idioms to make statements about modernity, and exhibited a willingness to move from modernist to 'traditional' identities: to change hats for different audiences (see also Werbner, 1991: 16–18). Such Janus-like behaviour was not a product of a weakness of character, or lack of political understanding: far from it. Hwesa chiefs and their allies consistently responded to the exigencies of the day. The strategies they have pursued have a clear internal logic, that of yielding the best chances of their dynasty's political survival.

The last word will not go to a colonial official. This study has shown that there are other, more convincing, versions of the Hwesa's past than one patterned on a European folk-tale. We finish with the voice of a key actor in Katerere's contemporary history. On one of my last visits to Katerere I visited a First Fruits Ceremony held at the home of the Mbudzi faction leader, Patrick Tsodza. The ceremony was attended by political and religious leaders from across the chiefdom, indicating that Tsodza was the popular and spiritually legitimate choice of leader despite the official recognition of the enemy Chifodya faction. Now reconciled to his chiefly calling, Tsodza recounted to me the case for his election.[7] A literate Catholic school teacher, he began in the Christian idiom. The Chifodyas had committed an abomination in the roasting of Chief Gambiza's body. Henceforth they were cursed like Cain's descendants and could not be chiefs. They had been elected by procedures alien to Hwesa culture – white man's laws. Tsodza finished by making a powerful statement of tradition. Picking up a fistful of earth he declared: 'I stand as the Chief of the Soil. The soil represents the previous chiefs … If a new chief is appointed he is rooted in the previous chiefs. I have the power of the soil.'

# APPENDIX 1: METHODOLOGY

## THE ORIGINS OF THE RESEARCH

In January 1987 I took up a position as a history teacher at Emmanuel Secondary school, Elim mission in Katerere, north-east Zimbabwe. I am not a Pentecostal but an Anglican; nevertheless, I was welcomed and encouraged to participate in the life and work of the mission. As a historian trained in Zimbabwean social history I found myself in a first-class position to research local political and religious change. So began the 10 years of research and writing which led first to my doctoral dissertation, and then to this book.

I stayed three years in Katerere as a teacher. In January 1990 I moved to Oxford to begin my doctorate, returning to Zimbabwe in April 1991 for seven months' more fieldwork. Subsequent to the completion of the doctoral research, I spent another year in Zimbabwe, from September 1995 to September 1996. Loose ends were tied up and I commenced to write, in dialogue with my informants, and local scholarship at the University of Zimbabwe.

## WRITTEN SOURCES

A variety of archives were consulted. The National Archives of Zimbabwe proved useful for reconstructing the conjunctions of the state with local religious and political institutions. More contemporary records of these interactions were found in the District Administration offices in the town of Inyanga. I worked in four mission archives to reconstruct the changing encounter between missionaries and the Hwesa. These were the Jesuit Archives, Harare, and the Carmelite Archives, Dundrum, Dublin, for Catholic interactions; and the Elim Archives, Cheltenham, England, and Apostolic Faith Mission Archives, Lyndhurst, South Africa, for Pentecostal interactions. Personal diaries and letters lent to me by various missionaries helped reconstruct the period of the liberation war, as did reports from the Catholic Commission for Justice and Peace in Harare. David Beach kindly gave me rough verbal translations of Portuguese archival material deposited in Lisbon and Maputo, reconstructing pre-colonial Portuguese relations with Katerere.

## THE FIELD WORK LOCATION

As indicated above, rather than choosing the research location it chose me. Although Katerere covers a sizable area of approximately 1,200 square kilometres, my three-year stay there gave me time to drive or walk across most of it. I was fortunate to own a pick-up truck which made travel relatively easy, although a two-hour walk would sometimes await me at my destination. Inevitably, some areas, such as the homes of religious or political leaders, the bases of new religious movements, or the nearby mission stations, were visited more than others. Nevertheless, I attempted to gain an understanding of religious and political processes in less researched areas by interviewing their inhabitants as they stayed at or visited Elim mission.

## INTERVIEWS AND SELECTING INFORMANTS

Between November 1987 and September 1991 I conducted approximately 90 formal interviews. Another 12 or more were conducted between September 1995 and September 1996 while I was primarily researching another project. My own work was augmented by interviews and research carried out by research assistants and students. These comprise formal interviews, personal reminiscences and more general data collection. Full details of this oral data are to be found in the section on sources at the end of this study.

My work as a history and religious studies teacher at Elim mission helped establish a good rapport with informants. The history syllabi devoted much space to the liberation struggle, and often students older than myself would recount their experiences of guerrilla mobilisation. Some wrote down their accounts, whilst others told me more outside lessons. I founded a history club where these themes were explored in greater detail. Gradually word spread that I was interested in local history, and students would appear with a transcribed myth or legend that they had heard from a relative, or a piece of fascinating gossip about local politics. I sent other students to research in the holidays. Students were keen to conduct their own research out of a desire to improve their English. Other information about possible informants was picked up from conversations with adults around the school, hospital, church and workshops.

Once I had identified potential informants, I would attempt to find an intermediary who could introduce me to them. At times, the prospective informant was a relative of my students or friends and they would facilitate the meeting. When this did not occur, my research assistants would be at great pains to stress both their and my links to the area. Informants would be told that I was a history teacher with an interest in the local past. We would discuss how the youth appeared to show little interest in their history or culture, and that these things needed to be recorded for posterity. We stressed that both the Chief and the local ZANU/PF councillor had given me permission to research. Often people already knew of me.

My research assistants would go to great lengths to explain my research intentions, and this would be emphasised by replaying to informants parts of the taped interview as it progressed. Informants were told that we respected them if they wished not to discuss a subject. Occasionally, they preferred not to answer questions, usually concerning the war. Their reluctance normally stemmed not from fear but the pain of bereavement. Generally informants were very hospitable and pleased to recount their experiences. Often I was offered a meal, or I departed with handfuls of groundnuts or maize cobs.

There were a number of reasons for informants' openness. Part of the explanation was related to my own points of entry as researcher, which I explore in greater detail below. Informants also welcomed interviews because they found the experience affirming. Many expressed surprise that a white man should travel a long way to a remote place just to listen to them. Their perception was that whites did the talking and held their culture and history in low regard. As my last two chapters illustrate, informants also perceived me as a potential means through which to further their own agendas. As a researcher seeking to record local history in written form, I was seen as someone who had the power to bestow political and religious legitimacy. Informants representing different social constituencies were keen to make the *first* statement or at least convince me that they had the authentic one, in the same manner that male elders have consistently manipulated representatives of the state throughout this century. Thus royal faction leaders competing for the chieftainship did their best to derogate rival claims to succession. Religious leaders competing for both clients and sacred space, sought to discredit opposing religions.

Some Hwesa hoped that my work would result in the creation of a sharper definition of Hwesa ethnicity to match that of the Manyika élites who surrounded them. When I left Katerere in December 1989, friends and colleagues threw a party for me. The mission pastor thanked me for my research endeavours, remarking 'we Hwesa have been at the bottom of history for many years, but Mr Maxwell has recorded our traditions '*pamberi ne Hwesa*!' – forward with the Hwesa'. This study has attempted to explore the constructed nature of research data using it as a window into the dynamics of Hwesa society.

At times I was surprised by how outspoken my informants were. Some were highly critical of their neighbours, and others were vociferous about the failings of the ruling party. Although I am committed to revealing my sources so that other scholars may assess their representative character, at times I have found it necessary not to reveal specific identities in order to protect informants, or their neighbours. However, where slander takes the form of political argument between well-established political élites, as in the case of the succession dispute investigated in Chapter 6, the informants are named. These political élites are positively disinterested in anonymity and have even sought out the Zimbabwean popular press (*Kwayedza*) in pursuit of their claims to succession.

## PARTICIPANT OBSERVATION

Both the Hwesa succession dispute detailed in Chapter 6, and the proliferation of Pentecostalism and subsequent revival of mission Christianity examined in Chapter 7, were events which I lived through during my stay in Katerere. Thus the last two chapters draw upon participant observation. Many of my insights into local religious and political interactions were gained in casual conversations whilst 'hanging around' football matches, church services and conventions, local stores, or the mission workshops. Other insights were gained through visiting students' families, or by accompanying one of my research assistants, Joseph Chitima, as he visited homes to evangelise, console the bereaved, or purchase goats. Some of my impressions I transcribed immediately; others I recalled at a later date.

## MEDIATING ISSUES

There were a number of factors which mediated or affected my position as a researcher. Being white seemed to be less of a problem than being male. In fact my European status appeared to be ameliorated by my relation with Elim mission. Few whites have had cause to live or work in Katerere. Occasionally, an ex-patriate NGO worker might pass through on the road. But white nurses, teachers and doctors attached to the missions are an accepted part of local society. As a teacher, I had a good reason for being there. Moreover, as a teacher of history and religious studies I had a legitimate reason for asking questions about these issues. In some senses, I *was* an insider. I attempted to reinforce this appearance by arriving at an informant's home accompanied by a friend or student, or with one of my well-chosen research assistants. Before engaging in formal research I already knew a great deal by virtue of my conversations, and research done for me by students. Many informants quickly realised there was no point concealing things from me, or misleading me. In another sense, I was an outsider and always will be. But the social distance created by being a European could work in my favour. Being outside so many of the local struggles I was less partisan – a person who could be confided in (or used).

In the past, anthropologists have held as one of their methodological tenets that it was unwise to conduct research in the vicinity of a Christian mission. Their reasoning was that informants would try to work out what the researcher wanted to hear in the same manner as they responded to missionaries. But when I arrived at Elim mission in January 1987, the time had long since passed when the missionary was regarded as a white chief: the mission was now in local hands and I had no administrative power. As this study has illustrated, for most of its existence the mission has had good relations with many in the local community. Even those whom it opposed on religious grounds could recognise the utility of its educational and health services. Moreover, my association with the mission also enabled me to research its social history, an important enterprise neglected by anthropologists and historians until recently. The written sources given to me by missionaries and ex-patriates in the field in the form of diaries, letters and reports also broke down the dichotomy researchers often create between the town as the location for archival work and the rural areas as the place for interviews and participant observation.

Despite being male, it was fairly easy to conduct interviews with young women within the safe confines of the school. Some girls also wrote down their reminiscences. Interviews with female elders were again not difficult. They were at liberty to talk to a young male. But discussions with married women proved problematic. A male household head would have to be asked first or, if he was absent, a 'responsible' male in the vicinity would appear. Although such men would respect our desire to want to hear the woman's perspective, they hovered in the background, and this may have affected the content of the interviews. Interviews with a woman-headed household, where the husband was deceased, and with local nurses in the vicinity of the hospital, provided other female perceptions.

The choice of research assistants was critical. My first was Augustine Mabvira. As an ex-combatant, Comrade Ranga (*Rangarirai mwana we povo* – Remember the child of the masses) had operated in the area. He opened many doors, particularly to traditional religious authorities who had assisted in wartime mobilisation. As one of the few guerrillas to operate in his home area, or its vicinity, he had been concerned to limit bloodshed. He was something of a local hero whom parents told their children about. I was impressed by his skills in diplomacy and his confidence in making relationships. Sadly, he never fully recovered from his war wounds, and died unexpectedly in 1995.

Of course, everyone had different experiences of the war and I realised Ranga's presence at some interviews may have intimidated informants. Increasingly I drew on the services of Joseph Chitima. Although he farmed like many others in the area, he had traversed Katerere in a number of guises: as a young hunter, a builder, part of a geological survey, a messenger for guerrillas, party official, evangelist, and now, finally, health worker. Like Ranga he seemed to know everyone and was particularly skilled at establishing some connection with the informant. He went to great lengths to explain my research, slowly easing me into the interview.

Both Ranga and Chitima spoke English well, but I was usually accompanied by Shupikai Chikutirwe whose English and Shona were of a very high standard. He taught me Shona five days a week for three years and had a very good understanding of my research. When I left Katerere in

December 1989, he conducted a number of interviews for me. Chikutirwe's task was that of a translator, though he also took notes. When he was not available I was accompanied by Samson Mudzudza, another secondary-school student. Mudzudza subsequently went on to the University of Zimbabwe and, to my delight, returned to Katerere in 1994 to conduct his own research for its Minority Languages Programme. His collection of oral traditions built on my research, and these he supplemented with a collection of songs, proverbs and folk-tales. Mudzudza read and discussed my doctorate with me, correcting the Hwesa orthography. We also discussed at length his own research.

All my research assistants lived in the area, though none were Hwesa. This slight distance proved particularly important when I was researching the succession dispute recounted in Chapter 6. Most important, they all possessed large amounts of a quality indispensable for successful interview work – charm.

Although a fair number of my interviews with whites and blacks were conducted in English, many involved translation from Chishona. After three years I could follow an interview enough to know when responses were being mistranslated, and sometimes even to grasp an important idea expressed obliquely. Generally, Chitima or Ranga would ask the questions and Chikutirwe would translate the response. It proved useful having a number of assistants at an interview because at times Hwesa dialect spoken by an elder was not immediately intelligible. My assistants would discuss responses, and ask clarifying questions before offering a translation. Another alternative translation was provided by those who transcribed the tapes: Richard Simbi, Emmanuel Nyarumba and Simba Chikodo. They were all ex-pupils of Emmanuel secondary school in higher education. Each offered his own reflections on the transcribed material.

Although I had a number of points of entry into local society, it would be fair to acknowledge that one perspective was stronger than others. I moved with young men and came nearest to seeing the world of Katerere through their eyes. These are my friends, and it has been good to grow up with them over the last 10 years. Hopefully, in the coming years, I will be able to make return journeys to visit friends in Katerere, and grow old with them. And doubtless as elders we shall see Hwesa history differently.

# APPENDIX 2: HWESA MYTHS OF ORIGIN

## MYTH 1: DEMBWETEMBWE & SAMAVANGA (SANHANI & KATERERE)

Dembwetembwe is said to be the first to arrive at Nhani mountain. Nyakasapa was already there living in a cave … Nyakasapa was said to be living without fire. He ate raw meat and fruits. Dembwetembwe made him fire … and was made chief because he was clever enough. Nyakasapa made himself *sahwira* (or *zunzu*) – blood brother – to the chief.

Dembwetembwe came from Mbire Dande. His migration from there was due to the fact they were looking for free land to settle with their family. This was the same period when many chiefs migrated, for example Mutoko and Saunyama. It is said they originated from Mbire.

Later on, Samavanga, the younger brother of Dembwetembwe, followed his brother. Dembwetembwe took him down to where Mhokore is. He wanted him to settle there and rule the present area of Katerere … Samavanga in Mhokore and Dembwetembwe in Nhani could see each other. They chose to live in these mountains because they could see any enemy *madviti* – Nguni raiders – coming and there are caves to hide in.

Because Samavanga was living nearer to Mozambique, Dembwetembwe gave him his ivory trade with the Portuguese in Sena. Their life was based on hunting. Samavanga's family grew very fast and he was very popular. Dembwetembwe had few sons and therefore his family was small. Samavanga used to give his brother some of his possessions after trading. But later he decided to fight his brother and bring the area under him. He called together soldiers and came to Duza. Dembwetembwe beat a drum which meant that Samavanga was to speak out his wishes. This is where the place-name Duza[1] came from. Dembwetembwe told his brother that he could not fight his relative and that the chiefdom and the trade were his.

Katerere is the name given to Samavanga after they had failed to spear him. When a spear was thrown at him it would slip off his body as if he was smeared with *derere* – okra. Sanhani (Nematombo) came from Dembwetembwe.[2]

## MYTH 2: SADOWERA & KATERERE

Chinoro is our forefather. They came from Mbire while they were three men and after more people came … The Sadoweras were the first to come and those who followed were many. And they outnumbered the Sadoweras and instead of sharing the chieftainship they were given the role they play now [in the coronation and burial of the chief]. The Katereres came after the Sadowera. From that time they were told that they would be chiefs because they were followers.[3]

## MYTH 3: SACHIWO & KATERERE

Sakudzamba is our forefather. He came together with Katerere from Mbire. They left Mbire while they were still four and settled together. Later Sakudzamba was told to explore the whole area and he did that. After exploring the area Sakudzamba made fire. When they wanted to make a chief Sakudzamba said that he should be chief because he had explored the area and created fire. In response the others said that Sakudzamba could not become chief because he had not performed the act of *kupinga nyika* – ritual incest – with his sister, necessary to protect the land. They had tricked him into the hut of a sister of one of the three in the company. In the end, Sakudzamba was given the position of honour of being the father of all the chiefs and his name was changed to Sachiwo. A place was allocated for him to live in. As father, Sachiwo had to do whatever Katerere and the other two wanted. Samavanga and then Samurirwa were the first two chiefs.[4]

# APPENDIX 3: RITUALS OF THE HWESA CHIEFTAINSHIP

### THE BURIAL OF THE CHIEF

Sachiwo anoints the swollen body so that it decreases in size. Sadowera buries the chief in a mountain grave. He is led there by a possessed medium. The chief is buried with his head facing Mbire.

### THE CORONATION OF THE CHIEF

Sachiwo enters the pool and takes the eggs of a crocodile. The *mhondoro* show him where to find them and give him courage. Sachiwo brings a crocodile from the Gaerezi River and the chief sits on the crocodile. Whilst Sachiwo dresses the chief, the eggs are placed in his hands. From this time forwards the chief no longer claps when greeting. Sachiwo chooses a site for the new chief's house.

Sanhani accompanies Nyakasapa who brings a baby baboon. Part of its skin will make up the chief's head dress. Nyakasapa is the chief's *zunzu* – blood brother. He encircles the chief's house with rattles. He is naked and shouts out both insulting and humorous things. Children must be locked inside. Anyone who laughs must pay a fine of a daughter.

### THE FIRST FRUITS CEREMONY

Seeds from the first harvest are brought to the chief's house by Sabvure. These are mixed with medicines and given to the *mhondoro* mediums to eat.[5]

# APPENDIX 4: HWESA LEGENDS

## The Flight of Nyamhute

Nyamhute was a magician who stayed on Cherenje mountain. Because Nyamhute was a magician he was stronger than his younger brother Nkota. When they wanted to assassinate him the whole mountain would be covered with fog which would protect him. The magic was stolen by Nkota's wife and Nkota brought an army to attack him. Nyamhute got hold of his magic but it would not work so he had to flee and go to Saunyama where his uncle lived. Later his people moved to Rusape in Makoni district.[6]

## The Murder of Chimucheka

The Mbudzi family called some Madzviti warriors. They wanted to kill [the current chief], Chimucheka, [of the Chirimunyati lineage]. Chimucheka fled to Sangano and from there he went to Barwe to seek protection from his grandfathers. His mother had come from Barwe. When the Mbudzi family heard that he was living in Mozambique with his grandfathers they followed him there. And when they arrived they asked to have Chimucheka but his grandfathers did not want to give him to these relatives. Because they disputed the grandfathers escorted the relatives to the cave where Chimucheka was hiding. The Mbudzi family called Chimucheka. When they caught him they wanted to kill him, but he said he first wanted to call his son. And when he called his son he came in the form of a dove. When he arrived where the people were he changed again into a person and greeted his father.

Because Chimucheka saw that his relatives wanted to kill him he said to them: 'If you relatives are killing me for my chieftainship how are you going to stay with my child?' He knew that it was impossible that they were going to live well with his son and as a result he said: 'You first kill my son and then kill me.' The relatives were furious and killed Hokoyo first and then Chimucheka. They stripped them of all of their clothes and left them bare and naked. And they came back here (Katerere).

When the grandfathers of Chimucheka realised that the relatives had gone they went to the cave to see if he was still alive. When they got there they were surprised to see him dead and naked. They went back and were told by their elders not to touch the bodies, but to take some pieces of *machira* – cloth which spirit mediums use – and just leave them by the corpses. And local *mhondoro* came and took the bodies and the pieces of cloth and buried the bodies. This was a bitter end to Chimucheka's life and so he created an atmosphere in Katerere unfavourable to rule in. Thus there were plenty of lions. Because of this atmosphere the people decided to send a delegation to Mozambique to fetch Chimucheka who was possessing one of the Makombe people. So when they went there they brought the medium. And Chimucheka said 'now because you have used my blood to perform ritual ceremonies and help you administer you must pay a fine'. A fine was paid by the killers as a punishment for the *ngozi* – avenging spirit – they had created by killing someone which they had tried to prevent returning by stripping the bodies of their clothes. They were charged a woman, a big cow and three oxen. These were paid to the medium. Three head of cattle are paid every time a new chief comes in.[7]

### LEGEND 3: THE MBUDZI HOUSE
## The Roasting of Chief Gambiza

The Chifodyas were impatient to succeed to the chieftainship. They recruited soldiers from Mutoko and marched to Katerere at the time of the installation of a new chief. Gambiza was still alive and living at Chikondokwe near Mt Nyazingwe. A battle took place at *Uswa Umonye* – the place of tangled grass –, where the Chifodyas killed Chief Gambiza [of the Mbudzi House]. They sliced his body. And by supporting it with poles, they roasted it on a spit. The dried corpse and the poles were eventually consumed by the fire. The ashes were taken and scattered in the Ruenya/ Inyangombe River. This was done to avoid the wrath of an *ngozi* – an avenging spirit. The lion spirit, Nyawada, saw what was happening to his people and organised resistance, hiding the chief's drum. The usurpers were defeated and when the Katereres returned from their refuge with Makombe in Mozambique, they restored the chiefdom with Nyawada choosing the chief from this present house. And when they said: 'We have no drum because it has gone to the Chifodyas,' Nyawada told them to bring him a servant. Together they collected the drum and presented it to the chief. The Chifodyas were declared outcasts and forbidden from inheriting the chiefdom forever. The clan spirits punished them in this way because they had angered the *mhondoro* by preventing a dead chief from being buried in the correct manner.[8]

LEGEND 4: THE CHIFODYA HOUSE
## The Murder of Nyamande

Gambiza was not a chief but a chief's servant. Gambiza left the Matitima [Mbudzi house of Katerere] and wanted to take the chieftainship from Nyamande. Nyamande had a dog called Dzava Hwesa which only barked at people who wanted to kill the chief. When Gambiza arrived at Nyamande's court to kill him they met a woman called Njesera, a daughter of Dzvukutu. Njesera warned the chief about the coming of Gambiza and the others. Njesera was Nyamande's wife and with the help of the dog acted as a lookout.

Gambiza and the others waited for the woman when she was coming from the *dambo* – field. They captured her and cut off her legs. They then attempted to find the chief, but he had already hidden. Gambiza realised the bad thing he had done and fled. This happened when the chief's *machinda* – retainers – were not there. They followed Gambiza and when they caught him they cut his body into pieces and put his flesh onto a mesh of sticks and burned it to ashes.

Nobody helped kill Gambiza. But the Matitima brought an army from Mutoko to kill Nyamande. Nyamande is the one who owns the chief's drums which he brought from Makombe. Even Nkota had no drum. Soldiers from Mutoko arrived when Nyamande's servants had gone to search for food and to buy grain at Nyakomba because it was a year of drought. The dog barked but there was nobody there to respond to it. They attacked Nyamande and injured him, but he never died. He called out that if they were to kill him they must use one of the roofing poles of his house. They tried to chop him but he never died.

After this Nyamande was hidden and given food by his servants. Where he was hiding was kept a secret and people were told that he had gone to Sena. Njesera was also hiding and her brother Dzvukutu used to go and see her where she was recovering. She told her brother where the chief was. She told him to move towards that place as a hunter and visit the chief. Dzvukutu met him and told him what had happened to his sister and was told that the children of Nyamande had gone to look for grain since it was a year of hunger. When coming from the mountain where the chief was hiding, Dzvukutu came past a beer party and the Matitima asked where he was coming from and he told them that he had been to see his son-in-law. They gave him beer so that he would reveal the secret when he got drunk. When he got drunk he revealed where Nyamande was hiding and in the morning the Matitima went to that place stealthily. Dry grass was spread at the mouth of the cave where the old chief used to lie during the day. They speared him, but he would not die. Since they had failed to kill him he told them to burn him with the grass he was lying on. After killing him they took his crown, the drum and another article called *madzamanga* used in rituals for making rain.

# APPENDIX 5: GENEALOGIES

A SUGGESTED GENEALOGY FOR THE KATERERE
RULING LINE[9]

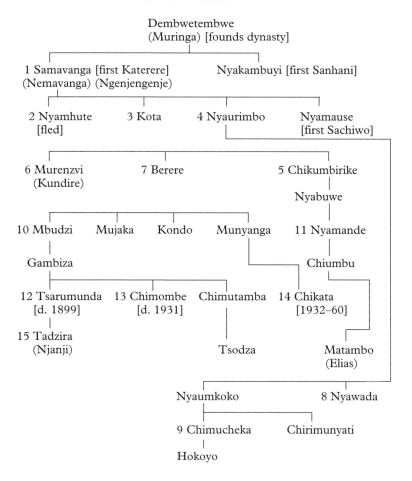

Note: Numbers denote those who became chiefs, and in which order they did so. Alternative
names are shown in round brackets.

## STATE GENEALOGY 1931–2[10]

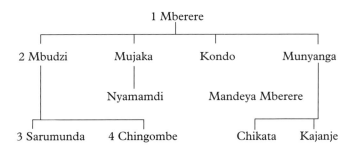

## STATE GENEALOGY 1960[11]

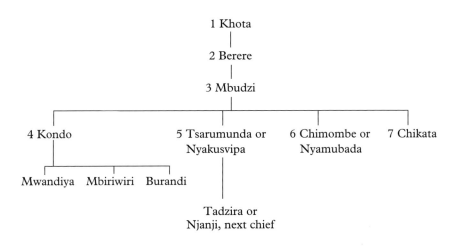

## CHIFODYA GENEALOGY[12]

## CHIRIMUNYATI GENEALOGY[13]

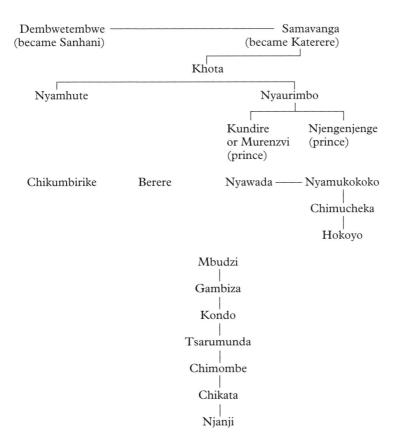

Note: Information on these genealogies (Chirimunyati and Mbudzi) is often incomplete
because informants are only interested in lines of descent which relate to their faction.
They also tend to screen out the genealogical claims of rivals' factions.

## MBUDZI GENEALOGY[14]

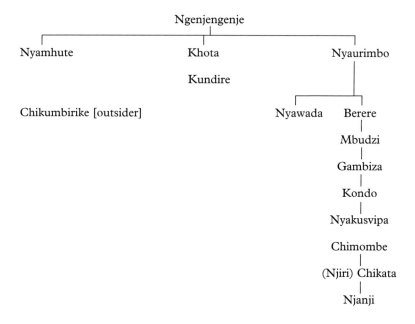

# NOTES

## INTRODUCTION

1. It is difficult to find an appropriate term to describe non-Christian African religion. 'Indigenous', 'African' and 'local' are all problematic for I will argue that Christianity is all of these. Although 'traditional' conveys a static character, I find it the best option.
2. This body of work is considered in chapters 3 and 4.
3. For other examples of the growing interest in the history of Christian mission see two recent 1995 editions of *The Journal of Religion in Africa* 25, (1) and (4).
4. In her recent history of African Christianity Elizabeth Isichei observes that there have been few in-depth studies of village Christianity. Isichei, 1995: 261.
5. Useful collections of essays can be found in James and Johnson, 1988 and, 1987, *American Ethnologist* 14 (1). For a recent syntheses of work on African Christianity, see Hastings, 1994a, and Isichei, 1995.
6. See Chapter 4 of this study.
7. I am currently making a study of an urban-based Zimbabwean pentecostal movement and hope to offer phenomenological insights into various pentecostal practices such as healing, exorcism, and possession by the Holy Spirit.
8. A good example of the characterisation of chieftainship in nationalist historiography is Ranger, 1969: 293–324. On 'peripheral' theories of imperialism, see for instance Robinson, 1972: 116–42. As this study will show these interpretations still find their way into the modern literature.
9. For examples of recent scholarship which recognise the contemporary importance of chieftainship see Molutsi and Holm, 1990; Van Binsbergen, 1987; Alexander, 1995; Geschiere, 1993.
10. For recent scholarship beginning to consider these issues see Beinart and Bundy, 1987; Vail, 1989; Ranger, 1993c.
11. On religious interactions see various essays in Schoffeleers, 1979; and the various essays in Werbner, 1977; Murphree, 1969; and Bhebe, 1979a. For studies on local political institutions see Alexander, 1993; Kriger, 1992. For studies that weave together the religious and the political see Ranger, 1985.

## CHAPTER 1

1. NAZ, SE 1/1/1, folios 211–16, F. C. Selous, General Correspondence, 1890–1.
2. Of course, *parts* of this repertoire were shared even more widely with other Bantu-speaking peoples.
3. See Storry, 1976: 13–30.
4. In low-lying areas these took the form of wooden stockades.
5. For a fascinating case study on the role of women in factional politics see Barnes, 1992.
6. NAZ, MA14/1/2 Jason Machiwanyika, lesson 28.

7. See also NAZ, MA14/1/2, Jason Machiwanyika, lesson 15.
8. Machiwanyika writes of Chief Mutasa exchanging women for gold. NAZ, MA14/1/2, Jason Machiwanyika, lesson 1.
9. NAZ, NUC 3/1/1, Annual Report, Inyanga, 1903.
10. Beach, 1989: 38. Beach is writing about an area which was particularly fragmented politically but his observation holds for Katerere.
11. Personal correspondence from David Beach, 6 January 1992.
12. NAZ, N9/4/1, Monthly Report, Mtoko, October 1898.
13. NAZ, N9/4/14, Monthly Report, Inyanga, January 1903.
14. In 1913 it was decreed by the Native Administration that the African population in each district would be calculated by multiplying the figure of adult male tax payers by a multiple of 3.5. The Annual Report for Inyanga, 1903, recorded 1,084 males, NAZ, NUC 3/1/1, Annual Report, Inyanga, 1903. Another estimate for the same year put the 'Hwesa' figure at 750, N9/4/16, Monthly Report, Inyanga, July 1903. The pursuit of accurate demographic figures is extremely problematic in this early colonial period. The exercise of population count, undertaken to facilitate tax collection, was not likely to yield the greatest of cooperation, and would have been compounded by Katerere's remoteness from administrative control. For more detailed discussions see Beach, 1990b: pp.31–83.
15. NAZ, NUC 3/1/1, Annual Report, Inyanga, 1903.
16. In 1903 it was estimated that the Hwesa possessed 55 sheep, 166 goats and seven head of cattle. NAZ, NUC 2/1/1, Out Letters, Inyanga, 12 September 1903.
17. Burke, 1969: 238. NAZ, NUA 2/1/5, Half Yearly Report, Inyanga (forwarded), September 1903.
18. Mukaranda, 1988: 9–10. NAZ, NUC 3/1/1, Annual Report, Inyanga, 1903.
19. See the Dembwetembwe and Samavanga myth, Appendix 2. This will be discussed in greater detail below.
20. NAZ, N9/4/2, Monthly Report, Mtoko, January 1899. Interview with Headman Robson Maroo and Kampira Maroo, Kodzaimambo, 23 March 1996.
21. NAZ, NSJ 1/1/1/, NC Mtoko to CNC, 17 August 1898.
22. NAZ, NSJ 1/1/1, Half Yearly Report, Mtoko, October 1898.
23. For early colonial references to family ancestor cults see NAZ, NUA 2/1/3, Yearly Report, Umtali, 1898. NUC 2/1/3, Out Letters, Inyanga, 28 May 1908.
24. Interviews, Pitodya Chifodya; Kaburunge Magadu; Mathias Sachiwo.
25. Bourdillon, 1987a: 253. *Svikiro* is a general term referring to all mediums.
26. Mudenge, 1988: 119–26. Isaacman, 1976: 128. See also the accounts of F. C. Selous and Andrada cited below.
27. See Mudenge, 1988: 127–34, for an explanation of the complex relationships between these High Gods and legendary figures. There is some disagreement concerning the description of this cult. Michael Bourdillon contends that the north-east Shona have no concept of a 'High God' but rather that Karuva and Dzivaguru are large and impressive autochthonous spirits. I choose to use the term 'High God' because Hwesa accounts of Karuva ascribe notions of a creator and a judge to him or her. Bourdillon's different conclusions may be explained by the fact that he draws his data from a different part of the north-east. However, contrary to Horton's well-known proposition about a two-tiered traditional cosmology of lesser spirits and a Supreme Being, I see no need to make a categorical distinction between larger ancestors and a Creator. While some missionaries and African clergy wish to uphold such a clear-cut separation it would appear that many significant spirits oscillate between the two positions over time. Bourdillon, 1979: 249, 251. Horton, 1971.

28. Interviews, Diki Rukadza, medium of Nyawada, 22 January 1989, 15 August 1991.
29. On this process of 'gleaning', see Bourdillon, 1988.
30. Dr and Mrs C. Brien, 'Gospel Advances in Southern Rhodesia' in *Elim Evangel*, 3 December 1951. On the relationship between Karuva, Dzivaguru, Murungu and Chikara see Mudenge, 1988: 127–34.
31. Hwesa informants told the German adventurer Carl Peters much the same when he visited Katerere in 1900, Peters, 1977: 159–63. This lack of local knowledge about the terraces may well be explained by the fact that the Hwesa did not consider it worth remembering them. Robert Soper, an archaeologist working on the area, contends that the terraces were widely used in the eighteenth century and that some of the stone enclosures were in use around 1900. Personal communication, Robert Soper, June 1997.
32. This squares with David Beach's dating of the dynasty. Beach, 1995: 14. For the methodology of dating using genealogies see Beach, 1994b, pp.275–8.
33. Willis, 1976; Miller, 1978: 75–102. Although I consider these scholars' work as part of the same school, there are differences in their approach. Though Miller arrives at the same tripartite scheme for oral traditions as Willis, he arrives at it through a line of reasoning which begins with myth rather than chronicle. Miller also differs from Willis over the composition of the second strata. He sees it as a series of repetitive processes in the state's history, rather than a representation of the attempts of the performer to demonstrate the importance of a class of recurrent events.
34. For example the folk tales: '*Tika ridabzvira nyama*' (The Hyena that dances to get meat) and '*Kondo na Khunguwo*' (The Eagle and the Crow); or the song '*Ndingafaresei?*' (How can I be Happy?). Samson Mudzudza, 1994, Minority Languages Project, University of Zimbabwe.
35. Informants from Makombe in Mozambique corroborate this idea on Hwesa origins. See Isaacman, 1976: 130.
36. For example, in Dande, northern Zimbabwe, autochthons still hold considerable ritual power. See Lan, 1985.
37. The Sanhani faction is remote from the politics of the recent past, and it does not bother to preserve a full genealogy. This may be because it is so secure that it does not need to. It is also physically separated from the rest of the polity by the Ruangwe Range. The Sachiwo faction is physically much closer to the centre of the contemporary chiefdom and is immersed in its politics. The Sachiwo tree is much longer than the Sanhani one, running to seven generations and 18 rulers. This may be because it was much closer to the Katerere faction proper, winning its territory more recently, and hence more fearful of expropriation. I am grateful to David Beach for discussing this point with me. Personal correspondence, 1 February 1993 and 15 April 1993.
    It is likely that the Nyakasapa faction diminished in influence as the political centre shifted.
38. Machiwanyika provides many examples in his History of the pre-colonial Manyika, see NAZ, MA14/1/2, History and Customs of the Manyika Peoples, n.d.
39. For example Chiefs Nyaurimbo and Kundire, interview, Mathias Sachiwo, 5 June 1991.
40. Andrada noted this as he travelled throughout the east in the 1880s. Arquivo Histórico Ultramarino, Lisboa, henceforth AHU, Andrada Expedition, 1/2, Andrada ao Ultramar, Massanga, 10 Junho, 1887.

41. Interview, Mathias Sachiwo, 5 June 1991.
42. Thus Sabvhure is associated with Mt Tsetera, Sadowera with Mt Nyazingwe, Tsengerai with Mt Nyakatondo, Nyamhengura with Mt Mutambwe and Gohoto with Mt Nyambuyo. Interview, Osius Nyamhute, 30 May 1991. Interview, Diki Rukadza, medium of Nyawada, 31 May 1991.
43. Interview, Martin Gande, 31 May 1991. The coming of the Gandes may well have been later. The choice of Chikumbirike as the incumbent chief may reflect the fact that they live in his spirit ward.
44. Interview, Harry Tsengerai. Personal communication, Samson Muzdudza.
45. Interview, Diki Rukadza, medium of Nyawada, 15 August 1991. Interview, Headman Robson Maroo and Kampira Maroo, Kodzaimambo, 23 March 1996. Maroo traditions state that they arrived during the time of Tsarumunda in the late nineteenth century.
46. Interview, Diki Rukadza, medium of Nyawada, 31 May 1991.
47. Interview, Patrick Tsodza. Tsodza claimed the Kazozo family had previously helped bury and crown the chief.
48. One such local family was Satuku. Personal communication, Ephraim Satuku.
49. One informant told of how the people of Mutoko came with knives killing most of the Hwesa. Interview, Zuze Chitima.
50. Interview, Diki Rukadza, medium of Nyawada, 15 August 1991.
51. NAZ, CT 1/15/3, Report, M. D. Graham, Fort Salisbury, 19 January 1892. Graham estimated that Makombe could turn out some 8,000 men.
52. NAZ, N3/33/8, NC Umtali, History of the Mashona Tribes, 18 January 1904. MA14/1/2, Jason Machiwanyika, lesson 25. NUC 2/4/2, NC Inyanga, Resume of Tribes, 13 January 1913.
53. Interview, Patrick Tsodza, 14 August 1991. Gelfand, 1974: 66.
54. NAZ, SE 1/1/1, F. C. Selous to Administrator, Mashonaland, 25 January 1891. CT 1/15/3, Report, M. D. Graham, Fort Salisbury, 19 January 1892. Burke, 1969: 232–5.
55. Interview, Patrick Tsodza.
56. Interview, Kwadigepi Nyahwema. See Beach, 1980: 151–2 on this type of *sahawira* or *shamwari* relationship.
57. Personal correspondence from David Beach, 24 April 1992.
58. Arquivo Histórico de Mocambique, AHM, Governo Geral Cxa, 38 ML (2), Andrada ao Governo Geral Toué, 19 Augosto 1889.
59. AHU, Andrada Expedition 1/2, Andrada ao Ultramar, Massanga, 10 Junho 1887.
60. NAZ, SE 1/1/1, F. C. Selous to the Administrator, Mashonaland, 25 January 1891.
61. AHU, Andrada Expedition, 1/2 Andrada ao Ultramar, Massanga 10 Junho 1887.
62. AHM, Governo Geral Cxa 38 ML (2), Andrada ao Governo Geral Toué, 19 Augosto 1889. The arming of Katerere to fight Mutoko was an event recounted by a good number of elderly informants: e.g. interviews, Oripa Chikutirwe and Ronia Sangarwe, Frank Matambo Sanhani and Kagonda Sanhani. Others could recount in some detail the places Andrada visited: interview, Matambo Chifodya.
63. NAZ, N9/4/2, Monthly Report, Mtoko, February 1899.
64. NAZ, N9/4/1, Monthly Report, Mtoko, October 1898. NUA 2/1/3, NC Umtali, Out Letters, 24 February 1899. NUA 1/1/1, NC Inyanga to NC Umtali, 21 October 1901.
65. NAZ, N9/4/14, Monthly Report, Inyanga, January 1903.
66. Andrada, 1891a; NAZ, CT 1/15/3, Report, M. D. Graham, Fort Salisbury, 19 January 1892.

67. Ranger, 1963: 59; *Cape Times*, 8 April 1892; *O Economista*, 10 March 1892. For Taungwena's involvement see NAZ, MA14/1/2, Jason Machiwanyika, lesson 80.
68. NAZ, CT 1/15/3, Report, M. D. Graham, Fort Salisbury, 19 January 1892. See also Isaacman, 1976: Chapter 3.
69. Interview, Langton Muromowenyoka, 7 December 1989.
70. See NAZ, MA14/1/2, Jason Machiwanyika, lessons 79 and 80. Hwesa tradition may be confusing Gouveia with the Portuguese soldier Fereta whose men were allied to Gouveia in the revolt, and were responsible for the rape of girls. However, an 1899 map, marking the place of Gouveia's death at the confluence of the Gaerezi and the Rwenya, puts his last battle well in Katerere's reach. See NAZ, N1/1/6, L. Armstrong to NC Mtoko, 21 July 1899.
71. NAZ, N9/4/1, Monthly Report, Mtoko, October 1898. NUA 2/1/3, NC Umtali, Out Letters, 24 February 1899.
72. NAZ, N9/4/4, Monthly Report, Mtoko, August 1899.
73. NAZ, N9/4/5, Monthly Report, October 1899.
74. NAZ, NUA 2/1/3, Annual Report, NC Umtali, 1898.
75. NAZ, NUA 2/1/1, Out Letters, NC Umtali, 2 April 1902.
76. NAZ, NSJ 1/1/1, Half Yearly Report, Mtoko, October 1898.
77. NAZ, N1/1/4, Out Letters, NC Inyanga to CNC Salisbury, 10, 12, 14 July 1902.
78. Interview, Langton Muromowenyoka, 7 December 1989.
79. NAZ, A/11/2/12/12, P. Gwynne S/Inspector, British South Africa Police to Chief Inspector Straker, 27 March 1904.
80. NAZ, N9/4/18, Monthly Report, Inyanga, April 1904.
81. Ibid.
82. Ibid. There was much debate within the administration over the meaning of the reports from the north-east. See NAZ, A/11/2/12/12, Unrest in Inyanga District, March–April 1904.
83. See Iliffe, 1995: chapter 9. Lonsdale, 1985; P. Martin, 1983: chapter 1.

## CHAPTER 2

1. NAZ, N9/4/4, Monthly Report, Mtoko, August 1899.
2. Interview, Headman Martin Grande, 11 August 1996.
3. NAZ, N/9/4/37, Monthly Report, Inyanga, October 1919. S2403/2681, Annual Report, Inyanga, 1953.
4. There were 126 prosecutions for possession of arms in Inyanga District between 1902 and 1922. NAZ, D4/21/1, Criminal Register, Inyanga, July 1902 to December 1922.
5. For a brief account of pre-colonial Inyanga chiefs' powers see NUC 2/3/1, Out Letters, NC Inyanga, 28 May 1908. Chiefs did carry on hearing criminal cases. Sometimes this happened in a clandestine manner, in other instances it occurred because they did not recognise such a rigid Western distinction between 'criminal' and 'civil'. See Holleman, 1969: 92.
6. Alexander, 1993: 7, citing Steele, 1972: 80–6. In 1907 the NC Inyanga looked forward to 'the tribal communal system being broken up in favour of the individual system', NAZ, NUC 2/1/2, Annual Report, Inyanga, 1907.
7. NAZ, D4/21/1, Criminal Registers, Inyanga, 1902–22.
8. *Gekeke* in this context means a person who constantly moves around.
9. Interviews, Harry Tsengerai; Headman Martin Gande, 11 August 1996; Kajiwa Nyakasapa.
10. NUC 2/3/3, Out Letters, NC Inyanga, n.d. 1918. S604, Out Letters, NC Inyanga, 17 January 1925.

11. NAZ, S2827/2/2/2, vol.5, Annual Report, Inyanga, 1952.
12. Interview, NAZ, Oral/Ha1, Walter Hughes Halls. Hughes-Halls was an NCO who patrolled the district in the 1910s.
13. Interview, Mary Brien.
14. NAZ, D/3/22/3, Rex versus Katerere et al., Criminal Cases Inyanga, 1921.
15. NAZ, NUA 2/1/5, Half Yearly Report, September 1903. Other inhabitants of Katerere quickly relocated. In 1901 it was noted that some Hwesa had moved into the previously deserted terrace land of the Inyanga 'civilization' around Nhani area. NAZ, N9/4/8, Monthly Report, Inyanga, April 1901.
16. Interview, Patrick Tsodza.
17. See also Mukamuri, 1989. I am not arguing that sacred wood lots were an invention in the colonial period, but that they took on a greater significance. For evidence of sacred wood lots in pre-colonial Katerere, see Burke, 1969: 237.
18. NAZ, S604, NC, Inyanga to Superintendent of Natives, Umtali, 17 May 1924.
19. NAZ, S1542/C6, Chiefs and Headmen, vol.7, NC Inyanga, 26 March 1936.
20. NAZ, S1561/10, Chiefs and Headmen, vol.14, NC Inyanga, to CNC, 21 April 1932.
21. Interview, Diki Rukadza, medium of Nyawada, 15 August, 1991.
22. Interviews, Oripa Chikutirwe and Ronia Sangarwe; Osius Nyamhute, 8 June 1989.
23. Interviews, Taimo Kapomba, medium of Chimucheka, 5 July 1989 and 11 December 1989.
24. Holleman (1969: 118–19) makes these points, although it is striking the extent to which his own case study on Chief Mangwende contradicts this general statement.
25. NAZ, N3/1/8, The Administrator, Salisbury, to the Governor, Tete, 23 November 1903.
26. Holleman, p.35. Holleman makes this argument for the 1940s, but it would hold for Katerere in earlier decades where NCs found messengers essential for retaining contact with distant chiefs. NAZ, N3/4/2, Out Letters, NC Inyanga, 22 December 1920.
27. DAI, NC, Inyanga to PNC, Manicaland, 25 July 1960, Chief Katerere.
28. NAZ, S1561/10, Chiefs and Headmen, vol.14, 1931–2. In April 1932 the NC spent four days in Katerere and reported that all the 'kraals' except one were in favour of Chikata. The Chifodyas told me in conversation that the NC camped in the southern part of Katerere near Mt Nhani, 40km away. It is more than possible that he was unaware of their rival claim. An example of a very similar case in the Makoni chieftainship is recounted by Donald Abraham. See 1951: 77–81.
29. NAZ, NUC 3/1/1, Annual Report, Inyanga, 1903.
30. NAZ, NUA 2/1/5, Monthly Report, Inyanga (forwarded), September 1903.
31. NAZ, NUC 3/1/1, Annual Report, Inyanga, 1903.
32. NAZ, N3/4/1, NC Inyanga to Superintendent of Natives, Umtali, 10 September 1914.
33. The NC Inyanga in 1937 wrote with pleasure of how the previously ambulatory Barwe had begun to settle and were 'amenable to tribal control'. NAZ, S1563, Annual Report, Inyanga, 1937.
34. NAZ, NUC 3/1/1, Annual Report, Inyanga, 1903. In 1901, Katerere was also the refuge of two criminals who had committed 'extensive thefts' in Tete. NAZ, NUA 1/1/1, NC Inyanga to NC Umtali, 20 and 21 October 1901.
35. On refugees from Barwe see Ranger, 1963: 60. On movement of Hwesa and Tangwena peoples to avoid tax payment see NAZ, NUC 2/3/1, Monthly Report, Inyanga, July 1906.

36. NAZ, NSJ 1/1/2, NC Mtoko to CNC, 3 September 1903.
37. NAZ, NUC 2/1/3, Out Letters, Inyanga, 28 May 1908.
38. This is certainly true for the Katerere, Maungwe and Saunyama dynasties. For Sawunyama the NC Inyanga in 1918 decided for the sake of continuity to restrict succession to the incumbent house and give a headmanship to a powerful rival house, in exile in the early years of the occupation. NUC 2/3/3, Out Letters, NC Inyanga, 3 September 1918. For Maungwe see Abraham, 1951: 77–9.
39. Burke, 1969; Andrada, 1891b. See also in the early colonial period a map by L. Armstrong NC, Mtoko, showing 'Cattarari'. NAZ, N1/1/6, Armstrong to Col. Alderson, 21 July 1899.
40. Portuguese Government, 1890: 264, no. 113. Andrada Expedition, 1/2 Andrada ao Ultramar, Massanga, 10 Junho 1887.
41. NAZ, S2076, Annual Report, Inyanga, 1920.
42. NAZ, NUC 2/1/4, Out Letters, Inyanga, 30 September 1911.
43. NAZ, NUC 2/1/3, Out Letters, NC Inyanga, 28 May 1908. NUC 2/4/2, Out Letters, NC Inyanga, 'Resume of Tribes', 13 January 1913.
44. NAZ, MA14/1/2, J. Machiwanyika, lesson 36, n.d.
45. NAZ, NUA 2/1/4, Monthly Report, February 1901.
46. NAZ, NUC 2/3/1, NC Inyanga to CNC Salisbury, 10 March 1906.
47. NAZ, NUC 2/3/2, NC Inyanga to Superintendent of Natives, 31 October 1911.
48. NAZ, NUC 2/1/4, Annual Report, Inyanga, 1909.
49. NAZ, S1561/10, Chiefs and Headmen, vol.6, Inyanga, January 1925.
50. NAZ, S138/17/1, NC Inyanga to Priest in Charge, Triashill Mission, 2 January 1927.
51. NAZ, S604, NC Inyanga to CNC Salisbury, 9 November 1927.
52. NAZ, S544, Criminal Cases Inyanga, 1928–33. Examples here are too numerous to cite.
53. NAZ, S1561/10, Chiefs and Headmen, vol.10A, 1928–9.
54. NAZ, S2076, Annual Report, Inyanga, 1920.
55. For a fuller discussion of women's varied experience under colonialism see Phimister, 1988: 203–5.
56. The Chief Native Commissioner used this phrase in his submission to the Phelps Stokes Education Committee of East Africa when elaborating on his system of administration. NAZ, S138/17,1924–25.
57. Schmidt reminds us that a few pre-colonial Shona women did have power as midwives, healers, spirit mediums and chieftainesses (1992: 24–5). Although she warns us (p.16) that such power may well have perpetuated a male dominated system.
58. Schmidt, 1992: 62–70. Schmidt also argues that the state's attack on peasant option in the 1930s further increased women's labour.
59. Personal communication, Ken Wilson.
60. For instance, interview, Kaburunge Magadu, Mutengapasi Magadu and Katoya Katerere.
61. NAZ, S604, NC Inyanga to CNC Salisbury, 5 August 1924.
62. Conversation, Joseph Chitima, 30 May 1991. In dry season women used the leaves of okra and cow peas. In wet season they used pumpkin leaves and sour cabbage. On the importance of gardens see Moore & Vaughan, 1987: 534.
63. For a review of the literature on theories of conversion see Ifkenga-Metuh, 1987: 11–27.
64. The reconstruction of religious change is particularly difficult to footnote as my argument is based on a synthesis of fragmentary oral and archival evidence.

Where possible I will indicate the archival sources, but the interviews are often too numerous to cite. The oral data comes from a collection of interviews with approximately 50 elders from the Katerere area. These comprise spirit mediums and their acolytes, Hwesa royals and commoners, and outsiders – male and female.

65. Michael Gelfand also found traces of a High God Cult amongst the Hwesa in 1970–1 during his research on Shona spiritual beliefs. Gelfand, 1977: 135.

66. Mazambani, 1990: 163. Conversations with David Mazambani, Harare, Zimbabwe, August 1991. Gelfand, 1977: 156.

67. Interviews, Pitodya Chifodya; Kaburunge Magadu; Mathias Sachiwo, 14 August 1991.

68. On the arrest of religious leaders seen as subversive in the north-east, see for instance, NAZ, N/9/4/2, Monthly Report, Mutoko, March 1899. NSJ 1/1/3, NC Mutoko to CNC, 4 September 1904. NSJ 1/1/5, NC Mutoko to CNC, 5 October 1910.

69. Kingsley Garbett's study of regional cults in the 1960s suggests that the state's concern did not extend to flows of messengers or pilgrims. Garbett, 1976.

70. Fields, 1985: 61–6. It is generally accepted that the Southern Rhodesian State was strong enough to engineer direct rule. However such rule was often tenuous in the early decades of colonialism, particularly in marginal areas.

71. McGregor, 1991: 292–3. Personal communication, JoAnn McGregor.

72. This point is also made implicitly by Kingsley Garbett, 1966, 'Religious Aspects of Political Succession among the Valley Korekore (N. Shona)' in E. Stokes and R. Brown (ed.), *The Zambesian Past*, Manchester: Manchester University Press, p.151; cited in Mudenge, 1988: 126.

73. K. Wilson, 1990: 637. I differ from Wilson in that I stress the adaptation of ancestral religion rather than its 'creation'.

74. For a similar argument about the decline of 'a man controlled ecological system', see Kjekshus, 1977.

75. Between 1902 and 1922 there were approximately 45 prosecutions for Game Law offences and approximately 125 prosecutions for possession of arms in Inyanga District. See NAZ, D4/21/1, Criminal Register, Inyanga, 1902–22. Hunting continued, particularly in Portuguese East Africa, but fear of stiff penalties if apprehended in British territory led to its decline. The adjacent territory of Mutoko employed two men to patrol the district and enforce Game Laws. NAZ, NSJ 1/1/5, Acting NC Mutoko, to CNC Salisbury, 3 September 1910.

76. For a decline in net making and other crafts see Acting NC Mutoko to CNC Salisbury, 24 January 1911, NAZ, NSJ 1/1/5. Dogs were used in hunting and to scare off predators. A tax on them led to a decline in their numbers. See S2076, Annual Report, Inyanga, 1920.

77. Accounts of baboons destroying crops are too numerous to record here. Particularly detailed examples are found in N9/4/36–45, Monthly Reports, Inyanga, 1918–23.

78. S615, Reports by E. Rossiter and Major P. H. Van Niekerk, 9 March 1927. Rossiter wrote to the NC: 'It will be noted that practically all fauna is increasing, being no doubt due to our isolated position, and scarcity of hunters.' NAZ, S603. E. Rossiter to NC Inyanga, 18 February 1927.

79. Interview, Kaburunge Magadu, Mutengapasi Magadu and Katoya Katerere.

80. During the 1903 famine the NC Inyanga was surprised to find the Hwesa still well nourished by means of roots and fruit, particularly the Ndiya root. NAZ, NUA 2/1/5, Monthly Report, Inyanga, 1903. On the ability of the peoples of pre–colonial Zimbabwe to survive famine see Iliffe, 1990: 15–20.

81. NAZ, NUC 3/1/1, Annual Report, Inyanga, 1915.
82. Interview, Janet Nyamudeza. Winnie Loosemoore, 'Demon Possessed Africans Delivered', *Elim Evangel*, 11 December 1954. These cults were known as *maromba* (*romba* sing.) in Hwesa.
83. For example, '*Suro Murezi*' (The Nurse Hare), '*Mwana Adatogorwa NaKuruwa*' (A Child Picked up by Baboons). Samson Mudzudza, 1994, Minority Languages Project, University of Zimbabwe.
84. NAZ, NUC 2/3/2, Monthly Report, Inyanga, September 1913.
85. Anselm Corbett, 'St Anna Rori', *White Friars*, September 1950.
86. Dachs and Rea, 1979: 72. JAH, Box 196, Hilda Richards, 'A History of Triashill', n.d.
87. Anselm Corbett, 'St Anna Rori', *White Friars*, September 1950.
88. JAH, Box 196, Richards, 'A History of Triashill', n.d. Isodore Coraghlan, 'Triashill Under the Marianhill Fathers 1896–1929', *White Friars*, March 1962.
89. Interviews, Father Tony Clarke; Oripa Chikutirwe and Ronia Sangarwe.
90. JAH, Box 196, Richards, 'A History of Triashill', n.d.
91. Anselm Corbett, 'St Anna Rori', *White Friars*, September 1950.
92. Informants here are too numerous to mention.
93. Interviews, Oripa Chikutirwe and Ronia Sangarwe; Harry Tsengerai. Interview conducted by Shupikai Chikutirwe with Douglas and Emily Sangarwe.
94. Interview, Frank and Kagonda Sanhani. JAH, Box 139/3, Outstations served by Triashill, n.d.
95. Interview, Muchato Madhenya (sub-Chief Sanhani).
96. One priest wrote: 'In Inyanga and Nyamaropa Reserve are up to today no Protestant mission and the utmost should be done to keep them out.' JAH, Box 139/3, Fr. Arndt to Rev. Msgr Brown, 15 April 1929.
97. NAZ, S2810/4203, D. Lamont to Mr Gardener, 4 June 1952.
98. NAZ, S1542/W6, CNC to Staff Officer, BSAC, 23 October 1933.
99. NAZ, S1542/W6, NC Mutoko to CNC Salisbury, 14 October 1933.
100. For a general survey, see Ranger, 1982a.
101. Interviews, Petros Sadowera; Pitodya Chifodya; Diki Rukadza, medium of Nyawada, 15 August 1991.
102. Matthew Schoffeleers, 1966, 'M'bona. The Guardian spirit of the Mang'anja', B.Litt dissertation, Oxford; cited in Ranger, 1982a: 40.
103. Keith Rennie, 1972, 'Some Revitalisation Movements Among the Ndau and Inhambane Thonga 1915–1935', Conference on the History of African Religious Systems, Lusaka, September, pp.16–17; cited in Ranger, 1982a: 26.
104. Interviews, Petros Sadowera; Mathias Sachiwo, 14 August 1991.
105. Audrey Richards, 1935, 'A Modern Movement of Witch-finders', *Africa* 40 (3), 448–61; cited in Ranger, 1982a: 21.
106. Ibid.
107. NAZ, S1561/10, Chiefs and Headmen, vol.6, 1925.
108. NAZ, S1561/10 vol.10, Chiefs and Headmen, 1929.
109. See NAZ, S1542/W6, Witchcraft, correspondence between 1933 and 1934.
110. For files on the AFM's history and links with the *Vapostori* see: S2810/2358/1, Apostolic Faith Mission, Hartley, 1931–45; S1542/MB8 vol.1, CNC's Correspondence 1919–34; S1542/MB8 vol.2, CNC's Correspondence, 1934–38; S1542/P10, Pseudo Religions, 1934–6. Interviews, Pastor Jeries Mvenge (ex-Superintendent of the AFM); Pastor Constantine Murefu (Principal of AFM Living Waters Bible College). I am currently researching the history of the AFM as part of a wider study on the history of Zimbabwean Pentecostalism.

111. Mchape, of course, operated throughout east and central Africa, whilst the *Vapostori* later developed transnational linkages. The AFM was also subject to suspicion due to its origin in South Africa, from which liberal or Bolshevik influences were believed to emanate.
112. Rennie, cited in Ranger, 1982a: 27.
113. Ibid.: 28–29.
114. Interview, Pitodya Chifodya.
115. Interviews, Peter Marova; Harry Tsengerai.
116. On demonisation see Schoffeleers, 1979: 30; and Weber, 1963: 28.
117. Interview, Harry Tsengerai.

## CHAPTER 3

1. NAZ, S988, Natural Resources Board, Native Enquiry, 16 July 1942.
2. Interview, Martin Gande.
3. NAZ, S1051, Annual Reports, Inyanga, 1946 and 1948. S2827/1977/1, Land, Inyanga, Assistant Secretary, Native Affairs to CNC, 6 September 1951.
4. NAZ, S2827/2/2/1–4, Annual Reports, Inyanga, 1951–6.
5. Etherington, 1983: 129. Except, perhaps South Africa, see Sundkler, 1976.
6. Hastings, 1994a: 559–61. Of course, as Hastings observes, Pius XI inherited a strong missionary concern from his predecessor, Benedict XV. Others would see this expansion in the 1920s as part of a whole process set in train by Gregory XVI (1831–46) or even Gregory XV in 1622.
7. *Elim Evangel*, 13 March 1950.
8. *White Friars*, September–October 1946.
9. Interview, Tony Clarke. For the wider background to the Irish impulse see Hogan, 1990.
10. *White Friars*, November–December 1946.
11. *Elim Evangel*, 'Elim Penetrates the R.C. Curtain', 1 February 1958.
12. *White Friars*, November–December 1946.
13. EAC, 'Correpondence with J. Williams', October 1947–July 1957, J. Williams to Reverend Thomas, Elim HQ, 27 April 1949.
14. Interview, Harry Tsengerai.
15. *The Comforter*, 'Our Missionaries in Southern Rhodesia', September–October 1945.
16. AFM, Jesse Williams, Lyndhurst, South Africa.
17. Ibid.
18. Ibid.
19. Interview, James Kaerezi.
20. Interview, Oripa Chikutirwe and Ronia Sangarwe.
21. Cathal O'hAinle, 'Carmelites in Africa', *Zelo*, summer 1958.
22. The Drs Brien, 'AFRICA: Entering New Areas with the Gospel' *Elim Evangel*, April 1954.
23. Donal Lamont, 'Missionary Journey' parts 1 & 2, *White Friars*, March–April, May–June 1949.
24. Ibid.
25. Cathal O'hAinle, 'Carmelites in Africa', *Zelo*, spring 1958.
26. An excellent account of the social teachings and practices of British Elim churches in the 1950s is found in B. Wilson, 1961: 77–88. Jeanette Winterson's work of *faction*, *Oranges are Not the Only Fruit* (1985), is based on her childhood experiences in an Elim Church in Lancashire in the 1960s. The Elim movement questioned the validity of her account.

27. Interview, Peter Griffiths.
28. Cecil Brien, 'Meet Our Missionaries', *Elim Evangel*, 14 January 1961.
29. Dr and Mrs Brien, 'Gospel advances in Southern Rhodesia', *Elim Evangel*, 3 December 1951. Winnie Loosemore, 'Demon Possessed Africans Delivered', *Elim Evangel*, 11 December 1954. A. Nicholson, 'Living Epistles', *Elim Evangel*, 7 September 1963.
30. Interview, Mary Brien. *Elim Evangel*, 10 November 1956; Brenda Hurrell, 'Journey to Katerere', *Elim Missionary Evangel*, July–September 1957.
31. I do not use the term 'eradication movement' because the Pentecostals dealt with a multitude of individual cases and did not administer a cure collectively. I deal in greater depth with the difference between cleansing and eradication in Chapter 7.
32. Winnie Loosemore, 'Demon Possessed Africans Delivered', *Elim Evangel*, 11 December 1954.
33. Interview, Mary Brien.
34. Ibid.
35. Interview, Peter Griffiths.
36. EAC, 'Elim missionaries A–J to 1966', Mary Brien to Elim HQ, 12 December 1950. Cecil Brien to Pastor L. Green, c.1950. *Elim Evangel*, 23 April 1951.
37. Interview, Peter Griffiths.
38. Mary Brien, 'Healing of the Sick', *Elim Evangel*, 7 July 1952.
39. Ibid. 'Elim Doctors working in the School' (no author), *Elim Evangel*, 3 January 1953.
40. *Elim Evangel*, 3 July 1953.
41. Dr and Mrs C. Brien, 'Gospel Advances In Southern Rhodesia', *Elim Evangel*, 3 December 1951.
42. Interview, James Kaerezi.
43. *Elim Evangel*, 25 June 1955.
44. For example, see interviews, Ephraim Satuku; Rinos Mukwewa; William Mukwata.
45. Alexander, 1993: chapter 2; NAZ, S2827/2/2/1–8, Annual Reports, Inyanga, 1951–61.
46. *Elim Evangel*, 5 May 1956.
47. Interview, Paul Makanyanga.
48. Interview, Peter Griffiths.
49. Personal correspondence from Comrade Ranga, 13 July 1990. For evidence of Pentecostal activity along the river see *Elim Evangel*, 4 March 1961 and 23 January 1971.
50. Personal correspondence, Comrade Ranga, 13 July 1990.
51. Interview, Paul Makanyanga.
52. *The Zambezi Mission Record*, October 1912.
53. Anselm Corbett, 'The Feast of the Little Flower in Africa', *White Friars*, November–December 1947.
54. *Zelo*, summer 1958.
55. Mel Hill, 'The Scapular in Africa', *White Friars*, July–August 1950.
56. *Zelo*, summer 1958.
57. Interview, Donal Lamont.
58. Tony Clarke, 'Our Missions and some Methods', *Zelo*, autumn 1960, pp.81–2.
59. *White Friars*, July–August 1959.
60. Interview, Paddy Stornton. For the theological context, see Ad Gentes, 'Decree on the Church's Missionary Activity' in Abbott, 1966: 604, 611–13.

61. Interview, Paddy Stornton.
62. A statement on 'Faith and Inculturation' issued by the International Theological Commission of the Catholic Church in 1987 stated: 'The process of inculturation may be defined as the Church's efforts to make the message of Christ penetrate a given socio-cultural milieu, calling upon the latter to grow according to all its particular values, as long as these are compatible with the Gospel.' Cited in Sherer and Bevans, 1992: 87.
63. Interview, Luke MacCabe (Dr R. J. MacCabe).
64. Berthold Dowd, 'Mashona Tribal Beliefs', October–November 1960; 'Carmelite African Mission', February–March 1961; 'A World of Spirits', December 1961–January 1962 in *The Scapular*.
65. Interview, Paddy Stornton. For the wider context see Dachs and Rea, 1979: chapters 14 and 16.
66. Mel Hill, 'Young Africa', *The Sword*, summer 1953.
67. Anselm Corbett, 'The Feast', *White Friars* Nov–Dec 1947.
68. Interview, Paddy Stornton. See Linden, 1980: 32–4, for a more detailed consideration of how the varied social sources of Catholic Church's missionary organisations affected patterns of missionisation throughout the country as a whole.
69. EAC, 'Correspondence with J. Williams', J. Williams, Report, 30 April 1952.
70. *White Friars*, July–August 1949.
71. Cathal O'hAinle, 'Carmelites in Africa', *Zelo*, spring 1958.
72. 'Consecration Ceremony', *White Friars*, August–September 1957.
73. Mrs J. Williams, 'Southern Rhodesia', *Elim Evangel*, 9 June 1952.
74. Dr and Mrs C. Brien, 'Southern Rhodesia: An S.O.S. for Prayer', *Elim Evangel*, 23 June 1953.
75. NAZ, S2810/4203, Acting Secretary to the PNC, Manicaland, 6 June 1952.
76. Cathal O'hAinle, 'Carmelites in Africa', *Zelo*, summer 1958, p.85.
77. Cecil Brien, *Elim Evangel*, 10 March 1952.
78. EAC, 'Mission Correspondence 1944–57', Mrs A. Nicolson to Elim HQ, 30 July 1956.
79. Interview, Mary Brien.
80. Tony Clarke, 'Our Missions And Some Methods', *Zelo*, autumn 1960, p.71. A. Nicholson, 'Africa', *Elim Evangel*, 7 July 1956.
81. NAZ, S2810/4203, Secretary for Native Affairs to PNC Manicaland, 10 August 1953.
82. NAZ, S2810/4203, Donal Lamont to Mr Gardener, 4 June 1952.
83. Ibid.
84. NAZ, S2827/2/2/3, Annual Report, Inyanga, 1955.
85. NAZ, S2810/4203 NC Inyanga to PNC Umtali, 5 April 1956.
86. NAZ, S2827/2/2/4, Annual Report, Inyanga, 1956.
87. For example, EAC, 'Mission Correspondence 1944–57', A. Nicholson to Elim HQ, 31 May 1956. *Elim Evangel*, 22 November 1951, 31 May 1956.
88. EAC, 'Elim Missionaries A–J to 1966', Zimbabwean Sons of the Soil to The Missionaries, 1 March 1964.
89. EAC, 'Elim Missionaries A–J to 1966', Cecil Brien to Reverend Gorman, Elim HQ, 26 March and 31 March 1964.
90. EAC, 'Elim Missionaries A–J to 1966', Zimbabwean Sons of the Soil to The Missionaries, 1 March 1964.
91. Interview, Paul Makanyanga.
92. EAC, 'Mission, Statistics', Annual report for year ended 31 January 1966. Reports and Notes, South Africa and Rhodesia, Minutes of the Field Council held 11 December 1972.

93. EAC, 'Rhodesia-Zimbabwe', Cecil Brien to Reverend J. Smyth, Elim HQ, 4 October 1970.
94. Mel Hill, 'Young Africa', *The Sword*, May 1952.
95. *Elim Evangel*, November 1955. See also Mel Hill, *The Sword*, May 1952.
96. EAC, 'Elim Missionaries A–J to 1966', Peter Griffiths to Mr Wiggleswoth, 24 August 1966.
97. Mel Hill, 'Young Africa', *The Sword*, May 1952.
98. Antony Clarke, 'Our Missions and Some Methods', *Zelo*, autumn 1960.
99. EAC, 'Vumba Press Cuttings', Catherine Picken, Field Report, c.1974.
100. Personal communication, Pious Munembe.
101. EAC, Reports and Notes, 'South Africa and Rhodesia', Don Evans, Personal Report of one year spent in the Rhodesian Field, August 1971–August 1972.
102. Interview, Paul Makanyanga.
103. Ibid.
104. Personal communication, Peter Griffiths.
105. EAC, 'Elim Missionaries A–J to 1966', Schools Disturbances, May–June 1966, Circuit Inspector, Manicaland North, to Provincial Education Officer, 29 July 1966.
106. EAC, 'Joan Caudell', Circular from Joan Caudell, December 1974.
107. 'A Thrilling Sequel', *Elim Evangel*, January 1975.
108. EAC, Missionaries: Beardwell–Gywnne, Mary Brien to Pastor Gorman, 25 July 1961; Margaret Gwynne to Mr Thomas, 30 April 1962; Margaret Gwynne to Mr Gorman, 9 November 1962. For the 1970s, see also Chapter 5.
109. Peter Griffiths, 'Emmanuel Secondary School, Rhodesia', *Elim Evangel*, 23 January 1971.
110. Personal communication, Des Cartwright.

## CHAPTER 4

1. Interview, Forichi Koso and family.
2. Research by Gloria Nyamazuve, March 1989.
3. 'The Story of the Foundation and Growth of the African Sisterhood in Rhodesia', *The Scapular*, January–February 1966.
4. *White Friars*, September–October 1960.
5. For a brief history see JAH, 'Handmaids of Our Lady of Mount Carmel, Rhodesia 1977', Box 300/5.
6. Interviews, Sister Michael Nyamutswa, Plexaides Musona.
7. Mel Hill, 'Young Africa', *The Sword*, summer 1953.
8. *Elim Evangel*, 10 March 1952, 11 December 1954, April 1954.
9. *Elim Evangel*, 10 November 1956.
10. EAC, 'Mission Correpondence 1944–57', W. Loosemore to Elim HQ, 8 October 1954.
11. Interviews, Peter Griffiths, Mary Brien.
12. Interview, Pious Munembe.
13. *Elim Missionary Evangel*, October–December 1957. *Elim Evangel*, 24 January 1970.
14. *Elim Evangel*, 5 December 1964. Interview, Mary Brien.
15. *Elim Evangel*, 11 December 1954. Interview, Mary Brien.
16. *Elim Evangel*, 10 March 1952.
17. Sermon preached by Mary Brien, Elim Mission, 12 June 1988.
18. Margaret Gwynne, 'My first four Months on the Field', *Elim Evangel*, 3 January 1958.

19. Interview, Pious Munembe.
20. Interview, Paul Makanyanga.
21. Interviews, Paul Makanyanga; Rinos Mukwewa; Pious Munembe; Ephraim Satuku.
22. Interview, Pious Munembe.
23. Margaret Gwynne, 'The Gems', *Elim Evangel*, 2 June 1962.
24. Conversation with David Mazambani, Oxford, 2 May 1992.
25. Ignatius Farragher, 'Vocations in Africa', *The Scapular*, November–December 1965.
26. J. K. Rennie (1973) describes a similar process in the construction of Ndau ethnicity.
27. NAZ, S1563, Annual Report, Inyanga, 1938.
28. In the first decade of the century many permits were issued for the purpose of allowing the movement of people and cattle out of the district. See for instance, NAZ, NUC 2/1/2, Monthly Report, Inyanga, July 1907.
29. NAZ, NUC 3/1/1, Annual Reports, Inyanga, 1915 and 1916.
30. NAZ, S1563, Annual Report, Inyanga, 1934.
31. NAZ, S1563, Annual Report, Inyanga, 1936.
32. NAZ, NUC 3/1/1, Annual Report, Inyanga, 1908.
33. NAZ, S988, Natural Resources Board, Native Enquiry, 1942, p.2.
34. NAZ, S1051, Annual Report, Inyanga, 1947.
35. NAZ, S2588/1977, C. G. Hamner to the CNC, 28 January 1948, and 23 March 1951, Acting Ass. CNC to C. G. Hamner, 28 April 1951.
36. NAZ, S517, CID Files on African Organisations, 1948–9, 'Manyikaland: Memorandum to the Government'.
37. Ibid.
38. Interview, Frederick and William Mukwata.
39. NAZ, S1563, Annual Reports, Inyanga, 1937, 1938; NUC 2/3/3, NC Inyanga to CNC, c.1920.
40. NAZ, NUC 2/1/5, Out Letters, NC Inyanga, 26 September 1914.
41. Conversation with Davis Mazambani, Oxford, 5 May 1992.
42. Father Anselm Corbett, 'St. Anna-Rori', *White Friars*, September–October 1950.
43. Interview, Pious Munembe.
44. Interviews, Pastor Pious Munembe; Rinos Mukwewa; Frederick and William Mukwata; Paul Makanyanga. Interviews conducted by Ewart Mapara with the Maparas.
45. Sermon, Mary Brien, Elim mission, 12 June 1988.
46. Interviews conducted by Ewart Mapara with the Maparas.
47. Interview, Mary Brien.
48. Interview, Mary Brien. Mary Brien to Mrs D. Smyly, 16 March 1985, in the possession of Dr A. Smyly. Interview, Janet Nyamudeza. See also Winnie Loosemore, 'Demon Possessed Africans Delivered', *Elim Evangel*, 11 December 1954.
49. Interview, Frederick and William Mukwata.
50. Interviews conducted by Ewart Mapara with the Maparas.
51. Interview, Tony Clarke.
52. Interview, Cyprian Pasipanodya and Camillo Mudondo.
53. Interviews, Paddy Stornton; Dr Robert MacCabe (Father Luke); Cyprian Pasipanodya and Camillo Mudondo.
54. Interviews, Pious Munembe; Paul Makanyanga; Tony Clarke.
55. I am grateful to David Mazambani for drawing my attention to this.

## CHAPTER 5

1. A useful section on the changing goals and strategies of the nationalist movements is found in Kriger, 1992: 82–93.
2. See, for instance, K. Wilson, 1992.
3. EAC, Reports and Notes, 'South Africa and Rhodesia', J. C. Smyth and L. Wigglesworth, Report of Delegation's Visit to Southern Rhodesia and South Africa 13 June–6 July 1976.
4. Diary, Brenda Griffiths, 14 September and 15 October 1976.
5. Ibid., 28 July 1977.
6. Ibid., 4 August 1976, 7 October 1976. Diary, Joy Bath, 7 June 1976. Headmen Chifambe and Mungezi were killed together with another unnamed headman in the Ruangwe area. Mungezi was unpopular for collecting contour ridge fines. Mungezi's headmanship was the creation of the ultra-traditionalist Rhodesia Front Government. The other two assassinated were probably 'kraal' heads.
7. DAI, 'Chief Katerere', DC Inyanga to Secretary for Home Affairs, 31 March 1980. 'Headman Sachiwo', minute from DC Inyanga, 16 October 1980. Interviews, Herbert Turai (Comrade Sam Zvaitika); Augustine Mabvira (Comrade Ranga), 31 May 1988; personal correspondence from Augustine Mabvira, 12 May 1992. Interviews, Corporal Archibald Maziti (Comrade Howard Shaka); Richard Simbi.
8. Diary, Brenda Griffiths, 4 August 1976, 28 July 1976. Diary, Joy Bath, 24 June 1976.
9. DAI, 'Chief Katerere', DC Inyanga to Secretary for Home Affairs, 31 March 1980.
10. Interview, Sister Michael Nyamutswa.
11. EAC, Reports and Notes, 'South Africa and Rhodesia', J. C. Smyth and L. Wigglesworth, Report of Delegation's Visit to Southern Rhodesia and South Africa 13 June–6 July 1976.
12. JAH, Box 195/3, Father Jerome O'Hea to the Monsignor, Triashill, 11 September 1930. NAZ, S604, NC Inyanga to CNC, 20 November 1930.
13. NAZ, S2827/2/2/4, Annual Report, Inyanga, 1955.
14. EAC, 'Missionaries: Beardwell–Griffiths 1963–4', Cecil Brien to Rev. G. H. Thomas, 17 November 1961. Elim missionary, Cecil Brien, wrote of a Joshua Nkomo holding a large rally near Regina Coeli mission in Nyamaropa.
15. NAZ, S2827/2/2/8, Annual Report, Inyanga, 1961.
16. NAZ, S2827/2/2/3, Annual Report, Inyanga, 1955.
17. Conversation with David Mazambani, Oxford, 5 May 1992.
18. Interview, Augustine Mabvira (Comrade Ranga), 3 June 1991.
19. Ibid.
20. Interview, Corporal Archibald Maziti (Comrade Howard Shaka).
21. Interview, Augustine Mabvira (Comrade Ranga), 3 June 1991.
22. Some Hwesa were still using bark blankets at this time. Ibid.
23. Ibid. Interviews, Corporal Archibald Maziti (Comrade Howard Shaka); Herbert Turai (Comrade Sam Zvaitika).
24. Interview, Augustine Mabvira (Comrade Ranga), 3 June 1991.
25. Ibid. Guerrillas used the Manyika of Sedze village in a similar manner. Interviews conducted by Ewart Mapara with the Maparas.
26. Conversation with David Mazambani, Oxford, 2 May 1992.
27. Interview, Frederick and William Mukwata.
28. Jeremy Brickhill, seminar on ZIPRA mobilisation, St Antony's College, Oxford, 1990.
29. Interview, Augustine Mabvira (Comrade Ranga), 31 May 1988.

30. For an extended treatment of the relation between Katerere's Christian missions and guerrillas see Maxwell, 1995a.

31. EAC, Reports and Notes, 'South Africa and Rhodesia', J. C. Smyth, Final Report of Visit to Rhodesia, July 1977.

32. Ibid. Diary, Joy Bath, 8 June and 20 October 1976. Diary, Brenda Griffiths, 27 August 1977.

33. Diary, Brenda Griffiths, 9 May and 6 August 1977.

34. EAC, Rev. and Mrs McCann, S. and P. McCann to L. Wigglesworth, Elim HQ, Cheltenham, 1 January 1977.

35. EAC, 'Rev. and Mrs Lynn', R. and J. Lynn to L. Wigglesworth, Elim HQ, Cheltenham, 31 January 1978.

36. For a detailed consideration of Avila mission's wartime relations with guerrillas see McLaughlin, 1995.

37. Interview, Father Peter Egan.

38. Interview, Father David Weakliam.

39. Interview, Father Paddy Stornton.

40. Interview, Brother Ignatius Moore.

41. Interview, Dr Robert MacCabe (Father Luke).

42. Interview, Diki Rukadza, medium of Nyawada, 22 January 1989.

43. Interview, Diki Rukadza, medium of Nyawada, 31 May 1991.

44. Gelfand, 1982: 134–5. Rukadza also gave Gelfand an interesting account of protective nature, pp.133–4.

45. For example, interviews, Oripa Chikutirwe; Zuze Chitima. Interview conducted by Shakewell Nyamahumba with Sub-Chief Fore Nyamahumba. Of Rukadza, Sub-Chief Nyamahumba of the Sawunyama dynasty said: 'He helps to organise Shona culture of Katerere ... and prevent them from doing bad things ... [he] was made spokesman because he is well known for his works.' Interview, Aluwizi Sanyamahwe, medium of Nyamande, and Advice Chifodya. Some officials in the District Administration considered Rukadza the 'Chief-maker'. DAI, 'Chief Katerere', Report on the Katerere Chieftainship Visit, 5 June 1991.

46. Interview, conducted by Shupikai Chikutirwe with Madzeku Chifodya.

47. Sing. *chapungu*.

48. Interviews, Osius Nyamhute; Frederick and William Mukwata. This was a well-known story. One woman told me that the *mhondoro* had the capacity to blur the vision of pilots so that the comrades would not be seen. Interview, Aquiline Kaerezi.

49. Interview, Richard Simbi.

50. Interview, Right Katerere.

51. Interview, Forichi Koso, ex-medium of Mbudzi, and daughter.

52. Interviews, Mathias Sachiwo, 5 June 1991; Forichi Koso, ex-medium of Mbudzi, and daughter (his daughter was the major informant in this case); Diki Rukadza, medium of Nyawada, 22 January 1989.

53. For instance the figure of medium Taimo Kapomba believed that many of the taboos on food were a product of the guerrillas' desire to be well fed. Interview, Taimo Kapomba, 6 June 1991.

54. 'Leading' families are those which have no claim to the chieftaincy but hold important ritual functions within it.

55. Interview, Michael Mudzudza.

56. These were the Gande people, who were of Jindwe origin. Interview, Martin Gande. Interview, Councillor Todd Mazambani, 1 June 1991. Conversation with David Mazambani, Oxford, 2 May 1992.

57. Interview, Augustine Mabvira (Comrade Ranga).
58. These were given to me whilst I was teaching history at Emmanuel Secondary School, Elim mission, 1987–9.
59. On 18 July 1976, six girls were killed at a party with comrades when it was attacked by security forces. There had been beer, dancing and records. Diary, Brenda Griffiths, 19 July 1976. Another informant at the Elim mission expressed his displeasure at the way young nurses would leave the station to spend time with guerrillas. Two of the ex-combatants I interviewed returned to Katerere to marry local women whom they had 'met' during the war.
60. Interview, Rumbidzai Bhande.
61. Interview, Anna Chikwiramakomo.
62. Interviews, Solomon Ndarowa; Philip Dhokotera; Corporal Archibald Maziti (Comrade Howard Shaka) and Captain N. Xechs Nyangari (Comrade Carl Marx); Augustine Mabvira (Comrade Ranga), 31 May 1988. This material conflicts with Martinus Daneel's work on the *Vapostori* in Masvingo. Here Independent church informants gave him an oral tradition of resistance which claimed connection with the victorious side in the war. See Daneel, 1991.
63. Personal correspondence from Augustine Mabvira (Comrade Ranga), 13 July 1990.
64. Interview, Pious Munembe.
65. Interview, Augustine Mabvira (Comrade Ranga), 3 June 1991.
66. These *mhondoro* were Chidana and Nyamchimbichara (Mutota). Interview, Mathias Sachiwo. Another influential Hwesa medium close to the border was Bracho, host of Dzihambo.
67. Interview, Taimo Kapomba, medium of Chimucheka, 5 July 1989.
68. Kapomba's homestead was en route to an airfield which was an important guerrilla target in the early stages of the war, before it was effectively closed down.
69. These differences were pointed out to me by Jeremy Brickhill (ex-ZIPRA guerrilla) and Nyasha Masiwa (ex-ZANLA guerrilla) in a presentation of this chapter in seminar at St Antony's College, Oxford, 3 March 1992.
70. Interviews, Herbert Turai (Comrade Sam Zvaitika); Augustine Mabvira (Comrade Ranga), 3 June 1991.
71. Interviews, Plexaides Musona; Archibald Maziti (Comrade Howard Shaka).
72. For example, conversation with Joseph Chitima, Gande village, 19 August 1991. Conversation with David Mazambani, Harare, 3 September 1991.
73. Personal correspondence from Augustine Mabvira (Comrade Ranga), 9 March 1992.
74. Interview, Archibald Maziti (Comrade Howard Shaka).
75. Interview, Councillor Todd Mazambani.
76. For example, interview, Taimo Kapomba, medium of Chimucheka, 6 June 1991.
77. Interview, Corporal Archibald Maziti (Comrade Howard Shaka). Personal correspondence from Augustine Mabvira (Comrade Ranga), 12 May 1992.
78. Interview, Herbert Turai (Comrade Sam Zvaitika).
79. The informant will remain anonymous.
80. See Davidson, 1981: 116 on the transformative limitations of anti-colonial nationalism. I am aware that Davidson's heralding of liberation movements, in Lusophone Africa, as models, is problematic in the light of their subsequent development.
81. I borrow this phrase from Ranger, 1986c: 386–90.

82. Even RENAMO have discovered this. Ken Wilson, personal communication.
83. See Maxwell, 1995a: 81. Neither does Kriger consider the implications for mobilisation of her district being a stronghold of American Methodism.
84. Jocelyn Alexander makes this point in a review (1992) of Kriger's book.
85. DAI, 'Chief Katerere', 'Development needs of the Mangezi Area', 1980.

## CHAPTER 6

1. A general survey of what I describe as 'lineage politics' can be found in Michael Bourdillon, 1987a, chapters 4 and 10.
2. Interview, Chief Katerere (Njanji).
3. DAI, 'Chief Katerere', DC Inyanga to PC Umtali, 5 February 1981. DA Inyanga to Zimbabwe Republic Police Force, Raungwe, 24 January 1989. Minute, DA Nyanga, 3 February 1989.
4. I use the term 'lineage politics' as a statement of the pervasiveness of this patrilineal idiom.
5. Many Hwesa acknowledge that the Nyamhute family could justifiably launch a campaign for the chieftainship. Nyamhute is a senior ancestor in the dynasty who was said to have fled to Makoni. Members of the Nyamhute faction live in southern Nyanga district, and others were evicted back to Katerere in the 1950s, as seen in Chapter 4. Osius Nyamhute returned to Katerere in the 1950s as a businessman. He built up a relationship with Forichi Koso, medium of Mbudzi, and one can surmise that he was interested in claiming the chiefdom. In the late 1980s Koso fell sick and the spirit left him. Nyamhute also lacked a significant local following. He has made no claims in the present dispute. Interview, Osius Nyamhute, 30 May 1991. Conversation with Joseph Chitima, Ruangwe, 19 August 1991.
6. Interviews, Diki Rukadza, 22 January 1989, 12 August 1989, 31 May 1991, 15 August 1991.
7. Interview, Diki Rukadza, medium of Nyawada, 31 May 1991.
8. NAZ, S1561/10, Chiefs and Headmen, vol.14, Inyanga, 1931–2. DAI, 'Chief Katerere', 1 November 1960. See also Appendix 5.
9. NAZ, S1542/C6, Chiefs and Headmen, vol.7, NC Inyanga to CNC, 26 March 1936.
10. Interview, Chief Katerere (Njanji).
11. Interviews, Langton Muromowenyoka, 3 June 1988 and 7 December 1989.
12. Generally, commoners or outsiders could only give me the names of the last four chiefs, the tradition stretching only as far back as their grandparents' memories. They seemed little interested in such lists, but were able to supply me with very detailed histories of their own families.
13. For more detail see Maxwell, 1994: 272.
14. Interviews, Diki Rukadza, medium of Nyawada, 22 January 1989, 12 August 1989.
15. These terms vary in meaning between those using them. Sanhani and Sachiwo who are locally known as 'sub-chiefs' are officially regarded as 'headmen'. Locally the term 'headman' is applied to the second most important tier of 'big men': Sabvure, Sanyamwere and Maroo. These are also popularly known as *sa dunhu* – 'ward heads'.
16. Interview, Frank Matambo and Kagonda Sanhani.
17. Interviews, Mathias Sachiwo, 5 June 1991, 14 August 1991.
18. DAI, 'Chief Katerere', Minutes of meeting held at Nyamasara Secondary School, 9 March 1990.
19. Interviews, Mathias Sachiwo, 5 June 1991, 14 August 1991.

20. DAI, 'Chief Katerere', NC, Inyanga to PNC, Manicaland, 25 July 1960.
21. DAI, 'Chief Katerere', J. C. Masuka, Report on the Katerere Chieftainship meeting held at Nyamasara Secondary School, 7 July 1989.
22. DAI, 'Chief Katerere', J. M. Gabaza, Report on the Katerere Chieftainship Visit, 5 January 1991.
23. Interview, Diki Rukadza, medium of Nyawada, 31 May 1991.
24. Conversation with Osius Nyamhute, Katerere, 11 June 1991.
25. DAI, 'Chief Katerere', J. M. Gabaza, Report on the Katerere Chieftainship Visit, 5 January 1991.
26. Ibid.
27. For example, interviews, Oripa Chikutirwe, Zuze Chitima. Interview conducted by Shakewell Nyamahumba with sub-Chief Fore Nyamahumba.
28. Weber's definition of charisma is problematic here because he opposes it to traditional authority to which Rukadza is inextricably linked. See Eisenstadt, 1968. I would define charisma in a more 'popular' Christian sense as possessing a halo of grace derived from impressive performance in ritual and seance.
29. I am grateful for the insights in this section given to me by David Mazambani.
30. NAZ, S1561/10, Chiefs and Headmen, vol.14, 1931–2. In April 1932 the NC spent four days in Katerere and reported that all the 'kraals' except one were in favour of Chikata. The dissenting 'kraal' was the family of the previous chief who resented loss of influence. The Chifodyas claim that the meeting took place at the southernmost part of Katerere. It is very possible that the NC was unaware of their existence.
31. DAI, 'Chief Katerere', NC Inyanga to PNC Manicaland, 25 July 1960.
32. Mazambani, 1990: 154. Conversations with David Mazambani, Harare, August and September 1991.
33. Conversation with David Mazambani, September 1991, Harare, Zimbabwe.
34. Interview, Taimo Kapomba, medium of Chimucheka, and Esther Kapomba, 11 December 1989.
35. Interview, Diki Rukadza, medium of Nyawada, 12 August 1989. At the meeting of 5 January 1991, the Chifodyas accused the Mbudzis of bribing Kaerezi with a daughter. DAI, 'Chief Katerere', J. M. Gabaza, Report on the Katerere Chieftainship Visit, 5 January 1991.
36. Interview, Patrick Tsodza.
37. Much of the inside information I have collected here was given to me by David and Amos Mazambani. For an even more detailed history of the Chirimunyati/Mazambani faction see De Wolf, 1996: chapter 6.
38. DAI, 'Chief Katerere', J. C. Masuka, Chirimunyati House, 26 June 1989.
39. At the meeting of 9 March 1990 Langton was accompanied by three men whilst the Chifodyas numbered 128 men. DAI, 'Chief Katerere', Minutes of the meeting held at Nyamasara Secondary School, 9 March 1990.
40. Interview, Aluwizi Sanyamahwe, medium of Nyamande, with Advice Chifodya.
41. Interview, Charles Madakwenda. The District Administration was not cognisant of Madakwenda's mediumship. DAI, 'Headman Sachiwo', Ref: Ch K14/Headman Sachiwo/89, reads 'Mhondoro Nyakapini used to speak through the voice of the late Kushanja Madakwenda'.
42. DAI, 'Chief Katerere', J. M. Gabaza, Report on the Katerere Chieftainship Visit, 5 January 1991.
43. Ibid.
44. DAI, 'Chief Katerere', J. C. Masuka, Report on the Katerere Chieftainship Meeting Held at Nyamasara Secondary School, 7 July 1989.

45. DAI, 'Chief Katerere', J. M. Gabaza, Report on the Katerere Chieftainship Visit, 5 January 1991.
46. Report on Katerere Chieftainship and Community, September 1965, in possession of Marshall Murphree.
47. DAI, 'Chief Katerere', J. S. N. Makoni, Meeting with the Mbudzi House, Sachiwo Primary School, 24 November 1989.
48. DAI, 'Chief Katerere', J. S. N. Makoni, Katerere Chieftainship Meeting, Nyamasara School, 9 March 1990.
49. Ibid.
50. DAI, 'Chief Katerere', J. S. N. Makoni, Meeting, Nyamasara Secondary School, 3 April 1992.
51. DAI, 'Chief Katerere', J. S. N. Makoni, Katerere Chieftainship Meeting, Nyamasara School, 9 March 1990.
52. Interview Patrick Tzodza and elders, 19 April 1996.
53. DAI, 'Chief Katerere', Appendix C, Katerere Chieftainship, 3 April 1992.
54. DAI, 'Chief Katerere', J. S. N. Makoni, Report on the Appointment of Matambo Chifodya, c.April 1992.
55. DAI, 'Chief Katerere', J. S. N. Makoni, Combined Meeting of All Three Houses, 8 December 1989.
56. DAI, 'Chief Katerere', Katerere Chieftainship Meeting, Nyamasara School, 9 March 1990.
57. DAI, 'Chief Katerere', Minute to the PA, Manicaland, Appointment of Matambo Chifodya as Chief Katerere, Inyanga District, 26 April 1990.
58. DAI, 'Chief Katerere', Meeting, Nyamasara Secondary School, 3 April 1992.
59. DAI, 'Chief Katerere', J. S. N. Makoni, Report on the Appointment of Matambo Chifodya, c.April 1992.
60. Interview, Choto Chabundo and Champion Sachiwo.
61. DAI, 'Chief Katerere', DA Makoni to PA, Manicaland, 6 April 1992. Senior Secretary for Local Government to PA Manicaland, 24 March 1993.
62. DAI, 'Chief Katerere', Acting DA Makoni to the Officer in Charge, ZRP, Ruangwe, 3 February 1994.
63. DAI, 'Chief Katerere', Ins Masuku, ZRP, to Office of the DA Nyanga, c.February 1994.
64. DAI, 'Chief Katerere', J. A. Masuka, Office of DA, Inyanga to Councillor Nyamamupondo Ward 2, c.April 1996.
65. Interview with Matambo Chifodya and *dare*.
66. Interview, Patrick Tsodza and elders, 19 April 1996.
67. Interviews, Councillor Todd Mazambani, 21 May 1988 and 1 June 1991. DAI, 'Chief Katerere', J. S. N. Makoni, Meeting with Nyaurimbo house, Kambarami village, 23 November 1989.
68. '*Makakatanwa mambishi ohushe hwaKaterere*' ('A Serious Tug of War over the Katerere Chieftainship'), *Kwayedza*, 8–14 December 1995.
69. Interview, Patrick Tsodza.
70. DAI, 'Chief Katerere', DC Inyanga to Secretary of Home Affairs, 31 March 1980.
71. Michael Gelfand wrongly translates *nyakwawa* as a specific Hwesa woman, 1982: 131.
72. Interviews, Kaburunge Magadu, Mutengapasi Magadu and Katoya Katerere; Pitodya Chifodya.
73. I have only come across requests for councils made by the more literate Manyika who worked in the capital. These occurred in the mid 1950s and were resisted by the Native Commissioner. See NAZ, S2827/2/2/3, Annual Report, Inyanga, 1955.

74. Interviews, Richard Simbi; Councillor Todd Mazambani, 21 May 1988.
75. Dr P. A. Smyly, Oxfam Progress Reports, 1985 and 1986, Elim mission hospital. Dr Smyly found that the local health committee was dissolved into a ward development committee. Further, resources from a cooperative development project were only channelled into the homes of prominent people.
76. For a very similar account of the party's decline at local level in Chimanimani district see Alexander, 1995.
77. DAI, 'Meetings and Assemblies', Minutes of a meeting of Chiefs held at the Chiefs' Hall on 12 December 1986, and Minutes of Chiefs' and Headmen's Meeting held at the District Administrator's office, Nyanga, 2 September 1987.
78. DAI, 'Meetings and Assemblies', Minutes of the Provincial Council of Chiefs' Meeting Held in the Chiefs' Hall Mutare, 5 January 1989.
79. Personal communication, Jocelyn Alexander.
80. DAI, 'Meetings and Assemblies', Minutes of the Provincial Council of Chiefs' Meeting, February 1984, and minutes of the Manicaland Provincial Council of Chiefs' Meeting Held in the Chiefs' Hall, Mutare, 5 January 1989.
81. DAI, 'Meetings and Assemblies', Minutes of the Manicaland Provincial Council of Chiefs.
82. DAI, 'Succession Claims and Disputes', Minute from the Provincial Administrator to all DAS Manicaland, 7 February 1989.
83. Interview, Todd Mazambani, 21 May 1988.
84. Martinus Daneel also found this in Masvingo Province; see Daneel, 1991: 20.
85. Interview, Diki Rukadza, medium of Nyawada, 22 January 1989.
86. Interview, Aquiline Kaerezi.
87. Interview, Diki Rukadza, medium of Nyawada, 15 August 1991.
88. There were frequent complaints concerning the lack of local post office and telephone facilities, the slow progress of the tarred road and villagisation.
89. For instance, the initial opposition of medium Kaerezi to the dam in the Mbiriyadi area. Interview, Aquiline Kaerezi.
90. This was the line eventually taken towards the Mbiriyadi dam when its benefits were eventually realised, and to projects drawing water from the Gaerezi. Interviews, Aquiline Kaerezi; Osius Nyamhute.
91. Interview, Emmanuel Nyarumba.
92. It is not always clear where Ladley is drawing his data from, but much of his argument seems focused on urban courts. However, it is my impression that much of the time of Katerere community courts was taken up with 'women's' issues. Andrew Ladley, 1990: 15.
93. Interview, Diki Rukadza, medium of Nyawada, 15 August 1991.
94. The cock is a Hwesa symbol for chief.
95. I am grateful to Terence Ranger and Richard Werbner for helping me to clarify this point. Personal communication from Richard Werbner, 6 February 1992.
96. DAI, 'Headman Sachiwo', Minute, ChK 14/Headman Sachiwo/89, 'Appointment of Headman Sachiwo', 1989.

## CHAPTER 7

1. The oral sources in this chapter are drawn from approximately 50 formal interviews which I conducted between November 1987 and September 1993. To my own observations I add research carried out by students at Emmanuel Secondary School, Elim mission, and more particularly on work conducted by Tom Riyo and Joseph Chitima in April and May 1993.
2. Interview, Paul Makanyanga.

3. Adrian Smyley, Oxfam Progress Report, Elim Hospital, 19 February 1984.
4. Adrian Smyley, Oxfam Progress Report, Elim Hospital, 27 August 1987. EAC, 'Zimbabwe Reports 1984-88', Brian Edwards, Record of Visit to Zimbabwe, January 1987.
5. This phrase is taken from J. Kerkhofs, 1982, 'The Church in Zimbabwe: The Trauma of Cutting Apron Strings.' *Pro Mundi Vita Dossiers*, January. Though this chapter paints a less simplistic picture of the issues concerning the de-institutionalisation of the church.
6. Interviews conducted by Tom Riyo with Israel Chibisa, and J. Kadzima.
7. An earlier version of this chapter contains a number of errors on the origins of these movements. I correct them here after subsequent research on the hitherto understudied Apostolic Faith Movement. See Maxwell, 1995b: 313–14.
8. Interview, Pastor Jeries Mvenge. See also NAZ, S2810/2340, Apostolic Faith Mission of South Africa, Salisbury Section, Revised List, 16 June 1945.
9. Torpiya may be a 'pentecostalised' version of Torpia the Ethiopian type independent church. See Daneel, 1971: 369–74.
10. 'Independent' is often used to stress these churches' difference from mission churches. But given their descent from, and resemblance of, the Apostolic Faith Mission, the utility of this term needs to be reconsidered. I use the term Pentecostal to emphasise their continuities with the world Pentecostal movement.
11. This was the case with Zviratidzo. Interview, Peter Katerere. See also Daneel, on attempts by Marange to explain the origin of his church in his own terms. 1971: 320.
12. Interview, Solomon Ndarowa.
13. I would categorise separately the township Pentecostalism of artisans, manual and domestic workers.
14. Research conducted by Tom Riyo and Joseph Chitima, April–May 1993.
15. Written reminiscences by Calista Chikafa, Elim mission, 1988.
16. For a more in-depth study of this imagery see Werbner, 1989: 239–330.
17. Sundkler, 1948: 55, 109. Sundkler subsequently changed his interpretation, 1976: 66, 317.
18. For instance, Sundkler, as committed Lutheran, was concerned with the threat of syncretism. This is clear in his first (1948) edition of *Bantu Prophets*. See Gray, 1995: 343.
19. Rosalind Shaw and Charles Stewart, 'Introduction' and Richard Werbner, 'Afterword', in Shaw and Stewart, 1994.
20. Exorcism is practised in other churches. On the Zimbabwe Catholic position see, Theological Commission of the Zimbabwe Catholic Bishops' Conference (ZCBC), 1989, *Healing and Salvation in the Church*. However, Pentecostals place a far greater emphasis upon what they call 'deliverance' and use it with great regularity. For a fascinating study of a Zambian Catholic Archbishop who was marginalised for his elevation of exorcism see Ter Haar, 1992.
21. Max Weber, in Eisenstadt 1968: 54–61.
22. See 'Sermons on "Sacred" Mountain', *Sunday Mail*, 3 September 1989, for examples of this contestation outside Katerere. In Shurugwi, Zionists attempted to pray on a holy mountain to 'dethrone' the spirits of the Shiri people.
23. Interview, Tobias Kasu.
24. Interview, Diki Rukadza, medium of Nyawada, 22 January 1989.
25. Research conducted by Christine Chatindo, December 1988.
26. On interviewing the husband and wife team leading Torpiya, my impression was

that the wife was *de facto* leader of the church. Interview, Elizabeth and Nicholas Pfunguro.

27. Similar trajectories of witchcraft eradication can be traced for other regions of Central Africa; see for instance Auslander, 1993: 176–7.

28. On Mchape, see NAZ, S1542/W6, NC Mtoko to CNC, Salisbury, 14 October 1933. On Makombe, discussions with David Mazambani, Harare, 3 September 1991, and Ernest Masiku, Ruangwe, 5 September 1991.

29. This is not true for other parts of Central Africa where Mchape agents operated. See Ranger 1982a: 16.

30. Discussions with Joseph Chitima, 19 August 1991, Pious Munembe 5 September 1991, Ernest Masiku, 5 September 1991.

31. Murphree, 1969. Makombe's ritual was similar to that of Dr Moses in Zambia and the more famous Chikanga. For a wide-ranging account of the symbolic meaning of Dr Moses's campaigns see Auslander, 1993.

32. This does not mean that individuals cannot progress from one cult to the other over time.

33. On the minimal level of female participation in party politics in Ruangwe, Katerere, see De Wolf, 1996: 63.

34. I am grateful to Terence Ranger for his insight on this point.

35. Interviews, Phineas Chitsatse; Angeline Masamba. See also Boddy, 1989: 145.

36. Interviews, Rosemary and Teresa Ndoma; Maria Mabvira.

37. For example, interviews, Nyanzara Bhande; Sister Michael Nyamutswa.

38. This sentiment was forcefully expressed by Hwesa women in interviews with the popular monthly, *Parade*, when it researched the issue in August 1991. See also *Sunday Mail*, 21 July 1991.

39. Interview, Razau Kaerezi, medium of Chikumbirike, 4 May 1991.

40. Interview, James Kaerezi.

41. This image was most powerfully deployed by Diki Rukadza, medium of Nyawada, 31 May 1991.

42. Interviews, Osius Nyamhute, 8 June 1989; Jesse Jim.

43. Reynolds, 1990. Obviously, the civil war intensified the need for healing in the west of Zimbabwe.

44. Schoffeleers, 1991, citing Jean Comaroff, 'Healing and the Cultural Order: The Case of the Baralong boo Ratshidi', *American Ethnologist* 7 (4), 1980, 639.

45. For example, interviews, Elizabeth Pfunguro; Rumbidzai Bhande.

46. It is important to stress that exorcism and healing sessions are not entirely the province of Pentecostals. On Jesuit responses to war trauma see Ranger 1987a: 154–5. Weller, 1991: 29.

47. Interview, Tobias Kasu.

48. Interview, Elizabeth Pfunguro.

49. The revival of the *sangoma* cult in Matabeleland appears to be meeting the same popular need to memorialise the dead. See Werbner, 1991: 186–93.

50. For incidence of witchcraft accusation and *chikwambo* outside Katerere see *Sunday Mail*, 16 June 1991, on Muzarabani where 'Development in the district has ceased because people are afraid of doing anything that is better than a witch [neighbour].'

51. Interview, Davis Matambo.

52. On human rights see Auret, 1992; Catholic Commission for Justice and Peace/ Legal Resources Foundation, 1997; ZimRights, 1997. On development see Sylvester, 1991: chapter 4. A useful essay tracing the ruling party's loss of legitimacy is Ncube, 1989. See also Zimbabwe's popular monthlies: *Parade*, *Horizon*, and *MOTO* from c.1990 onwards.

53. The discourse of civil society is found in the following local journals: *Southern African Political and Economic Monthly*, (SAPEM), *Transformation*, *African Communist*.
54. Personal communication, Paul Gifford.
55. MOTO 34, 1985, p.3, cited in Gundani, 1988: 241. Although Gundani believes that MOTO's critique is 'not quite fair', he notes that the CSSD changed its name to CADEC, Catholic Development Commission, because people confused it with a government department! (p.233)
56. Recent examples, *The Herald*, 1 October 1991 and *The Herald*, 13 November 1992.
57. DAI, 'Chief Katerere', 'Development needs of the Mangezi Area', 1980.
58. Ibid.
59. ZANU leadership declared 1978 *Gore re Gukurahundi* – The Year of the People's Storm, which would spread the war across the country.
60. Songs collected by Shupikai and Laiza Chikutirwe, 1988.
61. Oskar Wermter, 'Time to Choose', MOTO, Nov–Dec 1992.
62. For useful statistics on the impact of structural adjustment in Zimbabwe, see Chakaodza, 1993: 68–71.
63. On the issue of imitation see the Catholic magazine *Crossroads*, October 1993.

## CONCLUSION

1. NAZ, S2827/2/2/6, Annual Report, Inyanga, 1958.
2. For a summary of the debate's resolution see Etherington, 1996.
3. DAI, 'Chief Katerere', J. C. Gabaza, Report on the Katerere Chieftainship meeting held at Nyamasara Secondary School, 7 July 1989.
4. *The People*, 1995.
5. See Peel's critique (1994) of Andrew Apter's *Black Critics and Kings: the hermeneutics of power in Yoruba Society* (1992), Chicago, Chicago University Press, in 'Historicity and Pluralism', p.155.
6. See Peel, 1994: 155–56 on Nigeria and Ranger, 1986b: 55–6 on Zimbabwe.
7. Interview, Patrick Tsodza with Right Katerere, Thomas Katerere, Eric Katerere and Sylvester Kauwe, 19 April 1996.

## APPENDICES

1. *Kuduza* is translated as to 'speak out'.
2. Interview conducted by Andrew Chifodya with Madzeku Chifodya. Interview, Frank Matambo Sanhani and Kagonda Sanhani.
3. There is a play here on the verbs: *Kutevera* – to follow and from which it is suggested Katerere derives, and *Kudowera* – to become accustomed to (also has connotations of following). Interview, Petros Sadowera.
4. Interview, Mathias Sachiwo, 5 June 1991.
5. These rituals were recounted to me by 15 informants who came from either the royal houses or 'big families' involved in them, or were spirit mediums representing their interests. Two of the informants were outsiders who had spent their lives amongst the Hwesa. The accounts were fairly uniform. There were slight differences concerning Sanhani's role. Some said he nominated the chief, whilst one informant claimed he came with a baboon skin bag filled with grain. Concerning Sachiwo, there was confusion over the contribution made by the *mhondoro* spirit Sachiwo alongside the sub-chief. Some accounts missed out the eggs and others the crocodile. Sabvure is an important Hwesa family living south of Mhokore mountain in territory currently under Chief Saunyama.
6. *Mhute* is the Shona word for fog. Interview, Osius Nyamhute, 8 June 1989.

Interview, Matambo Chifodya. Matambo Chifodya's rendition of the legend was different in a number of places; most significantly, it did not identify Nkota as the cause of Nyamhute's flight, seeing him as in fact the elder brother.

7. Interview, Taimo Kapomba, medium of Chimucheka, and Esther Kapomba, 5 July, 1989.

8. Interviews with Diki Rukadza, medium of Nyawada, 22 January 1989, 12 August 1989, 31 May 1991, 15 August 1991. I collected this legend from numerous other informants. Their accounts were not too different from Rukadza's. I have stuck to his own account because he is the story's major proponent.

9. My oral sources are supplemented by the 1965 Delineation Report for Katerere containing genealogies, and a recent family tree by J. S. N. Makoni, DAI, 'Chief Katerere', 20 April 1990. These administrative sources are far too detailed to include in appendix form.

10. NAZ, S1561/10, Chiefs and Headmen, vol.14, 1931–2.

11. DAI, 'Chief Katerere', 1 November 1960.

12. Interview, Matambo Chifodya, 3 May 1991.

13. Interview, Langton Muromowenyoka, 3 June 1988. Initially the spirit Nyawada was not mentioned. Muromowenyoka was unable to elaborate many of the relationships between the ancestors.

14. Interview, Diki Rukadza, medium of Nyawada, 12 August 1989. Chimucheka was omitted.

# SOURCES AND BIBLIOGRAPHY

ORAL SOURCES

## Interviews conducted by David Maxwell

(m=male)
(f=female)
Rumbidzai Bhande, (f), Dumba, 25 November 1987.
Nyanzara Bhande, (f), Dumba, 25 November 1987.
Mary Brien, (f), Elim mission, 13 June 1988.
Pastor Wilson Chibisa, (m), Elim mission, 19 July 1996.
Choto Chabundo (*Zibaba* Sachiwo) (m), and Champion Sachiwo (m), 18 July 1996.
Pitodya Chifodya, (f), Chiwarira, 19 August 1991.
Matambo (Elias) Chifodya, (m), Chiwarira, 3 May 1991.
Chief Matambo (Elias) Chifodya and *dare* – council: Joseph Chapatarongo, (m), Advice Chifodya, (m), Enock Chifodya (m), Elisha Kambara, (m), Richard Mutukamira, (m), Tsekete Mutukamira, (m), Chinyama Nyatondo, (m), Denias Tsengo, (m), Chiwariria, 24 February 1996.
Furai Chikodo, (m), medium of Nyamudzva, Mhokore, 30 May 1991.
Dias Chikodo, Chiwarira, (m), 30 May 1989.
Tendai Chikumbindi, (m), Ruangwe, 21 April 1996.
Oripa Chikutirwe (f) and Ronia Sangarwe, (f), Gotekote, 2 December 1989.
Anna Chikwiramakomo, (f), Elim mission, 5 November 1988.
Zuze Chitima, (f), Gande village, 4 November 1988.
Enoch Chitsatse, (m), Sanhani, 4 June 1991.
Phinias Chitsatse, (f), Gande village, 27 April 1989.
Father Tony Clarke, (m), Carmelite Priory, Mutare, 21 April 1989.
Philip Dhokotera, (m), Elim mission, 29 May 1991.
Enoch Dzihwema, (m), Regina Coeli mission, 11 August 1991.
Father Peter Egan, (m), Carmelite Priory, Hatfield, Harare, 28 December 1988.
Headman Martin Gande, (m), Samakande Business Centre, 31 May 1991.
    11 August 1996.
Peter Griffiths, (m), Mt Pleasant, Harare, 15 August 1987.
Jesse Jim, (f), Elim mission, 4 May 1991.
Catherine Kadzere, (f), Chiwarira, 6 June 1991.
Aquiline Kaerezi, (f), Nyamagoromondo village, 18 April 1989.
James Kaerezi, (m), Gande village, 27 May 1989.
Razau (Manyeri) Kaerezi, (m), medium of Chikumbirike, Nyamudeza village, 4 May 1991.
    21 April 1996.
Taimo Kapomba, (m), medium of Chimucheka, Nyagato village, 5 July 1989.
Taimo Kapomba and Esther (f), Kapomba, 11 December 1989.
    6 June 1991.

Noel Kasu, (m), Nyamudeza village, 20 April 1996.
Tobias Kasu, (m), Nyamudeza village, 2 May 1991.
Louisa Katerere, (f), Chibisa village, 11 November 1989.
Chief Njanji Katerere, (m), Katerere village, 3 June 1988.
Peter Katerere, (m), Nyamagoromondo village, 18 April 1989.
Right Katerere, (m), Munemo village, August 1988.
Forichi Koso, ex-medium of Mbudzi, (m), Mapara village, 12 December 1988.
Colin Kuhuni, (m), Eastlea, Harare, 12 April 1991.
Bishop Donal Lamont, (m), Terenure College, Dublin, 8 September 1990.
Augustine Mabvira (Comrade Rangarirai mwana we povo – Ranga), (m), Elim mission,
    31 May 1988.
    3 June 1991.
Maria Mabvira, (f), Elim mission, 3 May 1991.
Father Luke MacCabe (Dr Robert), (m), Carmelite Priory, Dundrum, 7 September
    1991.
Charles Madakwenda, (m), medium of Nyakapini, Nyamagoromondo village, 13
    August 1991.
Muchato Madhenya (sub-Chief Sanhani), (m), Nyakakweto village, 20 April 1996.
Kaburunge Magadu, (f), Mutengapasi Magadu (f), and Katoya Katerere, (f), Buseta
    village, 30 April 1991.
Paul Makanyanga, (m), Alexander Park, Harare, 7 January 1989.
Headman Robson Maroo (m), and Kampira Maroo, (m), Kodzaimambo, 23 March
    1996.
Peter Marova, (m), Waterfalls, Harare, 22 December 1995.
Angeline Masamba, (f), Gande village, 1 June 1991.
Davis Matambo, (m), Nyamudeza village, 29 April 1991.
Mr Mateta, (m), Ruangwe, 16 April 1989.
Councillor Todd Mazambani, (m), Elim mission, 21 May 1988.
    1 June 1991.
Archibald Maziti (Comrade Howard Shaka), (m), and Captain N. Xechs Nyangari
    (Comrade Carl Marx), (m), Dakota Barracks, 25 July 1991.
Nyautonga Mbota, (f), Nkosi village, 30 April 1991.
Brother Ignatius Moore, (m), Carmelite Priory, Dundrum, 7 September 1991.
Michael Mudzudza, (m), Elim mission, 8 November 1987.
Samson Mudzudza, (m), Elim mission, 29 April 1991.
Frederick Mukwata, (m) and William Mukwata, (m), Nyamudeza village, 9
    December 1988.
Rinos Mukwewa, (m), Gande village, 10 December 1989.
Pastor Pious Munembe, (m), Elim mission, 19 April 1989.
Pastor Constantine Murefu, (m) (Principal of AFM Living Waters Bible College), 30
    July 1996.
Langton Muromowenyoka, (m), Sachiwo, 3 June 1988.
    7 December 1989.
Plexaides Musona, (f), Samakande village, 31 May 1991.
Gilbert Mutsapata, (m), Elim mission, 20 November 1988.
Pastor Jeries Mvenge (ex-Superintendent of the AFM), (m), Mutare, 19 July 1996.
Soloman Ndarowa, (m), Ruangwe 1991.
Rosemary Ndoma, (f), and Teresa Ndoma, (f), Nyamudeza village, 5 June 1991.
Samson Nyaguze, (m), Elim mission, 15 August 1988.
Kwadigepi Nyahwema, (f), Mukwewa village II, 22 April 1991.
Kajiwa Nyakasapa, (f), Mazaruwa, 10 August 1996.
Gwara Nyambuya, (m), Elim mission, 13 August 1987.

Morgan Nyambuya, (m), Elim mission, 13 August 1987.
Osius Nyamhute, (m), Katerere, 8 June 1989.
    30 May 1991.
Janet Nyamudeza, (f), Nyamaropa, 31 April 1991.
Francis Nyamusamba, (m), Nymaropa, 3 June 1991.
Sister Michael Nyamutswa, (f), Avila mission, 31 May 1991.
Emmanuel Nyarumba, (m), Elim mission, 16 June 1991.
Sophia Nyandoro, (f), and Stella Masiku, (f), Ruangwe 19 April 1996.
Cyprian Pasipanodya, (m), and Camillo Mudondo, (m), Bumhira school, Nyamaropa,
    3 June 1991.
Elizabeth Pfunguro, (f), Gotekote, 16 August 1991.
Diki Rukadza, (m), medium of Nyawada, Chifambe, 22 January 1989.
    12 August 1989.
    31 May 1991.
    15 August 1991.
Mathias Sachiwo, (m), Sedze village, 5 June 1991.
    14 August 1991.
Petros Sadowera, (m), Katerere, 7 June 1991.
Frank Matambo Sanhani, (m), Kagonda Sanhani, (m), Sanhani, 4 June 1991.
Aluwizi Sanyamahwe, (m), medium of Nyamande, with Advice Chifodya, (m),
    Chiwariwa, 19 August 1991.
Silas Sarukato, (m), medium of Nyauriri (Chiuriri), Chapatarongo, 17 July 1989.
Pastor Ephraim Satuku, (m), Elim mission, 14 August 1987.
    18 July 1996.
Richard Simbi, (m), Elim mission, 10 August 1988.
Dr David Smyly, (m), and Veronica Smyly, (f), Elim mission, 11 December 1988.
Father Paddy Stornton, (m), Carmelite Priory, Dundrum, 11 September 1990.
Harry Tsengerai, (m), Nyamahumba village, 2 May 1991.
Patrick Tsodza, (m), Munemo village, 14 August 1991.
'Chief' Patrick Tsodza with elders: Eric Katerere, (m), Right Katerere, (m), Thomas
    Katerere, (m), Sylvester Kauwe, (m), Munemo village, 19 April 1996.
Herbert Turai (Comrade Sam Zvaitika), (m), Chitungwisa, 9 August 1988.
Father David Weakliam, (m), Carmelite Priory, Dublin, 12 September 1990.

## Interviews from the Oral History Collection at NAZ

Walter Hughes-Halls, Highlands, 28 March 1969, Oral/Ha1
Patrick Pazarangu, Salisbury, 19 June 1979, AOH/56

## Interviews Conducted by Students, Colleagues, and Research Assistants

By Christine Chatindo with Ivy Mutandakamwe, Juliasdale, December 1988.
    with Christie and Mark Chatindo, Juliasdale, December 1988.
By Andrew Chifodya with Madzeku Chifodya, Sanhani, August 1989.
By Shupikai Chikutirwe with Madzeku Chifodya, Sanhani, 20 January 1990.
    with Ernest Masiku, Ruangwe, 13 January 1990.
    with Wilson Masiku, Ruangwe, 7 January 1990.
    with Douglas and Emily Sangarwe, Tsengerai village, 28 February 1990.
By Stephen Griffiths with Angeline Masamba, Gande village, 3 November 1987.
By Ewart Mapara with Rhoda, Edwina and Tongesai Mapara, Sedze village, August
    1989.
    with Rhoda, Edwina and Tongesai Mapara, Sedze village, August 1992.

By Shakewell Nyamahumba with sub-Chief Fore (John) Nyamahumba, Nyamahumba
    village II, 5 December 1989.
    with Lamious Nyamahumba, Nyamahumba village II, 4 December 1989.
By Tom Riyo with Israel Chibisa, Chibisa village, 30 April 1993.
    with Mr J. Kadzima, Chiwarwira, 23 May 1993.

## Written Personal Reminiscences

Calista Chikafa, 'The Liberation Struggle', 8 March 1988.
Erica Chikodo, 'MNR Abductions', December 1988.
Ewart Mapara, 'The Liberation Struggle', November 1987.
Michael Mudzudza, 'The Liberation Struggle', December 1988.
Patrick Mudzudza, 'The Liberation Struggle', November 1987.
Samson Mudzudza, 'An MNR attack on Zimbabwe', November 1989.

## Local History Projects

Joseph Chitima, Informal Local Church Survey, April–May 1993.
Shupikai and Laiza Chikutirwe, a collection of songs, poems and 'traditions', 1988.
Joseph Katerere, 'Hwesa Religion', September 1988.
Gloria Nyamazuve, 'Hwesa Religion', July and December 1988, March 1989.
Tom Riyo, Informal Local Church Survey, April–May 1993.

## University of Zimbabwe Minority Languages Project

Research by Samson Mudzudza on Hwesa, 1994.

### PRIMARY WRITTEN SOURCES

## Apostolic Faith Mission, Lyndhurst, South Africa (AFM)

Jesse Williams.

## Archivo Histórico de Moçambique, Maputo (AHM)

Governo Geral Cxa, 38 ML (2), 1889.

## Archivo Histórico Ultramarino, Lisboa (AHU)

Andrada Expedition, 1/2, 1887.
Andrada Expedition, 111/2, 1889.

## Catholic Commission for Justice and Peace Harare (CCJP)

Documents Concerning Prosecution of the Executive 1977–8.
'Terrorist Attitudes Towards Christian Religion'.
'Intervention of Donal Lamont', October 1971.
Notes and Reports Concerning Avila Mission 1976–9.

## District Administration, Inyanga (DAI)

*Files Relating to Chiefs and Headmen*
'Chief Katerere'
'Headman Sachiwo'
'Headman Sanani'
'Meetings and Assemblies'
'Succession Claims and Disputes'

# Elim Archives Cheltenham (EAC)

*Files Relating to Rhodesian Missionaries*
'Mission Correspondence 1944–57'.
'Correspondence with J. Williams' 1947–57.
'Correspondence with Missionaries prior to 1958:
        Picken, Renshaw, Loosemoore, Nicholson'.
'Correspondence with Missionaries prior to 1958:
        Hurrell'.
'Missionaries: Beardwell–Griffiths: Brien, Griffiths 1961–1964'.
'Missionaries: Beardwell–Gwynne' (n.d.).
'Elim Missionaries A–J: Briens, Caudell, Griffiths, to 1966'.
'Elim Missionaries L–T: Loosemoore, Renshaw', 1966.
'Drs Brien', (n.d.).
Joan Caudell, (n.d.).
'Missionaries: McCann, Norton', 1971.
'Mission, Statistics', (n.d.).

*Files Relating to the Liberation War and the Zimbabwean Church*
Reports and Notes, 'South Africa and Rhodesia' c.1971–80.
'Peter and Mrs Evans', (n.d.).
'Rev. and Mrs Lynn', (n.d.).
'Miss W. White', (n.d.).
'Rhodesia-Zimbabwe c.1970–1983'.
'Vumba Press Cuttings'.
'Zimbabwe Reports 1984–1988'.
'Zimbabwe General' 1989 – .

# Jesuit Archives Harare (JAH)

Box 139, Correspondence on Triashill.
Box 195, Correspondence relating to Triashill.
Box 196, Hilda Richards, 'A History of Triashill'.
Box 198, Correspondence relating to Triashill.
Box 300, Correspondence on African Nuns.

# National Archives of Zimbabwe (NAZ)

MA14/1/2, Jason Machiwanyika, History and Customs of the Manyika Peoples. (n.d.).
A 1/6/4, Manica, Reports on Events, 1890–1891.
A 11/2/12/12, Unrest in Inyanga District, March–April 1904.
Borrow 11/1/1, Correspondence of Henry J. Borrow, 1890.
CT 1/12/1, Manica, General, December 1890 to September 1892.
CT 1/12/2, Manica, Boundary, Portuguese, 1896.
CT 1/12/8, Manica, Reports, September 1890.
CT 1/15/3, M. D. Graham, Makombe-Gouveia, 19 January 1892 and press cuttings
        from *Cape Times* & *O Economista*
SE 1/1/1, Folios 211–32, F. C. Selous, General Correspondence, 1890–1.

*Native Department, Inyanga District*
NUC 1/1/1 to NUC 1/1/3, In Letters, NC Inyanga, c.1905–6.
NUC 1/4/1, In Letters, Miscellaneous, c.1908–15.

NUC 2/1/1 to NUC 2/1/6, Out Letters, NC Inyanga, November 1901 to October 1916.
NUC 2/3/1 to NUC 2/3/3, Out Letters, NC Inyanga, July 1904 to 1923.
NUC 2/4/1 to NUC 2/4/3, Out Letters, NC Inyanga, July 1904 to November 1923.
NUC 3/1/1/, Annual Reports, Inyanga, 1903–16.
NUC 3/2/1, Monthly Reports, Inyanga, 1914.
NUC 3/3/1, Special Report on the Social Condition of the Native Population.
NUC 7/2/1, Report, District Surgeon, March 1905.
S604, Out Letters, Inyanga, 1924–30, 1934–5.
S603, In Letters, Inyanga, 1924–9.

*Native Department, Mtoko District*
NSJ 1/1/1 to NSJ 1/1/5, Out Letters, NC Mtoko, December 1897 to March 1911.

*Native Department, Umtali District*
NUA 1/1/1 to NUA 1/1/2, In Letters, April 1897 to April 1908.
NUA 2/1/1 to NUA 2/1/12, Out Letters, NC Umtali, October 1896 to September 1919.
NUA 2/2/1, Out Letters, Confidential, September 1899 to April 1919.
S1012/87, NC Umtali, Correspondence and other papers, particularly Jehovah's
    Witnesses, 1948–52.

*Monthly, Quarterly and Annual Reports for Inyanga and Other Districts*
N9/3/1, Quarterly Reports, March 1896 to December 1900.
N9/4/1–45, Monthly Reports, October 1898 to September 1923.
S2076, Annual Report, 1920.
S1563, Annual Reports, 1934, 1936–8, 1940–2, 1944.
S1051, Annual Reports, 1943, 1945, 1946–8.
S2403, Annual Report, 1953.
S2827/2/2/1–8, Annual Reports, 1951–61.
S2827/1977/1, Land, Inyanga District.

*Civil and Criminal Law Files, Inyanga*
D3/22/1–5, Criminal Cases.
D4/21/1–2, Criminal Registers.
S2220, Civil Cases, March 1942 to November 1950.
S544, Criminal Cases, February 1928 to December 1933.
S644, Criminal Cases, January 1939 to June 1942.
S1518, Criminal Cases, March 1935 to January 1950.
S2221, Criminal Cases, September 1952 to December 1957.
S549, Criminal Registers, February 1928 to November 1933.
S1526, Criminal Registers, November 1933 to August 1955.
S2222, Inquests, February 1936 to November 1943.

*Chief Native Commissioner's Correspondence*
N1/1/4, Inyanga, July to December 1902.
N1/1/6, Mazoe South, October 1895 to August 1898 (including July 1899).
N1/1/7, Mtoko, March to November 1897.
N3/1/8, Inyanga, 1903 to 1907.
N3/24/12, Native Reserves, Inyanga, 1903 to 1907.
S1542/MB8 vol.1, CNC's Correspondence 1919–34.
S1542/MB8 vol.2, CNC's Correspondence, 1934–8.

*File Series on Chiefs and Headmen*
N1/2/1, Chiefs and Headmen, 1899–1900.
N3/4/1, Chiefs and Headmen, 1911–14.
N3/4/2, Employment of Messengers, 1920–1.
N8/1/1, Chiefs and Headmen, 1890–1930.
S1561/10, Chiefs and Headmen, 1915–34.
S1542/C6, Chiefs and Headmen, vols 1–16, 1935–52.
S2796/2/2, Assemblies of Chiefs, Manicaland.

*Other Files*
N3/33/8, History of the Mashona Tribes, 1903–4.
N3/31/1, Witchcraft, General, c.1900–10.
SS138/196, Suggestions for Closing Inyanga District, 1924–5.
S138/17, Phelp Stokes Education Committee of East Africa, 1924–5.
S138/17/1, Missions and Churches, 1925–7.
S138/106, CNC Appendix J, Control of Unrecognised Religious Denominations, 1923–8.
S138/34, Game and Pest Control, 1924–34.
S138/66, Tsetse Fly Control, 1927–30.
S535/495, Agriculture Department, Tsetse Fly, 1929.
S615 Inyanga Game Reserve Fauna, 1925–7.
S1542/W6, Witchcraft 1933–9.
S1542/P10, Pseudo Religions, 1934–6.
S2391/3626, Correspondence, Tsetse Fly, 1938–51.
S2585/1038/1–2, Demonstrators, 1939–56.
S2810/2340, Apostolic Faith Mission of South Africa, Salisbury Section, Revised List, 16 June 1945.
S2810/2358/1, Apostolic Faith Mission, Hartley, 1931–45.
S2810/2371, Missions and Churches, Umtali, 1940–56.
S2810/4203 Missions and Churches, Inyanga, 1950–7.
S988, Natural Resources Board, Native Enquiry, 1942.
S517, CID Files on African Organisations, 1948–9.
S2588/1977, Inyanga, Land, 1948–53.

# Sources in Private Hands

Diary, Joy Bath.
Elim Hospital Annual Reports 1989 and 1990, Dr Roger Drew.
Letters in the possession of Father Peter Egan.
Diary, Brenda Griffiths 1976–7.
Cuttings and Letters in the possession of Brenda Griffiths 1978.
Letters and Cuttings in the possession of Dr Stephen Griffiths.
Policy Document, Carmelites of the Irish Province in Rhodesia, in the possession of Janice McLaughlin.
Delineation Report, Katerere Chieftainship and Community 1965, in the possession of Marshall Murphree.
Letters in the possession of Dr Adrian Smyly.
Oxfam Progress Reports 1983–7, Dr Adrian Smyly.
Elim Hospital Psychiatric Reports, 1984 and 1987, Selmer Smyly.

## MISSIONARY PUBLICATIONS

*The Comforter*
*Elim Evangel*
*Elim Missionary Evangel*
*The Missionary Magazine*
*The Scapular*
*The Shield*
*The Sword. A Carmelite Quarterly of the Province of the Most Pure Heart of Mary*
*The Zambezi Mission Record*
*White Friars. The Magazine of the Brown Scapular*
*Zelo. Issued by Students of the Irish Province*

## NEWSPAPERS AND MAGAZINES

*Cape Times*
*O Economista*

## Zimbabwean Newspapers and Magazines

*Crossroads*
*The Herald*
*Horizon*
*Kwayedza*
*Manica Post*
*MOTO*
*Parade*
*The People*
*Sunday Mail*

## BIBLIOGRAPHY OF SECONDARY SOURCES

Abbott, W. M. (ed.). 1966. *The Documents of Vatican Two*. London, Geoffrey Chapman.

Abraham, Donald. 1951. 'The Principality of Maungwe: its history and traditions.' *NADA* 28, 56–83.

Alexander, Jocelyn. 1990. 'Modernization, Tradition and Control. Local and National Struggles over Authority and Land: a case study on Chimanimani District Zimbabwe', Balliol College, Oxford, ms.

— 1992. Review of Norma Kriger's *Zimbabwe's Guerrilla War. Peasant Voices*, *Journal of Southern African Studies* 18 (2), 443–6.

— 1993. 'The State, Agrarian Policy and Rural Politics in Zimbabwe. Case Studies of Insiza and Chimanimani Districts, 1940–1990', D.Phil, Oxford.

— 1995. 'Things Fall Apart; The Centre *Can* Hold: the process of post war political demobilization in Zimbabwe's rural areas', in Ngwabi Bhebe and Terence Ranger (eds), *Zimbabwe's Liberation War* vol.II, *Society*, pp.175–91. London: James Currey.

Alexander, Jocelyn, and Terence Ranger. 1998. 'Competition and Integration in the Religious History of North Western Zimbabwe', *Journal of Religion in Africa* 28 (1), 3–30.

American Ethnologist. 1987. 'Frontiers of Christian Evangelism' 14 (1).

Anderson, Benedict. 1991. *Imagined Communities: reflections on the origin and spread of nationalism*. London: Verso.

Andrada, J. C. Paiva de. 1886. *Relatório de uma Viagem ás Terras do Changamira*. Lisboa: Nacional.

1891a. *Report and Protest of the Affairs occurred at Manica.* Cape Town; Hofmeyr & Regter.

1891b. *Manica: being a report addressed to the Minister of the Marine and the Colonies of Portugal.* London: George Philip & Son.

Appadurai, Arjun. 1990. 'Disjunction and Difference in the Global Cultural Economy', *Theory, Culture and Society. Explorations in Critical Social Science* 7 (2–3), 295–310.

Auret, Diana. 1992. *Reaching For Justice. The Catholic Commission For Justice and Peace 1972–1992.* Gweru: Mambo.

Auslander, Mark. 1993. '"Open the Wombs!": the symbolic politics of modern Ngoni witchcraft', in Jean and John Comaroff (eds), *Modernity and its Malcontents. Ritual and Power in Post Colonial Africa*, pp.167–92. Chicago: University of Chicago.

Bailey, F. G. 1969. *Stratagems and Spoils: a social anthropology of politics.* Oxford: Basil Blackwell.

Barnes, Sandra. 1992. 'The Politics of Support and Protection in West African Communities of the early 19th Century', ASA Conference, Stirling, ms.

Baur, John. 1994. *2000 Years of Christianity in Africa. An African History.* Nairobi: Paulines Press.

Bayliss, Carolyn, Doris Burgess and Pepe Roberts. 1984. 'Editorial', special issue on 'Women, Oppression and Liberation', *Review of African Political Economy* 27–8, 3–7.

Bazeley, Selwyn. 1926. 'A Manyika Marriage Custom', NADA 4, 48–50.

Beach, David. 1980. *The Shona and Zimbabwe 900–1850.* Gweru: Mambo.

1984. *Zimbabwe Before 1900.* Gweru: Mambo.

1986. *War and Politics in Zimbabwe 1840–1900.* Gweru: Mambo.

1989. *Mapondera. Heroism and History in Northern Zimbabwe 1840–1904.* Gweru: Mambo.

1990a. 'Shona Oral Traditions', University of Zimbabwe History Seminar Paper, 81.

1990b. 'Zimbabwean Demography: early colonial data', *Zambezia* 17 (1), 31–83.

1991. 'The Origins of Moçambique and Zimbabwe: Paiva de Andrada, the *Companhia de Moçambique* and African Diplomacy 1881–91', University of Zimbabwe, Dept of History, ms.

1994a. *The Shona and their Neighbours.* Oxford: Blackwell.

1994b. *A Zimbabwean Past.* Gweru: Mambo.

1995. 'Archaeology and History In Nyanga, Zimbabwe', University of Zimbabwe, Dept of History Seminar Paper, 97.

Beinart, William. 1990. 'Empire, Hunting and Ecological Change in Africa', *Past and Present* 128, 162–86.

Beinart, William and Colin Bundy. 1987. *Hidden Struggles in Rural South Africa.* London: James Currey.

Beherend, Heike. 1990. 'The Holy Spirit Movement and the Forces of Nature in the North of Uganda (1985–87)', Conference on Religion and Politics in East Africa Since Independence. Roskilde.

Berger, Iris. 1981. *Religion and Resistance. East African Kingdoms in the Pre-colonial Period.* Tervuren: Musée Royale de l'Afrique Central.

Bernard, F. O. (ed., trans.). 1971. *Karl Mauch. African Explorer.* Cape Town: C. Struik Ltd.

Bhebe, Ngwabi. 1979a. *Christianity and Traditional Religion in Western Zimbabwe, 1859–1923.* London: Longman.

1979b. 'The Ndebele and Mwari before 1893: a religious conquest of conquerors by the vanquished', in Matthew Schoffeleers (ed.), *Guardians of the Land. Essays on Central African Territorial Cults*, pp.287–95. Gwelo: Mambo Press.

1988. 'The Evangelical Lutheran Church in Zimbabwe and the War of Liberation 1975–1980', in Carl Hallencreutz and Ambrose Moyo (eds), *Church and State in Zimbabwe*, pp.163–94. Gweru: Mambo.

Boddy, Janice. 1989. *Wombs and Alien Spirits. Women, Men and the Zar Cult in Northern Sudan*. Wisconsin: University of Wisconsin.

Bond, George. 1987. 'Ancestors and Protestants: religious coexistence in the social field of a Zambian community', *American Ethnologist* 14 (1), 55–72.

Boulton, E. C. W. 1928. *George Jeffreys. A Ministry of the Miraculous*. London: The Hubert Publishing Co.

Bourdillon, Michael. 1979. 'The Cults of Dzivaguru and Karuva amongst the North-Eastern Shona Peoples', in Matthew Schoffeleers (ed.), *Guardians of the Land. Essays on Central Africa Territorial Cults*, pp.235–55. Gwelo: Mambo.

1987a. *The Shona Peoples. An Ethnography of the Contemporary Shona, with special reference to the religion*. Gweru: Mambo, 3rd edn.

1987b. 'Guns and Rain: taking structural analysis too far?' *Africa* 57 (2), 263–74.

1988. 'Gleaning: Shona selections from Biblical myth', in Wendy James and Douglas Johnson (eds), *Vernacular Christianity. Essays in the Social Anthropology of Religion*, pp.120–30. Oxford: JASO.

Bourdillon, Michael, and Paul Gundani. 1988. 'Rural Christians and the Zimbabwe Liberation War: a case study', in Carl Hallencreutz and Ambrose Moyo (eds), *Church and State in Zimbabwe*, pp.147–61. Gweru: Mambo.

Bucher, Herbert. 1980. *Spirits and Power. An Analysis of Shona Cosmology*. Cape Town: Oxford University Press.

Burke, E. E. (ed.). 1969. *The Journals of Carl Mauch. His Travels in the Transvaal and Rhodesia 1869–1872*. Salisbury: National Archives of Rhodesia.

Burton, Willie. 1933. *God Working with Them. Being Eighteen Years in the Congo Evangelistic Mission*. London: Victory Press.

Caplan, Lionel. 1987. 'Introduction', in Caplan (ed.), *Studies in Religious Fundamentalism*, pp.1–24. London: MacMillan.

Catholic Commission for Justice and Peace/Legal Resources Foundation. 1997. *Breaking the Silence. Report on the 1980s Disturbances in Matebeleland and the Midlands*. Harare: Catholic Commision for Justice and Peace.

Caute, David. 1983. *Under the Skin. The Death of White Rhodesia*. London: Allen Lane.

Chakaodza, Austin. 1993. *Structural Adjustment in Zambia and Zimbabwe. Reconstruction or Destructive?*. Harare: Third World Publishing Co.

Cliffe, Lionel, Joshua Mpofu and Barry Munslow. 1980. 'Nationalist Politics in Zimbabwe: the 1980 elections and beyond', *Review of African Political Economy* 18, 44–67.

Comaroff, Jean. 1985. *Body of Power. Spirit of Resistance: the culture and history of a South African people*. Chicago: University of Chicago.

Comaroff, Jean, and John Comeroff. 1991. *Of Revelation and Revolution. Christianity, Colonialism and Consciousness in South Africa*. vol.1. Chicago: University of Chicago.

1993. 'Introduction', in Comaroff and Comaroff (eds), *Modernity and its Malcontents. Ritual and Power in Post Colonial Africa*, pp.xi–xxxvii. Chicago: University of Chicago.

Cross, Sholto. 1978. 'Independent Churches and Independent States: Jehovah's Witnesses in East and Central Africa', in Edward Fashole-Luke, Richard Gray, Adrian Hastings and Godwin Tasie (eds), *Christianity in Independent Africa*, pp.304–15. London: Rex Collins.

Dachs, A. J. and W. F. Rea. 1979. *The Catholic Church and Zimbabwe 1879–1979*. Gwelo: Mambo.

Daneel, Martinus. 1971. *Old and New in Southern Shona Independent Churches*. vol.I: *Background and Rise of the Major Movements*. The Hague: Mouton, Afrika-Studiecentrum.

——— 1991. 'Healing the Earth: traditional and Christian initiatives in southern Africa.' Utrecht, ms.

Davidson, Basil. 1981. *The People's Cause. A History of Guerrillas in Africa*. London: Longman.

Dayton, Donald. 1987. *Theological Roots of Pentecostalism*. Michigan: Zondervan.

De Craemer, W., R. Fox and J. Vansina. 1976. 'Religious Movements in Central Africa: a theoretical study', *Comparative Studies in Society and History* 18 (4), 458–75.

De Wolf, Judith. 1996. 'Practices of Local Governance. A Sociological Study into the Functioning of Local Government in Nyanga district, Zimbabwe', MSc thesis, Wageningen Agricultural University.

Doke, Clement. 1931. *Report on the Unification of the Shona Dialects*. Hertford: Stephen Austin and Sons.

Döpcke, Wolfgang. 1991. 'Chiefs and the State in Colonial Zimbabwe: some preliminary thoughts', St Antony's College, Oxford, ms.

Eisenstadt, S. N. (ed.). 1968. *Max Weber. On Charisma and Institution Building*. Chicago: University of Chicago.

Elbourne, Elizabeth. 1994. 'Colonialism, Conversion and Cultural Change: shifting paradigms of religious interaction in South African history', *Journal of Southern African Studies* 25th Anniversary Conference, 'Paradigms Lost, Paradigms Regained', York University.

Etherington, Norman. 1983. 'Missionaries and the Intellectual History of Africa. A Historical Survey.' *Itinerario* vii (2), 116–43.

——— 1996. 'Recent Trends in the Historiography of Christianity in Southern Africa', *Journal of Southern African Studies* 22 (2), 201–19.

Featherstone, Mike. 1990. 'Global Culture: an introduction', *Theory, Culture and Society. Explorations in Critical Social Science* 7 (2–3), 1–14.

Feierman, Steven. 1990. *Peasant Intellectuals. Anthropology and History in Tanzania*. Wisconsin: University of Wisconsin Press.

Fields, Karen. 1985. *Revival and Rebellion in Colonial Africa*. Princeton: Princeton University.

Folbre, Nancy. 1988. 'Patriarchal Social Formations in Zimbabwe', in Sharon Stichter and Jane Parpart (eds), *Patriarchy and Class. African Women in the Workforce*, pp.61–80. Boulder: Westview.

Fry, Peter. 1976. *Spirits of Protest. Spirit Mediums and the Articulation of Consensus among the Zezuru of Southern Rhodesia*. Cambridge: Cambridge University Press.

Garbett, Kingsley. 1976. 'Disparate Regional Cults and a Unitary Ritual Field', in Richard Werbner (ed.), *Regional Cults*, pp.55–92. London: Academic Press.

Gelfand, Michael. 1974. 'The Mhondoro Cult of the Manyika Peoples of the Eastern Region of Mashonaland', *NADA* xi (1), 64–95.

——— [1977] 1982. *The Spiritual Beliefs of the Shona*. Gweru: Mambo, 2nd edn.

Geschiere, Peter. 1993. 'Chiefs and Colonial Rule in Cameroon: inventing chieftaincy, French and British style', *Africa* 63 (2) 151–75.

Gifford, Paul. 1989. *Religion and Oppression*. Ecumenical Documentation and Information Centre (EDICESA), PO Box H94, Harare.

——— 1991. *The New Crusaders. Christianity and the New Right in Southern Africa*. London: Pluto.

1994a. 'Ghana's Charismatic Churches', *Journal of Religion in Africa* 24 (3), 241–65.

1994b. 'Some Recent Developments in African Christianity', *African Affairs* 93 (373), 513–34.

Gluckman, Max. 1963. 'Rituals of Rebellion in South-East Africa', in Gluckman (ed.), *Order and Rebellion in Tribal Africa*, pp.110–163. London: Cohen & West.

Gray, Richard. 1995. 'Bengt Sundkler's African Encounters', *Journal of Religion in Africa* 25 (4), 342–6.

Griffiths, Peter. 1978. 'The Process for Determining a Christian Religious Education Curriculum for Forms 1 and 2 in a Rhodesian African Secondary School', MA thesis, Institute of Education, University of London.

Grubb, Norman. 1973. *Rees Howells. Intercessor*. Guildford and London: Lutterworth Press.

Gundani, Paul. 1988. 'The Catholic Church and National Development in Independent Zimbabwe', in Carl Hallencreutz and Ambrose Moyo (eds), *Church and State in Zimbabwe*, pp.215–49. Gweru: Mambo.

Hagland-Heelas, Anna Marie and Paul Heelas. 1988. 'The Inadequacy of Deprivation as a Theory of Conversion', in Wendy James and Douglas Johnson (eds), *Vernacular Christianity. Essays in the Social Anthropology of Religion*, pp.112–19. Oxford: JASO.

Hallencreutz, Carl, and Ambrose Moyo (eds). 1988. *Church and State in Zimbabwe*. Gweru: Mambo.

Hastings, Adrian. 1994a. *The Church in Africa 1450–1950*. Oxford: Clarendon Press.

1994b. 'Editorial', *Journal of Religion in Africa* 24 (3).

Henriksen, Thomas. 1978. *Mozambique: A History*. London: Rex Collins.

Hobsbawn, Eric. 1983. 'Introduction: Inventing Traditions', in Eric Hobsbawn and Terence Ranger (eds), *The Invention of Tradition*, pp.1–14. Cambridge: Cambridge University Press.

Hogan, Edmund H. 1990. *The Irish Missionary Movement. A Historical Survey 1830–1980*. Dublin: Gill and Macmillan.

Holleman, J. F. 1969. *Chief, Council and Commissioner. Some Problems of Government in Rhodesia*. London: Oxford University Press.

Hollenweger, Walter. 1972. *The Pentecostals*. London: SCM.

Horton, Robin. 1971. 'African Conversion', *Africa* 41 (2) 85–108.

Howman, E. G. 1936. 'Notes and Anecdotes', *NADA* 14, 16–24.

Ifkenga-Metuh, Emefie. 1987. 'The Shattered Microcosm. A Critical Survey of Explanations of Conversion in Africa', in Kirsten Holst-Peterson (ed.), *Religion, Development and African Identity*, pp.11–27. Uppsala: Scandinavian Institute of African Studies.

Iliffe, John. 1979. *A Modern History of Tanganyika*. Cambridge: Cambridge University Press.

1990. *Famine in Zimbabwe 1890–1960*. Gweru: Mambo.

1995. *Africans. The History of a Continent*. Cambridge: Cambridge University Press.

Isaacman, Allen. 1976. *The Tradition of Resistance in Mozambique: anti-colonial activity in the Zambezi Valley 1851–1921*. London: Heinemann.

Isichei, Elizabeth, 1995. *A History of Christianity in Africa. From Antiquity to the Present*. London: SPCK.

Jacobs, Susie. 1984. 'Women and Land Resettlement in Zimbabwe', *Review of African Political Economy* 27/28, 33–50.

James, Wendy and Douglas Johnson. 1988. 'Preface' and 'Introduction: On "Native" Christianity', in James and Johnson (eds). *Vernacular Christianity*.

*Essays in the Social Anthropology of Religion*, pp.vi–viii and pp.1–12. Oxford: JASO.

Jeater, Diana. 1993. *Marriage, Perversion and Power. The Construction of Moral Discourse in Southern Rhodesia 1894–1930*. Oxford: Clarendon.

Jeffreys, Edward. 1946. *Stephen Jeffreys. The Beloved Evangelist*. London: Elim Publishing Co.

Jeffreys, George. 1932. *Healing Rays*. London: Elim Publishing Co.

— 1933. *Pentecostal Rays. The Baptism and Gifts of the Holy Spirit*. London: Elim Publishing Co.

Kalhari, G. P. 1981. 'The History of Shona Protest Song: a preliminary study', *Zambezia* 9 (2), 79–101.

Kaplan, Steven. 1995. 'The Africanization of Missionary Christianity: history and typology', in Kaplan (ed.), *Indigenous Responses to Western Christianity*, pp.9–28. New York: New York University Press.

Kerkhofs, J. 1982. 'The Church in Zimbabwe: the trauma of cutting apron strings', *Pro Mundi Vita Dossiers*, January.

Kjekshus, Helge. 1977. *Ecology, Control and Economic Development in East African History. The Case of Tanganyika 1850–1950*. London: Heinemann.

Kriger, Norma. 1988. 'The Zimbabwean War of Liberation: struggles within the struggle', *Journal of Southern African Studies* 14 (2), 304–22.

— 1992. *Zimbabwe's Guerrilla War. Peasant Voices*. Cambridge: Cambridge University Press.

Kuper, Adam. 1982a. *Wives for Cattle. Bridewealth and Marriage in Southern Africa*. London: Routledge & Kegan Paul.

— 1982b. 'Lineage Theory: a critical retrospect', *Annual Review of Anthropology* II, 71–95.

Ladley, Andrew. 1990. 'Just Spirits? Chiefs, Tradition, Status and Contract in the Customary Law Courts of Zimbabwe.' ms.

Lan, David. 1983. 'Making History. Spirit Mediums and the Guerrilla War in the Dande Area of Zimbabwe.' PhD, London School of Economics.

— 1985. *Guns and Rain. Guerrillas and Spirit Mediums in Zimbabwe*. London: James Currey.

Landau, Paul. 1995. *The Realm of the Word. Language, Gender and Christianity in a Southern African Kingdom*. London: James Currey.

Lewis, Ioan. 1976. *Social Anthropology in Perspective. The Relevance of Social Anthropology*. London: Penguin.

— 1989. *Ecstatic Religion. A Study of Shamanism and Spirit Possession*. London: Routledge, 2nd edn.

Linden, Ian. 1980. *The Catholic Church and the Struggle for Zimbabwe*. London: Longman.

— 1991. 'Church and Liberation: the difference between the Zimbabwean and South African experiences'. Utrecht, ms..

Lonsdale, John. 1985. 'The European Scramble and Conquest in African History', in J. D. Fage and Roland Oliver (eds), *The Cambridge History of Africa*, vol.6, *From 1870–1905*, pp.680–766. Cambridge: Cambridge University Press.

— 1992. 'African Pasts in Africa's Future', in Bruce Berman and John Lonsdale, *Unhappy Valley. Conflict in Kenya and Africa*, Book 1, *State and Class*, pp.203–23. London: James Currey.

MacCabe, Robert. 1972. 'Medicine in Nyamaropa: a study of the pattern of disease among Africans living in a remote part of Rhodesia.' PhD, University College, Dublin.

MacGaffey, Wyatt. 1983. *Modern Kongo Prophets: religion in a plural society*.

Bloomington: Indiana University Press.

McGee, Gary. 1988. 'The Azuza Street Revival and Twentieth-Century Missions', *International Bulletin of Missionary Research* 12 (2), 58–61.

McGregor, JoAnn. 1991. 'Woodland Resources: ecology, policy and ideology. An Historical Case Study of Woodland Use in Shurugwi Communal Area, Zimbabwe'. PhD, Loughborough University of Technology.

MacKenzie, John. 1988. *The Empire of Nature: hunting, conservation and British imperialism.* Manchester: Manchester University Press.

McLaughlin, Janice. 1991. 'The Catholic Church and the War of Liberation', PhD, University of Zimbabwe.

— 1995. 'Avila Mission: a turning point in church relations with the state and the liberation forces', in Ngwabi Bhebe and Terence Ranger (eds), *Zimbabwe's Guerrilla War*, vol.II, *Society*, pp.90–101. London: James Currey.

Mandaza, Ibbo. 1991. 'The Church and State', *Southern African Political and Economic Monthly* 4 (11), 2.

Marshall, Ruth. 1993. '"Power in the Name of Jesus": social transformation and Pentecostalism in Western Nigeria "revisited"', in Terence Ranger and Olufemi Vaughan (eds), *Legitimacy and the State in 20th Century Africa*, pp.213–46. Oxford: St Antony's MacMillan Series.

Martin, David. 1990. *Tongues of Fire. The Explosion of Protestantism in Latin America.* Oxford: Blackwell.

— 1993. 'The Evangelical Expansion South of the American Border', in Eileen Barker et al. (eds), *Secularization, Rationalism and Sectarianism. Essays in Honour of Bryan Wilson*, pp.101–24. Oxford: Clarendon Press.

Martin, Phyliss. 1983. 'The Violence of Empire', in David Birmingham and Phyliss Martin (eds), *History of Central Africa.* vol.2, pp.1–26. London: Longman.

Maxwell, David. 1993. 'Local Politics and the War of Liberation in North-east Zimbabwe', *Journal of Southern African Studies* 19 (3), 361–86.

— 1994. 'A Social and Conceptual History of North East Zimbabwe, 1890–1990', D.Phil, Oxford.

— 1995a. 'Christianity and the War in Eastern Zimbabwe: the case of Elim mission' in Ngwabi Bhebe and Terence Ranger (eds), *Zimbabwe's Guerrilla War*, vol.II, *Society*, pp.58–89. Harare: Baobab.

— 1995b. 'Witches, Prophets and Avenging Spirits: the second Christian movement in north-east Zimbabwe', *The Journal of Religion in Africa* 25 (3), 309–39.

Mazambani, David. 1990. 'Labour Migration Impacts on Communal Land Agriculture: case studies from Manicaland Province Zimbabwe.' PhD, Clarke University.

Miller, Joseph. 1978. 'The Dynamics of Oral Tradition in Africa', in B. Bernardi, C. Poni and A. Triulzi (eds), *Oral Sources: anthropology and history*, pp.75–101. Milan: Franco Angeli.

Molutsi, Patrick, and John Holm. 1990. 'Developing Democracy When Civil Society is Weak: the case of Botswana', *African Affairs* 89 (356), 323–40.

Moore, David. 1993. 'The Zimbabwean People's Army and ZANU's Interregnum: innovative military, ideological and political strategies', in *Annual Report of Uppsala Studies of Mission*, Uppsala.

— 1995. 'The Zimbabwe People's Army: the struggle for unity in ideology' in Ngwabi Bhebe and Terence Ranger (eds), *Zimbabwe's Liberation War*, vol.I, *Soldiers.* London: James Currey.

Moore, Henrietta, and Megan Vaughan. 1987. 'Cutting Down Trees: women, nutrition and agricultural change in the northern province of Zambia, 1920–1986', *African Affairs* 86 (345), 523–40.

1994. *Cutting Down Trees: gender, nutrition, and agricultural change in the northern province of Zambia, 1890–1990*. London: James Currey.

Moyo, Ambrose. 1987. 'Religion and Politics in Zimbabwe', in Kirsten Holst Peterson (ed.), *Religion, Development and African Identity*, pp.59–72. Uppsala: Scandinavian Institute of African Studies.

Moyo, Jonathan. 1992. 'State Politics and Social Domination in Zimbabwe', *Journal of Modern African Studies* 30 (2), 305–30.

Mudenge, S. I. G. 1988. *A Political History of the Munhumutapa c.1400–1902*. Harare: Zimbabwe Publishing House.

Mukamuri, Billy. 1989. 'Rural Environmental Conservation Strategies in South-Central Zimbabwe: an attempt to describe Karanga thought patterns, perception, and environmental control', ms. ENDA, Zimbabwe, PO Box 3492 Harare.

Mukaranda, Constance. 1988. 'The Late Pre-Colonial and Early Colonial History of Nyanga', BA Honours Dissertation, History Dept, University of Zimbabwe.

Murphree, Marshall. 1969. *Christianity and the Shona*. London: The Athlone Press.

Ncube, Welshman. 1989. 'The Post Unity Period: developments, benefits and problems', in Canaan Banana (ed.), *Turmoil and Tenacity, Zimbabwe 1890–1990*. Harare: College Press.

Newitt, M. D. 1988. 'Drought in Mozambique 1823–1831', *Journal of Southern African Studies* 15 (1), 15–35.

O'Dwyer, Peter. 1989. *James Carmel O'Shea, O. Carm*. Dublin: Gort Muire.

Peel, J. D. Y. 1994. 'Historicity and Pluralism in Some Recent Studies of Yoruba Religion', *Africa* 64 (1), 150–64.

   1995. 'For Who Hath Despised the Day of Small Things? Missionary Narratives and Historical Anthropology', *Comparative Studies in Society and History* 37 (3), 581–607.

Peters, Carl. 1977. *The Eldorado of the Ancients*. Bulawayo: Books of Rhodesia Publishing Co.

Petheram, R. W. 1974. 'Inyanga: with special reference to Rhodes Inyanga Estate', *Rhodesiania* 31, 36–50.

Phimister, Ian. 1988. *An Economic and Social History of Zimbabwe 1890–1948: capital accumulation and class struggle*. London: Longman.

Portuguese Government. 1890. *Memória e Documentos acera dos Direitos de Portugal aos Territórios de Machona e Nyassa 1890*. Nacional, Lisboa.

Ranger, Terence. 1963. 'Revolt in Portuguese East Africa. The Makombe Rising of 1917', in Kenneth Kirkwood (ed.), *St Antony's Papers* 15, pp.54–80.

   1969. 'African Reactions to the Imposition of Colonial Rule in East Central Africa', in L. H. Gann and Peter Duigan (eds), *Colonialism in Africa 1870–1960* vol.1. *The History and Politics of Colonialism 1870–1914*, pp.293–324. Cambridge: Cambridge University Press.

   1981. 'Women in the Politics of Makoni District, Southern Rhodesia 1890–1980', ms.

   1982a. 'Mchape: a study in diffusion and interpretation', ms.

   1982b. 'The Death of Chaminuka: spirit mediums, nationalism and the guerrilla war in Zimbabwe', *African Affairs* 81 (324), 349–69.

   1982c. 'Tradition and Travesty: chiefs and the administration in Makoni District, Zimbabwe, 1960–1980', *Africa* 52 (3), 20–41.

   1982d. 'Medical Science and Pentecost: the dilemma of Anglicanism in Africa', in W. J. Sheils (ed.), *The Church and Healing*, pp.333–365. Oxford: Blackwell.

   1983. 'Holy Men and Rural Communities in Makoni District, Zimbabwe, 1970–

1980', in W. J. Sheils (ed.), *The Church and War*, pp.443–61. Oxford: Blackwell.

1985. *Peasant Consciousness and Guerrilla War in Zimbabwe*. London: James Currey.

1986a. 'Promises, Promises: an alternative history of the Rhodes Matopos National Park', ms.

1986b. 'Religious Movements and Politics in Sub-Saharan Africa', *African Studies Review* 29 (2), 1–69.

1986c. 'Bandits and Guerrillas: the case of Zimbabwe', in Donald Crummey (ed.), *Banditry, Rebellion and Social Protest in Africa*, pp.373–96. London: James Currey.

1987a. 'Religion, Development and African Christian Identity' and 'Concluding Summary', in Kirsten Holst-Peterson (ed.), *Religion, Development and African Identity*, pp.29–57 and 145–63. Uppsala: Scandinavian Institute of African Studies.

1987b. 'Taking Hold of the Land: holy places and pilgrimages in twentieth century Zimbabwe', *Past and Present* 117, 158–94.

1987c. 'An Africanist Comment', in *American Ethnologist* 14 (1), 182–5.

1989. 'Missionaries, Migrants and the Manyika: the invention of ethnicity in Zimbabwe', in Leroy Vail (ed.), *The Creation of Tribalism in Southern Africa*, pp.118–50. London: James Currey.

1990. 'The Origins of Nationalism in Rural Matabeleland: the case of Wenlock.' ms, St Antony's College, Oxford.

1991a. 'The Meaning of Violence in Zimbabwe.' ms.

1991b. 'Religion and Witchcraft in Everyday Life in Contemporary Zimbabwe', in Preben Kaarsholm (ed.), *Cultural Struggle and Development in Southern Africa*, pp.149–66. London: James Currey.

1993a. 'The Local and the Global in Southern African Religious History', in Robert Hefner (ed.), *Conversion to Christianity. Historical and Anthropological Perspectives on a Great Transformation*, pp.65–98. Berkeley: University of California Press.

1993b. 'Introduction', in Ranger and Olufemi Vaughan (eds), *Legitimacy and the State in Twentieth Century Africa*, pp.1–28. Oxford: St Antony's MacMillan Series.

1993c. 'The Invention of Tradition Revisited', in Ranger and Olufemi Vaughan (eds), *Legitimacy and the State in Twentieth Century Africa*, pp.63–111. Oxford: St Antony's MacMillan Series.

1994. 'JSAS and the Study of Religion', *Journal of Southern African Studies* 25th Anniversary Conference, 'Paradigms Lost, Paradigms Regained', York University, pp.1–7.

Rennie, J. K. 1973. 'Christianity, Colonialism and the Origins of Nationalism among the Ndau of Southern Rhodesia 1890–1935', PhD, Northwestern University.

1979. 'Transformations in the Musikavanhu Territorial Cult in Rhodesia', in Matthew Schoffeleers (ed.), *Guardians of the Land. Essays on Central African Territorial Cults*, pp.257–85. Gwelo: Mambo.

Reynolds, Pamela. 1990. 'Children of Tribulation: the need to heal and the means to heal war trauma', *Africa* 60 (1), 1–38.

Robinson, Ronald. 1972. 'Non-European Foundations of European Imperialism: sketch for a theory of collaboration', in E. R. J. Owen and R. B. Sutcliffe (eds), *Studies in The Theory of Imperialism*, pp.116–42. London: Longman.

Schmidt, Elizabeth. 1992. *Peasants, Traders and Wives. Shona Women in the History of Zimbabwe 1870–1939*. London: James Currey.

Schoffeleers, Matthew. 1979. 'Introduction', in Schoffeleers (ed.), *Guardians of the Land. Essays on Central African Territorial Cults*, pp.1–46. Gwelo: Mambo Press.

1985. *Pentecostalism and Neo-Traditionalism: the religious polarization of a rural district in southern Malawi*. Amsterdam: Free University Press.

1991. 'Healing and Political Acquiescence in African Independent Churches', in Carl Hallencreutz and Mai Palmberg (eds), *Religion and Politics in Southern Africa*, pp.89–108. Uppsala: Scandinavian Institute of African Studies.

Scoones, Ian and Ken Wilson. 1988. 'Households, Lineage Groups and Ecological Dynamics: issues for livestock research and development in Zimbabwe's communal areas', Masvingo, ms.

Scott, Leda. 1990. *Women and the Armed Struggle for Independence in Zimbabwe 1964–1979*. Edinburgh: Centre for African Studies, Edinburgh University, Occasional Papers, 25.

Shaw, Rosalind and Charles Stewart. 1994. 'Introduction', in Shaw and Stewart (eds), *Syncretism/Anti-Syncretism: the politics of religious synthesis*, pp.1–26. London: Routledge.

Sherer, James and Stephen Bevans (eds). 1992. *New Directions on Mission and Evangelisation 1: Basic Statements 1974–1991*. New York: Orbis.

Sindima, Harvey, J. 1994. *Drums of Redemption. An Introduction to African Christianity*. Westpont: Greenwood Press.

Sundkler, Bengt. 1948. *Bantu Prophets in South Africa*. London: Lutterworth Press.

1976. *Zulu Zion and Some Swazi Zionists*. Oxford: Oxford University Press.

1987. 'African Church History in a New Key', in Kirsten Holst-Peterson (ed.), *Religion, Development and African Identity*, pp.73–83. Uppsala: Scandinavian Institute of African Studies.

Steele, Murray. 1972. 'The Foundations of a Native Policy: Southern Rhodesia, 1923–33', PhD, Simon Fraser University.

Storry, J. G. 1976. 'The Settlement and Territorial Expansion of the Mutasa Dynasty', *Rhodesian History* 7, 13–30.

Sylvester, Christine. 1991. *Zimbabwe: the terrain of contradictory development*. Boulder: Westview.

Taylor, Guy. 1924. 'The Genealogical Method of Anthropological Enquiry', NADA, 33–48.

Taylor, John V. 1958. *Processes of Growth in an African Church*. Edinburgh: SCM.

Ter Haar, Gerrie. 1992. *Spirit of Africa: the healing ministry of Archbishop Milingo of Zambia*. London: Hurst and Co.

Theological Commission of the Zimbabwe Catholic Bishops' Conference (ZCBC). 1989. *Healing and Salvation in the Church*. Harare: ZCBC.

Thompson, Phyllis. 1979. *The Rainbow or the Thunder*. London: Hodder and Stoughton.

Tomlinson, R. W. 1973. *The Inyanga Area. An Essay in Biogeography*. University of Rhodesia, Series in Science, Occasional Paper, 1.

Vail, Leroy. 1989. 'Introduction', in Vail (ed.), *The Creation of Tribalism in Southern Africa*, pp.1–19. London: James Currey.

Van Binsbergen, Wim. 1981. *Religious Change in Zambia. Exploratory Studies*. London: Kegan Paul International.

1987. 'Chiefs and the State in Independent Zambia', in *Journal of Legal Pluralism* 25 and 26, 139–201.

Van Rouveroy van Nieuwaal, Emile. 1987. 'Chiefs and African States: some introductory notes and an extensive bibliography on African chieftaincy', *Journal of Legal Pluralism* 25 and 26, 1–46.

Vansina, Jan. 1985. *Oral Tradition as History*. London: James Currey.

Warner, Marina. 1976. *Alone of All Her Sex. The Myth and Cult of the Virgin Mary*. New York: Alfred Knopf.

Weber, Max. 1963. *The Sociology of Religion*. (trans., Ephraim Fiscoff). Boston: Beacon Press.

Weinrich, A. K. H. 1979. *Women and Racial Discrimination in Rhodesia*. Paris: UNESCO.

Weller, John. 1991. *Anglican Centenary in Zimbabwe 1891–1991*. Mutare: Zimbabwe Newspapers Ltd.

Werbner, Richard (ed.). 1977. *Regional Cults*. London: Academic Press.

1989. *Ritual Passage, Sacred Journey. The Process and Organisation of Religious Movement*. Manchester: Manchester University Press.

1991. *Tears of the Dead. The Social Biography of an African Family*. Edinburgh: Edinburgh University Press for the International African Institute.

1993. 'The Making of Moral Knowledge: local-global displacements', IV Decennial Conference, ASA, Oxford, 26–30 July 1993.

1994. 'Afterword', in Rosalind Shaw and Charles Stewart (eds), *Syncretism/Anti-Syncretism: the politics of religious synthesis*, pp.212–15. London: Routledge.

Willis, Roy. 1976. 'On Historical Reconstruction from Oral-Traditional Sources: a structuralist approach'. Twelfth Melville J. Herkovits Memorial Lecture. Evanston, Ill.

Wilson, Bryan. 1961. *Sects and Society. A Sociological Study of Three Religious Groups in Britain*. London: Heinemann.

Wilson, Ken. 1988. 'Indigenous Conservation in Zimbabwe: soil erosion, land-use planning and rural life', African Studies Association, UK Conference, Cambridge, 14 September.

1989. 'Trees and Fields in Southern Zimbabwe', *Journal of Southern African Studies* 15 (2), 369–83.

1990. 'Ecological Dynamics and Human Welfare: a case study of population, health and nutrition in southern Zimbabwe', PhD, University of London.

1992. 'Cults of Violence and Counter Violence in Mozambique', in *Journal of Southern African Studies* 18 (3), 527–82.

Winterson, Jeanette. 1985. *Oranges are Not the Only Fruit*. London: Pandora.

Wright, Marcia. 1993. *Strategies of Slaves and Women. Life-Stories from East/Central Africa*, London: James Currey.

Young, Michael. (ed.). 1979. *The Ethnography of Malinowski. The Trobriand Islands 1915–18*. London: Routledge and Kegan Paul.

ZimRights. 1997. *The Matabeleland Conflict*. Harare: A Zimbabwe Human Rights Association Publication.

Zvobgo, C. J. M. 1991. *The Wesleyan Methodist Missions in Zimbabwe 1891–1945*. Harare: University of Zimbabwe Publications.

# INDEX

adultery, 50, 62
adventurer, 5, 17, 29, 30, 40
   *see also* Andrada; Mauch; Peters; Selous
agriculture
   among Hwesa, 1, 15, 19, 38, 51, 52,
     114, 218
   among Manyika, 51–2, 111–12, 113–14
   European, 70, 112
   opposition to colonial policy, 112–13,
     133–4
   *see also* famine; Land Apportionment
     Act; Native Land Husbandry Act;
     women
Agritex, 182, 208
agro-ecological stress, 53, 56–8
Alexander, Jocelyn, 179, 222–3
American Methodist Church, 59, 62, 110,
   111
Andrada, J. C. Paiva de, 17, 18, 29–31, 32,
   57, 62
Anglican, 59, 110, 111, 115, 116
Apostolic Faith Mission, AFM, 65–6, 67,
   75, 76, 85, 128, 189, 191, 192, 193,
   194, 196, 202, 225
autochthons, 20–4, 56, 75
   *see also* Nyakasapa
Avila Mission, 91, 92, 93, 95, 98, 99, 102,
   109, 116, 118, 164, 188, 191, 194
   and liberation war, 129–30, 137, 138

Barwe, 15, 19, 25, 26, 28, 29, 31, 32, 34,
   44, 46, 47, 55, 108, 113, 114, 115,
   116, 123, 138, 139, 141, 170, 234
Beach, David, 14, 17, 242n
'big men', 12, 13, 14, 18, 19, 186
Boddy, Janice, 4, 58, 202, 205
Borngaes-Njenje Church, 191, 192
Bourdillon, Michael, 136, 162, 242n
Brickhill, Jeremy, 124–5
bride price, 36
bride service, *ugariri*, 12, 13
Brien, Cecil, 70, 76, 81–6, 87, 88, 94, 95,
   97, 98, 106, 108, 126
Brien, Mary, 70, 76, 82–6, 94, 95, 97, 98,
   106, 108, 115, 126

British, 28, 31, 32, 34, 38, 42, 100, 110,
   112, 119, 223
British South Africa Company, BSAC, 1,
   30–2, 33, 34, 36, 38, 48, 50
bureaucratisation, of Christian movements,
   97–100, 197, 220

Carmelites, 70, 71–3, 76–8, 88–101, 105–6,
   129, 130, 225
   initial encounters with Hwesa, 77–8
   localisation of Christianity, 88–93
catechists, 59, 98
Catholics, 2, 59–62, 70, 71–3, 76–8, 88–
   101, 111, 116, 129, 130, 169, 175,
   198, 202, 215, 217, 223
   *see also* Avila Mission; Carmelites;
     Jesuits; Marianhill missionaries;
     Marianism; Regina Coeli mission;
     Trappist; Triashill Mission; Ugandan
     Martyrs Mission
cattle, 12, 13, 111, 206, 235, 242n
chiefs, traditional leaders, 4–5, 14, 18, 19,
   22, 25, 27, 30, 36, 37, 38, 39–47, 49,
   64, 74, 113, 151, 179, 180, 181, 182,
   184, 185, 186, 198, 209, 211, 212,
   217, 219, 221, 223, 226, 233, 235,
   245n, 261n
   authority, 39–41, 173–4, 185
   burial, 41, 135, 143, 158, 168, 198, 221,
     232, 233
   genealogies, 20, 25, 44–5, 155, 156–7,
     159, 168, 169, 170, 177, 219, 237–
     40
   installation of, 22, 41, 42, 104, 158, 159,
     170, 173, 180, 183, 232, 233
   legitimacy, 39–41, 57, 65, 149, 155, 166,
     170, 173, 174, 175, 182–5, 210
   Provincial Council, 179
   regalia, 41, 151, 173, 174, 180, 235–6
   relation to mediums, 18–19, 29–30, 39–
     42, 143–4, 149–51, 180–5, 186, 211
   succession, 11, 25, 150–1, 153–80, 185–
     6, 227, 228, 230
chieftainship, 22, 34, 150, 153, 177, 183,
   201, 227, 233, 241n